Pelican Books
The Pelican Guide to Modern Theology
Editor: R. P. C. Hanson

Volume 1:
Systematic and
Philosophical Theology

William Nicholls was born in Hitchin in 1921, and read classics and theology at Cambridge, his studies being interrupted by war service in the Middle East and Italy. After going down from Cambridge in 1949, he joined the staff of the World's Student Christian Federation as a travelling secretary, based on its Geneva headquarters. In 1951 he returned to England to prepare for ordination in the Church of England at Wells Theological College. His first book, *Ecumenism and Catholicity*, a study of the theological implications of the ecumenical movement, inspired by his Geneva experience, was published in 1952. Later that year he was ordained to the curacy of Wendover, Buckinghamshire, a post he combined with work as Deputy Chaplain to aircraft apprentices at R.A.F., Halton. In January 1955 he became Chaplain to Anglican Students in Edinburgh, where he took up his ecumenical interests again, joining in discussions between the Scottish Episcopal Church and the Church of Scotland, and in the work of the European section of the Theological Commission on Christ and the Church of Faith and Order. In 1960 he moved to Canada, where he and his wife and three children now live. He is at present Professor and Head of the Department of Religious Studies at the University of British Columbia, Vancouver. There his interests have increasingly turned from the study of theology to the study of religion, and from dialogue between churches to dialogue between faiths, and between religion and the secular world. He has done some broadcasting and TV work with the Canadian Broadcasting Corporation, and writes regularly on religion for the Canadian monthly, *Saturday Night*. His recreation is photography.

William Nicholls

Systematic and Philosophical Theology

Penguin Books

Penguin Books Ltd, Harmondsworth,
Middlesex, England
Penguin Books Inc., 7110 Ambassador Road,
Baltimore, Maryland 21207, U.S.A.
Penguin Books Australia Ltd, Ringwood,
Victoria, Australia

First published 1969
Reprinted 1971
Copyright © William Nicholls, 1969

Made and printed in Great Britain by
Hazell Watson & Viney Ltd, Aylesbury, Bucks
Set in Monotype Times

Contents

Theology used to claim to be able to give authoritative information about all the phenomena in the universe, or at the least to share this privilege with philosophy. Now through the vicissitudes of the history of thought theology usually occupies a lowly place in those institutions which exist to train men and women in all the important intellectual disciplines, and in some it does not appear at all. And its sister, philosophy, has fared little better. Theology has been chastened by adversity, by discovering that its claims were disputable, and in many cases manifestly false. The brash confidence sometimes displayed by the newer disciplines may encounter a similar experience. In consequence of this development it is thought by some that theology is dying: theology is the scientific study of religion, and religion is dying. The answer to this suggestion is simply that theology is not dying as long as there are people who believe it worth while to practise it. There are still plenty of people interested enough in theology to study it and to contribute to it.

Theology is the science of thinking about God. It has to cover a vast field, including ancient history, ancient languages, church history, philosophy of religion, literary criticism (including textual criticism of two or three different types), the history of Christian thought and comparative religion. Men have always thought about God, often passionately; some of the best minds in history have been devoted to thought about God. Theology has therefore behind it a long, varied and fascinating history.

But what and how is God? This is one of the first questions handled by *The Pelican Guide to Modern Theology*. A guide of this sort should explain how people today think and in the past have thought about God. And as this is a Christian country (or at least a post-Christian one) this guide has thought it right to

7

explain how Christians think about God. This has involved devoting a volume to the philosophy of religion (the interaction of Christian thought and philosophy), a volume to the Bible, describing how it is studied today, and a volume to historical theology, demonstrating in three different fields how scholars today handle the tradition which Christianity has formed in the course of its journey through history. We have not covered the whole field; we have had to omit, for instance, a treatment of the medieval period and we have made no reference to comparative religion. But this series will have done enough if it causes its readers to understand how it is that some people find theology the most attractive, the most exacting and the most satisfying intellectual pursuit of all.

R. P. C. HANSON

Introduction to Volume 1

In the first volume of this series the reader is being plunged immediately into modern theology. The first volume deals with theology as it presents itself to experts in the subject today, in its purest and acutest form, with the question of what we mean by God and how, if at all, God can be encountered and understood. The other two volumes will deal with the raw material, as it were, for Christian theology, with the biblical evidence and how it is handled today, with various aspects of Christianity as it has developed since it first began, and with how these aspects are treated today. Volumes 2 and 3 therefore in a sense lie behind Volume 1. If the reader finds Volume 1 of interest and concern to him, he should want to go on to the other two volumes in order to explore the foundations of theology further.

If he reads as far as Volume 1, however, he will be left in no doubt that the science of theology is facing a number of radical, indeed of ultimate, questions which constitute one of the most acute crises that theology can ever have faced, that is, all those questions involved in the root problem of how God can be conceived of or known at all. How searching this question is, why it faces theologians with peculiar intensity today, and what answers have been and are being given to it, all this is expounded lucidly in the first volume. It falls to the editor of the series only to make a few introductory, perhaps no more than marginal, remarks about the subject.

First, it should be observed that theology is not alone in this acute crisis. The crisis may appear to theologians to be affecting them particularly, but in fact it is only one form of a crisis which is affecting the whole of contemporary western European and Anglo-Saxon culture, involving philosophy, ethics, literature, art, sociology, psychology and politics as well. It is simply the crisis brought about by the advance of scientific technique. Have we no reliable form of knowledge apart from scientific knowledge? Above all, is our only reliable form of knowledge about ourselves, about man, scientific knowledge? The crisis is really a crisis of anthropology, but more, a crisis of the human spirit. Decision one way or the other will clearly have far-reaching and immensely important consequences, far beyond merely theological circles. This does not make the crisis less acute for theologians, but it should prevent them from feeling isolated. And it might perhaps, if more widely appreciated, cause some students of other disciplines to cooperate with theologians in a common search to resolve a common dilemma. Theology is not the odd man out among disciplines. It is one end of a spectrum.

Next, the reader will certainly gain the impression that theologians are not running away from their proper problems. They might indeed be represented, if we wished to dramatize the situation, as pioneers and heralds pointing to the cultural crisis to which we have been referring, and they are performing this function with a remarkable freedom and seriousness. The word 'theologian' has for the ordinary reader associations of dogmatism, narrow-mindedness and remoteness from reality. Nobody who reads this volume could imagine that these qualities could be ascribed to the theologians mentioned in it. Openness, liveliness and a determination to follow where the facts and the truth lead are surely their main characteristics. The theological student today has to face problems more acute and questions more searching than his predecessors for many generations had to face. But, whatever else he learns, he will be taught not to run away from unpleasant truths nor to stop short of drastic conclusions. It will be his own fault if he does not discover that the debates in which he will be involved are lively debates, dealing with living issues.

Finally, is this liveliness and awareness evident in theological discussion no more than the jerking and writhing of a dying body? Is it the frenzy of despair? The reader must decide for himself. But it would be curious if a century which had produced figures as great as those of Barth, Bultmann, Tillich, Bonhoeffer and Niebuhr were really witnessing the end of a dying tradition.

Ancient pagan thought did not die like this, nor did Gnostic thought. That we are in a period of theological confusion, change, heart-searching, re-assessment, reinterpretation, even revolution, nobody could deny. But the proposition that this period heralds the death of theology, that there is nothing left for the theologians to trouble themselves about, is, in the light of the account given in this volume, a highly doubtful one. On the contrary, the strong impression which one gains from this account is that, whatever else is lacking to the pursuit of theology, life, vitality, is not.

R. P. C. HANSON

Preface

This is not a book about what I think, but about the work of others. I have tried to understand what they mean, to think their thoughts after them as far as possible, and to express them again, in my own words and theirs, for the benefit of newcomers to the subject. I have not offered criticism, except indirectly through discussion of their criticisms of one another. This does not mean that I have no criticisms of my own to offer, but to present mine would have meant writing a different kind of book from the one I was asked to write.

My own opinions on these topics, so far as they are of interest to anyone, can partially be inferred from the decisions I have taken about the way to present the material. Since another writer would have taken different decisions, it may be worth while drawing attention to mine. Other decisions, as I am well aware, could be convincingly defended. No single book, especially of this length, could say everything worth saying about so large a subject. My first decision was not to write a small encyclopedia, but to discuss in the central portion of the book a few authors of particular significance as adequately as possible, while setting them in their historical and intellectual framework. My own view of modern theology presumably comes out most clearly in the choice of those to be given this fuller treatment.

They all belong to the German tradition, or are closely related to it intellectually. I am convinced that during the past century and a half or so work unrelated to this tradition has been of less intellectual importance, and should not engage the attention of anyone who wants to understand modern theology until he has gained some understanding of the German tradition and the problems it deals with. In that tradition the intellectual issues confronting theology in the modern world were first isolated and defined, and the most important solutions so far were first proposed.

The German tradition is Protestant. This book does not offer guidance in understanding Catholic theology, except indirectly. Those who miss such guidance may be asked to remember that Catholic theology is a separate subject, with different intellectual roots and social purposes. Writing within a powerfully cohesive tradition, Catholic theologians are more concerned to express a corporate faith than a personal vision, religious or intellectual. Their differences from one another are subtle and not obvious to the general reader without much preliminary study of the inherited tradition. Nor has it until recently been the aim of Catholic theologians to confront the problems that have occupied Protestant theologians in the period under discussion. Now that a fresh generation of Catholic theologians has started to confront them, they necessarily find themselves in considerable debt to the German Protestant tradition described in this book. Hence my book may also be of help in understanding the latest developments in Catholic theology, though it does not deal with them explicitly, except for a few brief references.

Among the writers here discussed, and among the themes that occupy their attention, everyone will have his own preferences and special interests. Mine are doubtless exhibited in the arrangement of the material that appears below. Perhaps it may be worth saying, therefore, that it is not necessarily my view, as a glance at the table of contents might easily suggest, that Karl Barth is about twice as important as anyone else mentioned here. The magnitude of his published work and of his achievement does indeed call for a somewhat lengthier account of his work than that of other writers. But since he comes first in any case, as the leader of a revolutionary movement that has been the principal point of orientation in contemporary theology, I have used the chapter on Barth not only to mention other theologians who shared in his revolution, but also to explain many matters mentioned there for the first time, and useful in understanding the other theologians dealt with as well. This has considerably swollen the size of that chapter. The reader who does not think he is interested in Barth must accept my apologies, for he will find the book more difficult than I meant it to be if he does not read the chapters in order. In fact, there are many links between earlier and later chapters of the book.

In general, I have concentrated upon questions of theological orientation and method, rather than trying to give a complete account of the positions of each writer on every major topic. I have assumed that a guide is for intending travellers, though one who does not mean to make the journey can also derive some enjoyment from reading a guidebook. I have tried to point out a clear way through this landscape, without describing everything that is to be met with on the way. I have discussed philosophical matters from a theological angle, and only at such length as seemed necessary to clarify a writer's theological position. More specialized works will be needed by a reader who is led by what he finds here to greater interest in a particular writer, and hence in his view of questions I have treated briefly or not at all. The names of some of these books are given in a brief bibliography at the end. I am myself much in debt to these writers for the clarification and interpretation they have undertaken. In one or two instances I have ventured to differ from well-established interpretations.

The most important thing I want to say to the reader before he begins this book will already be apparent. This book cannot be as rewarding to read as the works of the writers it deals with, and I would consider that I had failed if anyone were tempted to use it as a substitute for reading them. In its incompleteness, it is intended to lead to its subject, not to be a permanent resting-place. I hope it will not mislead such a reader seriously, and that it will not long detain him from his own encounter with contemporary theology.

My thanks are due to the Board of Governors of the University of British Columbia for leave of absence, and to the Canada Council for a Senior Fellowship, which enabled me to undertake, among other work, the writing of the first draft of this book. My wife and John Gerrard acted as guinea-pigs by reading the book in typescript as it was written, and pointing out many obscurities that an academic reader might have missed. Two senior students in our own department, Christopher Hamilton and Ruth Nichols,

Preface

were of invaluable assistance during the final revision of the manuscript. I am especially grateful to Mrs Lynda Spratley, who compiled the Indexes. For the errors and obscurities that remain, I am myself wholly responsible.

WILLIAM NICHOLLS

Department of Religious Studies
University of British Columbia
July 1968

One

Modern Theology and the Modern World

THE SUBJECT AND PURPOSES OF MODERN THEOLOGY

Theology is the literature in which the faith of Christians finds intellectual expression. A theological writer expresses the faith he shares with the Christian community in the intellectual terms available to him in his time, and so helps himself and his fellow believers to understand what they believe, so far as that is possible. Modern theology does this for our own time. It does not differ from the theology of the past in any essential way. It is distinguished by a set of problems, and by proposals for their solution, not present in previous theological work. These problems first came to the notice of theologians at around the beginning of the nineteenth century. The contemporary theologians to be discussed below were therefore not the first to deal with them. On the contrary, these writers show themselves acutely aware of, and in varying degrees in reaction to, the solutions offered by their nineteenth-century predecessors. Behind the theology of today lies a whole generation of modern theological work. We cannot understand contemporary theology without some knowledge of the work already done in modern times, or indeed without knowing a little of the earlier history of theology, from the New Testament up to the birth of modern theology at the beginning of the nineteenth century.

The purpose of this introductory chapter is to provide such a background in brief compass, and incidentally to explain why a modern type of theology came into existence. To understand that is immediately relevant to seeing why nineteenth-century theology took the form it did, but it will be hardly less useful for understanding more recent work. As we shall see, the work of our own time more closely resembles traditional theology than does that of the writers of the nineteenth century, but for all that, it must try to solve the same problems as theirs did. The problems confronting nineteenth-century writers have not disappeared, though their solutions did not prove acceptable to their successors. If the solutions proposed have undergone radical change, the problems have not.

Modern theology is the product of a cultural and intellectual situation that is familiar to us in every aspect of modern life. It is a response offered by Christian believers to the development of the modern world itself, under the influence of the rise of science and technology. The intellectual consequences of the rise of science have been no less far-reaching than their influence upon our way of life. Science, particularly the physical sciences, has acquired unrivalled intellectual prestige in the modern academic world, and in society as a whole. It is very widely believed to be the most reliable method open to us of finding out how things are in any sphere of reality. What is not scientific, at least in method, is thought to be unreliable, or to have abandoned the encounter with reality. A great deal of intellectual effort is devoted today to criticism of literature and the arts, and the public attention devoted to this work suggests that people find it meaningful for understanding their own lives. But such work is not thought to add to our stock of information about reality: it deals with meaning rather than fact, with values rather than with mapping the world in which we live. Thus both philosophy and religion, which once had the sort of prestige today enjoyed by science, have become discredited as sources of information about reality. There is the suspicion that they too deal with values and meaning, rather than with what is the case.

During the period that modern theology has been under development, philosophy encountered the same situation. It too had to come to terms with science, and particularly in the English-speaking world largely conceded to it the ground of reality. The type of philosophy most familiar to the English-reading public regards science as our way of finding out how things are, and confines itself to the discussion of logical and ethical questions, on which science has no contribution to offer, and where philosophy is competent, not only to speak in its own name, but to assist the scientist. Where the influence of science is strong, we find other disciplines preoccupied with questions of method. As scientists do not tire of telling us, what is important in their work is not so much a body of findings, for these are in any case under constant revision, but the method which produced them and leads also to their revision and extension. Scientific method is a means of making sure that we do in fact learn by our experience. It forces us back to experienced fact at every point. No theory is allowed to stand without constant and rigorous confrontation with the test of fact. Every other discipline has had to meet that test since science invaded the traditional scene. Either a discipline must renounce the claim to deal with reality, or it must show that it too is scientific, in that it has a clearly demonstrated object for its inquiries, and can show how every statement it makes refers back to this object. It must show how it knows that what it says is true. And to know that a statement is true means for the scientific mind that it is known to reflect a state of affairs in the object of study. Statements that do not reflect such a state of affairs are false, statements that by their form are incapable of doing so are empty.

Philosophy could meet this difficulty by retreat, even if the retreat proved to be strategic. Most modern philosophers profess to have abandoned metaphysics, considered as the attempt to speak about reality on some other ground than that of scientific method. Could theology do the same? Even more than philosophy, theology had been committed to reality. It professed to inform us about God, about the creation and end of the world, about eternity, about the invisible work of grace. None of the topics on which theology traditionally believed that it could inform us had the same kind of evidence that science could refer to. No experiment, it seems, could inform us about the existence of God, or any other of the realities which theology regarded as its subject-matter. Theology could not continue its traditional role and still become scientific. Alternatively, should it seek to become scientific, it might have to change its subject-matter, and confine itself to that which enters into human experience as an evident phenomenon. In that case, it would be very difficult to continue to speak about God and his work.

Modern Theology and the Modern World

It is not an objection to theology, from the point of view of the scientist, that its findings may seem to run counter to common sense and its view of the world. Those of science do the same, and its 'counter-intuitive' character may even be said to be among its distinctive features. On the contrary, the scientist is apt to suspect the theologian of relying altogether too much upon common sense and intuition, instead of correcting them by a rigorous method that can break through their hypnotic influence to the reality behind. Science is critical of everything we think we know, and the scientific temper is characteristically iconoclastic. If theologians are thought to be gentle and reverent men, tenderly guarding a received tradition, scientists often seem brash and rude, disbelievers by temperament of what is received, and supremely confident in their ability to find out what is really the case. If these are caricatures, they are surely illuminating ones, and incidentally help to explain the appearance in modern times of theologians of a different and critical stamp, much more closely resembling the stereotype of the scientist. Like every other discipline today, modern theology is haunted by science, and cannot disengage itself from a constant internal debate about its own scientific character.

Whether or not we think what theologians (or some of them) say is true, we must be aware that theology has lost most of its traditional authority since the rise of science. Theologians were once thought to be able to speak with quasi-divine authority about a mysterious realm beyond this world, and yet of the highest importance to man. Now we are doubtful whether any-one can speak about such a realm, even if it exists. The more confident the claim of the theologian to do so, the less he is likely to inspire an answering confidence in his hearer. No one thinks he gains authority simply from his status as a spokesman of the church, for that sort of authority inspires no conviction. Individual writers can have a personal authority which status cannot confer upon them, but which they win, as any highly gifted person may, by their display in their work of what is taken to be wisdom. The authority of the scientist, which is so great today, is of another sort. We trust scientists as authorities (and we do, even more than we are justified in doing) partly because science is not authoritarian. If we ask scientists why they say something is the case, they do not in general reply that the competent authority has said so. They appeal, or ought to appeal, to a body of evidence, and to theories whose persuasiveness lies not just in their elegance or coherence, but in the knowledge that they have stood the test of repeated confrontation with relevant facts. Science is not static; it is in continual process of correcting itself, and its theories must constantly grow more powerful in order to organize intellectually a growing body of factual evidence. Is theology like that? Can it meet the modern demand for factual information, or is it confined to the spheres of meaning and ethics?

These are, I believe, the sort of questions the educated layman wants to ask the theologian. In default of clear replies to them, he is likely to exhibit a spectacle that is painful, though by no means unfamiliar, to the theologian today. As they talk, the theologian must watch the layman's eyes glaze, not in boredom or rejection, but in simple incomprehension. What is the man talking about? Is he indeed talking about anything? The conservative theologian, who does not deal with the questions raised for theology by science, or, if he does, deals with them by a reiteration in stronger terms of the traditional position, does not get this response. In a way he seems to enjoy a surprising popularity with layman and sceptic alike. His advantage is that they know what he means. The simple-minded layman often supposes he knows that 'the old faith' is true. The sceptic with equal assurance knows that it is false. Both feel clear about the man's meaning. The modern theologian is often under cross-fire from both the lay and the sceptical ranks. Each accuses him of mystification, and unnecessary mystification at that. What is unclear is not so much his method as his subject. The propositions of conservative theology look as factual in their own way as those of science. Unfortunately, where they are indeed factual in this way, they are often in conflict with the findings of present-day science. Thus the sceptic feels himself on solid ground in rejecting them, while the conservative himself has to engage in a counter-apologetic, denying the right of science to lay down the law at points where he himself wishes to speak on behalf of

God. The modern theologian avoids this direct encounter and conflict with science, at the cost of obscurity on the vital question of whether he is speaking about reality.

If this obscurity characterized modern theology as a whole, the sceptic would be well justified in rejecting it. However, as it will not be difficult to show below, this is not the case. Reputable writers are sharply aware of these questions, and deal with them in the forefront of their work. Since the problems are so difficult, the solutions proposed will not commend themselves to every reader, but it may reasonably be claimed that the problems receive clear and honest discussion, and that genuine attempts at solution are proposed. But the layman has surely seized upon the central problem of modern theology, its subject-matter, or in scientific terms, the object with which it deals. Traditional theology was clear on this point. It dealt with revealed truth, with propositions known to be true on the authority of God revealing, whether that revelation was located as for Catholics primarily in the teaching of the church, or as for Protestants in the Bible as the inspired Word of God. Since this object could be taken as given, theology could proceed in a clear way to develop its own system of thought upon its basis. It is just this given object in the form of revealed truth that science, as we shall see, has called in question. Still, most modern theology has continued to suppose that it could speak about the revelation of God. It simply located this revelation somewhere else than in inspired propositions vulnerable to scientific criticism. Modern theology has maintained the traditional task of speaking about God and his work, in a world increasingly unable to conceive of either.

Theological literature is of many kinds. We are here concerned with a particular sort, called systematic and philosophical theology, or, loosely, theology without qualification. This is the discipline in which the substantive contentions of theology are set forth in the clearest possible way. It is supported by a number of historical disciplines, to be dealt with in other volumes in the present series, concerned with the Bible and with the past of Christian thought. It leads in turn to the disciplines of practical or applied theology, in which the understanding of the Christian faith, set forth by the systematic or philosophical theologian in contemporary terms, is applied to the life of the church and in particular to the work of the ministry. Practical theology belongs largely to the professional training of future ministers, and though it interacts both with education, and with medicine and psychiatry, is of less intellectual interest.

The distinction between systematic and philosophical theology is a fine one, and varies with every writer according to the view he takes on the traditional and perennial question of the relation between theology and philosophy. For our purposes it is best not to attempt to define the difference, but to recognize that the literature we have in mind, which it is most convenient to call simply theology, following popular usage, will always exhibit some systematic and some philosophical characteristics. Every writer of theology is concerned, nowadays at least, to organize his thought in some systematic way, and to exhibit some relationship between what he thinks on one point and what on another. Writers are likely to differ on what the principle of organization should be. Barth, for example, insists that philosophy must not provide it, that the interior logic of the Christian faith provides its own organization, which he prefers not to call systematic. Tillich, on the other hand, calls his major work *Systematic Theology*, yet of all the writers here discussed he is the one most appropriately called a philosophical theologian. He proposes a philosophical as well as a theological position, using his philosophical work to organize and give conceptual coherence to his theological vision. Bultmann to a certain extent does the same, though he does not offer a systematic account of the Christian faith as a whole. None of these writers holds the traditional view of the relationship of philosophy to theology in any recognizable form, for none of them believes that metaphysics can provide a preamble to faith, in which the Christian faith in God is harmonized with the findings of reason on the origin of the world. Philosophy is used (even by those who deny it any role in theology) to give conceptual clarity to a faith derived primarily from the Bible and the traditional experience of the Christian community, and vitalized by personal vision.

Modern Theology and the Modern World

THE SOURCES AND
TRADITIONAL INHERITANCE OF THEOLOGY

As we have seen, modern theologians are by no means the first to attempt to give intellectual expression to Christian faith, and they cannot ignore the past of their discipline, however modern they find it desirable to be in their own work. Christian theology begins in the New Testament itself. According to the most influential of modern students, Christian faith began in the response of those who had been Jesus' disciples to the mysterious events faith calls his resurrection. The church continued Jesus' own preaching of the Kingdom of God and its imminent and present coming. It added a proclamation of Jesus himself as the one through whom God had established, was establishing and would in future finally establish his own Kingdom. The earliest confession of this faith seems to have consisted in only two words: *Iesous Kyrios*, Jesus is Lord. To explain the meaning of these words, theology was necessary.

The word Jesus clearly refers to Jesus of Nazareth, the son of Joseph and Mary, the rabbi who preached the imminence of God's Kingdom, and was crucified by the Roman authorities, perhaps as a Messianic pretender. To say that he is Lord already involves a strange kind of affirmation, even before we make up our minds what attributing Lordship to him must mean. For those who speak of him in this way, his personal existence and influence in the world, apparently decisively terminated by the action of the authorities in putting him to death, have not terminated at all. On the contrary, his influence is now, it is asserted, so great that only absolute terms are adequate to qualify it. To say that he is Lord is, for Jews, to identify him with the God of the Old Testament, the LORD himself, and, for Gentiles, to consider him as ruler of the universe. To both, the faith of the earliest Christians was highly offensive. For Jews, it constituted, as it still does, idolatry, prohibited by the first commandment. For Gentiles, it was ridiculous as well as offensive, because Jesus was an unimportant person who had been executed as a criminal. Even then there was nothing simple or immediately acceptable about the Christian faith. It required explanation if it was to be believed with the mind. Explanation could hardly render it less offensive, but it might make the nature of the offence intelligible.

As the theologians of the earliest church confronted the task of explanation, they were faced with a cultural difficulty. Christianity had begun on Jewish soil. The early Christians constituted a Jewish sect, differing in degree rather than kind from such a sect as the Essenes, who also believed in the imminence of the Kingdom. Like the other sects, the Nazarenes (or Christians, as they came to be called outside Palestine) held to the presuppositions of Judaism. Over against all their rivals, they alone believed, however, that the hope of the Jews had been fulfilled in Jesus. Believing this, they thought the time had come to extend the privileges of Israel to the rest of the world. They preached to Gentiles as well, which Jesus had not, and soon the church acquired a mixed membership. The many problems thus created dominated the life of the first-century church. Among these was a cultural one. Gentiles of Hellenistic culture could be attracted by the monotheism of the Jewish faith, along with its high ethical teaching. Christianity made monotheism available in a religious form, and not just as a philosophical theory. Judaism also did this, and hence attracted a considerable number of adherents, or 'fearers of God'. But these adherents often hesitated to take the step of circumcision, and so never became full members of the Jewish community. Christianity admitted these people on easier terms: profession of faith and baptism were sufficient to admit them to the full enjoyment of what they had looked upon in Judaism from the outside. But these cultivated Gentiles did not share with the Christian leaders a full Jewish tradition of life and thought, nor could they understand Christianity fully if it continued to be expressed in Jewish terms. Thus, even before the first books of the New Testament came to be written, the primitive community had begun on the task of translating Christianity into the terms of the Gentile Hellenistic world.

To do this involved more than simply to translate Aramaic terms into Greek ones. The basic theological vocabulary of the church was inherited from the Old Testament, and that had already been translated into Greek for the benefit of Hellenistic synagogues outside Palestine. Hence a stock of Greek equivalents for the basic theological terms already existed and was at the disposal of the church. But for Christians as for Jews the question now was, what happened to the meaning of Jewish terms when they were not only translated into Greek but transferred into a Gentile cultural milieu? Could that meaning remain unaltered? It would receive something from the new milieu; would it not also lose something that had been vital to it in the old?

Hellenistic culture was not simply a neutral medium for the reception of the new ideas. It was permeated with religion. This Hellenistic religious outlook had already received a simplified and subtle formulation from the philosophers, Stoic and Platonic. It would not be difficult for a Jewish or Christian monotheism to ally itself with the monotheistic thought of the philosophers; this step had already been taken before Christianity came on the scene. But the Gentile did not understand his human existence and his relation to God in the same way that the Jew did. At a popular level, he might be accustomed to the awe-inspiring rites of the mystery religions, and so fail to be content with synagogue services based on Bible-reading, or with the simple though solemn domestic rites from which the Christian eucharist had grown. Could the eucharist itself be interpreted as a mystery rite, and so taken from a domestic setting that meant little, and become what we call a 'service' or 'liturgy'? Could Jesus himself be fitted into the slots of a Greek philosophy of religion? The Stoics and Platonists in differing ways spoke about the Word, as the Christians did. They meant universal reason, permeating the creation and uniting it to the one God, its origin. Was Jesus also that Word, come to earth and manifested in human form? To answer these questions needed the judgement of a theologian. So we find Paul, John and the other theologians among the New Testament writers grappling with them. The answers must be faithful to the Jewish background which had formed these men, and still meaningful to their Gentile converts, evoking the memories of their religious past too.

The New Testament itself can be regarded from this point of view as an enterprise of translation from one culture to another, strikingly analogous to the work of contemporary theologians in its aims. By the time that the documents of the New Testament had been written and assembled, the process of translation had already proceeded a considerable distance. The original Jewish form of Christianity has been almost lost to view. It can only be inferred by scholars from traces it has left upon the largely Greek idiom of the New Testament. Before the composition of the later books of the New Testament, Jerusalem itself had fallen to the Romans, and Christianity, as well as Judaism, had been deprived of its world-centre. The sect of the Christians had been found unorthodox by the leading rabbis, and the Christians themselves expelled from the synagogues. They now had a distinct new religion on their hands, instead of a sect within Judaism. Henceforward the church would be overwhelmingly Gentile in membership, and would think its faith out theologically in Gentile terms.

By the middle of the fifth century, the process of thinking out was virtually complete. The primitive Christian faith on Jewish ground had centred on the impingement of the future upon the present through the coming of God's Kingdom. But Christ had not returned in triumph. Jewish Christians had been succeeded by Gentiles, for the most part concerned not with a historical hope for the Kingdom of God, but with problems of death and mortality. Some of them did continue to hope for the thousand-year reign of Christ on earth, but this expectation was soon to be declared by the authorities alien to the true faith. The historical hope of the Jews, their *eschatology* as theologians call it, had been almost completely transmuted into the hope of eternal life beyond the death of the individual. Christianity came to be presented as the gift of light for the darkened mind, as immortality for mortal man. The Second Coming of Christ was too prominent in the New Testament to be forgotten by the church, but it became a symbol, even an optional one, and men set their hope on immortality for their souls. The Second Coming was assimilated to another image, far less prominent in the New Testament documents themselves, that of the Last Judgement.

Modern Theology and the Modern World

The main problems of theology were now no longer seen in historical terms but in cosmological ones. Jesus was no longer thought of as the Messiah who had brought in the Kingdom of God, but as the Word, or Logos, who mediated between God and the world. The doctrine of the Trinity was thought out to solve the complex problems of mediation involved in the relationship of God to his creation and its redemption from the powers of darkness and death. The doctrine of the Trinity is the triumph of Greek theology. In Greek it has great lucidity, in spite of its paradoxical character, and granted the set of problems it was designed to solve, offered an elegant and even definitive solution. So far from being nonsense, as it must often appear to those modern Christians who cannot easily make real to themselves the problems it is concerned with, the doctrine is deeply satisfying to the mind, and leaves no loose ends. The solution of the other great problem of Greek theology, the Incarnation, proved more intractable. The earliest Christians had apparently not thought in incarnational terms, but of the action of God in the events of a human life. Once Christian thought made use of Greek terms, a new problem was set. What is the relation of the being of God and the being of man within the unity and individuality of Jesus Christ? From the point of view of the official doctrine of the institutional church, the matter was brought to a conclusion at the great Council of Chalcedon in 451, which brought together in a perhaps somewhat unstable unity the two emphases dominant in previous controversy, upon the unity and divinity of Christ on the one hand, and upon his real humanity on the other. But the formulation of Chalcedon did not satisfy all competent thinkers, and later history suggests that its solution could not easily be held in the minds of Christians as a balanced whole. Traditionally, it appears that Christians have had little difficulty in thinking of Christ as God, but have been less successful in thinking of him as fully human. In modern times, his humanity has been evident enough to them, but his divinity has become more problematic. Theologians who have studied the traditional solutions, and supposedly understand them thoroughly, have not escaped the same difficulties.

The first few centuries of the history of the church are known

28

as the patristic period, that is, the period of the church *fathers*, such as Irenaeus and Tertullian, Clement and Origen, Athanasius, Basil and the two Gregories, Augustine, Cyril and Leo. These men and their contemporaries gave Christian theology its traditional form and language, and theirs is the thought that influenced the great Councils, or ecumenical conferences, that authorized the Creeds now normative over the greater part of Christendom. These men were heirs of the classical culture of the ancient world, and they thought in metaphysical terms derived from the Platonic, Aristotelian and Stoic traditions.

The theologians of the patristic period seldom used the ideas of a particular philosopher to the exclusion of those of others; they regularly drew on several of the great philosophical traditions for their theological purposes. After initial hesitation, for then as now there were conservative churchmen who wished all official statements of faith to be made in the language of the Bible, philosophical terms were used freely, but they were also used eclectically. They were pressed into service to clarify ideas which were theological, not philosophical in their origin. The Council of Nicaea in 325 first introduced a philosophical term into the Christian creed, when it defined the consubstantiality of Christ with the Father, using the Greek word *homoousion*. The word contains the important idea of *ousia*, being. But what does 'being' mean, here or elsewhere? Being can mean one thing to a Platonist, another to an Aristotelian and a third to a Stoic. When the Council of Nicaea invoked it, they can hardly have had the concrete notions of any of these traditions in mind. They must have used the word in a more popular sense, to signify that whatever the Father is, the Son is likewise. Individual theologians, interpreting the common faith, may have had closer associations with particular philosophical schools, but even so they were theologians first and philosophers second.

This principle holds good even when we come to the medieval period, and find among the scholastic theologians of the west thinkers who do come to terms with a particular school of philosophy. Even there, as in the most eminent of the Christian Aristotelians, Aquinas, philosophical terms are transformed in meaning by their Christian use. When Aquinas speaks of 'being' he does not mean what Aristotle meant, for he has applied the term to the living God who said of himself, I am that I am. The *actus purus* of Thomistic thought is not identical with the unmoved mover of Aristotle's theology. Hence it has become fashionable to speak of the existentialism of Aquinas, but this is a confusing usage, for the existence which is spoken of is not the same as that which is central in the thought of modern existentialist philosophers. Aquinas thought of being as an act: *esse* is the infinitive and means 'to be'. So the act of being, or existing, which differs analogically in every being, from God himself to the most insignificant of his creatures, is what gives to each being its distinctive ontological status. When God is called *ipsum esse subsistens*, therefore, he is not, as modern theologians frequently allege, necessarily thought of in a static manner, drawn from the theology of the ancient Greeks. Nevertheless, the preoccupation of the metaphysicians of the Middle Ages with 'being' determined the shape of their thought, and the resulting philosophical theology appeared to their successors to have moved away from the dynamic and personal terms employed by the Bible.

The Reformers were responsible for the re-introduction of biblical terminology into the centre of Christian thought. Luther was a professor of Old Testament studies in a German university, and his theological innovations were intimately connected with his studies of biblical language. Justification by faith had been explained by Latin theology since Augustine in a way which did violence to its original meaning in biblical Greek, and to the Hebrew background of Paul's Greek. Luther was able largely to recover the biblical meaning of the word, though the theological language of the day still imposed some false alternatives upon him when his ideas came into sharp controversy. Luther asserted that, in New Testament usage, 'justify' does not mean 'make righteous', as the Latin theologians had been explaining, but 'to regard as righteous', 'impute righteousness to' someone. Similarly, 'grace' does not mean an influence from God working in the human soul to produce goodness, but the divine favour, given freely out of love. And 'faith' does not mean an intellectual virtue whereby we believe the propositions of the creed when

they are presented to us by the teaching church, but man's openness to the justifying grace of God. From the point of view of the
modern biblical scholar, Protestant or Catholic, Luther was
essentially on the right lines in his interpretation, but the imputa-
tion-impartation alternative, in explaining the meaning of
justification, now appears as a false one. Luther did not always
remain consistent in his own use of terms like faith. When he
suggests that a man is justified when he believes *that* his sins
have been forgiven for Christ's sake, he is vulnerable to the
objections of his opponents that the idea that one is justified is
in danger of being substituted for the reality. In spite of these
difficulties, doubtless inevitable at that time, Luther's new
distinctions have become a permanent part of the heritage of
Christians, especially when confirmed by modern biblical scholarship. The new meaning of justification, and the all-important
distinction between the Law and the Gospel, or the imperative
and the indicative of God, as it has been called in recent theology,
have become basic especially to Protestant theology, and used
as systematic principles of interpretation even in areas of
theology where one might not suppose they could have any
application.

After the Reformation, both Catholics and Protestants
assumed defensive postures, and little creative advance was made
in theology until the nineteenth century. Hence the periods just
described have provided modern theology with both its sources
and the traditional heritage which it must adapt to a new culture.
The problem which it faces will already be apparent. Christian
theology was first developed and thought out in the ancient world.
The men of the middle ages and the Reformation were far closer
to the mind of the ancient world than we are to theirs. Even the
Reformation was a less decisive event in cultural history than
the birth of the modern world. It is not just the Bible, therefore,
but the whole heritage of theology which requires reinterpretation if it is to be easily intelligible to the modern mind.

How can we sum up this heritage? To do so in the space at
our disposal is almost impossible, but the task must be attempted.
First, there is the Bible itself, with its Jewish monotheism and
ethics, creatively developed by Jesus and the theologians of the

primitive church. Then the contribution of the ancient church
gave Christians their creeds, centring on the great doctrines of
the Trinity and the Incarnation, which the theologians had
worked out intellectually in great detail and with much brilliance.
The scholastics provided a total view of the world in which everything from God to the meanest of his creatures could be thought
of as part of a great chain of being. The same clear and consistent
categories of thought could be applied to all. Thus reason
seemed to have moved into harmonious concord with faith. The
Christian who could understand and take in these men's work
could view a vast and sublime picture with rational joy in believing. The Reformers, without destroying this scheme, introduced
new and painful tensions by their insistence on the corruption of
man's will and intellect, and the consequent total need of man for
grace. The Christian picture of the world remained in its essential
outlines, but so fierce were the tensions now present within it
that the picture could hardly be seen as a whole. The Protestant
Christian saw a drama, where the Catholic had seen a beautiful
landscape stretching from Heaven to Hell. In the Protestant
drama God and the devil wrestled in conflict over the soul of man,
but the might of God in Christ prevailed. Believing often against
experience, the Protestant was to go out into the world despising
the demons overcome by Christ, and build a secular life under
the justifying grace of God.

For the Protestant, the dialectic of human corruption and
divine grace meant that the sacred sphere of religion was not
nearer to God than the secular sphere of worldly life and work.
Luther's doctrine of the calling meant that the father of a family,
the magistrate or the peasant was as pleasing to God in his daily
life as the monk had thought to be in his monastery. Hence
Protestantism, which began in the re-assertion of the radical
insufficiency of anything man could do in this life to please God,
even in his most religious activities, ended in affirming this world
more than Catholicism. Secularity is thus for good or ill in great
part the fruit of Protestantism. The Protestant Reformers were
themselves medieval men, occupied with medieval problems,
yet latent in their theology were ideas that combined with other
and independent cultural developments to bring about the

modern world. That world however was not to be born for another two centuries after the Reformation.

THE MAKING OF THE MODERN WORLD

The Reformation gave western man the idea of the intrinsic religious worth of secular life, needing no validation from the sacred. But it preserved the sacred sphere, in which man experienced his vertical relation to God. Protestant man experienced it with a new intensity, formerly known only by the professionally religious man, the monk or the cleric. Protestantism also introduced changes within the sphere of the sacred which over a period of time would put its validity in question for the man of the world.

The Protestant Reformation led, not as a result of the intention of the Reformers, but as a result of their failure to carry the body of the church with them, to the break-up of Christendom, an event which has lately been called by many scholars the end of the Constantinian era. Both terms refer to the rise of a new situation in the relationship of the church to society, in which over a period of time the church became a voluntary organization for that section of society which is interested in religion, instead of being the bond of society as a whole. If society and the church have today moved decisively out of the Constantinian era, the term can remind us that there was once a state of affairs before that era began. The church can hardly regard the Constantinian era as normative for its relation to society, since it had a beginning and an end. The Constantinian era began in the fourth century, when Constantine, the first Christian Emperor, stopped the persecution of the church and made Christianity the state religion, transferring to it all the privileges formerly enjoyed by the pagan religions. From that time on, the church could assume that it lived in a Christian society, in which culture, including thought, law and customs, would be governed by Christian beliefs. The church and the state were two complementary organizations within the one body, the *corpus Christianum*. Thus the church sanctified the state, and the state gave legal sanction to the wishes of the church. This conception of the church's relation to society remained influential until the Enlightenment, and traces of it still linger, especially in Europe and Britain, though not in North America. In such a Christian theory of society, the one church was a bond of cultural unity. It gave intellectual and spiritual foundations to society, in which a serious and corporate attempt was made to organize and order the whole of life in the light of the Christian faith. The church was the principal source of ideas and values, and was afforded the opportunity, denied it in the centuries of persecution, of applying its convictions over the widest possible area of human life. Christendom was both a church to which, in principle, everyone belonged, and a society reflecting the Christian faith in its totality.

The Protestant Reformation did not abandon the ideal of Christendom. Certainly, the radical wing of the Reformation thought that the link between the church and the state should be broken, but its ideas had to wait several centuries before they gained wide acceptance, and then it was in considerably altered form. In their own time, the radicals were strenuously opposed by the leaders of the mainstream of the Reformation, especially Luther himself, and it was in large measure because they challenged the notion of Christendom that they were opposed. The Lutheran, Calvinist and Anglican forms of the Reformation all retained in essentials the notion of Christendom as a society in which all men shared the Christian faith, belonged to the church, and put Christianity into practice in their social as well as their individual life. What was new in the sixteenth century was not the abandonment of the ideal of the Christian society, for it was not abandoned except by the radicals, but the break-up of the unity of the one church. Now, instead of a single church, there were several competing claimants for the role of providing the foundation for a Christian society. Protestants no less than Catholics saw themselves as the inheritors in this respect of the tasks and privileges of the medieval church.

The first signs of the change which came to accomplishment in the modern period appeared when the wars of religion in Europe failed to lead to clear victory for either party. The competing confessions were forced to recognize each other, and allow one another a demarcated sphere of influence, within which each could independently pursue the attempt to create a Christian society, on the basis of their own confession. We can date the end of the medieval world not with Luther's posting of the Ninety-Five Theses on the door of the Castle Church at Wittenberg, but with the Peace of Westphalia (1648), which gave political effect well over a century later to the stalemate in the wars of religion. The Peace stabilized a state of affairs in which some countries would remain Roman Catholic, some Lutheran and others Calvinist.

The end of the medieval world did not lead immediately to the beginning of the modern world. The distinctively modern notion of religious tolerance had not arrived with the Peace of Westphalia. Each confession still enforced conformity in its own territory, and retained the positive ideal of the Christian body politic. In Britain under Cromwell the idea of tolerance made a brief and significant appearance, but even then it was not extended to members of the Church of England. After the Restoration the Act of Uniformity restored the establishment of the Church of England, and imposed penalties on non-conformists. Yet the experience of the Commonwealth and the Restoration had taken England a step nearer to the modern world. The Restoration failed to restore religious unity, and left a substantial body of Christians outside the established church. Their toleration and eventual acceptance could only be a matter of time.

One important effect of the wars of religion was intellectual. The Peace of Westphalia had a counterpart in the life of the mind. If rival embodiments of Christianity could co-exist socially, even though not yet to a significant degree in the same country, perhaps these conflicting embodiments were intellectually justified too. Toleration of theological differences was not just a political necessity: it might reveal aspects of truth hitherto unsuspected by the Christian mind. Men were disgusted with the ferocity with which the wars of religion had been fought, and it occurred to many that this ferocity might be a worse betrayal of the Christian gospel than any amount of heterodoxy. Church doctrine began to be seen no longer as life-giving truth upon which prayer and action could be securely based. Men now began to see it increasingly as a human structure, alienated from reality, and needing to call upon authority precisely because it lacked intrinsic truth. Thus people in Europe were prepared when the new ideas of the Enlightenment spread from Britain to Europe. The Enlightenment systematically exalted the natural reason against the positive doctrines of the warring confessions, and regarded Christianity as a way of life, an ethic, rather than a system of revealed truths. Lessing's fable of the three rings in his *Nathan the Wise* is perhaps the classic example of the new attitude. No one really knows which is the genuine ring (the true religion), but the Father will be best pleased by the endeavours of his sons to live up to the ethical demands they can see, whether the ring is genuine or not. Latent in the fable is the disturbing implication that perhaps none of the rings is genuine.

The late seventeenth and early eighteenth centuries saw the rise of two new forces within the religious world, representing twin expressions of the theological scepticism engendered by the religious wars. The first of these is to be seen in the rationalizing philosophical theology, called Deism in England and usually Free-Thinking in Germany. This type of thought disturbed the centuries old balance between nature and grace, philosophy and theology, reason and revelation, in favour of the first term of each of such pairs. Nature and the natural man were the great ideas that excited the men of the period. The natural was contrasted not just with the artificial in the sense of what is falsely sophisticated by civilization, but with the intellectual structures erected by theology in the name of revelation. These had rendered what was truly natural and clear, mysterious and forbidding, and a source of conflict where none need arise, if men would only hold to what they knew for certain by nature.

The second reaction to the wars of the confessions was a more spiritual one, sometimes combined with the first, but distinct in source and aim. This was the movement known as pietism, the forerunner of what is known in the English-speaking world as Evangelical Christianity. The pietist shared the deist scepticism about dogma, but unlike the deist he did not retreat to rationalizing philosophy and ethics. Instead, he saw the heart of Christianity as lying in devotion: his religion focused on repentance, conversion, regeneration, and cultivation of the new life in small groups of devoted men and women, nourished by bible-study and hymn-singing, and anxious to win others to the same manner of life.

Both of these reactions favoured the development of the new social situation which became a fact in the modern world. The rationalism of the Enlightenment led to the growth of a secular way of thinking, which broke with Christianity as the foundation for individual and social life. Its scepticism about dogma contributed to the modern conviction that religion is a private matter, which ought not to be regulated by social controls. The pietist concentration upon devotion rather than dogma led in the same direction; so did the preference of the pietist for small voluntary associations or groups of committed Christians, over the established churches which brought together the often luke-warm masses. The radical wing of the Reformation had offered a similar criticism of the established church: the pietists were not themselves the descendants of such movements, but their convictions made alliance with those of the descendants of the radicals in a new complex of ideas about the social form of Christianity which has increasingly become the dominant one today, and holds unchallenged sway in North America.

Thus was born the modern, or post-Christendom, situation of the church. Theology is only now beginning to take account of this situation. The church may still be legally established, as in England and in Scotland, but culturally it has ceased to be the effective establishment. It knows itself to be a minority group along with other minorities, in a society which is radically pluralist. No single cultural force is dominant enough to be the establishment, except perhaps applied science, especially as utilized by the military-industrial complex which dominates the acquisitive society of today. In such a society, religion is one possible option, not the cultural cement of the whole. It becomes a private matter, which can only have social implications for the individual and his actions within society, never for society as a whole. Religion now exalts tolerance as an essentially religious principle, and the foundation of human freedom. It claims toleration rather than privilege for itself from the secular state, tolerates its own religious rivals on principle, and gradually ceases to expect to lay down even moral standards for society. Where the full consequences of the new situation have been accepted, Christians are in alliance with humanists in demanding that the state refrain from interference in the private domain. To that domain, personal ethics as well as religion are now thought to belong. The law should confine itself to strictly public matters, and morals are not among them, except where the freedom of other individuals is involved.

No change could well be more complete. Yet this is no return to the pre-Constantinian era, as some have romantically assumed. No one can respond to the call: 'Back to the catacombs.' Western society may not be Christian any longer, at least in any traditional sense, but it is not pagan, and it has been Christian. Christianity has no need to fight rival religions, though some modern totalitarian regimes certainly have a strongly quasi-religious tone. It is not clear that martyrdom could even be relevant in the modern secular state. Its control of the means of communication could render the witness of the martyr totally ineffective, except on spiritual levels of which modern man takes no account. The totalitarian state is indeed in some sense pagan, but is not a genuinely modern development; it is rather a conservative, panic reaction to the freedom of the modern secular world, and draws upon the vestiges of emotions that once gave support to Christendom, though they have since become divorced from Christian thought and values. So far as Marxism is genuinely modern, it is at odds with the totalitarian tendencies of the institutional communism it has given rise to. It is not even clear that we can talk about a post-Christian era today, as many do, unless we are prepared to identify Christianity and Christendom. Many Christian values have won general acceptance, and are incorporated in the so-called secular view of life. The church is in a situation which is radically new, and the past provides no landmarks by which to orient oneself to it.

Underlying these changes, and others to be discussed shortly, is the transformation of the material basis of society brought about by the industrial revolution. This built upon the scientific discoveries of the seventeenth and eighteenth centuries, and gathered momentum, especially in Britain and Germany, in the nineteenth century, and from these countries spread to the whole western world. Perhaps this transformation was the most important of all the factors which brought the modern world into being. A Marxist would say that it was the cause of the others. To enter into adequate debate with those who contend that this is so would require both space and competence not at my disposal. But the present account implies a different view, that material changes involve technical capacities which a society does not possess until creative thinkers have developed the necessary fundamental theory. Once the theory is applied at the technical level, it then brings about transformations in social relationships, and hence cultural changes, which alter the way people think. Hence the relationship between the ideal and the material in human life is even more dialectical, in my opinion, than at least popular Marxism represents it as being. This is not to underestimate, I believe, the importance of material factors, and many of the theologians here discussed would incidentally regard it as a misunderstanding of Christianity if a theologian saw it as his duty to do so.

The transformation of society brought about by the industrial revolution and its contemporary successors, the electronic and perhaps now a biological revolution, is a familiar story which need not be told again. What is necessary here is to recall the way in which this transformation influenced theological thought. Pervasive as this influence is, we can especially see it, I think, at two points, firstly, the rise in importance of the middle class, along with the appearance of the working class as a new social group unknown in the days of classical Christian theology, and secondly, the transformation of man's relationship to nature, carrying with it profound changes in his understanding of what it means to be human.

Christianity, especially Protestant Christianity, is at the present time in the west the religion of the middle classes. To say this might lead to the conclusion, which would be false, that it is therefore a dominant cultural force. Rather, in becoming the religion of the middle classes, Christianity underwent changes, some of which have already been described, which rendered it a less powerful social force than it had formerly been. First, to say that Christianity is the religion of the middle classes is as much a negative statement as a positive one: it is no longer, to any significant degree, the religion of the upper classes, and it has never been the religion of the industrial working classes, which themselves came into being after the break-up of Christendom. Second, in becoming the religion of the middle classes, Christianity was adapted to its needs. In this role, it is neither a creative standpoint for individuals, stimulating art, literature, philosophy or social action, nor is it a programme for society. Its role is rather to reinforce the bourgeois social attitudes which give the middle class its identity. Popular middle-class Christianity is concerned with private morality, the realm left untouched by the national state. It leaves business and political morality autonomous, often on principle, usually unconsciously. What it is primarily concerned with is personal goodness, the morality of the family and the small group.

The rise of the middle class in western society has been associated with the growth of political democracy. The theological consequences of this development are harder to assess, but perhaps they lie in the field of authority and its meaning. In the democratic state, it is understood that the state may not dictate to its citizens what they should privately think. Of course it still does so in many ways, notably by the manipulation of the media of information. But the commonly held political theory assumes that it ought not to. Religious belief is understood, as we have noted, to belong to this private realm, and the theory fits in well with the middle-class assumption that religion is in any case concerned with private matters. There is a kind of truce between religion and society, an agreement on each side to leave one another alone. A man's religion is his own business, both in the sense that no one else can tell him what it should be, and that he must not live it out in such a way as to affect the privacy of others. Possibly this new attitude has altered people's views of the role of religious authority, reinforcing other influences destructive of the old authorities of Bible and church. The popular liberal Protestantism is strongly anti-clerical: the layman considers he has as much insight into religious truth as the priest, and he will not have the priest telling him what to think. This attitude gains force if it is assumed that religion is primarily concerned with ethics, for ethical practice needs no dogmatic authority. If a man cannot see his ethical obligations for himself, it is unlikely that he will be able to under the instruction of a religious authority.

Equally important for theology is the change in the view of man which characterizes the culture of today. Theology has always been interested in the relation of man to nature. Classical Christian thought reflects a period in which man felt himself to be other than nature, dependent upon it and its mysterious inner workings, able to live successfully with nature if he could understand and cooperate with these workings, but different from nature as belonging also to the realm of spirit. Perhaps this view of man reflects an economic basis in agriculture. Since the industrial revolution man has learned to understand nature much better, and in many ways to dominate and change it. In many parts of the world he has already drastically altered his environment, so that it has been to a great extent humanized. Curiously enough, the result is often felt to be inhuman, but the inhumanity, on reflection, turns out to be that of man, not of nature. Man now regards himself as the master of nature, as the agent of his own evolution. These changes, on the other hand, have been accompanied by developments in the biological sciences which stress man's continuity, even identity, with nature, in relation to the animals first, and then to the whole world of living creatures. Contemporary sensibility sees man as a part of nature, exercising the natural prerogative of transforming other parts of nature for his own purposes.

Such a view is different at almost every point from the one incorporated in classical Christian theology. It does not distinguish man from nature by relating him to a transcendent world. It sees him, on the contrary, as continuous with nature, though not dependent upon it in such a way as to constitute a model for conceiving his dependence on his creator. It does not advise him to live close to nature and its rhythms, through a liturgical round of seasonal festivals. There is no need to mythologize nature if you are simply part of it. This stress upon the continuity of man with nature, characteristic of present-day sensibility, also accommodates some aspects of man's nature which theologians have been apt to blame the modern world for ignoring.

In the nineteenth century, theologians often felt obliged to come to terms with evolutionary optimism about man. The twentieth-century theologians discussed below were in advance of many of their contemporaries in abandoning an optimistic view of man. Earlier than thinkers in many other fields, they warned people about the dangers to man in the totalitarian states of the nineteen-thirties. The view of man they had come to hold was thus somewhat better able than those of many of their contemporaries to absorb the moral shock of the concentration camps without being disrupted. In a sense they were already prepared, so far as anyone could be prepared for such a thing, to see man in the ghastly light shed by the burning fires of the extermination camps.

The contemporary secular view of man is also not an optimistic one, in the sense of expecting man to leave his animal past wholly behind him in some foreseeable future. It is highly optimistic technically, somewhat pessimistic in what it expects for man's spiritual development. Original sin has become a metaphor for theologians, but at the same time the metaphor has become a meaningful one within a widespread contemporary sensibility. The full implications of the concentration camps for our view of man have certainly not yet been absorbed either by theologians or by moral philosophers. What, for example, is the significance of the fact that they seem wholly to lack a counterpart in animal behaviour? Perhaps a future theology will be able to take more adequate account of these happenings.

One more consequence of the industrial transformation of society remains to be considered. The nineteenth century saw the beginnings of world-wide communications, and in the twentieth they were to be immensely speeded up, through the invention of flying, radio, TV, the orbital communications satellite, and other techniques. As the industrial revolution gathered momentum, the developing societies of the west needed communications with the primary producing countries of Africa and Asia which were the source of their raw materials. Hence the West found itself coming into much closer contact with other cultures. Associated with the colonizing efforts of the imperial powers, already begun before the industrial revolution got under way, were the endeavours of missionaries to spread the Christian faith outside the borders of the old Christendom. Again, it will be a matter of controversy between historians whether these missions were the result of the imperialism of the powers whose nationals the missionaries mostly were, or whether missions were an autonomous development of the Christian mind. The fact is that in the Protestant missionary movement which began at the close of the eighteenth century they were very closely associated. Before our own time very few missionaries, with the exception of some radical Roman Catholics who failed to carry their church with them, knew how to distinguish clearly between the export of western culture, and the propagation of the Christian faith.

Whatever the reasons why missions were undertaken at the particular period they were, they had an unforeseen effect. Missions brought to the intellectuals of Europe a new knowledge of other religions. They were no longer able to ignore either the 'primitive' religions, which appealed to the Enlightenment mind as specimens of the 'natural', or the 'higher' religions which were the cultural equals of Christianity itself, though not everyone could recognize them as such. From the end of the eighteenth century on, it was part of the intellectual awareness of philosophers and theologians that Christianity did not stand alone, as the true religion surrounded by nothing but pagan darkness, as had earlier been supposed, but that it is one among a number of higher religions flourishing in different cultures. Hence it was concluded that however much such religions might differ among themselves, and many were more struck by their likenesses than by their differences, they can be seen as parallel and formally similar types of response to the situation of man in the world. In any case, it was at once noted that the ethical teaching, in particular, of the higher religions is very similar.

The new consciousness of Christianity as set in the context of other religions paralleled the acceptance, tacit as it often was, by the various Christian groups in the west that they must co-exist in a pluralistic society. As man became increasingly conscious of himself as a member of a single world-wide human race, a consciousness becoming characteristic of educated people in our own time, he learned to think of the religions too as co-existing in a state of mutual tolerance, as the confessions had begun to do within the Christian group as a whole. The co-existence of the confessions had led to the idea that there is no one absolute version of Christianity, but that the differences between the confessions are only relative. A similar idea now grew up in relation to the religions as a whole: perhaps there is no one true religion, but these too are relative to one another and to the cultures in which they are found. The philosophers drew these conclusions very rapidly, the theologians slowly and reluctantly, with a clear realization that to do so would be to break with past tradition, and with New Testament teaching. Hence too there have been attempts to retain the notion of the absoluteness of Christianity, coupled with cultural respect for the other religions. The nineteenth century also saw the rise of a new academic discipline, the history of religions, which tried to study the religions from a neutral standpoint and for the sake of their inherent human interest, instead of the standpoint of the Christian missionary.

SCIENCE AND PHILOSOPHY

We have already seen reason to think of modern theology as haunted by science, for the latter has come to play the same integrating role in modern culture as theology played in the Middle Ages. In the eighteenth century, theology and science could meet upon the common ground of philosophy. Science was thought of as natural philosophy, a term still used in the Scottish universities. Theology, by the same token, could be regarded as the supernatural extension of philosophy. Theology and metaphysics bore upon a common object, which they studied from different points of view, while metaphysics drew upon natural philosophy, or physics, for some of its basic material. Theology started from metaphysics, or physico-theology, and went on to clarify with its aid the content of the revelation of the God whose existence metaphysics had established. Philosophy offered a language and a conceptual framework used by both science and theology.

While this state of affairs lasted, it could be taken for granted that theology and science could speak to each other, and the findings of one influence the other. Once science began to make progress, however, it learned that it must assert its independence of theology; it could not be free to make the discoveries of which it must be capable, if its findings were to be prescribed in advance by dogma. But was theology likewise independent of science? Today, it is commonly asserted by theologians that it is. It is often said that science and theology cannot conflict, since their objects are different: they belong to spheres which cannot intersect. In general, the theologians of the nineteenth century continued to assume that science is relevant to Christian theology, and that it would probably be necessary to modify both the method and the particular results of theological work in the light of the scientific advances constantly being made.

Eighteenth-century thinkers, on both the philosophical and the theological sides, had already begun to realize that science was far more than a way of finding out new facts about the Creation that it had not pleased God to reveal in Holy Scripture. Newton and other pioneers of science may have believed something like this, but once science turned its attention to the past, especially to the origins of man, such a view became peculiarly difficult to maintain. The new view of man's origin was apparently in simple conflict with the biblical story, which readers of the Bible were then tending to regard as divinely-inspired science, instead of myth. So, on the one hand, there could be a conflict between science and Scripture, and on the other, science was coming to be recognized as more than a body of theories and established facts. It was a method of arriving at truth, one so powerful that it seemed destined to supersede all others. In the middle of the nineteenth century, Auguste Comte, the positivist philosopher, put the matter with compelling simplicity:

According to the fundamental doctrine (sc. of positivism) all our speculations on every subject of human enquiry are bound to pass successively, both in the individual and the race, through three different theoretical stages, usually known as Theological, Metaphysical and

Positive. . . . The first of these states, though in every respect indispensable at the outset, must henceforth be regarded as purely provisional and preparatory. The second is but a modified and destructive form of the first, and thus has only the transitional office of leading gradually to the third. This last is the only normal and final state of human reason in all departments of knowledge. (Comte, *A Discourse on the Positive Spirit*, 1844, tr. 1905, p. 199.)

The 'positive' state referred to is of course the scientific one.

Science was always felt as a threat, while theology remained orthodox in the older Protestant sense, that is, based on the doctrine of the literal inspiration of the Bible, and holding that such inspiration applied as much to the historical as to the doctrinal passages. Science offered alternative and more plausible explanations for such matters as the origin and early history of man, where reliance had formerly been placed upon an inspired Bible. In the latter part of the century, when Darwin produced evidence for natural selection, placing philosophical speculation about evolution on a firmly scientific basis, the debate between theology and science centred upon the doctrine of man.

Theology received a profound shock from these discoveries of Darwin. Not only was it no longer possible to regard man as a creature fallen from a historical state of original righteousness, but it now seemed as if he was not the object of a special act of divine creation. In no essential respect could man be distinguished from the beasts whose descendant he was. Later, the psychological discoveries of Freud, and the work of the ethologists, would offer powerful reinforcement for the same view of man as simply a highly evolved animal. Hence conservative theologians fought evolutionary theory tooth and nail, as indeed their successors, the extreme fundamentalists, do today. They tried to break the theory down by every possible kind of *a priori* criticism, since they could hardly challenge Darwin's observations. Surely if the theory had possessed any fundamental logical weakness, the intensity of this criticism must have shattered it. But the theory of natural selection did not rely upon *a priori* reasoning, such as similar reasoning could defeat, but upon evidence. The defenders of Genesis could bring forward no fresh evidence in favour of the biblical story, to upset the compelling pattern of observed facts on which Darwin had brought public attention to bear in his work.

Earlier in the century, science had made further inroads upon the belief in the supernatural, first called radically in question by the Enlightenment. Science then seemed to be discovering immutable laws of nature which made miracle impossible, including those central miracles upon which argument for the divinity of Christ had rested. No doubt in every period men have regarded reported miracles with a certain scepticism, at least initially; otherwise, presumably, the notion of miracle would be an empty one. The New Testament does not fail to report the scepticism with which the first accounts of the resurrection of Christ were received by the leaders among his disciples. But the world-view of the first century could accommodate miracles. They were, no doubt, highly improbable, but it was agreed that they were possible, and so, given good enough evidence, reported miracles could gain credence. So it remained until the rise of science.

Whatever the laws of nature had been understood to mean in a pre-scientific age, God could clearly suspend them for his own higher purposes. Science, at least at first, changed all that: it replaced philosophical speculation about the laws of nature with the discovery of concrete laws, and thus began to give a new meaning to the concept of law. Nineteenth-century science tended to see the world on the model of a vast machine, and in this model, scientific laws were unbreakable. The regularity of the universe could not be infringed without destroying the basis of science, and rendering it once again unintelligible to the human mind. But since the regularity of nature was constantly being verified with every fresh experiment, and no new evidence of a convincing kind came in to support the occurrence of miracles, the scientists became extremely sure of their principle.

Present-day science operates with a less mechanistic model. The concept of unbreakable law, with its implications for a rigid causality operating throughout nature, is being replaced, if only to account for observations at the sub-atomic level, with a notion, going back to Hume in its origins, of statistical regularity. Thus, the present-day scientist is more likely to speak of a high degree of probability of one event following upon another, than of the first causing the second. Whether this makes the notion of miracle any easier to entertain scientifically, may well be doubted. The notion of statistical regularity only provides for the occurrence of a limited set of possible events following upon a given previous event. Miracle would involve the appearance of an event not belonging to this set, and even if the likelihood of this happening may be expressed in terms of probability, instead of being ruled out *a priori*, the probability assigned to a miraculous event is likely to be so near zero that the difference is academic. The statistical probability of a death being followed by its reversal in a resurrection will always be regarded, one supposes, as a very low one. Nor, indeed, is it clear that the concept of statistical probability, developed to account for observations of the behaviour of sub-atomic particles, has any application to the macroscopic events with which the theologian is concerned when he thinks of miracle. Whatever the problems created by scientific notions for such traditional topics as miracle and free will, they remain basically philosophical problems, and it is unlikely that they will be resolved or removed by any discoveries or theories emanating from science.

Whether a more contemporary understanding of scientific law makes miracle easier to incorporate into a scientifically-grounded picture of the world may therefore be doubted. At any rate, there is no agreement among the most influential of contemporary theologians that it does. In the nineteenth century, the conflict seemed direct and sharp. One must choose between science, and a theological defence of miracle involving clear breaches in the uniformity and regularity of nature. Miracles could no longer be simply *believed in*, as in the past. In order to maintain miracles, the theologian must now devise a special theory of the operation of the laws of the universe, and of God's relation to the world. Only theological exigencies made this theory necessary: philosophical considerations did not require it. Believing in miracles now involved not just faith, but a special philosophy for the purpose, or even much pseudo-scientific rationalizing of the biblical accounts. The concept of miracle acquired a meaning unprecedented in Christian history, whether one tried to retain it or not. It is not surprising that a number of leading theologians were willing to give it up.

If the miracles were to be discarded, theology was in for a difficult time. If it was no longer possible to believe in the Virgin Birth and the bodily resurrection of Jesus, let alone in the miracles reported in his ministry, without developing a special philosophy in order to do so, the wisest course might be to see if the doctrines of Christianity could be maintained without invoking miracles. But since the divinity of Christ had been bound up with these central miracles in the theology of the past, to give up the miracles meant for many to give up the divinity of Christ. Many nineteenth-century theologians took this step, either abandoning the divinity of Christ altogether, or more usually replacing it with an idea that functioned equivalently, such as his God-consciousness, or his Messianic consciousness. Later, theological critics such as Troeltsch came to see an 'internal miracle' in this idea too, and historical critics doubted that the evidence justified invoking it. Others tried to retain the divinity of Christ and the central miracles associated with it, while abandoning the nature miracles of the ministry, either offering rationalizing explanations, or suggesting that the gospel record of them was inauthentic.

I have already pointed out that the real importance of scientific method lies for theology at least not so much in any particular discoveries that may have resulted from it, as in its implications for the nature of knowing. Science appeared, as it still appears, to offer an uniquely reliable way of gaining information about reality. Thus from the time that Kant was 'awakened from his dogmatic slumbers' by reading the works of Hume, the question of how we come to have reliable information about reality became a central one for philosophers. Kant distinguished between the phenomena that we experience and what he called 'things in themselves', and showed that we cannot be supposed, without contradiction, to have knowledge of the latter. What we know, and know reliably, are the objects of our experience, the phenomena. To our knowledge of these the knowing mind contributes much, through the *a priori* concepts it brings to experience. Time, space, causality, substance and the like are not simply given with the phenomena to our experience. Our minds apply these *a priori* concepts to the objects of experience. Thus metaphysics, as a science of being, was judged impossible, and only empirical knowledge, along with the transcendental deduction of the categories, remained.

The combined impact of Hume's empiricism and Kant's critical philosophy proved destructive to the rational theology of the Enlightenment, brought to its highest pitch by Leibniz and Wolff. Hume had exploded the idea of causality upon which the cosmological arguments for the existence of God had rested, and Kant, besides drawing attention to fallacies in all the existing arguments for God, showed that in any case it is not possible for God to become an object of knowledge in experience. But Kant considered that in removing knowledge he had made way for faith. He considered it possible to restore in the sphere of the practical reason what he had removed in that of the pure reason. He regarded the Ideas of God, freedom and immortality as necessary postulates of the practical reason, entailed by the categorical imperative, the given reality of moral obligation. These Ideas were after all needed if moral life was to bear the supreme weight of importance Kant wished to attach to it. God must be postulated if the highest good, the equation of happiness with virtue, were to be realized. Though God could not become an object of theoretical knowledge, this practical knowledge was sufficient for the demands of the moral life. It was the knowledge afforded by a 'rational faith'. Kant regarded religion as simply morality interpreted as duty to God. Anything more than this was priestcraft and spurious service. Both Kant's transcendental idealism coupled with empirical realism, and his moralization of religion, were to have a great influence upon future theology, though the immediate effect of his work was favourable to scepticism. When we find theologians of the German tradition decrying metaphysics, while asserting that God is a transcendent person known only to faith, we can detect the influence of Kant. It is a commonplace of this tradition, right up to the present day, to follow Hume and Kant, ignoring the irony of the former, in believing that the destruction of metaphysics is a benefit to faith, and hence to theology.

For Hegel, however, the philosophy of his time had resulted in what he seems to have been the first to call 'the death of God'. When philosophy renounced God as its proper object, religion in turn was plunged into 'an infinite grief'. Hegel could see nothing but disguised atheism in the theologies that corresponded to or appeared in the thought of Kant, Fichte and Jacobi, the idealists of his time. For them the Absolute was above reason. Hegel took the opposite view, and developed a Concept of God. Ironically it was his influence, and not that of the Kantians, that underlay the systematic atheism of the nineteenth century, in Bruno Bauer, Feuerbach, Marx and Nietzsche. Hegel himself wished to overcome, much in the manner of the Enlightenment, the 'positivity' of traditional Christianity, in which God is simply given, by once more making God the object of rational thought, the supreme Concept in which his whole system of thought comes to rest. God is for him the Absolute Spirit, with which man's subjective spirit is ultimately one. The real meaning of Christianity lies in its revelation of the Concept of Godmanhood, the unity of man with God, as an eternal truth. Theologians and atheists alike were able to call on the rich thought of Hegel to justify their own ideas, and his influence on theology was second only to that of Kant. In either a Kantian or a Hegelian sense, virtually the whole of nineteenth-century theology was idealist.

HISTORICAL METHOD

Hegel had another sort of influence on theology, of a more indirect kind, for his work laid the foundations of the philosophy of history, and led to history being regarded as the basic academic method in virtually every arts subject. Like science, history goes back to the Greeks, but it experienced a revolutionary development at the beginning of the nineteenth century through the development of a critical method that greatly increased the reliability of its findings. The development of critical history was of even greater importance to the theologian than that of modern science, for the former took an immediate place in his own work, in the study of the Bible. In the eighteenth century Lessing had already advised people to read the Bible as they would any other book, then a revolutionary idea; Lessing added that the uniqueness of the Bible among books would then become apparent of its own accord. As it happened, Lessing had particularized: read the Bible, he had said, as you would Livy. It was the investigations of the Roman historian Barthold Georg Niebuhr into the sources of Livy's history of the Roman republic that did much to put critical history on a firm methodological basis. Niebuhr found that most of what Livy said about pre-republican Rome was of very little historical value.

When the same methods were applied to the Bible, by Niebuhr among others (they had been pioneered in the previous century by Reimarus), the results were equally destructive of traditional orthodoxy. It did not take the critic long to conclude that Moses was not (as tradition had affirmed) the author of the Pentateuch, the first five books of the Bible, containing precisely those stories which gave difficulty to the modern mind, the creation and fall of man, the flood, the call of Abraham, the captivity in Egypt and the Exodus, and the giving of the two tablets of the Law on Mount Sinai. This important conclusion, still not accepted by many fundamentalists, rests not upon a single decisive argument (though the fact that the Pentateuch records the death of Moses might do) but upon the cumulative effect of a mass of detailed evidence, compelling to the mind of anyone who has looked at all of it. The proof that Moses' authority could no longer rationally be invoked to support the historicity of these stories served to reinforce existing doubts entertained upon other critical grounds. It was likewise used to uphold *a priori* argument against their truth, based on the obviously legendary and miraculous character of much of this material. Soon it became commonplace among theologians to suppose that there was nothing, or virtually nothing, reliable in all this literature. The Old Testament came to be of low repute among theologians, both on historical and on ethical grounds, and it has regained much of its former position of importance and esteem only in contemporary times, as a result of scholarship that has concentrated more upon its theological meaning than on the attempt to convert its myths and legends into pseudo-history.

It was not, however, in the study of the Old Testament that the so-called 'higher criticism' made its greatest impact, but in that of the Gospels.

It quickly became apparent that the Gospels were not the work of immediate eye-witnesses of the events they record. Perhaps none of the Gospels is the work of any of Jesus' own disciples, though the traditional attribution of the Fourth Gospel to the beloved disciple was long clung to, and still finds scholarly upholders today; it cannot be ruled out as impossible. In any case, however, it was soon established that the Gospels were not the earliest parts of the New Testament, having been composed some time after the letters of Paul, perhaps one or even two generations after the lifetime of Jesus. For a time, a tendency prevailed among the critics to very late dating, pushing John, and even Matthew and Luke, well into the second century. About the middle of the nineteenth century, the priority of Mark was established reasonably securely, though it is not logically impossible that Matthew was written first, and the view has been ably defended in recent years. The Gospel of Mark had been little read in the past, in comparison with its companions. Almost everything it contained was to be found in the other Gospels, along with much else, such as the birth stories and the sermon on the mount, about which it was silent. Hence in pre-critical days it had hardly been noticed that Mark's Gospel offered a portrait of Jesus strikingly different from that of conventional piety, one which proved highly attractive to the modern age.

The Marcan portrait thus formed the foundation of many of the reconstructions of the historical Jesus produced by nineteenth-century scholars. Once criticism began to work on the Gospels, it was realized that Jesus may have been very different, in historical fact, from the picture of him offered by either piety or dogma. Many seized on this possibility as a way of escape from the bondage they found in these traditional pictures. Some of the earlier nineteenth-century reconstructions of the life of Jesus, such as those of Strauss and Bauer, were motivated as much by hatred of the dogmatic picture of Jesus as by love of their subject. However, they raised genuine historical questions, present in the material, though their reconstructions contain little of permanent value. Their achievement was to make it impossible for those who came after them to evade the questions. The story of the success and failure of the nineteenth-century 'quest of the historical Jesus' has been brilliantly told by Albert Schweitzer in his book of that name.

Historical method became an indispensable part of the equipment of all scholars working with the past. Since the quest of the historical Jesus was of such central importance to the theologians of the nineteenth century, they were able to contribute a great deal to the refinement of historical-critical techniques, and indeed the story of New Testament criticism is one of the most technically fascinating in scholarship, apart from the importance of the questions it undertook to solve. In essence, the critical method is an attempt to approach historical material with as few assumptions as possible. Only such an approach can tell us anything we do not already know. The historian tries to confine himself to asking what is the evidence, what is its value, and what conclusions can properly be drawn from it. The material available to the historian, in the form of documents and artifacts from the past, is of a very different kind from that at the disposal of the scientist. It seldom admits of anything comparable to an experiment, by which the predictive value of a theory can be tested. Apart from the inapplicability of prediction to the past, chance, rather than the power and accuracy of historical theory, largely dictates what fresh evidence will be found, to confirm or falsify historical hypotheses.

An instructive case is provided by the history of first-century Judaism, knowledge of which is vital for the proper understanding of Christian origins. The finding of the first of the Dead Sea Scrolls in 1947 led to the opening up of a whole body of fresh evidence which has transformed the scholarly picture of the Judaism of the time when Christianity was born. First reactions indeed suggested that a cultural matrix had now been found which completely accounted for Christianity, thus destroying the uniqueness on which some of its apologetic claims had traditionally rested. More sober assessment does not detract from the value of the discovery, but it does suggest that our new knowledge of the Essene community, which in all probability produced the scrolls, permits us to see early Jewish Christianity in less complete contrast to contemporary Judaism, and rather as one among a broad spectrum of sects, whose convictions are more intelligible against the background of this more complex Judaism. By the same token, many features of the New Testament documents previously thought accountable for only by Gentile influence are now seen to be entirely Jewish, and this discovery favours an early dating for some documents which had been previously assigned a late date on the ground of supposed Gentile influence.

If the chance discovery of a body of ancient documents has not wholly revolutionized New Testament studies in the most recent period, it has clearly led to a striking development, and since not all the scrolls have been edited and published, it is too early to say what the final result will be. What we learn from this about critical history is that however sophisticated its methods, and they are indeed sophisticated in biblical studies, it would have been impossible to produce our present picture of first-century Judaism and early Christianity's place within it unless that evidence had happened to turn up. Past events leave traces for the future investigator to find, not in accordance with his needs, but with the working of chance. Chance kept historians from knowing more than a very little about the Essenes, until chance in turn furnished them with a rich fund of information, throwing light on many more problems than it is possible to mention here. What else do we not know of first-century Judaism, or early Christianity, that might further alter our picture of both if we knew it? We cannot conclude from such reflections that historical method should be abandoned as wholly unreliable. Dependent as it is on chance for its evidence, it is still the most reliable method of investigating the past that we have. Its conclusions can only be successfully challenged by more rigorous application of its own methods, as has continually happened in the quest of the historical Jesus. What should be concluded is that the historian must be far more modest in his claims for the reliability of his findings than the scientist need be.

The aim of the historian is to reconstruct a situation which could have left just these traces and no other, but the aim is almost unattainable. Only if we knew that every significant aspect of the past situation had left a commensurate trace could we be assured that our reconstruction was authentic, given a perfect technique of assessment of the evidence and deduction from it. In practice, the traces are always incomplete and doubtless disproportionate to the structure of the situation that produced them. It is always possible that several different situations could have left the traces we have, and we have very few objective criteria for distinguishing between their relative probability. When it comes to connecting one reconstructed situation with another, to produce the history of a period, the possibilities of error are not added but multiplied. Hence the best historians are often the most modest in their claims for their own reconstructions of the past. The most that can be claimed for them is that they are compatible with the evidence we have at present. The appearance of fresh evidence would almost certainly compel their revision.

The historian's craft is therefore as much an art as a science. He is seldom dealing with material that can furnish him with a clear Yes or No to his questions. It is always a matter of probability, and in the assessment of this kind of probability personal factors, such as 'intuition', or 'having the feel of a period', enter in. Given the same evidence and the same method, one man will be better than another at reconstructing the past. How do we know if he has succeeded, in that relative sense in which success in historical investigation can be spoken of? The only success there is, normally speaking, is the agreement of the historian's own professional colleagues that his work stands up to their criticism. A historical statement is probable if it is thought to be so by the consensus of workers in a particular field, over a period of time sufficiently long for the possible objections and alternatives to have been fully discussed.

These observations encourage considerable scepticism about 'assured results' in history, whether in the realm of the Bible or of secular history. Hence there has been some reaction away from the objective view of history which arose in the nineteenth century, and many philosophers of history have asserted that presuppositionless historical investigation is impossible. Only the right presuppositions, it is claimed, can bring one into that

kind of relationship with the material that leads to fruitful communication between the past and the present, so that the past
can again speak to us with a living voice, as the theologian in
particular must hope that it will. On the other hand, the newer
views clearly open the way to dogma and prejudice in a way that
the older one in intention at least did not, and in the last resort can
only justify even greater scepticism on the part of the critic.
Even if a particular presupposition in approaching the evidence
permits a vivid reconstruction, only the evidence itself can tell
one whether the reconstruction is historical fiction or a distorted
but recognizable view of the past. If the evidence is incomplete,
so must be the reconstruction.

Nineteenth-century biblical critics were borne up on a wave of
optimism about the possibilities of the new science of critical
history. They believed it would sweep away the dust, confusion
and pious imagination of the centuries, and bring them face to face
with Jesus as he actually was. The vision was an intoxicating one,
and promised a quite new and far more reliable sort of theology,
from the modern point of view, as well as freedom from the
power of priestcraft and dogma. Countless lives of Jesus were
produced out of this conviction, and a trickle of them continues
to appear up to the present time. A fascinating twentieth-century
example of this typically nineteenth-century quest is to be found
in *The Passover Plot*, recently brought out by the independent
scholar Hugh J. Schonfield. The author has a gripping tale to
tell, but he ought not to be able to convince us that it is true. The
reason does not lie, of course, in the unorthodoxy of his picture of
Jesus, for there is nothing new or necessarily unacceptable about
that. The same objections would apply to a fully orthodox picture
produced by the same methods. Rather, the type of evidence
afforded by the Gospel writers as historical sources is not such
as to permit us to proceed to a reconstruction of the life of Jesus
as full and detailed as the one Schonfield presents. All reconstructions of this type must founder on the rock of the historical
inadequacy of the sources for such a purpose.

The vision of a truly historical Jesus, freed from the trappings
of dogma and piety, was to fade, for most scholars, before the
nineteenth century came to an end. Of the causes of its fading,

one had already been discussed in the last few paragraphs, the limitations of historical criticism as a means of finding out the truth about the past. Historical criticism is indeed, as pious people have complained, destructive. It destroys the credibility of traditional views of the past, without necessarily putting much of religious value in their place. Yet the study of the New Testament by critical means has greatly enriched our understanding of the early church, somewhat in proportion to the increase in our scepticism about the historical Jesus. Why is this?

The answer lies in what the critical method told New Testament scholars about the sources at their disposal. The more the Gospels were studied the more clear it became that they were neither 'the memoirs of the Apostles', as a second-century writer had naïvely put it, nor the first biographies of the man Jesus, as the nineteenth-century critics had more or less unanimously assumed. The Gospel writers had a clear purpose, which governed their treatment of all the material they transmitted. They wrote to evoke faith in Jesus as the present Lord of the church, ruling it through the Spirit; their own work was one medium of the Spirit's governance of the community. They and their readers were living, as they believed, in the last years of human history before the triumphant return of Christ. The Gospels are propaganda literature, in the original and literal meaning of the word. They were written to propagate the Christian faith, not to transmit historical information for the benefit of future scholars. They resemble sermons more than they do biographies. Perhaps this does not mean that the would-be biographer of Jesus can extract nothing of value to himself from their work, but there is in fact so little of what he needs, and so much that he must discard, that there remains little to support his project of writing a life of Jesus. This is the second reason for the fading of the vision of the Jesus of history.

Some far-sighted theologians, especially among the systematic theologians as opposed to the biblical scholars, were beginning to realize the significance of these facts before the nineteenth century came to an end. They began to pose the issue in the form of a dilemma, as Albert Schweitzer would a decade or more later as a biblical scholar. But their dilemma was a different one.

Schweitzer was interested in the original question of what could be learned from the sources about Jesus as a historical character. He was led to pose the alternative in terms of interpretation: either consistent eschatology or consistent scepticism. Either we admit that we can make no sense out of the Gospel record, or we must work on the assumption that Jesus was totally governed by an apocalyptic vision, in which his own ministry appeared as the key to open up the coming of God's kingdom within the lifetime of his own disciples. In that case, it would have to be admitted that the Jesus of history was a remote, even alien figure, a man who could have little attraction for a nineteenth-century liberal scholar holding a harmonious view of life centred round a strong ethical concern. Jesus as he really was would turn out to be, in short, a deluded fanatic, who tried to turn the wheel of history with his own shoulder, and was crushed by it. Yet, as Schweitzer thought, there was no escaping the power of this mysterious man and of his call to discipleship, even today. Not by scholarship, but in action, through following him, one might find out who he was and is. Schweitzer's *Quest* ends in words that for all their scepticism have become classic in modern devotional writing:

It is a good thing that the true historical Jesus should overthrow the modern Jesus, should rise up against the modern spirit and send upon earth, not peace, but a sword. He was not a teacher, not a casuist: He was an imperious ruler. It was because He was so in His inmost being that He could think of Himself as the Son of Man. That was only the temporally conditioned expression of the fact that He was an authoritative ruler. The names in which men expressed their recognition of Him as such, Messiah, Son of Man, Son of God, have become for us historical parables. We can find no designation which expresses what He is for us.

He comes to us as One unknown, without a name, as of old, by the lake-side, He came to those men who knew Him not. He speaks to us the same word: 'Follow thou Me!' and sets us to the tasks which He has to fulfil for our time. He commands. And to those who obey Him, whether they be wise or simple, He will reveal Himself in the toils, the conflicts, the sufferings which they shall pass through in His fellowship, and, as an ineffable mystery, they shall learn in their own experience Who He is.

Schweitzer acted on his own words. He threw up his brilliant career as a theological scholar and musician, acquired medical qualifications, and departed to Lambarene in West Africa as a missionary doctor.

Schweitzer's alternative to scepticism, consistent eschatology, seemed sceptical enough, when contrasted with the hopes in which the quest of the historical Jesus had begun, but it was a genuine, and once grasped imaginatively, a plausible, historical reconstruction of the life of Jesus. What of the alternative Schweitzer rejected, consistent scepticism? The weight of scholarly opinion would now move much closer to that alternative. Schweitzer failed to impress upon his colleagues the validity of his own consistent reconstruction, though elements in it have been thought of permanent value, and have been taken up into the on-going consensus of New Testament scholarship. Those who reached more sceptical conclusions came to believe that the nature of the sources precluded a plausible reconstruction of the sequence of events of Jesus' life, and of its development through his ministry to his crucifixion.

The leading systematic theologians of the end of the nineteenth century, Wilhelm Herrmann and Martin Kähler, already saw in the eighteen-nineties the way things were going in biblical scholarship, and posed a different dilemma from Schweitzer's. Their question was about the religious value of critical scholarship. Could faith be founded on the historical Jesus, as reconstructed by the scholars, or must his religious value today not enter into the decision of faith, and indeed be the decisive factor? Clearly the quest of the historical Jesus was producing far more meagre results than had been expected. Moreover, every scholar would produce his own version of Jesus. To which of these should faith be directed? Was it not, as Kähler in particular would contend, an intolerable legalism to make faith wait upon the findings of such scholars? Were not the professors usurping an authority that Protestants had denied even to the Pope, or to that 'paper Pope', inspired Scripture? The attempt to go back behind the New Testament's witness to the Christ of faith, in the hope of meeting an undogmatic historical Jesus, was a quest for a will-o'-the-wisp. So, they contended that the Christian's faith is not directed to some putative Jesus constructed by the professors of New Testament criticism, but to the Christ preached by the church. 'The real Christ is the preached Christ', said Kähler.

Thus, in a sense the wheel had come full circle. Only in a sense, for if the wheel had gone round once, its axle had also moved on, and the vehicle of theology was in a different place. The attempt to use the techniques of critical history to get behind dogma and find a Jesus immediately accessible to modern man had failed. But much had happened *en route*. The doctrine of biblical inspiration had been effectively destroyed. If faith needed, as it apparently did, an authoritative witness to respond to, such a witness must be sought elsewhere than in the letter of the Bible. As we have seen, very much has been learned and would subsequently be learned about the early church, for if the Gospels told us little of historical value about the life of Jesus, they told us all the more about the period in which they were written. No modern version of the Christian faith could ignore the findings of biblical scholarship, whether they were positive or negative. The issue of the relation of the Christ of the church's faith to the Jesus of the historians had been placed firmly in the centre of the problem of being a Christian today, and every theologian would have to deal with it. At the same time, it had become completely clear that the Christian faith in the modern world could not be identical with the faith of the first century, or the fourth, or the thirteenth, or even, most plausible of all to German Protestants, the sixteenth. Every historical epoch necessarily produced its own version of the Christian faith, in the terms set for it by its own culture. That was why the mind of the New Testament writers, and even that of Jesus himself, turned out when more skilfully investigated to be foreign to the mind of the nineteenth century. That was also why a modern theology would have to be bold enough to seize the opportunity of thinking out Christianity anew in modern terms.

GERMAN SYSTEMATIC THEOLOGY
IN THE NINETEENTH AND TWENTIETH CENTURIES

In this survey of the development of the cultural environment of the modern world, we have frequently referred to the way in which theologians reacted to it in their own thought. Almost every name we have had occasion to mention has been German. In the period we are interested in, German theologians were the first to come to terms with these modern developments. Decades ahead of the theologians of other countries, they defined the issues, presenting bold and original solutions to the problems, and then ruthlessly criticized and if necessary abandoned these solutions if they failed to withstand criticism. German theology has maintained this leadership into our own time. Though English-speaking theology, especially in America, is learning to assimilate the results of the German work much more quickly, so that it can now produce original work that does not merely repeat what has already been done in Germany, it is too early to speak of the German tradition losing its leadership.

Why German theologians made these dramatic advances, while others did not, is not easy to say. The question can be pushed back a stage further by remembering the astonishing constellation of talent in philosophy, music and literature that appeared in Germany from the close of the eighteenth century onwards. The stimulus of such company may have inspired the theologians to equal intellectual feats. On the other hand, this neither explains the appearance of talent in other fields, nor accounts for the fact that in Britain, for example, while British scientists were taking the lead in the world, no comparable developments in theology occurred. Certainly British historical scholarship could hold its own with German in the field of theology, then as now, but in the vital field of systematic and philosophical theology, British theologians, and to a great extent American ones, first resisted German innovations, and then took them up only when the Germans were ready to discard them. It is an interesting reflection that in the University of Cambridge, theology of the kind pioneered in nineteenth-century Germany only gained a firm hold on the Faculty of Theology at a time when the same theology was already under the most violent criticism in Germany from Karl Barth. The story can be repeated for different issues and different times.

Thus, if our interest is in systematic theology, it is with the German tradition that we must be principally concerned. The founder of modern systematic theology was F. D. E. Schleiermacher (1768–1834), who taught theology first at Halle and then at Berlin, where he was a contemporary and rival of Hegel. Influenced by Spinoza and the Romantic movement in philosophy, and by the Moravians, a pietist group, in religion, he was at the same time wide open to the cultural renaissance then going on in Germany. His project as a theologian, at least in his early years, is well defined in the title of his first important work: *On Religion, Speeches to the Cultured among its Despisers*. Schleiermacher wished to vindicate religion for his cultured contemporaries, but to do this he had to understand the culture and share it himself. Indeed he must identify himself provisionally with their own contempt for religion. Thus he had to be aware of the currents of thought we have been sketching, at the stage they had reached in his time.

When Schleiermacher was a young man, the intellectual climate was dominated by the influence of Kant. Kant's influence on religion was more destructive than his actual contentions. His criticism of metaphysical knowledge of God had more effect on the educated classes than his own rehabilitation of God in the sphere of the practical reason. Schleiermacher made no attempt to restore metaphysical knowledge of God, as Hegel did. Nor did he follow Kant along the path of insight through moral experience. This way would dominate popular interpretation of religion in the succeeding period, and play no small part in the work of the theologians. Schleiermacher's own aim was to vindicate religion, considered as something distinct from the rational activity of philosophy and science, on the one hand, and from morality on the other. In thus distinguishing religion as something *sui generis* he did not wish to cut it off from either reason or morality, both of which followed from religion, in his view. But he wanted to show that religion was a universal response to reality, found in the feeling of every man. 'Feeling' meant a non-cognitive relation to reality, having cognitive implications. At the very depth of his feeling, man found himself related to the Infinite, as Schleiermacher was later to say, in absolute dependence. 'Feeling' is hardly even a psychological category, as Schleiermacher explains it. It is almost a mystical participation in the world in its relation to God. Hence God is not deduced by any argument, nor is he even the presupposition of the pious feeling of man: God is 'originally given' to the religious feeling.

Schleiermacher begged his cultured contemporaries to look more deeply into their own experience, and they would find religion there at the deepest and subtlest level, at the point where their own being was united and separated from the being of the world around them. If this were so, a way of understanding Christianity was opened up that could survive the metaphysical scepticism of the time, and come into no conflict with the then developing science. If all men, simply because they were human, could experience the feeling of religion, Christians were those whose religious feeling was mediated by Jesus Christ. Hence Schleiermacher saw a way in which a whole theology could be constructed on these presuppositions, without ever getting into the difficulties of the old rational theology, which had been demolished by Hume and Kant, and yet preserving the religious character of the older theology, which the pietism in which he had been brought up had transmitted to his own time.

In his epoch-making work, *The Christian Faith*, Schleiermacher produced the first systematic theology of modern times, and perhaps the most elegant and highly organized of all. He made use of a simple but far-reaching methodological criterion. Every doctrine was to be understood as the formulation of a particular determination of the religious consciousness in its Christian form. Thus, the subject-matter of theology was not the Christian message, or the being of God and Christ; Kant had made it seem impossible to talk about these. Its subject was the contents of Christian faith, and so Schleiermacher did not call his book a dogmatics, but a *Glaubenslehre*, a doctrine of faith. What could not be formulated as a specific determination of Christian piety either did not belong to Christianity, or must be regarded as metaphysical speculation, of doubtful value to faith. In spite of the Romantic origins of his thought about religion, Schleiermacher's *Glaubenslehre* was given a highly formal organization, with numbered and related propositions heading each section. It left an indelible mark upon the subsequent history of systematic theology, and influenced Catholic as well as Protestant writers.

Nineteenth-century theology did not always follow Schleiermacher into the details of his thought, but in one respect his influence was altogether decisive. They began, as he had done, from religion, and spoke of Christianity within the terms of a philosophy of religion. The right way to begin, they thought, was to construct a philosophy of religion as a distinct and universal human phenomenon, and then to show how, within the total spectrum of the religions, Christianity had the best claim on one's attention. They did this in various ways, according to their philosophical background, whether Hegelian, Kantian or Romantic-realist. For the Hegelian, Christianity was the absolute religion, in which the highest concept, that of Godmanhood, the unity of God and man, had finally come to historical expression. Others saw Christianity as embodying the essence of religion; whatever was meant by religion, Christianity was this *par excellence*. The quest of the historical Jesus becomes important to the systematic theologian at this point. If historical research could uncover the religion of Jesus himself, instead of the religion which the church had built up around an un-historical picture of him, then it might be possible to show objectively by academic methods that this religion of Jesus was in fact the essence of religion, or at least the highest form of religion yet seen. On the other hand, the difficulties in the quest of the historical Jesus and the growing scepticism about it which appeared at the end of the nineteenth century threatened the success of the whole project of putting theology on a sound academic footing.

The leading Protestant theologian of the latter part of the nineteenth century was Albrecht Ritschl (1822–89). His most important work was *The Christian Doctrine of Justification and Reconciliation* (1870–89). Ritschl was under Hegelian influence at first, but later moved to positions closer to those of Kant and

Schleiermacher. In an age of science, he hoped to present religion from an empirical point of view, having nothing to do with metaphysical speculation or any theoretical considerations. Faith for Ritschl is pragmatic: it attains God in a value-judgement, an important term in this theology. A value-judgement involves 'an essential belief in the good and the possibility of attaining it'. 'In religion the thought of God is given', but it lies beyond the horizon of metaphysics, whose use must be forbidden to theology, at any rate for the purpose of conducting a rational argument for the existence of God. Religion is in effect the affirmation that the world is ultimately in accord with our own conviction of our worth as persons. Our self-valuation as superior to nature is the source of the value-judgement in which we attain God.

Metaphysics being forbidden, Christianity as Ritschl sees it rests heavily upon the foundations of historical research, and so is seen in Christocentric terms. The basis of Christian faith is the example of the historic Christ. Ritschl was aware of the difficulties of historical research, but he believed it yielded objective facts about Jesus, notably that in the light of a unique God-consciousness he found reconciliation between human worth and the apparent hostility of nature. Thus Christ's work is to reconcile man to his own existence in the world, and so to God. Ritschl's Christology, or teaching about Christ, is likewise non-metaphysical. Christ's God-consciousness formally replaces his divinity, as traditionally understood, and discussion of his work takes precedence over speculation about his person. What he thinks of Christ is likewise a value-judgement, but it is based on positive historical fact, as uncovered by objective research. The Christian makes a different value-judgement about the human implications of the historical facts from another person, but both have access to the same facts.

Ritschl's influence is very widespread in the later theologians of the period, and can be seen in certain respects even in the contemporary theologians who are most concerned to escape from the 'liberal' theology Ritschl founded. They too are hostile to metaphysics and highly Christocentric, though as we shall see they have a different conception of the relationship of Christology to historical research, since they have been through a sceptical discipline that came too late to influence Ritschl's thought. The highly influential church historian Adolf von Harnack, whose famous book *The Essence of Christianity* (tr. E. B. Saunders, 1900, Harper Torchbooks, 1957) is the classic summary of liberal Christianity, was a Ritschlian, though he did not profess to be a theologian but a historian. His influence is also to be seen in Wilhelm Herrmann, the teacher of Barth and Bultmann in systematic theology. Through Herrmann the influence of Ritschl was mediated to them.

On the whole, the theologians of the nineteenth century (which should be counted for our purposes as ending in 1914) did not question their decision to begin with the philosophy of religion. They expressed their religious presuppositions in various ways, but the movement from the general to the particular was common to them. The criticism of religion, as we shall see, was begun by Barth, but he continued the liberal emphasis upon Christ as central in theological knowledge, which he had learned from Herrmann. Herrmann, along with Martin Kähler, who came from the somewhat more conservative tradition of the 'mediating theology', did question the reliance upon the historical Jesus so prominent in Ritschl. Herrmann's theology centred upon religious experience, conceived as free self-surrender to God in Christ. God reveals himself wholly in Christ, so that we should not say, with tradition, Jesus is God, but 'God is Jesus'. Jesus is the ground of faith; his inner life is the saving fact, through which the divine forgiveness comes to us. Herrmann's approach to theology is through ethics rather than doctrine. The Jesus of whom Herrmann speaks in such sayings is not the Jesus of the historians. In 1892 he was already saying in an article that the main contribution of historical research to faith is that it removes the props. It cannot produce a biography of Jesus. 'We . . . know our faith created not through a fact that could be historically proved. Of course that would be meaningless. We owe our faith to a fact that each of us experiences for himself in a particular way from the same tradition.' (Quoted by James M. Robinson, in 'For Theology and the Church', *Journal for Theology and the Church* I, 1965, p. 15.)

Kähler put the point more sharply in his famous book, *The*

So-called Historical Jesus and the Historic, Biblical Christ, published in 1886 and translated in 1964 (Philadelphia, Fortress
Press, Seminar Editions). Kähler denied altogether that the
historical Jesus could be the foundation of faith. He went further
still and denied that the historical Jesus of the scholars was a
reality at all. 'The real Christ is the preached Christ' (op. cit.
p. 66). The total biblical picture of Christ as preached by the
church gives us the reality of Christ, as a historic figure whose
influence has worked upon us to bring about our faith. Kähler
contrasts the historical (*historisch*), by which he means that which
is open to and reconstructed by the methods of historical
research, and the historic (*geschichtlich*), that which is influential
in the actual events of history, in which men's existence is
determined.

The ideas of Herrmann and Kähler were to be extremely
influential in contemporary theology, and they constitute a kind
of preparation, in the theology of the nineteenth century, for the
revolutionary theology of the twentieth. While they remain
within the general presuppositions of the nineteenth-century
theology, they are already aware of contradictions within it,
which Barth and his friends would later emphasize in their
polemic against it. The theologies of Herrmann and Kähler
started from a different point from those of their predecessors
in the nineteenth-century tradition. To rest faith, with Kähler,
upon the preached Christ, or with Herrmann, upon a traditional
experience of liberation into which we enter today, is really to
break with both the philosophy of religion, in the form in which
the nineteenth century knew it, and the positivism of the historical
Jesus, which complemented the philosophy of religion in the
structure of nineteenth-century theology in the German tradition.
The theologians of the twentieth century would draw out the
fuller implications of these new thoughts, and of even newer
ones of their own, in the sharpest contradiction to the whole
tendency of the theology of which Herrmann and Kähler were
among the last and not least distinguished representatives.

THE ISSUES

We are now in a better position to understand and summarize the set of problems which distinguish modern theology from its more traditional predecessors. At the beginning of the nineteenth century, theologians confronted the break-up of the foundations of the traditional theological structure. The two main elements in this foundation had been for both Catholics and Protestants the metaphysical arguments for the existence of God, and a doctrine of authority, whether of church or Bible. The arguments contained in natural theology rendered what the theologian had to say about God intelligible by relating the propositions of faith to those of reason. More crudely, they were supposed to demonstrate the existence of God. The doctrine of authority was intended to show that the God thus established had made himself known to men, that he had spoken, through an inspired Bible or through an authoritative teaching church. Thus the human mind could know not only the existence of God but also his character and intentions towards men.

The critical philosophy made it seem impossible, for very large numbers of Protestants at least, that the human mind could have knowledge of God. Not only were the traditional arguments for the existence of God shown to be fallacious, so far as they were regarded as in any sense proofs of God's existence, but God was placed outside the region of which we can have reliable knowledge in any case. Thus, what is today commonly called God-talk has been questionable for over one hundred and fifty years. During this whole period, if the theologian wanted to talk about God he must do so on some other ground than that of rational knowledge. While Kantians and positivists denied metaphysical knowledge of God, Hegelians asserted it, but in an idealist form which involved breaking down the traditional distinction between God and man. Thus, while Hegelian theologies were in fact produced, right up to the twentieth century, and indeed show signs of reappearing at the present time, the more important area of Hegel's influence lay among the great atheists of the century. The theologians more generally followed Kant in regarding God as above rational knowledge. Hence they produced a non-metaphysical doctrine of God, resting upon moral or religious experience, instead of upon a rational analysis of the world and of man's being. The first issue confronting modern theology was thus how and even whether to speak of God.

While critical philosophy broke down the rational metaphysics which had been the foundation of the doctrine of God, critical history broke down the authority of the Bible, and implicitly that of the church which supported its own teaching by reference to the Bible. If the Bible contained statements which critical investigation showed to be factually false, or misleading if taken literally, it would no longer be possible to regard it as inspired. In an educated milieu at least, theologians would have to support statements drawn from the Bible not by the old argument from its divine inspiration, but by a historical-critical treatment of the text. It might be possible to modify the doctrine of inspiration, but for practical purposes it simply dropped out of academic theology, and was replaced by the critical treatment of the Bible. This left another huge gap in the traditional structure of thought, and it must be filled in some way. The second issue confronting theologians was, therefore, how to speak about revelation, or the authority of doctrinal statements, in the absence of an inspired Bible.

These two issues were faced more by Protestants than by Catholics, until very recently. The scholastic natural theology, though by this time known only in a decadent form, continued to carry considerable conviction in the Catholic community, and in the latter part of the nineteenth century underwent a substantial if transitory revival through the growth of Thomistic scholarship, which in our own time has made it possible to criticize the decadent scholasticism of the post-Reformation period in the light of a better understanding of the meaning of thirteenth-century theology and philosophy. Likewise, the continuing respect for the authority of the church in the Catholic community helped to preserve its traditional role as the foundation for the positive statements of theology long after the Bible was being treated critically, first on Protestant and then on Catholic ground. Here too however the processes of criticism have recently gained momentum. The findings of biblical scholarship are now being widely disseminated among Catholics. On the other hand, the notion of the authority of a teaching church is being eroded by the mistrust, general in the modern world, of any kind of authority in intellectual matters resting upon status. Hence Catholic theology is moving into a crisis comparable to that in which Protestant theology has been living for more than one hundred and fifty years. It is accordingly becoming apparent that if Catholic theologians wish to confront the problems Protestants have been living with they will have to take into account Protestant proposals for their solution.

Clearly associated with the two major problems were others generated by them. These are in particular the problem of the relation of faith to religion, and hence to human culture generally, and the relation of the Christ of faith to the Jesus of history. Every modern theologian has been compelled to confront these questions, and types of modern theology can be easily distinguished by the answers given. As we have seen, nineteenth-century theologians generally regarded faith as a manifestation of religion, and placed God's self-disclosure to man within religion, or religious experience. Twentieth-century theologians on the contrary considered that the effect of this procedure was to reduce faith to an epiphenomenon of human culture. Faith then became the final achievement of man at his highest, instead of the gift of God to lost sinners, as it had been for the Reformers. So they called radically in question the nineteenth-century association of faith with religion, and established a critical distance or opposition between the two. This contrast between faith and religion is highly characteristic of the theology of the period to be considered.

Nineteenth-century theologians, up to Herrmann and Kähler, viewed the Christ of faith critically, and tried to reconstruct their faith in the light of the picture of Jesus offered them by the historians. Thus they largely abandoned the structure of traditional Christology. Modern Christology generally takes the humanity of Christ as its starting-point, characterizing his uniqueness in terms of divine operation in redemption rather than divine substance in incarnation. Twentieth-century Christ-

71

ology, however, reverses the emphasis of the nineteenth. It views the Jesus of history with critical scepticism, and subordinates him to the Christ of faith. Christ is given to us in the Word, the proclamation of the church, not by the critical historian; it is neither possible, nor important for faith, to know much about Jesus' historical life. The link between Jesus and the contemporary Christian runs through the church's proclamation. In this respect, the legacy of Herrmann and Kähler is particularly evident. With this emphasis upon the proclaimed Christ goes the Christocentrism of twentieth-century theologians, though this goes back even deeper into nineteenth-century roots. Here too however the emphasis is different. Where nineteenth-century Christocentrism refers to Jesus, that of the twentieth century directs attention to the proclaimed Christ. Both had to face the question of the relationship between the two.

Commonly, the contrast between the two periods of modern theology which we have discussed is expressed by calling nineteenth-century theology 'liberal' and twentieth-century 'neo-orthodox'. The latter term in particular will receive fuller discussion below. Neither term is very satisfactory, and in any case, if used accurately and significantly, each would have to be considerably restricted in its application. Liberal theology would then mean the work done in the Ritschlian school in Germany and elsewhere in the late nineteenth and early twentieth century, and neo-orthodoxy would for all practical purposes mean the work of Barth. However, I shall use the terms much more loosely in what follows to express a general contrast in aim and atmosphere between the thought of the nineteenth- and twentieth-century theologians in the German tradition. Nineteenth-century writers clearly aimed to situate their work within the tradition of liberal scholarship as practised in universities. They addressed in the first instance the academic community, and through it the public at large. Their relationship to the church was ambiguous, sometimes even negative. They grounded their thought not in the life of the Christian community but in a philosophy of religion and in the critical study of Christian origins and history. Both of these pursuits are open to any qualified person, whatever his personal religious position.

Twentieth-century theologians take as their starting-point the proclamation of the church and its confession of faith. Thus they cut many of their links with the academic community, though they continue to work in the theological faculties of universities, and have re-forged traditional links between theology and the community of the church, including its preaching and practical concerns in its ministry. Their new adherence to the community causes them to view with fresh respect the formulations of traditional orthodoxy, discarded by their predecessors, and they often use them with a minimum of re-interpretation. To this extent the term neo-orthodoxy seems not to be misapplied. The question of the relationship of the church to society, and of the church to the churches, their division and their unity, become important minor themes of twentieth-century theology, though we shall have space to do them no sort of justice in what follows.

It will now be clear that modern theology as a whole is faced with the invigorating question of its own proper starting-point, having been deprived of a traditional one by the changes that have taken place in culture in modern times. It must answer the question of its starting-point, of what is most evident, or given, for its discipline, in the presence of a supremely confident science, which knows just how to answer this question for itself, and so far as it turns its attention to the theologians, is more than half convinced that they do not know the answer. Nineteenth-century theology first became aware of the urgency of the question, and hence is preoccupied with the question of intel-ligibility, of how to speak clearly of religion in a time when the traditional basis for doing so had gone. As twentieth-century theologians reviewed the history of their own discipline in modern times, they became convinced that something vital had been sacrificed to the quest for intelligibility, that man had been told something he knew already by those who were so eager that he should understand. But the Christian gospel, they thought, is not something man knows already. It is something that comes to him from beyond himself and his culture, and it will always be strange to him. Hence twentieth-century theologians, until very recently, have turned first to the question of the Gospel. What is the substance of the Gospel, sacrificed, as they supposed, by their predecessors? To express this adequately they were prepared to let the question of intelligibility fall into the background. In the last few years it has become plain that it continues to be urgent, and that it cannot be separated from the twentieth-century question of the substance of the Gospel.

Two

Barth's
Theological
Revolution

In the words of the Roman Catholic theologian Karl Adam, Barth's early theology 'fell like a bomb on the playground of the theologians.' It was not so much that the effect of what he said was destructive to the prevailing theology, though it was destructive, and was intended to be. Rather, the inspiration of his thought came from a totally different direction from the sources of the theology which at that time held the field in the German universities. Where the leading theologians of the day followed the nineteenth-century tradition in starting from religion, and so from man, Barth started from God and from his self-revelation in Christ. What was more, he tried to be as consistent and rigorous in conforming to his new method as they had been in relation to theirs. Hence his theology appeared as a shattering novelty, and immediately created a storm of controversy which has not altogether died down fifty years later.

Looking back on his own early days in a lecture delivered in 1956, Barth himself used the somewhat milder metaphor of a change of direction. 'Beyond doubt what was then in order was not some kind of further shifting around within the complex of inherited questions ... but rather a change of direction. The ship was threatening to run aground; the moment was at hand to turn the rudder an angle of exactly 180 degrees.'[1] Barth had come to believe that the whole enterprise of academic theology was going in the wrong direction, and so heading straight for disaster. Only the most drastic action could save it. Barth's early utterances are characterized by a highly dramatic and rhetorical tone, and by the choice of language and of images suggestive of total contradiction of the thought of his immediate predecessors, indeed, of all merely human thought. He appeared in the guise

1. Karl Barth, *The Humanity of God*, Collins, 1961, p. 41.

of a revolutionary. His task was destruction, not building. Perhaps the building would be carried out in due course by other hands, but in any case there could be no true building until the ground had been cleared, and fresh foundations dug.

In fact, such language probably exaggerated the novelty of Barth's enterprise; he cannot be fully understood without some knowledge of what nineteenth-century theology was about, and he was in many ways indebted to it. Later, he would have little difficulty in admitting that. At the time, the emergency seemed too great for such qualifications, and his opponents saw the issue between them in just as absolute terms as he did himself. We must therefore begin our understanding of Barth by considering why he wanted to be so sharp a critic of his predecessors, and then follow his development as he turned to more constructive tasks. The second part of our job is no less important than the first, and has until recently been much neglected, except by specialists. In the English-speaking world, one constantly hears the thought of Barth described in terms that, if they apply to him at all, apply only to his early revolutionary phase. At the same time, the total effect of his theology is a revolutionary one, and as time goes on it becomes more and more clear that he stands virtually alone among the leading theological figures of our time, for all his peers remain in much closer relationship to the nineteenth century than he does himself.

Some of his critics would apply very different terms to Barth. They would call him a reactionary, or his thought obscurantist. It is possible to believe Barth mistaken in many of his criticisms of other theologians, especially those of the nineteenth century, without judging such language appropriate, or even illuminating in its exaggeration. Against such misunderstandings, it is important to grasp that Barth is a modern, and that, even at points where he is most uncompromising in his preference for traditional over nineteenth-century theological positions, his version of the traditional doctrine is again and again one which could never have entered anyone's head before the twentieth century.

What is perhaps most characteristic of him, his total refusal to have anything to do with apologetics, his determination to take his stand at all times coolly upon the intrinsic certainty of faith in the Christian message, presupposes a modern situation in which so many other theologians are on the defensive, itching to offer proof of the unprovable. His disdain for proof is even, perhaps, itself an oblique witness to the magnitude of the problems attending talk about God in our time. Whether you think Barth right or wrong when you have begun to understand him, you are bound to admit that he has tackled the great problems of theology in our time on an impressive scale, and that anyone who wants to put forward different answers will have to reckon with Barth's on the way. This could hardly be said without restriction and qualification of any other contemporary theologian.

BACKGROUND AND EARLY INFLUENCES

Karl Barth was born in Basel, Switzerland, on 10 May 1886, the son of Fritz Barth, a professor of New Testament. His theological education took place at the universities of Bern, Berlin, Tübingen and Marburg. He studied under some of the greatest teachers of the prevailing theological outlook, among them Adolf von Harnack and Wilhelm Herrmann, in their different ways the finest exponents of the Ritschlian theology.[2] Barth did not lose his reverence for these men, though he found it necessary to differ sharply from them, especially from Harnack, with whom he carried on a public controversy about his own new ideas. Barth found in Herrmann, the leading systematic theologian of the day, a congenial and inspiring teacher. He was able to claim later that he had remained faithful to Herrmann's fundamental insights, but had taken them further than Herrmann himself. According to Barth's own testimony, it was from Herrmann that he learned his characteristic refusal to engage in apologetics. Herrmann also mediated to Barth the liberal emphasis upon the centrality of Christ, strongly marked in Herrmann's own saying, 'God is Jesus', which in somewhat different form reappears as a key feature of Barth's own mature theology.

In his early days as a theologian and minister of the Swiss Reformed Church, Barth felt no discontent with the teaching he had received. His own earliest writings were entirely in the liberal

2. See above, pp. 66 ff. Barth died in 1968.

tradition in which he had been trained. At this time, however, he was also undergoing influences of a different kind, which were to mature and come to fruit later on. Along with his lifelong friend Eduard Thurneysen, he got to know Christoph Blumhardt, a remarkable preacher and pastor, whose ideas cut across many of the theological antitheses of the time. He was the son of Johann Christoph Blumhardt, who had founded a retreat centre at Bad Boll in Württemberg. As a preacher, the elder Blumhardt had revitalized the pietist tradition by a new emphasis upon the Kingdom of God. The Blumhardts were ahead of their time in the way they understood this idea. Liberal theology in its later phases also made much use of the idea of the Kingdom of God, but the liberal theologian meant by it the fulfilment in this world of the ideals of the Fatherhood of God and the brotherhood of man, brought about by human ethical endeavour, in obedience to the teachings of Jesus. The Blumhardts understood the notion much more as twentieth-century biblical scholarship would, to mean the sovereignty of God in the world, effectively reasserted through the victory of Jesus over the demonic powers that keep men bound by evil and alienated from God. Their message is summed up in the phrase, 'Jesus is Victor', which Barth has recently told us is the best summary of what he himself wants to say as a theologian.

The Blumhardts, especially the younger, Christoph, differed from the conventional pietist also in their social concern. Christoph Blumhardt was deeply interested in the modern world, and wished to come to terms in his theological thought with the challenge both of science and of socialism. From 1900 to 1906 he sat as a member for the Socialist Party in the state legislature of Württemberg. This was an unheard-of action for a pastor in those days. Up until today very few anywhere have followed his example, and those who have have usually been subjected to intense criticism. Blumhardt had grasped that Christianity was popularly identified with the interests of the middle class, and he thought that he ought to try to right the balance in his own actions. When Barth himself became minister of a parish containing many industrial workers, he reached the same conclusion, and though he did not enter political life in the narrow sense of the term, he did join the Social Democratic Party in Switzerland, in order to carry out his ministry better. Barth's own socialism, which he learned in part from Blumhardt, and also from the religious socialists Kutter and Ragaz, has given scandal to many throughout his life. It is an additional pointer to the mistakenness of the interpretation of Barth that regards him simply as a reactionary. Those who are genuinely conservative in theology are almost always equally so in politics.

Barth's pastoral ministry began in 1909, when he became an assistant in the parish of Geneva. After two years he was appointed to the parish of Safenwil, where he remained until his theological notoriety brought him the call to a professorial chair, ten years later. Safenwil is a small town in the Aargau, in the Swiss Alps. It was not, as students of Barth sometimes imagine, just a farming village. The majority of those under his spiritual care were workers in a factory, and Barth found himself taking sides with them in industrial disputes. However, the most important of the formative experiences that came to him in this period was that of having to preach regularly. Traditionally, the Reformed Church, to which Barth belongs, has, like the Lutheran, taken preaching with extreme seriousness. It sees the sermon as the central act of public worship, having the same sort of solemnity and importance as Catholics attach to the sacrifice of the Mass. If the worshipper today still goes to church primarily to hear the sermon, that is not because he hopes to be passively entertained, but because he expects God to address him and his fellow-worshippers through the words of the preacher. Even in the heyday of liberal theology, this expectation survived in the parishes, and it placed upon the shoulders of the preacher an unique burden.

Confronted by such expectations, and believing in their justification, the preacher enters the pulpit on Sunday, having first solemnly tolled the bell for the people to come and hear. He stands up in the pulpit and looks down at a sea of faces, turned to him, and to him alone, in the expectation that God will speak to them. But the preacher is not God; he is only a man. He cannot but disappoint such expectations, if he preaches from human resources. His spiritual wisdom, intellectual understanding and theological learning are not enough. However much he may have perfected his powers by study and diligence, however experienced he may be in pastoral matters, however well he knows his people, when he enters the pulpit he has taken on something that is beyond him. This is the truth, Barth was not slow to see, not only about a young man like himself, whose experience is limited and whose powers are not yet fully developed, but about every preacher. All he can offer is a human discourse about religious matters. In Barth's Reformed way of putting it, he can only offer the word of man, not the Word of God.

Barth also knew, however, of the traditional faith of his Reformed Church that this is not the last word to be said about preaching, and perhaps therefore not even the first word. According to one of the Reformation formularies, '*praedicatio verbi dei est verbum dei*'. The preaching of the Word of God is the Word of God. This must mean that there is a divine promise attached to preaching. When a preacher in faith sets out to proclaim the message of God, and when the congregation listens in faith and expectation, God can make himself heard, even through the human limitations of the preacher.

Liberal theology was not well adapted to preaching. It did not understand the relationship of God and man through the Word in the traditional way we have just examined. It started from an academic analysis of man's religion, and spoke of God and his being and acts only as they became manifest in a religious response. It was more apt to suggest to man that he should heighten his religious responses, than that he should abandon human activity and listen to the Word. We have seen that the motives behind this liberal way of explaining Christianity were academic: the liberals wished to find an objective starting-point for the study of Christianity in an age when the prestige of science was rapidly growing. But the fact that they chose this one perhaps tells us something very important about the way they understood Christianity. In any case, Barth found their way useless, once he was confronted with the crushing awareness of the distance between the legitimate expectations of the people, and his own power to satisfy them. So Barth turned away from the liberal tradition in which he had been trained, and began to look for another way. He studied the Bible intensively, and looked in it for a central message, which he could identify as God's Word to man.

So, under the influence of the Blumhardts, of the religious socialists and of experience of pastoral ministry, Barth's theology began to move from its liberal foundations, and to gather weight as it moved. Soon it would crash down upon the theology of Barth's own teachers and of his contemporaries, like the bomb that Karl Adam called it. But the decisive break with the nineteenth-century theology had not yet come. The final break was brought about for Barth by the events attending the outbreak of the First World War. As he wrote later:

> One day in early August 1914 stands out in my personal memory as a black day. Ninety-three German intellectuals impressed public opinion by their proclamation in support of the war policy of Wilhelm II and his counsellors. Among these intellectuals I discovered to my horror almost all of my theological teachers whom I had greatly venerated. In despair over what this indicated about the signs of the times I suddenly realized that I could not any longer follow either their ethics and dogmatics or their understanding of the Bible and history. For me, at least, nineteenth-century theology no longer held any future.[3]

If the mature Barth is here correctly reporting the insights of his early manhood, he already had at that time a conviction later to find formal expression in the structure of his greatest work, the *Church Dogmatics*. Ethics and dogmatics go together. What you believe, and what you think you ought to do, can't be separated. In that case, ethics can be used to test the validity of a theology. The ethics of his own teachers had now been shown up as faulty by their support of the Kaiser's war policy, so there must be something (perhaps even everything that mattered most) wrong with their theology too. One must look for a theology that led to the right ethical conclusions. Such a theology could not come about without a complete breach of the prevailing harmony between theology and culture.

At this time Barth was also reading some of the nineteenth-century writers whose thought did not reflect the evolutionary

3. *The Humanity of God*, p. 14.

v.s. optimism

optimism that had influenced his own teachers. Among these writers, who were ahead of their time in not sharing the prevalent nineteenth-century optimism about religion, were Kierkegaard, Dostoyevsky, and the Basel theologian Overbeck. These writers could be read as a commentary upon what Barth had heard the Blumhardts say about the Kingdom of God, which is precisely not the Kingdom which man establishes by his own ethics and religion. The existentialism of Kierkegaard would for a while greatly influence Barth's own theology, and even more perhaps the language in which it was expressed. Later, however, he came to believe that there was no escape by the route of existentialism from the nineteenth-century starting-point in man's religiousness. Existentialism really only offered a more profound and searching account of that religiousness at its best, but it did not provide the intellectual foundation for a theology seeking to speak about God in rational and intellectual terms, as Barth eventually wished to do. Nevertheless, Kierkegaard was an important bridge for Barth into the new world of his developed theology, and perhaps he has never fully shaken off his influence.

The most important effect upon the young Barth of all these influences has already been mentioned. They pressed him to go back to the Bible and find out for himself what its message was, when read with eyes from which the liberal spectacles had been removed. Once that happened, he saw something very plainly, which no one in the German academic tradition (except the minority figures mentioned) had seen for a long time.

The theme of the Bible, contrary to the critical and to the orthodox exegesis which we had inherited, certainly could not be man's religion and religious morality and certainly not his secret divinity. The stone wall we ran up against was that the theme of the Bible is the deity of *God*, more exactly God's *deity* – God's independence and particular character, not only in relation to the natural but also to the spiritual cosmos; God's absolutely unique existence, might and initiative, above all, in his relation to man. Only in this manner were we able to understand the voice of the Old and New Testaments. Only with this perspective did we feel we could henceforth be theologians, and in particular, preachers – ministers of the divine Word.[4]

4. *The Humanity of God*, p. 41.

The theme of the Bible, Barth had now come to believe, was the opposite of the theme of German liberal theology. Moreover, German academic theology was totally discredited in his eyes by its failure to meet the challenge of the war situation with an appropriate ethical response. There was no point in going back, however, to the theology which had prevailed before the rise of liberalism, and which still lingered on in conservative circles, what he calls 'orthodoxy' in the quotation in the last paragraph. Orthodoxy was no better than liberalism: it too started from man and failed to give place to the uniqueness and absolute initiative of God. Barth found no model for what he now wanted to do theologically except in the Reformers, and behind them in the biblical writers themselves. He must develop a new kind of theology which would enable him to stand in the twentieth century where the biblical writers had stood in the first, and see what they saw. His theology was not, of course, to be a fundamentalist repetition of what 'the Bible said'. Rather, it would be a re-appropriation in twentieth-century terms of the thought that arises from confrontation with the deity, the Godness, of God, proclaimed by him in his own Word.

THE EPISTLE TO THE ROMANS AND ITS IMPACT

Biblical commentary was inevitably the first theological work in which Barth's new approach to his task was reflected. During his years at Safenwil he studied the Bible profoundly, and tried with the help of his friend Thurneysen to understand its message in the new terms they were discovering. There grew from all these studies a massive commentary on a single book, the Epistle of St Paul to the Romans.

Barth's theme, the most important of the epistles of St Paul, was by no means a new one for theologians to take up. The epistle has inspired revolutionary theologians many times, notably Augustine and Luther, to mention two in the tradition Barth inherited. What was new, at least for modern theology, was the manner of Barth's commentary. It shocked the biblical scholars by its apparent indifference to the critical questions that occupied their own attention, and by its dogmatic, rhetorical tone. The book suggested that the task of the commentator was not to reconstruct the historical situation from which Paul wrote, but to stand before the theological realities before which Paul stood, and share his understanding of man's situation before God. 'If we rightly understand ourselves, our problems are the problems of Paul; and if we are to be enlightened by the brightness of his answers, those answers must be ours. . . '[5]

The great themes of *Romans*. the righteousness of God, and the faith by which man is made partaker of God's righteousness, through grace alone, were ideally suited to what Barth now wished to say. He wanted above all to reverse the general direction of theology: instead of moving from man to God, it must move from God to man. The first step was to show that if it started from man it could not reach God. The early chapters of Romans provided abundant material to support this contention, and Barth had only to apply them to the contemporary cultural situation. He did so in a new kind of theological language, derived from many sources, among them neo-Kantian transcendentalism, in which the thought of God is pushed up beyond the reach of reason, the existentialism of Kierkegaard, which understands faith as passionate subjectivity taking man beyond the limitations of reason, and some jargon of his own using mathematical expressions as metaphors. The aim of all this language was to show that no knowledge of God can arise from a starting-point in man's religiousness, and that the true knowledge of God can never be taken over by man as a possession and incorporated into his religious attitudes. This was Barth's fundamental breach with the nineteenth century, and it remained basic in his later theology, as well as providing the inspiration for other developments in contemporary theology which go even beyond Barth himself in the divorce between theology and religion.

Barth was the first major writer to begin the criticism of religion from a theological standpoint.[6] Since Schleiermacher,

5. Preface to Barth's *Epistle to the Romans*, Oxford University Press, 1933, p. 1.

6. As a critic of religion, Barth had some nineteenth-century forerunners, such as Overbeck, and in England F. D. Maurice, whose ideas anticipate Barth's at more than one point. But they had no comparable influence on other theologians.

nineteenth-century theologians had considered that one must begin by establishing religion either as a distinctive and universal phenomenon, or (in later writers) as a universal human *a priori* in the interpretation of experience. Given this, the theologian would proceed to show the distinctiveness of Christianity among the religions, as the highest or the absolute religion, and ground this claim in the religion of Jesus himself, as recovered by historical scholarship. Such a procedure was both academically respectable and apologetically useful. When Barth repudiated it, his own ideas seemed neither. If theology were to follow his lead, his critics (including some of his own teachers) objected, theology would cease to be academic and be useless in the modern world. Barth had come to believe, however, that the modern world needed a theology that did not tell it what it knew already, but something that left to itself it could never know. It needed to receive a message that it had never entered into the heart of man to conceive.

So Barth tried to speak of God, not as the 'whence' of man's own piety, but in his utter distinctiveness from everything that he has made, including man. As he was later to write:

What forcibly began to press itself upon us about forty years ago was not so much the humanity of God as his *deity* – a God absolutely unique in his relation to man and the world, overpoweringly lofty and distant, strange, yes even wholly other. Such was the God with whom man has to do when he takes the name of God upon his lips, when God encounters him, when he enters into relation with God. We were confronted by the mystery comparable only to the impenetrable darkness of death, in which God veils himself precisely when he unveils, announces and reveals himself to man, and by the judgement man must experience because God is gracious to him, because he wills to be and is his God. What we discovered in the change that occurred at that time was the majesty of the crucified, so evident in its full horror, just as Grünewald saw and depicted him. We saw the finger of John the Baptist, by the same artist, pointing with authority to this Holy One: 'He must increase, but I must decrease.'[7]

So Barth's theology at this time was filled with what he calls the 'pathos of distance'. As he wrote after he had become

7. *The Humanity of God*, pp. 37 ff.

famous, in the second edition of his commentary on *Romans:* 'If I have a system it consists in the fact that I keep as consistently as possible before me the negative and positive significance of what Kierkegaard has called "the infinite qualitative distinction" between time and eternity. "God is in heaven and thou on earth." The relation of this God to this man, and this man to this God, is for me the theme of the Bible and the sum of philosophy.'

The 'pathos of distance', or the theme of the 'diastasis' between revelation and culture, as Barth also called it, meant using every available device of rhetorical language to suggest that infinite qualitative distinction between God and man, and man's consequent incapacity to grasp this God within his understanding, or to reflect his righteousness in his behaviour. This apparently one-sided stress upon the otherness of God was necessary, Barth thought at this time, to correct the at least equally one-sided stress of liberal theology on continuity between God and man's highest aspirations. If God could be contained within man's religiousness, Barth thought, it was no long step from this to the position of Feuerbach, who had maintained that the attributes of God really belonged to man. In liberal theology, he now believed, God had been simply man spoken of in a louder voice. Man's 'secret divinity' had been the real theme. The anti-theologian Feuerbach had simply let the cat out of the bag.

From such a theology there could be only two roads. One led to Feuerbach's cultural atheism. Feuerbach had held that the divine attributes should be returned to man, since they really belonged to him all the time; they could only be attributed to God by being alienated from man, and man in consequence impoverished of what belonged to his substance. The other was the road Barth himself took, the road of 'diastasis', in which total discontinuity was asserted between God and human culture, and God affirmed not as man writ large, but as wholly other. This phrase became widely associated with Barth's theology, both among his friends and his critics, and has stuck to him even after he had repudiated it as firmly as his critics could reasonably desire. If God were wholly other, it would presumably be impossible to speak a word about him. Along with the 'wholly other' went other catchphrases of the new theology, the famous 'infinite qualitative distinction', already mentioned, the 'vertical from above' in which the wholly other broke in to man's world, the 'mathematical point' or 'tangent', in which alone God and man can 'intersect' and meet, the 'vacuum' of human possibilities in which alone man can be open to God.

This theology also led to a new way of interpreting the Bible. Perhaps it would be better to say that it actually found its initial expression in biblical interpretation. The new understanding of the Bible was first offered in Barth's commentary on *Romans*. God was beyond reason or spirituality, and as the wholly other must be spoken of as indissolubly Subject. Thus the great words of the Epistle were to refer to God and his acts, not to man and his response. 'Righteousness' meant not human goodness, but the righteousness of God, God's active power of goodness whereby he subdues all evil under his own sovereign rule. 'Faith' meant in the first place not man's religious response to God, but God's own faithfulness to his purpose and promises. Of course these terms had sometimes to be applied to man. But Barth showed that, far more often than anyone else had supposed, they could be applied to God with a gain in depth of meaning. Thus their meaning when applied to man was similarly transformed.

The theology of Barth and those who thought on roughly similar lines became known as the 'theology of crisis', or the 'dialectical theology', or sometimes 'neo-orthodoxy', the term which later gained the widest currency. Each of these terms finds a certain basis in the thought of Barth and his colleagues in the movement of the nineteen-twenties. Thurneysen was his closest theological ally throughout. There were also Friedrich Gogarten, who took a different direction from Barth in the thirties and is now close to Bultmann, Emil Brunner of Zürich, of whose relation to Barth's theology more will be said below, and even for a time Rudolf Bultmann himself. Barth made abundant use at this stage of the idea of crisis, though he afterwards dropped it, and it does not figure prominently in his mature thought. Crisis is a literal translation of the biblical Greek word *krisis*, which means judgement. Crisis could mean 'the power of God as the crisis of all other power or the *Heilsgeschichte*[8] as the crisis of all history or grace as the crisis from death to life or, above all, the crisis which had been brought on man in Jesus Christ, namely in the judgement whereby God has judged man in and through the death of Jesus Christ on the cross.'[9]

Barth himself admits, a little ruefully, that he is himself to blame for the use of the term 'dialectical' to describe his own theology. It has often been used abusively; alternatively, as by Tillich, Barth has been criticized for not being really dialectical, in the critic's own understanding of the term. The fact is that 'dialectical' is a term that lacks a fixed meaning, though its origins and background are broadly clear, and one has normally to infer its precise meaning in a particular writer from the way he uses it. In its origins the term denoted that kind of thinking which goes on in a conversation or dialogue between two partners. In a dialogue, one commonly finds that each party stands for an aspect of truth that the other cannot successfully represent in his own contribution. Neither side is wholly wrong or wholly right. By the clash of ideas in the dialogue each standpoint is refined and purified, becoming more complete in itself. In this way, the positions of the two participants can assume a form in which each emerges in its full distinction from the other, and yet there is no victor in the debate, since each position has been shown to be both false and true. There is no third position, however, which transcends or synthesizes the positions of the opposing partners (at least in Barth's understanding of dialectic), for the truth that would fully embody what each in its partiality contends for separately cannot be conceptualized: its only expression is found in the two positions *and* in their opposition to each other. If a conversation is the model for dialectical thinking, it is not the only form of it. The dialectic can and

8. *Heilsgeschichte* is a technical term in German theology, not easily translatable, meaning the chain of events leading up to and including the death and resurrection of Christ, and the emergence of the church. Literally, history of salvation.

9. H. Hartwell, *The Theology of Karl Barth*, Philadelphia, Westminster Press, 1964, p. 12.

commonly does go on in a single mind, and it is to this sort of inner dialectic within a single developing position that the term more commonly refers in a philosophical or theological context.

Dialectical thinking thus works by negation, leading to the affirmation of what survives negation, though that cannot, in this form of dialectic, be expressed positively, or undialectically. Dialectic need not however work in the triadic or three-step form commonly (and it seems largely incorrectly) associated with Hegel, where thought proceeds by thesis, antithesis and synthesis (the negation of the negation). According to Walter Kaufmann in his recent book on Hegel,[10] these terms are not used by Hegel himself, except where he is criticizing Kant, who noted the frequency of the triad in human thought, for falling under its spell. Such precedents, real or supposed, are not of much help in understanding what Barth means by dialectic. For him, it was the paradoxical way of speaking arising from the fact that the object of theology, God, cannot be objectified in human statements. His grace, too, is always judgement, and his judgement always grace; more, it is judgement precisely because it is grace, and grace because it is judgement, that is, the judgement of *God*. Such a mode of speech can become a mannerism, which does not illuminate an author's contentions, and then it merits the parody of a friend who said that Barth says black is white, precisely because it is black.

Barth himself wrote:

The genuine dialectician knows that this centre (the living Centre of theology) cannot be apprehended or beheld, and he will not if he can help it allow himself to be drawn into giving direct information about it, knowing that *all* such information, whether it be positive or negative, is *not* really information, but always *either* dogma or self-criticism. On this narrow ridge of rock one can only walk: if he attempts to stand still, he will fall either to the right or to the left, but fall he must. There remains only to keep on walking – an appalling performance for those who are not free from dizziness – looking from *one side to the other*, from positive to negative and negative to positive.

Our task is to interpret the Yes by the No and the No by the Yes

10. Walter Kaufmann, *Hegel*, Weidenfeld & Nicolson, 1966, p. 168.

without delaying for more than a second in either a fixed Yes *or* a fixed No. . . .[11]

Dialectic thus became for Barth a way of speaking about the ineffable indirectly. To fall into direct speech would – apart from involving a contradiction, if there is any force in the word ineffable – be to fail to speak about *God*, to refer to him as if he were, as Barth puts it, 'a bit of the world', and would thus become idolatry. In Barth's later thought, this characteristic dialectical idiom also falls into the background, though he never wholly loses it, and his speech becomes more direct and positive, as it also becomes more biblical and less philosophical in tone.

The term neo-orthodoxy, widely used especially in America to characterize the theology not only of Barth but of most of the other writers in this book, is somewhat easier to understand. It too was originally a pejorative term, used by liberal critics to draw attention to aspects in the thought of Barth and his colleagues which struck them as reversion to the past. Indeed, in the 1960s even Brunner was using the term in criticism of Barth's later theology, reproaching him for departing from the dialectical way of speaking originally common to both, and for reviving the objectivism of orthodoxy. The orthodoxy referred to is usually the theology of Protestant scholasticism in the period after the Reformation, rather than the orthodoxy of the ancient church, formulated in opposition to the important Trinitarian and Christological heresies, Arianism, Apollinarianism, Nestorianism and Eutychianism. The later orthodoxy of the Protestants was characterized by a stress on doctrinal formulations well beyond anything found in the Reformers themselves, so that it almost came to be the view of orthodox theologians that a man was justified by believing a correct doctrine of justification by faith, instead of by faith in Christ himself. Faith had come to mean belief in correct doctrinal propositions. The orthodox doctrinal structure thus rested on two propositions: the demonstration of the existence of God by the scholastic arguments, and the doctrine of biblical inspiration. Liberalism, or neo-Protestantism, as Barth usually calls it, broke with both parts of this

11. *The Word of God and the Word of Man*, New York, Harper, 1957, p. 206.

foundation, believing the first proposition discredited by critical philosophy, and the second by critical history. As a result, liberalism tended to abandon not only the general structure of Protestant orthodoxy, but also certain individual doctrines central to the orthodoxy of the ancient church, notably the Trinity, the divinity of Christ, original sin, and the objective atonement by Christ for men's sins.

Neo-orthodoxy, if we accept the term, resembles traditional orthodoxy in these respects more than its Protestant successor. It revives the particular doctrines of the ancient church which liberalism had supposed must be given up, but it does not revert to the basis of Protestant scholasticism in rational metaphysics and biblical inspiration. Though perhaps less impressed than the liberals by the philosophical arguments against metaphysics, neo-orthodox theologians laid great emphasis upon religious ones, suggesting that metaphysics must inevitably be the idolatrous speculation of minds corrupted by sin. Nor did they revert to the doctrine of biblical inspiration. Neo-orthodoxy replaced both elements in the foundation of orthodoxy with a new and dynamic doctrine of revelation, or the Word of God, which is perhaps its most important distinctive feature.

To have a doctrine of revelation was not in itself a novelty. In one form or another, Christian theology had always had one: it had always affirmed that there are some distinctive truths known to Christians about God and his relationship to man which could never have become known on the basis of human reason or insight. Man could only know these truths because God had made them known. Even liberalism could not dispense with a doctrine of revelation, in spite of its wish to set the study of Christianity on as objective a footing as possible. But the form of the liberal doctrine of revelation was conditioned by its setting within the liberal analysis of religion. Like the theologians of neo-orthodoxy, who were in this respect their heirs, liberal theologians had located revelation in Christ, since they had repudiated metaphysics, and with it the idea of a general revelation in nature accessible to the human reason. What they meant by revelation in Christ was determined by their view of Christ and the way in which theology knows him; it was in these respects that neo-orthodox writers broke with their predecessors, constructing a new form of the traditional doctrine of revelation. Liberal theologians saw revelation in a static way, as a kind of constant, because they linked it with man's religious faith. Religion was the point at which their thought entered the Christian world of belief and experience.

Barth and his friends wished to call in question this constant, in which revelation remained immanent in religion, and to render it no longer obvious that man could know God. If men indeed did know God, this was not the result of something in the nature of man and of God, and hence a property of their permanent relationship with one another, but a miracle of grace. They wished to see revelation as a special act of God, bound up with his act of saving man from his condition of being lost as a result of sin. Their doctrine of revelation can be called dynamic as well as new, because it regarded revelation as an event and not a condition, founded in a gracious decision of God identical with his decision to forgive and rescue lost humanity. 'Normally', if this word is permissible to describe a condition they regarded as altogether abnormal, man cannot possibly know God, even through his highest religious, moral and intellectual aspirations. Before God, man is utterly lost, and this applies to his reason and to his religion as much as or more than it does to his moral capacities. If man is to come to the saving knowledge of God, this must happen as a result of God's good pleasure, of his own free decision to make himself known. God decides to do this as and when he pleases, but when it happens it always is an event, calling for a corresponding decision of faith from man.

Barth's aim was to break with the structure of liberal theology, which had founded everything upon the phenomenology[12] of

12. 'Phenomenology' was not used in this sense as early as nineteenth-century theology, though the term appears in Hegel in important contexts, e.g. in the title of his book, *The Phenomenology of Mind*. The word is widely used in contemporary theological writing, as here, in a sense derived from the work of the philosopher Edmund Husserl, whose writings belong to the twentieth century (he published his first important work in 1900, and died in 1938). Husserl, the 'father of phenomenology', sought for a starting-point for philosophy in what is truly evident, in the hope of making it a 'rigorous science'. He considered that he had found this starting-point in

faith. As such, it could be followed by the interested non-believer in every detail, though he would not regard it as descriptive of an outlook he shared himself. Because the phenomenology in question bore upon religious faith, and not upon God revealed, it struck Barth as man-centred. It inevitably exalted beyond what Barth thought proper or plausible limits the inherent religious capacities of man. But he did not wish, in breaking with liberalism, to revert to the contemporary form of the old orthodoxy, which for somewhat different reasons he thought equally man-centred.

He only gradually came to see what would be involved in his attempt to turn the helm of the theological ship, and though his aim did not alter, it was not without great intellectual struggle that he reached his mature position. In consequence of these struggles, he began to see more clearly that the liberal position had not lacked strength. It would not be so easy to leave it behind without falling back into a rationalistic theology on the one side or toppling over on the other into complete scepticism. The theology of his early period often came close to the latter peril, while the more rational thought of his later theology attracted criticism from his early associates as a new orthodoxy. It is clear, at any rate, that Barth did not at once succeed in shaking himself free from the presuppositions of the nineteenth century. In his early period he conspicuously shared the neo-Kantianism of some of his predecessors, with its incapacity to say anything directly about the being of God.

He began by denying what liberalism had taken for granted, that there is a constant of faith, in which God is present or immanent, through a revelation in man's religious experience.

---

the phenomenon as it appears in our experience, before we give it an interpretation. In order to concentrate attention upon the phenomenon, he practised what he called an '*epoché*', 'bracketing' questions of truth and reality. He then tried to analyse the structure of the phenomenal 'essence' thus disengaged. Phenomenological method has been widely applied in the study of religion, e.g. by van der Leeuw in *Religion in Essence and Manifestation*, and also in existentialist philosophy. The 'existential analysis' of Heidegger, which provides the philosophical groundwork of Bultmann's theology, is indebted to the phenomenology of Husserl, who was Heidegger's predecessor at Freiburg. See further, below, p. 170.

He did not intend to deny that God is present in faith; he wished to rest faith not on religion but on revelation; his assertion of the 'diastasis' was aimed at rendering once more miraculous and astonishing what liberalism had domesticated. Later, he would also find it necessary to affirm what liberalism had denied. He would contend that God gives himself to man's faith as an object, so that faith is also knowledge, as well as being experience, trust and obedience, and that theology is accordingly dogmatics, the elucidation of the Christian *message*, and not simply of the Christian *faith*.

Thus Barth's own doctrine of revelation, especially in his early period, was founded upon the famous 'infinite qualitative distinction'. If God and man are not in relationship naturally, or even through religion, revelation must acquire a fresh meaning. God can *only* be known through God, and specifically through an act of God. As the wholly other, he is not properly speaking knowable at all. Indeed, only when Barth had become critical of his own theological language at such points could he find a way of speaking positively about God. At this stage in his development, the 'knowledge' of God open to man is only the reflection of God's prior knowledge of man, an 'ac-knowledge-ment' of this divine knowledge. Revelation is understood negatively and dialectically: God as absolute subject remains hidden even in his revelation; he does not become the object of faith-knowledge which can be expressed in propositions.

Why did Barth assert this paradoxical position? Certainly not as a result of any failure to notice that it was paradoxical. Indeed, he gloried in the many paradoxes it generated. He had at least three motives. He was convinced of the truth of the old Reformed saying: *finitum non capax infiniti*, the finite cannot grasp, or contain, the infinite. Thus for Barth the unknowability of God depended not so much on Kant's critique of pure reason, whose language he sometimes borrowed, but upon the difference between God the creator and man the creature. Man's status as the creature is too remote from that of the creator for him to grasp the being of God with his reason. Secondly, he wished to affirm another traditional but neglected Reformed doctrine, the corruption of the human reason by sin. This corruption of reason was inherent in the radical lostness of man before God which Barth thought he perceived, along with the older theologians, and in opposition to the liberals. Calvin had thought, along with Paul, that man ought to have been able to know God, though not necessarily his being, because the creation as his handiwork bore upon it the stamp of its maker; but in the fall man had turned wilfully away from this knowledge, and could not regain it by his own efforts. In the present condition of man, only the revelation of God in Christ could restore to him his original capacity to know God in the creation. Thus, man ought to know God through his creation, but could not; he was 'without excuse', in the words of Paul. A third and connected reason was that Barth and his friends wished to see in man's knowledge of God a fruit of God's grace, not the achievement of human effort.

Many writers of the period, though less characteristically Barth himself, regard the knowledge of God as relational, not merely in the sense, with which Barth would fully agree, that it cannot be had outside the commitment of man to faith and obedience, but in the sense that it is actually part of this relation of commitment. Such a view also has roots in the nineteenth century. Those who today emphasize this form of the doctrine of revelation often refer to word-studies of the Bible, which show that the word for 'to know' in the Old Testament is the one also used of sexual union. This is held to imply that knowledge of God can only be had in intimate and loving relation to God, and that it is quite distinct from intellectual knowledge, which can be expressed in propositions, and possessed neutrally and objectively, without self-commitment. The denial that revelation is given in propositions is generally characteristic of the neo-orthodox school, and indeed of all modern writing on the subject. But it is not characteristic of Barth's own later thought. He would agree that revelation is in the first instance of God himself, not of propositions about him, and he certainly has no wish to minimize the importance of relationship to God, or the connexion between knowledge and obedience in faith. But he goes beyond all his colleagues in insisting that the knowledge given in faith is real, rational knowledge, not some ineffable understanding mediated in 'encounter', or relationship. We shall return to this point when we come to consider the transition in Barth's own thought as his mature theology emerges.

Barth's doctrine of revelation was not the least shocking of his innovations. It challenged liberal theology at a point very dear to it, the point at which it tried to ground theology in an objective academic method. If liberalism had been right, analysis of the problem of religion would have provided a basis for talking about God objectively and publicly, in spite of the collapse of the philosophical demonstration of his existence. Thus theology could remain in the community of learning in the university. If Barth were right, theology could only arise from specifically Christian faith. It must be an activity of the church, oriented to preaching, not a public activity open to anyone willing to think objectively about religious problems. Barth seemed to the liberals to be putting the clock back, to be undercutting the ground on which they considered they had made progress in rendering theology intellectually respectable in the modern world. No wonder that charges of reaction and obscurantism were levelled at him.

Barth was, however, more of a revolutionary than a reactionary. If his revolution had conservative features, his doctrine of revelation was far from being a reaction back to past views. No one before Barth, not even Calvin, had so stressed the unknowability of God and the inadequacy of human reason, faced with it, to know not just the nature of God but even his existence. Many have thought that his view went so far in denying all knowledge of God outside the revelation in Christ that the early chapters of *Romans*, in which Paul argues that man is without excuse for his ignorance, are an embarrassment to his position, to be reconciled with it only by strained exegesis. This is surely a point at which Barth is a modern. His total denial of rational argument for the existence of God surely reflects not just a religious sense of the otherness of God, but a specifically post-Kantian agnosticism about the power of reason outside the empirically given world.

Negatively, he went further than anyone else had done before him in asserting the 'diastasis' between God and all human culture. God is radically misunderstood if he is conceived as in any sense whatever to be found on this side of the limits of all human possibilities. God is always the beyond, never to be confused with 'a bit of the world', which man can know empirically. This meant the total exclusion of all natural theology, as a matter of theological principle and not just of philosophic scepticism. Even if such arguments did lead anywhere, they would only be able to reach an idol, 'the god of the philosophers, not the God of Abraham, Isaac and Jacob', whom the Bible also calls 'the living God'. Positively, on the other hand, the doctrine of revelation replaced a shaky natural theology with something Barth held to be more secure and reliable. As Barth's thought matured, this positive emphasis overcame the negativity of his early polemics. Natural theology ceased to be an enemy to be rooted out, as the Israelites under Joshua and his successors believed they ought to root out the pagans from the land of Canaan; it was now regarded rather as a pathetic substitute for the true knowledge of God by faith. The believer need have no concern with such substitutes. But it would be lacking in pastoral charity if the theologian devoted his energies (as his old colleague and rival Brunner had come to think desirable) to destroying natural theology for those who still need it as a prop, because they have not attained to a clear faith. When faith is fully come, the prop will fall away under its own weight, without needing to be pushed.

Barth's doctrine of revelation is also distinctively modern in the way it replaces biblical inspiration, the other pillar of the old Protestant orthodoxy. The latter located revelation in the letter of inspired Scripture, and so lost the freedom with which the Reformers themselves had approached Scripture, even when they appealed to it as the sole authority over against Catholic tradition. Orthodoxy was perhaps not quite so rigid and rationalistic in its view of Scripture as twentieth-century fundamentalism, for it could make use of the allegorical methods of the ancient church to find an acceptable meaning in passages which caused difficulty for the Christian mind on ethical or similar grounds. Even with the aid afforded by such devices, a theology treating the letter of the Bible as inspired consorted ill with Paul's view of the Gospel, as superseding the law for the Christian, and of the Spirit, who gives life where the letter kills. To abandon the idea of biblical inspiration is thus to abandon a legalism, a legalism which is neither Pauline nor in keeping with the Reformation distinction between the Law, leading to condemnation, and the Gospel, leading to forgiveness and life. Accordingly, the Christian cannot be compelled to believe by the legal authority of an inspired document: he is *invited* to believe by God in his gracious self-disclosure.

On these grounds, Barth had no wish, in attempting to escape from liberal theology, to go back behind its critical view of the Bible to the orthodox view of biblical inspiration. Accordingly, in devising a doctrine of revelation even more uncompromising in its assertion of man's remoteness from God than anything in orthodoxy, he could not follow its example in locating revelation in the inspired propositions of biblical documents. Revelation must be the self-disclosure of God himself, and so in the first instance it could be located nowhere else but in the person, words and works of Jesus Christ, as God incarnate, the Word made flesh. However, since the death and resurrection of Christ, the original revelation is located in the past, though its significance continues.

So revelation must be proclaimed, and its proclamation must be an event, an act of God, still reaching out to lost man. The second form of revelation is the proclamation of Christ as Lord, first uttered by apostles and prophets, and still uttered in the preaching of the church. But the testimony of the prophets and apostles has been recorded in Scripture; once canonized, Scripture remains the permanent basis of the proclamation of the church. Revelation is not a static property of the Scriptures, even though the church has canonized them in recognition of their permanent authority, and they alone must govern the proclamation. Even through Scripture, revelation happens as an event, in which the written word, like the proclamation of the church, becomes the Word of God. Scripture and preaching are spoken of as the medium, even the occasion, of God's self-disclosure, rather than its substance. God remains sovereign Lord, even in his revelation of himself.

By means of this doctrine of revelation Barth was able to allow for the results of the scientific, or critical, study of the Scriptures, while affirming an authoritative revelation, and while preserving, more successfully than his orthodox predecessors, the Reformation insights about the nature of the Gospel. If the old doctrine of inspiration could be described as two-dimensional, confined to the flat pages of a book, Barth's was three- or perhaps four-dimensional. Barth saw revelation as a historical event, behind and within Scripture and the life of the church out of which Scripture came, an event continually renewed, without being repeated, in the proclamation. This did not mean that revelation was at the mercy of biblical criticism.

Barth has always spoken of historical criticism with a certain reserve, from his earliest period on. He concedes the intellectual validity of its methods, but doubts the value to faith of what they can yield. If they fail to come to terms with what is most distinctive about Scripture, its own claim to record the apostolic witness to God's self-disclosure, the material under study will be misconceived. On the other hand, once this character of Scripture as mediating revelation is taken seriously, the response can no longer be that of the detached historical scholar, but must be either faith or rejection. Barth is inclined to detect the latter in much sceptical criticism. Barth's own route to the original form of revelation in the Word made flesh is not through a critical quest for the historical Jesus, but through the apostolic proclamation of the risen and ascended Christ.

From this apostolic proclamation descend the confessions of faith of the ancient church, and the contemporary church's proclamation and so its theology. Surprisingly, therefore, at first sight, Barth is willing to join with the radical critics who think that historical criticism can tell us very little about Jesus as a man, though he firmly insists upon the actual historicity of Jesus. Though Barth may not share their historical scepticism, he is convinced that it is not important for faith to know about Jesus as a particular man, but about Jesus as the one in whom God was present and acting for man's salvation; about this Jesus he is informed by the proclamation. At this point he comes very close to the position of his old associate Bultmann, who is himself a radical critic of the New Testament. For both men, faith is directed not to the results of historical criticism, but to the proclamation, in which revelation happens now. Clearly, the influence of Herrmann and Kähler is present in the thought of both.

Barth makes much of his theology dependent upon the doctrine of Christ, but the Christ he has in mind is not the human figure of the ministry and the crucifixion, as he might have been apprehended by some observer living at the time, or as he is now reconstructed by the techniques of critical history. Here he differs sharply from the older liberals who had looked for the historical Jesus. They too had been highly Christocentric in their theology, and they had been the first to say that Christianity is Christ. They spoke of following Jesus today in discipleship, and they wished to found contemporary religion upon 'the religion of Jesus', as they called it, in contrast to 'the religion about Jesus', for which they blamed Paul. In contrast, Barth has no fear whatever of the high Christological dogmas incipient in the thought of Paul, and explicit in the creeds of the ancient church. He thinks they follow inevitably from the apostolic faith in Christ as Lord and Saviour. So Barth's Christocentrism differs from that of the liberals in being a Christocentrism of what Kähler called 'the historic Christ' as opposed to one of the 'historical Jesus'. It starts from a view of Christ accessible only to faith, and formulated in the proclamation and the confessions of faith. Theology, for Barth, belongs to the believing church, the community of faith, rather than to the academic community.

FROM PROPHET TO DOGMATIC THEOLOGIAN

In trying to explain the meaning of the term neo-orthodoxy, and to show the force of both parts of the term, we have attributed to Barth an orthodox theology, but one which is highly novel, distinctively modern, and by no means reactionary (unless indeed it be thought that any form of orthodoxy is inherently reactionary). We must now go back to the story of his career, and continue to trace the course of his revolutionary theology, both in its own development and in its interaction with the events of the time. Before the second edition of his commentary on *Romans* had come out, Barth had already received and accepted a call to a theological chair in the university of Göttingen. At Göttingen he devoted most of his time to studying and lecturing about the past of theology. There he laid the foundations of the encyclopedic knowledge of the history of Christian thought which is manifest in his *Church Dogmatics*. At Göttingen he was not allowed to lecture on dogmatics proper, since he is a Reformed and Göttingen is a Lutheran university. Barth's chair was not of dogmatics but of Reformed theology, and endowed by a grant from the Presbyterian Church in the U.S.A. It was only after he left Göttingen for a regular chair at Münster that he launched out as a systematic theologian.

Barth had not at first thought of himself as a regular systematic theologian. He had seen his own theological contribution initially as a corrective to the prevailing theological tendencies, rather than as a comprehensive expression of the Christian faith as a whole. He had thought of himself, like Kierkegaard, as 'a pinch of spice', that flavours the whole dish without itself being tasted. Could he change from being a prophet to being a responsible exponent of the whole faith, in its full content and in the proper balance of its proportions? His historical studies helped him to take the measure of the task, and to develop his own positions on the principal topics. Others had seen him as a theologian before he had seen himself as one. They had professed to know what his theology was, when he himself only knew that theology must find a new direction, which would open up the message of the Bible for the preaching of the church. Perhaps after all he had a theology; more, perhaps he must assume the responsibility for the statement of the Christian faith as a whole in contemporary terms in accordance with the approach he believed to be necessary.

During the nineteen-twenties, his work remained for the most part polemical, though it increasingly found expression in historical studies, including repeated encounter with the thought of his great predecessor Schleiermacher, whom he took to be the most important and typical, as well as the most attractive, representative of the theology with which he was in conflict.

101

With his friend Thurneysen he founded a journal, *Zwischen den Zeiten* ('Between the Times') in which the ideas of the new theology were to be ventilated and fostered. He also published two more biblical commentaries, one on *Corinthians* (translated as *The Resurrection of the Dead*, 1933) and the other on *Philippians* (translated in 1962).

While he was at Münster, in 1927, Barth published his first attempt at the systematic expression of his theology. The book was intended to be the introductory volume of a larger work, to be called *Christian Dogmatics in Outline*. This first volume was entitled *Die Lehre vom Wort Gottes: Prolegomena zur christlichen Dogmatik* ('The Doctrine of the Word of God: Prolegomena to Christian Dogmatics'). The book has never been translated in full, for it never fulfilled the role Barth had destined for it, as the foundation of his own systematic theology. When he saw it in print, and read the criticisms of others, together with those he now found he himself wanted to direct against it, he decided to abandon the work, and to begin all over again. The point of his own self-criticism was that in the polemic against Schleiermacher and liberal theology, he had himself not sufficiently escaped from the nineteenth-century way of putting the questions of theology. In a subtle way, it could be said that underneath all the obvious, loudly proclaimed differences, Barth had so far done nothing more radical than stand Schleiermacher's theology on its head. He had put a negative where Schleiermacher had put a positive, and used existentialism and dialectic as a negative natural theology. God was to be reached by the systematic negation of human culture.

Barth could not escape from the nineteenth-century framework of thought without taking a more radical step. He must go on from his denial of what it affirmed about religion to a new affirmation of what it had denied about theology. He must develop a theology that could speak about the being of God, without dependence upon philosophy. So far, in his denial of continuity between revelation and religion, he had only sharpened the nineteenth-century agnosticism about the being of God. In his false start on a dogmatics, as in his *Romans*, Barth had understood the knowledge of God dialectically and relationally.

But God himself remained beyond all positive statement, and knowledge of him was only a reflection, arising in man who had accepted the impossibility not only of philosophical but of religious knowledge of God, of his grateful acknowledgement that he was none the less 'known of God'. There was nothing beyond Barth's negative dialectic except the vertical from above, the downward movement of God's knowledge of man. Was there here any foundation for Barth's project of writing a true dogmatics, or was he in fact still confined to the sphere of *Glaubenslehre*, teaching about the contents of human faith? To go any further would mean to understand revelation as a miracle, in which God, who is always and only subject, graciously permits himself to become object for man's understanding in his own self-disclosure in Christ. This was the step Barth now took, and he was greatly helped in taking it by his studies of St Anselm, which also bore fruit in a book which Barth has described as his own favourite among all his works, *Fides Quaerens Intellectum, Anselms Beweis der Existenz Gottes* (1931, translation by I. W. Robertson, *Anselm, Fides Quaerens Intellectum*, 1960).

Barth's *Anselm* is an indispensable key to the understanding of his mature position on the basic philosophical and theological questions involved in the attempt to say anything about the object of theology in the contemporary intellectual situation, and as such it is one of the most important documents of modern theology. Not surprisingly, like most of Barth's work, it is hardly bedside reading. Nor is the translation an unqualified success, and the current edition contains a number of misprints in the Latin of the work of Anselm with which it deals, his *Proslogion*. But for anyone who really wishes to come to terms with Barth's thought, the book is not only indispensable but exciting. It takes the form of a minute, often word by word, study of the *Proslogion*, the work that contains the second and more famous of Anselm's two proofs of the existence of God, the so-called ontological argument.

To a greater extent therefore than most of Barth's writings, his *Anselm* is a scholarly study of a theologian of the past. However, it is both more and in a way less than an objective attempt to reconstruct Anselm's own position. Barth identifies

103

himself with Anselm, and as he walks with him step by step along the road from faith to understanding, he is also working out his own mature position on the nature of theological thinking. The work is as thorough as the subject-matter demands, but perhaps Barth's interest is even more in the question itself than in Anselm's answer to it. The interpretation which emerges has not commended itself wholly to specialists in Anselm's thought, though it has certainly won their attention and respect. Though it throws much light on Anselm, it perhaps throws even more on Barth. He approaches Anselm as a colleague in a common task, not simply as an exegete whose sole aim is to expound the thought of an author exactly as it was.

I do not wish to minimize the seriousness of Barth's scholarly interest in this book, for he aims to clear away the mess of past interpretations in the best possible way, by attending to what the text itself says. Philosophers usually see Anselm through the spectacles of Descartes and Leibniz, who adapted Anselm's argument to their own somewhat different purposes, not to mention those of Kant, who certainly refuted them, but they do not necessarily see Anselm himself. In consequence, Barth will not permit Anselm's argument to be described as an ontological proof. An ontological argument would seek to prove God's existence from the notion of God, to 'define God into existence' as it has been put. Barth does not consider that this was Anselm's aim. Anselm does not treat existence as a perfection included in the definition of the most perfect being; he does not define God in this way, and is careful to avoid doing so, for he was aware of the fallacies in such an argument, if it purports to prove God's existence. Barth considers that Anselm's argument moves entirely within the sphere of believing theology, and finds support for his view in the fact that the argument is cast in the form of a prayer.

Anselm had long sought in prayer an argument for God's existence which would confound 'the fool who says in his heart that there is no God', and also give joy to the faithful by confirming them in their belief. Any such argument could only arise from faith itself, and it must move, not from faith to sight, which is not possible in this world, but from faith to understanding.

But the journey from faith to understanding is made within faith; at its conclusion, faith has not been left behind, but is confirmed, and finds fresh expression in joyful worship. As Anselm said, following Augustine, I know that if I did not believe, I should not understand. So the argument of the *Proslogion* can be no ontological argument, at the disposal of the unbeliever equally with the believer (in fact, it cannot belong to natural theology), but must be the work of *fides quaerens intellectum*, in Anselm's own phrase, faith seeking understanding.

Anselm believed that he had found the answer to his prayerful quest in the description of God as *id quo maius cogitari nequit*, 'that than which nothing greater can be conceived'. This description clearly does not define the essence of God. It is a dialectical description, giving directions for the manner of conceiving God. God is not correctly conceived, it implies, if one thinks of him as anything whatever that can be transcended by a further thought. But the description does not tell us positively how God is to be conceived. It is not derived from philosophical analysis of the concept of God, but from the biblical faith in God as creator, and the consequent prohibition against idolatry. In biblical language, Anselm's formula could be translated as, God is what is not an idol.

In the debate with the doubter about the existence of God, the believer takes the initiative by laying down the terms of the debate: God must be discussed in the terms of Anselm's formula. Now, if it is agreed that that is what is meant by God, it will follow that it is impossible to deny the existence of *id quo maius cogitari nequit* without falling into contradictions. The doubter can understand the phrase logically and grammatically, and he knows that those who use it do so in order to refer to God, though he himself does not at present suppose that it refers to anything in reality. It is therefore common ground that *id quo maius cogitari nequit* is in the understanding, though not yet that he also exists in reality. But if it is maintained that he exists only in the understanding, it can be shown that so to conceive him is not to conceive him. If one could think of him, as clearly one can, as existing in the understanding alone, one could likewise think of him as existing in reality also; the second thought is *maius*, greater, or more, than the first. Thus to satisfy the formula, the second thought must be preferred to the first. It follows that *id quo maius cogitari nequit* must exist not only in the understanding but in reality. Further, if he were to be conceived as merely happening to exist, this would also be not to conceive him, for he could be conceived as existing in such a manner that it is impossible for him not to exist, and this too is *maius*. So *id quo maius cogitari nequit* must be conceived as existing not merely in reality as well as in thought, but in such a manner that his non-existence is inconceivable. But this is God.

This is not the place to discuss either the correctness of Barth's interpretation, or the validity of the argument he finds in Anselm. Much could be said on both sides of these issues. In any case, Barth does not think the argument either is or was intended to be a proof of God's existence which can stand on its own feet outside faith. What principally interests us here is what Barth learned from Anselm about the nature of theology as *fides quaerens intellectum*. Faith's search for understanding is a rational quest. When understanding is reached, it is because the rationality of the believing mind has come to correspond with the rationality of the object of faith. Human reason, in this case, cannot be used to deny the necessary existence of God, because if it were so used it would fall into irrationality, into self-contradiction. It is a mystery how the fool can say there is no God, when he contradicts himself in saying so. But when the believer affirms with understanding of faith the necessary existence of God, the rationality of his knowing mind, which affirms the proposition that God exists necessarily, has come into correspondence with the rationality of God's own being. If the proposition that God exists is necessary, in the sense that it cannot be denied without contradiction, this is because God's existence in reality is also necessary. There is therefore a correspondence between proposition and reality, which Barth calls the correspondence between the noetic rationality of theology, and the ontic rationality of the object of theology.

Barth had now taken a crucial step beyond the positions of his early work. Faith can, in his new view, admit to rational knowledge of the object of faith. It gives rise to rational propositions about God, and these bear on the being of God, in this case on his necessary existence, though not yet on his essence. Barth has moved in principle beyond a dialectical theology to a positive theology, but since he has not withdrawn any of the critical strictures upon religion and natural theology from his earlier period, he has not fallen back into orthodoxy. For the mature Barth, as for Anselm, God remains not merely that than which nothing greater can be conceived, but that which strictly cannot be conceived by man at all. It follows that a rational theology rests upon a miracle, as Barth gladly affirms. The miracle, however, is not accidental but essential to the Christian faith. It is the central miracle of the Word made flesh. Even now, Barth does not consider that in revelation God communicates to man authorized propositions about himself which could constitute the immediate object of faith. This was the view of the old orthodoxy, but it is not Barth's. In revelation, God gives nothing less than himself. The Word made flesh is God and man.

Thus Christology enters into the substance of Barth's doctrine of revelation, as does the closely related doctrine of the Trinity. The latter therefore appears at the beginning of the *Church Dogmatics*, instead of at the end, as in Schleiermacher's *The Christian Faith*. The object of faith is not God in himself but God in his Word, God communicating himself to man while retaining his mystery and sovereignty. The mystery and sovereignty of God do not mean however that revelation is unreliable, that he might turn out ultimately to be something quite different from what he shows himself to be in revelation. Barth likes to talk in this connexion of the freedom of God. This term is connected with Anselm's favourite attribute of God, his *aseity*. This word comes from the Latin phrase *a se*: God exists from himself, not *ab alio*, from another. God's aseity, or freedom, is not to be conceived as a subtle limitation. His transcendence does not preclude his immanence, nor his omnipresence his ability to be present somewhere in particular. Likewise, his freedom is freedom *for* man, not *from* man.

Hence God is not locked up in his own eternal subject-hood. He is indeed absolute subject, but in his freedom he consents to become object in the incarnation, and this is the miracle. The

Word made flesh can be spoken of in human language, and what is true of him will be true of God. The incarnation discloses in history what God is 'antecedently in himself'. Everything that we find God to be in revelation he is already eternally and archetypically. Thus the later Barth can even speak of the humanity of God, in balance with his deity. His willingness to be with man is part of his eternal nature. So all that God is, is offered to man in Christ. In revelation we even enter into God's self-knowledge. Man participates in the mutual knowledge of the Father and of the Son. The act of God in his revelation cannot be separated, as in the earlier Barth, from the being of God. God is what he is in his word. Though we see in a glass darkly, and know God only in Christ crucified, we know. Faith is as such knowledge, and has a dynamic which leads to understanding. This movement within faith to understanding is theology.

Barth could now write his *Dogmatics*. He had already scandalized his liberal colleagues by proposing to write dogmatics at all. He now went further. When the first volume of the second version of his work appeared in 1932, it was seen that he had changed the title. The work was now to be called *Die kirchliche Dogmatik*. The authorized translation, probably inevitably, renders this as *Church Dogmatics*. But that is not precisely what *kirchlich* means in ordinary German. It has much the same connotations as the English word 'ecclesiastical'. Again Barth had scandalized the theological public. Not only would he write dogmatics, he would now write ecclesiastical dogmatics, dogmatics linked to the church and to its confession, instead of to the academic community and to free inquiry.

In the preface to the new volume on the doctrine of the Word of God, the first half-volume of the new and enlarged work, he says that his aim in revision had been to remove from his writing any trace of dependence upon existentialism or any other philosophy. Theology is to depend wholly on the Word of God, as found in the proclamation of the church and governed by the Scriptures. Thus it necessarily becomes an activity of the church. But this repudiation of philosophical support should not mislead us. Barth now intends to speak more rationally than before, not less so. Theology is defined as a science, in the sense that it has an object by which it is determined, and a discipline which renders it critical in its attempts to conform its own utterance to the given nature of its object. But the purpose of this science is ecclesiastical, not academic. Its aim is to criticize the church's proclamation at any given time to see that it remains in conformity with the revelation on which it is based, through those cultural changes which alter its expression in history. Theology is the science by which faith seeks understanding of its given object, leading to worship and rejoicing in the glory and beauty of that object. As a *critical* science, it has the highly practical purpose of keeping preaching in accord with the Word it is supposed to deliver.

THE CHURCH STRUGGLE

No sooner had Barth embarked once more on his enterprise, and set his course by what he considered a truer guiding star than before, than events put his theology to a searching test. Barth was still a professor in Germany, having by now moved from Münster to Bonn, and in 1933 Adolf Hitler became Chancellor of the German Reich. What had these political events to do with the theological themes with which Barth had been wrestling in the previous decade, ever since he had finished the second edition of his *Romans*? He already knew that faith had something to do with politics. In fact, as we noted, his whole theological enterprise appears to have been set in motion back in 1914 by a political and ethical judgement about liberal theology. The events of 1933 and the next year brought new clarity to this perception of the relation of faith to politics. He now saw clearly that faith is not only experience, not only knowledge, not only personal obedience, but commitment in the world. He found the severe discriminations he had been learning to make in the theological field turning out to have the sharpest political relevance. The rejection of natural theology in favour of Christocentric revelation turned out to be the theological ground for the German church's resistance to Adolf Hitler.

The Christians of Germany were ill-prepared for the task of resisting Hitler. For many, it was not easy to see why a Christian should want to resist Hitler. The Nazi Party represented itself as an instrument of national renewal, including moral renewal. The Germany of the twenties, involved in the collapse of values following on the defeat of the First World War, and all the negative as well as positive consequences of the removal of past standards of thought and conduct, scandalized very many in the churches, and especially their leaders. In a time of moral and spiritual decadence, as they thought, a movement was surely to be welcomed that stressed patriotism, discipline, heroism, and even sacrifice. The Nazis appeared as restorers of moral and spiritual values to a decadent and demoralized nation. Nor were the Nazis themselves slow to realize the value of church support, and did their best to enlist it on their side by emphasizing this aspect of their own aims, no doubt sincerely enough. It is not hard to imagine conservative churchmen in most countries, including Britain and America, responding in a similar way to an analogous situation. It is always easier to see through the speciousness of the moral appeal of Fascism when it is someone else's Fascism.

Even if churchmen were critical of many aspects of the Nazi regime, and saw that it would soon become a totalitarian tyranny, there were powerful influences in the German and especially the Lutheran theological tradition to restrain them from any active opposition. The Lutheran churches of Germany, like other state churches, including the Church of England, had historically taken very seriously the Pauline saying, 'the powers that be are ordained of God'. Traditionally, this had meant that an unjust regime should be endured with patience and prayer, and that however wicked one's rulers might be, rebellion was more wicked still. English Christians may compare the Litany of the Book of Common Prayer, 'from all privy conspiracy, sedition and rebellion, Good Lord deliver us'. The Lutheran doctrine of the *Obrigkeit*, the authorities, or powers that be, existing by divine permission, and demanding the obedience of the subject on pain of disobedience to God, prevented large numbers of churchmen from engaging in any active opposition to the Nazis, in spite of inner uneasiness about what their rulers were doing. It needed a different doctrine of the State from the traditional Lutheran one to free churchmen from this inhibition.

Roman Catholics, faced with these events, adopted for the

most part what was then (though hardly now) their normal stance. They endeavoured to protect the integrity of the church as an institution, and purchased its safety by restraining themselves from interference in politics. Certainly a number of brave bishops and others protested against the regime as such, and later some priests gave their lives for the Jews. But the official attitude was summed up in the concordat at 1934 between the German regime, represented by von Papen, and the then Cardinal Pacelli (later to be Pope Pius XII), for the Vatican. It won protection for the church itself against persecution at the cost of an oath of fidelity to the regime to be taken by the bishops, and the prohibition of political activity among the clergy.

Some Protestants tried to combine a form of Christianity with the Nazi ideology. These were the 'German Christians'. The church elections of 1933, held under government pressure, produced a majority for this group, and calling themselves 'The Evangelical Church of the German Nation' they issued the following statement: 'A mighty national movement has captured and exalted our German nation. An all-embracing reorganization of the State is taking place within the awakened German people. We give our hearty assent to this turning point of history. God has given us this: to him be the glory.' The doctrine of the German Christians was based on the key words of Nazism itself: Nation, Race, Führer:

We take our stand upon the ground of positive Christianity. We profess an affirmative and typical faith in Christ, corresponding to the German spirit of Luther and to a heroic piety . . .

We see in race, folk and nation orders of existence granted and entrusted to us by God. God's law for us in that we look to the preservation of these orders . . .

In the mission to the Jews we perceive a grave danger to our nationality. It is an entrance gate for alien blood into our body politic. It has no justification for existence beside foreign missions. . . . In particular, marriage between Germans and Jews is to be forbidden.

The Nazi *Führerprinzip*, or leadership principle, was also implemented in the church by the setting up of ten new bishoprics. (This partly accounts for later German opposition in ecumenical discussion to claims for episcopacy.) Just as in many Anglican churches, especially in the dominions or abroad, the Union Jack is displayed as a symbol of the union of patriotism and religion, so the swastika flag was brought into the churches, and the national anthem of Germany, and even the Nazi Horst Wessel song, were sung in the church services.[13]

In all this there was much that was both plausible and specious to a certain type of Christian mind, by no means confined to Germany, but totally incompatible, in the view of men like Barth, with faithfulness to Christ as the only Lord of the church. The task of providing the theology on which resistance in the church to these developments could be based fell to Karl Barth, along with some of his friends and colleagues, notably Martin Niemöller, Heinrich Vogel, Wilhelm Niesel, Hans Asmussen and others. At first Barth himself, like Catholic opponents of the regime, thought a distinction should be made between theological and political opposition to Hitler. At all times his own efforts were primarily directed against the threat to the integrity of the church constituted by the false doctrine of the German Christians within the fold. As time went on, the distinction became more difficult to maintain, and Barth saw with increasing clarity that theological opposition actually entailed political action, at any rate in a totalitarian state. He was himself still a Swiss citizen, but he felt strongly identified with the Christians of his adopted country, and he did not hesitate to join with them in all action rendered necessary by the task of defending the faith.

The immediate reaction of those who, like Barth, saw the necessity of opposition to Hitler, and in particular to the distortion of the Christian faith brought about by the doctrines of the German Christians, primarily in theological terms, was to draw up confessions of the true faith. These were based on the precedent of the confessions produced by the Protestant groups at the time of the Reformation: they do not deal with the whole faith, as do the creeds of the ancient church, but concentrate upon issues believed to be of supreme importance in the situation of the time. They are drawn up by groups of concerned Christians

13. For the events of 1933, see e.g. Georges Casalis, *Portrait of Karl Barth*, Garden City, N.Y., Doubleday Anchor Book, 1964, from which the above quotations are taken.

who believe that they experience the pressure of the Holy Spirit to confess their faith publicly, as the early Christians did before the Roman tribunals. In the years immediately following the accession to power of Hitler, a number of such documents were produced by various synods and assemblies, and those who made and held to these confessions of faith were known as the Confessing Church (*die bekennende Kirche*, sometimes incorrectly translated as the Confessional Church). The Confessing Church took its own status as the representative of the true faith with the utmost seriousness, not without reason; some of its spokesmen, such as Dietrich Bonhoeffer, regarded it as the sole embodiment of the true Christian Church in Germany at that time. Its members were perhaps insufficiently aware of their spiritual brethren in the Catholic Church, though Catholic opposition did not reach its full extent until the war years.

The most important document of the Confessing Church was actually the work of Karl Barth. This was the famous Barmen Declaration of 31 May 1934, the first draft of which was produced by Karl Barth in a few hours one day during the synod 'while the others were taking the afternoon nap', as he later recorded. The opening paragraph, including the theologically vital first article, read as follows:

In view of the errors of the 'German Christians' of the present Reich Church Government, which are devastating the Church and are also thereby breaking up the unity of the German Evangelical Church, we confess the following evangelical truths:
I. 'I am the way, and the truth, and the life; no one comes to the Father, but by me.' (John 14:6.) 'Truly, truly, I say to you, he who does not enter the sheepfold by the door but climbs in by another way, that man is a thief and a robber . . . I am the door; if anyone enters by me, he will be saved.' (John 10:1, 9.)
Jesus Christ, as he is attested to us in Holy Scripture, is the one Word of God which we have to hear and which we have to trust and obey in life and in death.
We reject the false doctrine, as though the Church could and would have to acknowledge, apart from and besides this one Word of God, still other events and powers, figures and truths, as God's revelation.

The confession then works out the implications of the doctrine for a number of spheres in the remaining articles, concluding with an invitation to all Christians in Germany to join with the Confessing Church.

The crisis in the German Church had found the man. Barth was uniquely prepared to give theological leadership in the confusion reigning in the church over the specious programme of the German Christians, and over the implications for Christians in general of the changes going on in the State. He and those who thought with him had worked out a theological position which gave them independence of judgement, and foresight to oppose the Nazi regime while it still seemed morally superior to the social situation it aimed at altering, long before its evil character had become publicly understood or even fully worked out in action. From his earliest days, Barth had affirmed a sharp distinction between the Gospel and human culture, even if that culture took a lofty religious and moral form. He had opposed every kind of synthesis between the Gospel and other spiritual forces, every kind of 'Christianity and . . .' programme, every kind of hyphen linking what he considered utterly distinct things. He was sure that whenever the Gospel was thus coordinated with other forces, it must become subordinated to them.

The choice was always, he thought, between the Gospel alone, and the Gospel in bondage to something alien to it. The programme of the German Christians seemed to be proving his point up to the hilt. The choice between Jesus Christ as the one Word of God, and Jesus Christ *and* some kind of human religious insight, was proving to be identical with the choice between Jesus Christ alone, and ultimate loyalty to race, nation and Führer. As the further events of the thirties and forties unrolled, culminating in the horrors of the concentration camps, and the martyrdom of many Christians who defended the Jews or opposed the regime of Hitler, Barth had only too much reason to believe that his original conviction, however polemically expressed, had always been correct.

To this period in Barth's life belongs also the breach with his early colleague Emil Brunner on the issue of natural theology. The polemical bitterness with which the dispute was conducted, especially on Barth's side, which had not wholly died down by the time of Brunner's death, can be explained by the intensity of the spiritual crisis in Germany. The issue between the two colleagues has sometimes seemed difficult to disentangle, but this is the context in which it becomes intelligible. While the two participants were then and always united by very much, over against theologians of a wholly different stamp, the argument was about a real issue, though it has often been presented in a misleading way to the English-speaking public. The principal essays and articles in which the debate was carried on were translated into English considerably before Barth's other relevant works of the period, and did much to fasten a negative image of Barth on the mind of the Anglo-Saxon theological public. Almost everyone accepted Brunner's interpretation of what Barth meant, and rather naturally sided with Brunner on the issue. Barth's famous *Nein* to Brunner on the issue of natural theology was added to a few snippets from the *Epistle to the Romans* to produce the standard picture of Barth as arrogant and hostile to humanity.

However, the issue was not as simple as that. Barth had no hostility to human reason, still less to man as such. What he wished to prevent was the return of the dialectical theologians to the nineteenth-century practice of grounding theology in a doctrine of man, and this he saw Brunner doing in his famous idea of 'the point of contact' for the Gospel in human nature. It was not because Barth considered man so fallen as to be utterly incapable of anything good that he refused to admit a point of contact, but because he wished to ground theology solely in the one Word of God. As we may infer from his activities in the Confessing Church at this time, he thought the cause of man himself bound up with this one Word of God, Jesus Christ. Brunner's reversion to the idea of natural theology, even a negative natural theology, was bound up with his defence of the orders of creation, as the foundation of ethics. But the German Christians were grounding their own support for Nazi ideology on these orders of creation, as the extract above suggests. As for the charge of irrationalism, Barth had already written his *Anselm* and moved into a positive, rational type of theological thinking, while Brunner was trying to use a negative natural theology to break down the pretensions of reason. The debate, however, never became a dialogue.

THE CHURCH DOGMATICS

In 1935 Barth was forced to leave his chair at Bonn, and quit Germany altogether. He moved to the University of Basel, just across the Rhine from Germany.

His earlier studies, coupled with his experience of the interaction of theology and life, had fully equipped him for the task to which he now set himself with increasing concentration, the task of writing his massive *Church Dogmatics*. The theology to be expressed in it was already present in its essentials in his mind, though his thought has at no time hardened into predictable lines. Always fresh encounter with the text of the Bible was capable of making him change his mind, or come up with some new interpretation of an old doctrine. By now he had a following, especially among younger theologians and students, but he always disavowed the Barthians, and tried above all not to become a Barthian himself. His advice to theologians who have been inspired by his theology has been to do what he did, and attack every problem freshly for themselves. Perhaps when they have done it he has sometimes shown the human weakness of not being pleased at their dissent from his own positions. More often, however, it must be admitted, his disciples have tended to turn his theology into an orthodoxy lacking the flexibility of his own thought.

The *Church Dogmatics* is altogether too vast a work for it to be possible even to outline it here. We shall have to be content with singling out a few of the points on which Barth's mature theology offers fresh and distinctive points of view on old questions. The size of the work is perhaps one of the facts about it which is significant. The first half-volume of the new version came out in 1932; the second (I/2) was issued in 1938. The translation did not until recently keep pace with the original. I/1 had been translated by 1935, though not so well as the later volumes, which have been done by a team of translators, under the general editorship of men who really understand Barth. I/2 was translated in 1958, and since then volume after volume has appeared in quick succession. Four volumes of the original have now been completed, amounting to twelve part-volumes, a total of approximately six million words. A fifth volume is part of the plan, but it will now never be written. This part of Barth's *oeuvre*, which would be more than enough for most men in a lifetime of work, is in addition to forty or fifty other books, and several hundred articles. So vast an output is both a considerable human achievement, and something of an obstacle to coming to terms with the thought of the man.

Many of Barth's critics refuse to have patience with a work of this size, and consider that if Barth wishes to be taken seriously, he must go to the trouble of condensing his ideas so that they can be taken in by readers who are not prepared to make the *Church Dogmatics* their sole theological reading. However, nowadays Barth is taken much more seriously than such critics, and the reports of those who have explored the region of the *Church Dogmatics* for themselves make it clear that something of great importance is to be found there. Hence it might be better to suppress one's impatience and consider if there are any good reasons for the exceptional length of the work. One reason, which is not perhaps in itself a justification, is the pressure under which Barth worked until his later years. We have just examined some of the pressures under which he wrote in the thirties, and seen reason to believe that they account in part for the polemical bitterness of some of his writings of the time. This bitterness is quite absent from the work of his later period. Such external pressures in any case gradually relaxed, and played no part in the latter part of his career. There has always, perhaps, been an internal pressure. Barth is not just a detached scholar, but a revolutionary and a crusader. He is engaged in constant struggle with himself and all other theologians to make way for the Word of God, and to let it prevail over human thoughts and imaginings. What he has heard must be communicated. Moreover, in a highly creative person such as Barth there is more labour in condensing what he has written than in producing it in the first place. Barth has always written out his lectures in full, and he does not subsequently revise much. When he does, the

revision is apt to be drastic and total, as in the case of his preliminary essay in dogmatics; in that case, too, the revision was very
much longer than the original. A considerable proportion of his
writings originated as lectures, of which he has been invited to
give very many. In the later years, when a new kind of pressure
came upon him to finish the *Church Dogmatics* before his energies ran out, or death brought the project to an end, he would
give the chapters as lectures to his students and send them straight
off to the press.

What I have said so far might suggest that Barth's work might
be better for pruning. This may perhaps be true, but it is nothing
like so true as one would suppose if one had not read him at
length. The extreme extent of the *Church Dogmatics* is not just
a consequence of his having so much to say. It is a result of his
method. He wishes to be responsible to his sources, Scripture
itself, and the writings of past theologians, including the confessions of faith of ancient and more recent times. All these must
be honoured, in accordance with the commandment, 'Honour
thy father and thy mother'. The theologians of the past have no
authority comparable to Holy Scripture, but they must be listened
to, before one decides to take up a different position of one's own.
So Barth's work contains great areas of fine print, playing a role
comparable to but greater than that of footnotes and appendices
in other writers, devoted to the exegesis of Scripture, discussions
of the positions taken up in the past on the point in question by
theologians both Catholic and Protestant, and reviews of contemporary writers in philosophy and theology. On a first reading,
one can omit the fine print, but a good deal will be missed by
one who never gets to it, and the theologian will find it too
fascinating to pass by.

On the other hand, his own thought moves in a way which
makes for length. There is a pattern in it, derived in part, presumably, from his early dialectical phase, which leads him to
take a proposition, divide it into two terms, and examine it by
laying the emphasis on each of them in succession. Sometimes
the original proposition contains more than two terms. Generally
speaking, Barth does not think in a linear way, moving in order
from point to point, disposing of each in turn. His thought

moves spirally, or centripetally. He circles round the matter under discussion, seeing how it looks from angle after angle, constantly returning to the issue from a new point of view.

On the larger scale, the organization of the volumes resembles that of music rather than argument: a striking example is the fourth volume, dealing with the doctrine of reconciliation, where theme after theme is integrated into the structure, and kept in relation with its companions throughout. Another example is the discussion of the perfections of God in II/1, where he constructs a kind of cat's-cradle of connected attributes of God, all related to a key pair, God's love and God's freedom. Here is a section of 500-odd pages which ought to be read, even by one who has no intention of reading the whole work. It will be apparent that Barth is an artist, not just a dry reasoner. He creates a world, and the reader has to accept it while he is within it; the more he learns to move freely about in this world, the greater satisfaction he will derive. Only when one goes out of it again does criticism easily arise. Of course, Barth does not consider for a moment that this theological world is simply his own creation.

We must now venture, in spite of these difficulties, to state in summary form some of Barth's conclusions. To my mind, Barth's most important and distinctive contribution to modern theology is his attempt to show how a form of rational speech about God is possible, leading to the development of a scientific and critical dogmatics. To come to terms with this approach is really more important than to discuss any particular feature of his teaching, though its formal character is here inseparable from his exposition of the content of the Christian faith. This feature of Barth's thought is the one that differentiates him most sharply, not only from the theology of the nineteenth century, but from that of his own contemporaries, except those he has most directly influenced. Since this question has now become a key issue in all contemporary theology, we may fittingly add something to what has earlier been said on this topic.

Barth's position on the understanding of faith cannot be separated from what he has to say about Christ as the one Word of God. So far, we have been somewhat preoccupied with the polemical content of these affirmations, in relation to the errors of the German Christians. Because Christ is the *one* Word of God, no other religious forms or figures can be the Word of God for us, even alongside Christ. Hence, not only must German Christianity be rejected, but so must natural theology in every shape and form, even the negative apologetic undertaken by Brunner. But the positive implications of this position are even more important. In Christ, God does speak. The Word has been made flesh, and God has given himself to man's knowledge in a human mode. This word that is also a deed is as such God's language. Hence theology can be objective and realist. It has an object, by which it can measure and control its own development and expression. This object is intrinsically, no doubt, above human reason, as the nineteenth century considered God to be. But this does not mean that God is not rational. He is the source of all rationality in man. Nor does it mean that man can say nothing that will be both rational and true about God, for Christ is himself the truth, as well as the way and the life, and in him divine truth becomes intelligible to us. The incarnation therefore replaces the metaphysical analysis of the world as the ground of rational theology. Theology need therefore neither renounce rationality in the name of the transcendence of God, or of the uniqueness of the religious relationship to God, nor need it borrow its rationality from outside, by taking over a particular philosophy as the basis of its rational exposition of the Christian message. It gains intrinsic rationality from its object, the Word of God. Philosophy can be exceedingly useful, indeed indispensable, in the service of this rationality, provided it never becomes a *Weltanschauung* in itself. Like the church fathers, Barth is perfectly prepared to use philosophy to explain theology, provided that this order is maintained, and the philosophy is used eclectically and not systematically.

A key feature in Barth's exposition of the rationality of faith is his doctrine of analogy, again based upon the incarnation of the Word, and not upon analysis of the being of the world. Any critically rational speech about God will have to make use of analogy in some form or other. Analogy is the only positive method that has been devised of employing terms drawn from the purposes for which we ordinarily use words, and to which our vocabulary applies in its original sense, for application to God, without falling into either anthropomorphism on the one hand or idolatry on the other. Barth's step from a purely critical and dialectical theology was a movement from negative to positive speech, and therefore if it was not to be a step into rationalized orthodoxy (or worse, into anthropomorphism and idolatry) had to be a step into the use of analogy. This meant that God could no longer be called the wholly other, and that the distinction between God and man could no longer without qualification be called infinite. Barth did not need to withdraw any of the critical aspects of his early theology in order to move into analogy, but he needed to make his language more precise and less rhetorical. He now devised a new conception of analogy which was strictly theological, and had nothing in common with at any rate the popular understanding of the analogy of being.[14] Barth's theological analogy works downwards (in a sense therefore the 'vertical from above' is retained even here) where philosophical analogy works upwards from the being of existents in the world to the being of God, which man cannot know directly. Barth calls his form of analogy the analogy of faith.

Here are terms which require explanation. Analogy arises where the same word is predicated of different subjects in appropriately differing senses. Analogical predication is distinguished, as by Aquinas, from 'univocal' predication on the one hand, and 'equivocal' predication on the other. Predication is univocal where the word is used in the same sense in each case. If the word 'father' were predicated univocally when applied to God, we should understand that he engendered men, as the gods do in some mythologies. In equivocal predication the words are the same, but the meanings have nothing in common. If theological predication were equivocal, we should not have the slightest idea what our words meant when we

14. The qualification 'popular' is important here. Barth did engage in many polemics about the analogy of being, without perhaps clearly grasping the subtler meaning of Aquinas' doctrine, which is much closer to his own than the popular version.

applied them to God. All language about God would be completely meaningless. (No theologian, until the present day, has ever taken the position that theological language is equivocal; if he did, he would have to be silent, which theologians are not apt to be, in most people's experience.)[15] We may remember that in non-philosophical language equivocation means lying. Analogy stands in the middle, between univocal and equivocal predication. It assumes that the meaning of a word predicated of a series of subjects of differing ontological status will differ in proportion, without the various meanings becoming so unrelated as to fall into equivocation.

Barth's original objection to analogy (his polemic against the analogy of being was not less violent than his general polemic against natural theology – he recently said that the analogy of being was the only serious reason for not becoming a Roman Catholic) was that the analogy of being brought God and man under the one category of being. But, as the church fathers said, *deus non est in genere*, God is not in a category. In fact, the objection is hardly relevant to the doctrine of Aquinas, which is the official one for Roman Catholic theology. Indeed, it attributes to the doctrine of analogy the very error it was designed to avoid. Being is not a category in Thomistic thought, but an 'analogical transcendental'. Thomists assume that we must talk of the being of God, if he exists, but cannot mean the same thing by it as when we talk of the being of man.

In Barth's reversed analogy, God is the analogy, and man, or the world, the analogate. He bases this position on the saying of Paul about the fatherhood of God, from whom all fatherhood in heaven and earth is named. God is the real father, we are fathers by analogy. We do not understand the divine fatherhood on the analogy of our own, but come first to understand our own when we see it in relation to the divine fatherhood. How then do we understand divine fatherhood? We understand this only by its revelation in the incarnation of the Son of God.

15. Modern logical empiricism does not recognize analogy, and uses all words univocally. In conformity with this, Paul van Buren, in *The Secular Meaning of the Gospel* (see Chapter Seven), denies analogy, but also refrains from speaking of God.

This is the analogy of faith, or the analogy of relation, as Barth calls it.

The phrase, analogy of faith, comes from the Greek of Romans xii, 6, where Paul says, 'If we prophesy, let us prophesy according to the proportion of faith'. The word for proportion in Greek is *analogia*, from which analogy comes. Whether Paul had any such notion in mind may be debated, but this does not invalidate Barth's use of the analogy of faith, or the Christological analogy, as it is also called, as a controlling principle in his theology. The analogy of faith figures even in his early thought, but the analogy of relation, or Christological analogy, is a feature of his mature thought, in the *Church Dogmatics* and writings of the period of its composition. The analogy of relation is what is technically, e.g. by Aquinas, called the analogy of proportionality, as opposed to the simpler analogy of proportion, as in the example of the meaning of 'father'. The analogy of proportionality follows the scheme $\frac{a}{b} :: \frac{x}{y}$, that is to say, the analogy is not between a and x or b and y as such, but between the relationship linking a and b, and the relationship linking x and y. Thus, the relationships themselves are to be thought of not univocally but analogically to each other. If the relationships were understood univocally, if we knew a and b and also x, we should know y. This might give us a theology which would have some of the advantages of automation, but not those of life. In fact, y is still mysterious to us, and can only be partially guessed at by means of the analogy.[16]

Barth's analogy of relation is, then, a case of the analogy of proportionality. An important example of his use of it is to be found in what he says of the image of God in man, one of his most interesting and novel reformulations of a traditional doctrine. Barth takes as his starting-point the Genesis i story of the creation of man. (This version comes from the source P, whereas the slightly different companion version in Genesis ii

16. The Thomistic analogy of being is also a case of the analogy of proportionality, since what is analogical in different sorts of being is the relation of essence to existence. In God these are identical, in other beings they are related proportionally.

comes from the JE material.) God is represented as saying 'Let *us* create man in *our* own image,' and the account at once goes on to say, 'male and female created he them,' apparently linking the creation of man as a pair with the image of God. Barth draws attention both to this connexion and to the plural forms used of God, corresponding to the Hebrew plural *Elohim,* used by this source as the term for God. He does not believe that either is accidental. Elohim, he thinks, is not just a plural of majesty, as the Hebraists suppose, like the royal or papal 'we'. Rather is it to be taken with full theological seriousness as prefiguring the Christian understanding of God as the Trinity. Thus the human pair are as such the image of God, who as Trinity is himself in a certain sense plural.

Barth sees an analogy between the 'I–Thou' relationship in the Trinity and the corresponding relationship in man. Man and woman, created in the form of a pair, are essentially vis-à-vis each other, and so their relationship, which they cannot avoid, both reflects the being of God as Trinity, and is the foundation of the social life of man. The 'I and Thou' relationship is constitutive of human nature, and cannot be effaced by the fall of man.[17] The image of God in man is indestructible, contrary to Reformed tradition, which Barth had earlier followed in his assertion of its destruction. Since Barth had never sought to find any point of contact in human nature for the Word of God, it does not embarrass him when he now discovers he must say that the image of God is intact. In any case, man loses the righteousness of God at the fall. It also follows from this doctrine that man's nature must be defined in terms of co-humanity, because he is in the image of God in this way, and also because Christ is his brother, and Christ is himself the man for others.

The idea of analogy therefore plays a part not so much in the understanding of God as in the understanding of man in the light of God. Here the theological analogy of relation is

17. The distinction between the relationships of 'I and Thou' and 'I and It' pervades contemporary theology. It originated, it seems, with Feuerbach, but finds striking formulation in the work of Martin Buber. See R. Gregor Smith's *Martin Buber* in the series Makers of Contemporary Theology, London, Carey Kingsgate Press, 1966.

reinforced by the Christological analogy. It is also a distinctive feature of Barth's doctrine of man that it is governed and controlled by his doctrine of Christ, instead of Christology being dependent on a doctrine of man, as is usual. It is fundamental to Barth's doctrine of man that we do not know ourselves until we know Christ. Not only does Barth reject, as we have seen, the nineteenth-century idea, very popular also in the twentieth, that anthropology, the doctrine of man, is the presupposition of a theology, but he refuses even to discuss the doctrine of man except in the context of the Trinity and the incarnation of Christ. He concedes that secular study of man can tell us much about man as a phenomenon, but if we wish to know what man really is, we must go to the revelation in Christ. On the other hand, he insists that the humanity Christ took from the Virgin Mary (Barth believes in the Virgin Birth as the sign of the incarnation of God) was nothing other than our humanity, under the conditions of original sin. It is not some privileged humanity, not held in common with the sinners he came to save. Christ takes it as it is in us, and makes it new by his faithful refusal to yield to any of the temptations common to the fallen humanity he shares.

Theologians influenced by Barth have tried to carry the implications of the Christological analogy further than he has himself done in the work so far published. Along with Barth, they understand the relationship of the two natures of Christ in the terms of the Council of Chalcedon, which defined Christological doctrine authoritatively for Catholic Christians in 451. Interestingly, Barth not only accepts the teaching of this Council, but also adds some refinements on it coming from Byzantine theology. Chalcedon summed up the relationship as being without confusion and without separation, in a personal unity. If this relation is taken as the analogy in an analogy of proportionality, it may be possible to understand better areas of theology which according to Barth and others depend on Christology, such as the church, ministry and sacraments. The church fathers and some of the Reformation theologians preceded them in using Christology to control the doctrine of the relationship of Christ's presence in the sacrament of the eucharist to the bread and wine. By analogy, this relationship too can be described as without separation and without confusion, though not as a personal unity. The Christological heresies also have their counterparts in sacramental doctrine. In these suggestions, other theologians have gone further than Barth has himself, though the topic is not due to come up until the unpublished IV/4 of the *Church Dogmatics*. It is not certain that Barth would have been as consistent as his followers had he come to the sacraments.

Commentators have seen in Barth's mature thought an unparalleled 'Christological concentration'. We have just seen how Christ is indeed central to Barth's doctrine of revelation, and to his doctrines of man. Much more could be said about these points. His doctrine of God is incomplete without his discussion of the covenant of grace between God and man, which is actualized in history in Christ. The mature Barth will not even discuss God except in relation to man, as *for* man. God's very being is for man. These are conclusions from his refusal to speak about God outside his one Word, Jesus Christ, for it is in Christ that God is for man. Since revelation does not lie, God in himself, in his eternal being, must be for man. This turning of himself to man must be part of his eternal decree in Christ. So Barth understands the covenant as preceding even the creation of the world, as its ground. Creation is thus the consequence of the eternal decree of God electing man to life in Jesus Christ. The world is created as the theatre for the history of salvation.

The idea of creation in Christ is present in the New Testament, but no one before Barth had known how to take it with full seriousness. Most of his predecessors were influenced by the traditional scheme relating creation to natural theology, not to Christology or the doctrine of redemption. Having freed himself from this inherited scheme, Barth could look with fresh eyes at the New Testament, and see what it was actually saying. The prologue of the Fourth Gospel, read in conjunction with the first chapter of Genesis, which it recalls, is the key text, along with many Pauline sayings. So creation itself is grace, and depends upon the covenant. These are startling ideas, when first met, and not easy to understand without much thought. But the more one thinks about them the more compelling they become, and their Scriptural basis is evident.

Following up an insight of one of his associates, Pierre Maury, Barth also rethinks predestination and election Christologically. The doctrine of double predestination, to life and also to death, had always been an obnoxious feature of Calvin's doctrine, and it was really of little help to point out, as his followers truthfully could, that the same doctrine is found in Augustine and Aquinas, even if not so prominently. One achievement of liberal theology had been to fasten firmly upon the modern mind the idea that God is a God of love, that if one must continue to speak of his wrath, it can only be as an aspect of his love. Luther had called the law and the wrath of God his strange or alien work, in contrast to the Gospel of love, which is his proper work. The attempt to question this subordination of the wrath to the love of God, and to coordinate them, as many fundamentalists do, simply meets with intense scepticism and rejection from most modern people. Likewise, the doctrine of double predestination simply strikes people as immoral. Maury was able to find a non-liberal ground for transforming the doctrine of double predestination into an aspect of the Gospel.

Barth and Maury note that Paul speaks of the election of mankind, not the election of individuals. The elected church, and the elected individual, are actualizing in themselves the election of man. This election is also unequivocally election to life. Man is elected to life in Christ. What then of the reprobation, the opposite of election, corresponding to the predestination to damnation? Just as man is elected in Christ, and predestined to life in him, so the reprobation falls on Christ. He is the reprobate, who has borne condemnation in our place, when he died on the cross. Hence he has exhausted all God's condemnation, and there is none for man. Does this mean that all men will be saved? Barth has been charged by conservative commentators with teaching the doctrine of universalism on this account. Barth would reply that he does not, simply because to do so would be to rationalize something Scripture leaves mysterious, not because universal salvation would be incompatible with what we know of God in Christ. And is universalism so wicked? As we shall see once more before we are done, Barth refuses to coordinate grace with wrath, or the power of God with the power of evil.

We can now return to Barth's epoch-making criticism of religion, in the systematic form that it has gained in the *Church Dogmatics*. In dealing with the last few topics, we have already moved into the territory of the third volume of the *Church Dogmatics*, whereas religion is treated considerably earlier, in the second part of the first volume, with the doctrine of revelation. However, after this discussion of his Christological concentration and some of its implications, it may be easier to understand his ideas on religion. The criticism of religion, like that of natural theology, with which it is bound up, looks at first like a negative feature of a theology we have learned to understand as essentially positive and optimistic. Like Barth's other negations, his criticism of religion is the other side of a great affirmation. This is certainly true of his mature view of the matter, but it is important to remember that the criticism of religion does not first appear in the *Dogmatics*. It is present also in his early revolutionary phase, as an essential part of the diastasis between the Gospel and culture.

The theological criticism of religion has become one of the most striking features of present-day theology, to the extent even of becoming something of a cliché. Its original meaning has consequently been largely forgotten by those who use it. Whatever view we finally take up on this matter, it is well to remember how the discussion started in the thought of Barth. Barth heads section 17 of the *Church Dogmatics*, 'God's revelation as the abolition of religion'. In the light of his earlier polemics, and in the new context of the discussion of non-religious Christianity initiated by Bonhoeffer's *Letters and Papers from Prison*, we are not surprised to find so strong a word as abolition used. But then it becomes a puzzle why, unlike Bonhoeffer, Barth seems finally to restore to religion its rights in the Christian scheme. Here it is helpful to look at the German. As Herbert Hartwell reminds us,[18] the word *Aufhebung*, here translated as abolition, has an ambiguous meaning. Literally, it means 'picking

18. H. Hartwell, *The Theology of Karl Barth*, Philadelphia, Westminster Press, 1964, pp. 87 ff.

up': thus it can mean both to remove and to exalt. Hegel, who was very fond of the word, regularly exploited this ambiguity, and according to his most recent commentator, both senses are normally present in his use of the word.[19] If we make the same assumption about Barth's usage, things become clearer. Perhaps we should take these facts into account, and not translate *Aufhebung* by 'abolition', but in some other way: Hartwell translates the title of the section as 'The Revelation of God as the Abolition and Exaltation of Religion'; Kaufmann in his book on Hegel renders *Aufhebung* as 'sublimation'.

For Barth, religion is essentially unbelief. As such, it is abolished by Christ, in 'the faith of the Son of God who gave himself for me'. But unbelief is a permanent characteristic of sinful man, even when justified by grace. So religion becomes the object of God's grace as well as his judgement. It is taken up into God's gracious approach to man, as the human response to the Word, and justified and sanctified in Christ, on the analogy of the assumption of human flesh by the Word in the incarnation.

As unbelief, religion is man's constant attempt to do for himself what only God can do for him, i.e. to form a concept of God, and to justify and sanctify himself in relation to it. Thus religion is idolatry, because its concept of God is man-made and based on man's arbitrary choice of what he will worship, and it is self-righteousness, because man uses his religious activities as a means of justifying and sanctifying himself, instead of letting God do it by grace.

This theological judgement on religion should not be confused with a cultural one, in which other forms of human religions are given a negative valuation by Christians on the basis of their own cultural superiority. There is no such superiority: even the doctrine of justification by faith is not an infallible distinguishing mark of true religion, for something very like it exists in the Pure Land sect of Japanese Buddhism, as the history of religions shows. Christianity itself as a historical and cultural form is simply one among the human religions, as liable to God's judgement on unbelief as any of them. The criticism of religion has nothing to

19. Walter Kaufmann, *Hegel*, Weidenfeld & Nicolson, 1966, pp. 52, 159, 191 ff.

do with Christian imperialism; it is made in the name of the great positive of the Gospel, in the light of which even historical Christianity comes under judgement.

But just because it is the Gospel and not some human value judgement that condemns religion, there is also justification for religion under the grace of God. Under grace, there is also 'true religion', and this is Christianity, considered not now as a historical and cultural form, but in its theological meaning. The Word of God is heard and believed in a human act of faith, it elicits human thanksgiving expressed in worship, and human action in deeds of witness. Through grace, these acts, which are in fact religious, are the true religion in this world. Only in the Kingdom of heaven, when we see God face to face, will religion come to an end. Has the meaning of religion for Barth shifted a little now from his original definition? Granted that faith is always accompanied by unbelief, the meaning of religion now seems to have shifted from unbelief to certain concrete acts and institutions which historically come into being as a result of the preaching of the Word, and these are neutral in value: they neither imply nor preclude unbelief. At any rate, from this point of view, Barth abandons the polemic against religion. The absurdities of human religion and religious culture appear lovable to one who sees them under the mercy of God. This is more or less the point at which Bonhoeffer's even better-known criticism diverges from Barth's, as we shall see below.

We have not the space to discuss Barth's views on every major topic of theology, though it would be profitable to do so. A number of other characteristics of his thought can be brought together if we end by looking at the positive spirit of his theology, several times mentioned already. The mature Barth is no longer a dialectical theologian in the sense that his thought moves by negation, affirming only what cannot be contained in words at all. When all the criticism is done, there is now something to be affirmed, and affirmation becomes more and more characteristic of Barth in his later years, while his manner becomes simpler and more tolerant. This is not just a question of tone and manner, but of the deepest movement of his thought.

Already in the thirties Barth saw that he wanted to affirm the priority of the Gospel over the Law. Particularly among Lutherans, this way of thinking was found revolutionary, and it has novel and interesting consequences. I suspect that it is in fact the fundamental insight that governs the structure of the later volumes of the *Church Dogmatics*, particularly where his thought departs from the established Protestant tradition. The distinction and unity between the Law and the Gospel is perhaps for Protestant theologians of the Reformation tradition the supremely important theological question. A clear new proposal on this question, effectively worked out, would mean a step forward within the Protestant tradition hardly less important than its origination by Luther, Zwingli and Calvin. Doubtless it is in such company that Barth belongs. The distinction between the Law and the Gospel may well be the most profound way of expressing the original insight of Luther, which was his most important contribution to Christian thought. For Luther, the distinction is very sharp: his own distinctive teaching about justification by faith alone, and the liberty and obedience of the Christian man, hang upon it. Both the Law and the Gospel are God's. The Law is an instrument of condemnation and killing, the Gospel of forgiveness and life. Hence God's work through the Law is his strange work, whereas his proper work is his work in the Gospel. In itself, the Law seems to be demonic for Luther, belonging with sin, death and the devil. Related to the Gospel, it becomes an instrument of God for good, since the condemnation it wields brings down human self-righteousness, and makes man see his need of the forgiveness and justification offered him in the Gospel. This is the unity of Law and Gospel. But the distinction comes in again when man believes the Gospel, for now he is no longer under the Law, but supremely free; this free man is also every man's servant through the obligation of love for which the Gospel frees him.

The Lutheran view of Law and Gospel is thus sharply dualistic, like the Lutheran view of much else: *either* the Law, *or* the Gospel, never both. Civil Law and the State belong under the Law: they have no function whatever within the sphere of redemption, except to provide a protected space for the preaching of the Gospel. On the other hand, since Law has no place in the Christian life, Christian ethics becomes a problematic notion for Lutherans.

Later Lutheranism borrowed from Calvinists the idea of the 'third use of the Law', as a guide to the justified man in living the Christian life. (The first and second were, roughly, the natural law, and the standards of the sermon on the mount, which are so unattainably high as to drive the Christian to the Gospel for justification.)

Barth wished to speak of one Word of God, which is necessarily Gospel first, and only then Law. God does not, in his opinion, first condemn man for the sake of subsequently having mercy on him. His fundamental and unwavering attitude to man is expressed in his grace, but grace is also judgement, and as the judgement of *God*, must abolish whatever is contrary to itself. So the Gospel contains the Law within it, or operates through the Law, which then becomes the external form of which the Gospel is the inner content. This has several important consequences. The Law is always the law of the covenant. Barth is surely on good biblical ground here. The Ten Commandments begin not with a legal prescription, but with God's proclamation of himself as the God who brought the people up out of Egypt into liberty, and so is their God. Thus the commandments are given within an already existing relationship of grace. Grace is not given to men because they keep the Law, as some late medieval Catholics thought, or even because they do not, as Lutherans supposed. It is given because God is God, the God of love and freedom. His grace confers freedom, but the form of that freedom is doing his will. There is no freedom apart from or in contradiction to God's will. When Barth talks about ethical questions, he habitually uses the form 'may and must'. He means that man is set free by the Gospel to do God's will; only if man does not take up this freedom, but turns away from it, does he experience its grace as compulsion. Then it is time to talk about what man *must* do.

It also follows that ethics is a part of dogmatics, not a separate subject that might precede or follow it. Ethics must be proclaimed along with the Gospel of which they are a part. We noted at the beginning that Barth has never wanted to separate ethics and dogmatics. In 1914, and again in the thirties, he used politics as a test of sound theology. Theology must have ethical consequences, including political ones, and correspondingly ethics must never be divorced from theology. So he puts his ethical teaching in with the principal doctrines in his dogmatics, instead of reserving it for a special section at the end, or a separate work. The volume on God has a section on the command of God. The volume on creation has a whole part-volume devoted to the command of God the creator. The volume on reconciliation was to end with a part-volume, on the command of God the reconciler.

Likewise, as I have already implied, his ethics is an ethics of freedom. He believes in ethical rules, though not the sort that do not admit of exceptions. But the meaning of ethics itself is that it gives concrete form to the exercise of the freedom conferred on man by grace. Enlightened by the Gospel, man can see that there is no freedom in his own way. As Augustine taught, the highest kind of freedom is not *posse non peccare*, to be able not to sin, but remaining 'free' to sin if one wishes, but *non posse peccare*, being unable to sin. Otherwise it would be very difficult to understand in what sense Christ or God is free. Freedom is so important for Barth that he regards it as one of God's two key perfections, along with love. Hence he needs a definition of freedom that will work for both God and man, at any rate analogically. What man thinks of as his free will, the ability to choose between good and evil, is not freedom at all. So the 'must' of God is there to protect the 'may'; even under grace, it is needed by sinners.

More surprisingly, Barth considers that we know nothing of our sin until we have been redeemed from it. Of course man can feel guilty, because he knows that he breaks the moral law. But this is not that sin, on account of which a man is lost before God. That terrible reality we can only know and understand when we have left it behind, by contrast with the grace of God which has defeated it. Hence Barth's theology does not lend itself to preaching to obtain conviction of sin, still less to playing on people's guilt feelings in order to make them want forgiveness. This too is the explanation of a saying of Barth's, often quoted against him by Anglo-Saxon theologians, that because Christ was born on Christmas Day we know that man is utterly lost. The point is that this is the only way in which we do know that man is utterly lost – total grace implies total need. We only know lostness through salvation, and through considering its cost. Thus his meaning is the opposite of the one attributed to him. But this misunderstanding is by no means unique in controversy about Barth.

The priority of the knowledge of reconciliation over the knowledge of sin is expressed in the structure of the fourth volume of the *Church Dogmatics*. Sin receives no full discussion until we reach this volume. Then it is discussed by relating each of its principal forms to corresponding affirmations about the person and work of Christ. Discussion of the obedience of the Son of God leads to a treatment of the pride and fall of man. From the exaltation of the Son of Man, he moves to the sloth and misery of man. In the light of the glory of the mediator, he considers the falsehood and misery of man. Immediately these three forms of sin have been analysed, Barth proceeds to the way in which their defeat is actualized, in the justification of man, the sanctification of man and the vocation of man. Thus the discussion of sin is totally enclosed in the discussion of the way in which God has overcome it.

An equally important consequence of the Gospel Law priority is to be seen in Barth's novel doctrine of the State. This too in an indirect way is brought under the Gospel, through the doctrine of the Lordship of Christ over both church and world. The idea is worked out in two essays, *Rechtfertigung und Recht* (1938, translated as *Church and State*, though 'Justification and Justice' might be nearer) and *Christliche Gemeinde und Bürgergemeinde* (1946, translated as 'The Christian Community and the Civil Community' in *Against the Stream*).[20] We have already discovered that for Barth faith means commitment in the world, including political commitment. He also relates the State to the redemptive work of God. Continental theologians often reproach Anglo-Saxon ones for confusing church and state, expecting the state to realize a community of love possible only under the Gospel. If this is a mistake, Barth does not make it when he relates the state to the Gospel.

20. ed. R. Gregor Smith, S.C.M. Press, 1954.

Barth knows how to distinguish church and state, but he does not consider that the state belongs with a law preceding the Gospel, which he in any case rejects. Following Paul, Barth sees the exalted Christ as the Lord of all forms of power and authority, making use of these, even when they do not acknowledge his authority and act evilly, to serve the will of God for good. The State, even when it is a bad state, provided it is not so evil as to be unrecognizable as a state at all, belongs within God's redemptive purpose. The order it confers on human life serves God's purposes for men, contributing to the freedom of the Gospel in their corporate life. The Lordship of Christ extends in fact to all spheres of human life. This idea has proved highly suggestive in the field of Christian ethics since the war, and is particularly associated with the social thinking of the World Council of Churches.

We may see this same thought of the priority of Gospel over Law, of good over evil, of God over his enemies, in one of the most difficult of Barth's doctrines, that of the *Nihil*.[21] The Nihil is Barth's term for what in other theologies is symbolized as the devil and his angels, the transcendent power of evil. Barth has been criticized by more conservative theologians for not having a devil in his theology. In a sense, this is correct. The Nihil is not a personal being, capable of confronting God on almost equal terms. Barth avoids the dualism of much traditional (and again especially Lutheran) theology. On the other hand, this does not mean that he in any way minimizes the reality and power of evil, especially in relation to man. By himself, without God, man is completely powerless against the Nihil. However, as its name indicates, the Nihil is not a positive force of evil, still less a concrete person. Positive existence and personality belong to what is good, to what God has created, and the Nihil is not a part of his creation. The term Nihil indicates that strictly speaking evil has no reality, if that word is to be given its full sense, still less the power to defeat God.

21. I render the German *das Nichtige* in this way, following Cochrane and Hartwell, where the official translation of the *Church Dogmatics* has 'the Nothingness'. 'The Nihil' carries the destructive connotations of annihilation and nihilism, missing in 'Nothingness'.

We appear to have sketched a series of paradoxes, incapable of resolution in an intelligible statement of Barth's meaning. Nor does the terminology he goes on to use do much to lessen our intellectual difficulty. He calls the Nihil 'unreal', 'an impossible possibility', and again, 'an ontological impossibility'. Yet he certainly means to affirm the actuality of evil in the strongest terms. We must do our best, within the limitations of space, to see what is and is not meant by such terminology. However, it is worth pointing out that Barth would not be pleased if we spent too much time and effort in understanding the Nihil. Part of his contention is that man should not dwell on the Nihil in thought, because it belongs to what God has not willed, and has overcome in Christ; speculative curiosity about evil and its ontological status may be risky, drawing the mind too far away from the proper objects of contemplation for the Christian. In the structure of his dogmatics he devotes relatively less space to it than most theologians do to their doctrine of evil, though in absolute terms the treatment is extensive.

When Barth calls the Nihil unreal and impossible, he certainly does not mean to say that it has no existence. He does wish to suggest that its mode of existence is unique, paradoxical and contrary to the mode of existence of God's creation. In denying ontological reality to transcendent evil, he does not deny that it has ontic existence, or actuality. We could say that while Barth diverges from the existentialist theologians in speaking about the being of God, he follows their practice when it comes to God's enemies. Here his language is existentialist, not ontological: his Nihil is a non-objective existential, in their terminology. It cannot have either reality or, strictly speaking, possibility, since God has not created and willed it. It is not a part of that good creation to which God has said Yes. But it has actuality and thus, though impossible, must be regarded as having an impossible possibility.

Barth here offers us, in fact, an up-to-date version of the old doctrine of evil as a *privatio boni*, an absence of good. But his version surely does far more justice than this way of speaking is usually able to, to the existential experience of the power of non-being, or evil. The power of evil is indirectly derived from the power of God: where else could it get anything positive, like power? It exists in the power of God's No. It is the utterly black shadow cast by the pure light of God. Without the light, there could be no shadow. But the shadow is not something, as the light is, though in its nothingness it has effective existence. It can plunge man into its darkness, though he was made for the light. It is then a consequence, not directly willed by God, but foreseen and ruled by him, of God's act of creation. It does not therefore pre-exist the creation of the world, as the devil was thought to. There can be no fall before the creation of the world, as some theologians have speculated. The Nihil is treated along with the doctrine of providence, not of creation as such. Its power is seen in the agony and cross of Christ, but there precisely it is overcome.

Finally, it will be illuminating to say something about Barth's doctrine of Mozart. He had a place in his dogmatics for his favourite composer. At first sight, this looks like a charming weakness on Barth's part, a piece of inconsistency, the imperfection in the marvellous fabric of his *Church Dogmatics* that makes it humanly acceptable. How could Barth above all slip in a bit of theology of culture like that? But Barth knows what it is he is doing. Mozart is not a theological authority, and he does not contribute any doctrine. (It is not really fair to talk about his *doctrine* of Mozart, as I did.) But if Barth is right in his musical judgements, Mozart does show in music exactly what I have been trying to convey about Barth's theology in the last few pages. Let us listen to Barth on Mozart:

Mozart's centre is not like that of the great theologian Schleiermacher, identical with balance, neutralization and finally indifference. What happened in this centre is rather a splendid annulment of balance, a *turn* in the strength of which the light rises and the shadow winks but does not disappear; happiness out-distances sorrow without extinguishing it and the 'Yes' rings stronger than the still existing 'No'. Notice the *reversal* of the great dark and little bright experiences of Mozart's life! 'The rays of the sun *disperse* the night' – that's what you hear at the end of *The Magic Flute*. The play may or must still proceed or start from the very beginning. But it is a play in which some Height or Depth is winning or has already won. This directs and characterizes it. One will never perceive equilibrium, and for that reason uncertainty or doubt, in Mozart's music.[22]

And from the *Church Dogmatics* itself:

It is possible to give him this position (sc. in theology) because he knew something about creation in its total goodness that neither the real fathers of the church nor our Reformers, neither the orthodox nor the liberals, neither the exponents of natural theology nor those heavily armed with 'the Word of God', and certainly not the Existentialists, nor indeed any other great musicians before him and after him, either know or can express and maintain as he did. In this respect he was pure in heart, far transcending both optimists and pessimists. 1756–1791! This was the time when God was under attack for the Lisbon earthquake, and theologians and other well-meaning folk were hard put to it to defend him. In face of the problem of theodicy, Mozart had the peace of God which far transcends all the critical or speculative reason that praises and reproves. The problem lay behind him. Why then concern himself with it? He had heard, and causes those who have ears to hear, even today, what we shall not see until the end of time – the whole context of providence. As though in the light of this end, he heard the harmony of creation to which the shadow also belongs but in which the shadow is not darkness, deficiency is not defeat, sadness cannot become despair, trouble cannot degenerate into tragedy and infinite melancholy is not ultimately forced to claim undisputed sway. Thus the cheerfulness in this harmony is not without its limits. But the light shines forth all the more brightly because it breaks forth from the shadow. The sweetness is also bitter and cannot therefore cloy. Life does not fear death but it knows it well. *Et lux perpetua lucet (sic!) eis* – even the dead of Lisbon. Mozart saw this light no more than we do, but he heard the whole world of creation enveloped by this light. Here it was fundamentally in order that he should not hear a middle or neutral note, but the positive note far more strongly than the negative. He heard the negative only in and with the positive. Yet in their inequality he heard them both together, as for example in the Symphony in G-Minor of 1788. He never heard only the one in abstraction. He heard concretely, and therefore his compositions were and are total music . . . I make this interposition here, before turning to chaos, because in the music of Mozart – and I wonder whether the same can be said of any other

22. 'The Freedom of Mozart', in ed. Walter Leibrecht, *Religion and Culture: Essays in Honour of Paul Tillich*, New York, Harper & Row 1959, p. 76 f.

works before or after that – we have clear and convincing proof that it is a slander on creation to charge it with a share in chaos because it includes a Yes and a No, as though oriented to God on one side and nothingness on the other. Mozart causes us to hear that even on the latter side, and therefore in its totality, creation praises its creator and is therefore perfect. (III/3, pp. 297 ff.)

Barth himself began his working day by listening to records of Mozart on the gramophone. In the light of these quotations, we can see that he did so, not only in order to begin the day with more zest, but in order to hear once more from Mozart what he himself heard. Barth's theology too has this *turn* to the positive, and it is the strongest of the impressions that it makes.

BARTH AND BRUNNER

As the total structure of Barth's theological achievement came gradually into view, its scale and quality began to be measurable. One opinion of him, coming from a source that could hardly be accused of being Barthian, and for this among more obvious reasons carries particular weight, is that of Pope Pius XII, who said that Barth was the greatest dogmatic theologian since Aquinas. Such an estimate began to be widely shared outside Germany after about 1950, when the *Church Dogmatics* began to appear in volume after volume of English translation, along with articles in a wide range of journals about the significance of his work. Before that period, he had been known outside Germany and Switzerland chiefly for his commentary on *Romans* and the debate with Brunner about natural theology, and this debate, as we have noted, was understood very much from Brunner's point of view, since the works that would have enabled the reader to set it in its proper context in Barth's thought were known only to a few specialists. Brunner at that time probably enjoyed the higher reputation of the two. His principal works were translated much earlier, several of them before the war, and he was widely regarded as the best representative of the dialectical theology. Barth was the extremist, known perhaps for his bravery in the Confessing Church, but as a theologian taken less seriously in the English-speaking world than Brunner. Now it does not seem necessary to accord Brunner more than relatively brief treatment as we draw near the end of this chapter on Barth's revolution in theology.

The fact is that if we can understand Barth, Brunner presents no difficulties. The points at which he differs from Barth are not hard to explain, and in any case Brunner is a very clear and readable author. He is undoubtedly a fine teacher, but as a creative theologian few would now place his contribution on a level with Barth's. Just because it is not so 'extreme' as Barth's, it offers a less distinctive solution to the problems of twentieth-century theology than his. From the point of view of the general reader, Brunner's contribution is likely to be thought of as included in Barth's; the reader who rejects Barth is not likely to find Brunner sufficiently different to meet his objections to Barth, and if Barth is accepted, he will be the one to be read.

Why then has there been so much conflict between the two, commonly believed to extend to a certain personal bitterness that made it hard for the two former comrades to meet, up to the time of Brunner's death? This is to be explained in part by the more charged nature of theological controversy in Europe: small differences are taken with greater seriousness, and total agreement sought in a way foreign to British and American traditions of debate. Moreover, the differences between them arose at just those points where Barth thought it vital to make a clean break with liberal theology, and Brunner thought it vital not to revert to orthodoxy. Where Barth wished to start from the Word of God, Brunner was ready to begin with a doctrine of man, and to find in it a point of contact for the Word of God. Brunner did not revert to natural theology in the old sense, but gave it a new meaning, as the 'eristic' task of theology, in breaking down rival world-views, to make way for the Gospel. He also maintained, as Barth did not, the nineteenth-century cleavage between faith and theology, though he gave it a novel and interesting form, which we must consider. On Brunner's side, too, there may perhaps have been a certain feeling of personal disappointment, that his own achievements were not recognized as fully as they might have been, once Barth's massive work grew to surpass and finally overshadow his own. It is clear that he never properly understood Barth on the points on which they differed. Nor can he be much blamed if he felt nettled by the vigour with which Barth criticized him.

It is not, I think, a misleading generalization if we say that all of Barth's associates of the nineteen-twenties who afterwards differed from him did so because they remained in essentially the same position that they had originally shared with Barth, while he moved on to a position they could not accept. Brunner is no exception. When Barth added to his denial of what nineteenth-century theology had affirmed, the continuity between religion and faith, his affirmation of what it had denied, the possibility of theological speech bearing upon the being of God, he lost them all. This is true of Bultmann, it is obviously true of Tillich, who had never been very close to Barth, and it is true of a number of lesser theologians not discussed here. The proof that it is true of Brunner is to be found in his criticism of Barth. Barth, he considers, has *objectified* faith: that is, he has seen faith as knowledge of an object, as expressible in true propositions. A cardinal principle of Barth's own theology is the priority of the object of faith over the act of faith. In these terms, Brunner's theology is constructed around the relationship of the object of faith and the act of faith, in an event which overcomes the distinction between subject and object. Truth lies not in the objective revelation, nor, as with the nineteenth century, in the content of man's faith, but in the encounter between revelation and faith. God and man meet as I and Thou. Brunner also remains closer to the existentialism of Kierkegaard and others than Barth, and he blames Barth for losing touch with Kierkegaard's discoveries.

Brunner's most original contribution to modern theology lies in this doctrine of truth as encounter, and it is one that has probably exercised a wider influence, at least on a semi-popular level, than any of Barth's distinctive ideas, except perhaps that of the Lordship of Christ. Among those who are influenced broadly by neo-orthodoxy, at least in the English-speaking world, the most frequently met with doctrine of revelation is not Barth's but a non-propositional, relational view of revelation, owing most to Brunner, whose thought is quite legitimately filled out with insights from Buber's philosophy of I and Thou. The strength of such a view is the freedom it gives its exponents in relation to biblical criticism and the difficulties about miracles. Interestingly, Brunner saw Barth's descent into objectivism beginning when he embraced the doctrine of the Virgin Birth, to Brunner an obvious myth. The Brunner-Buber view is strongly personalistic, and emphasizes the element of personal commitment in faith. It is less strong at the point where an explanation is needed of how theological propositions are related to faith. It deliberately places them on an altogether lower level than faith itself, and here it is unmistakably the heir of the nineteenth century.

Brunner's most important works have all been translated, with the exception of his first, *Die Mystik und das Wort* ('Mysticism and the Word'), a polemical study of Schleiermacher, which did much to establish the view of Schleiermacher with which the dialectical theologians worked. Accessible in English, however, are for example *The Mediator*, the first major study of Christology in contemporary theology, *Man in Revolt*, and *Revelation and Reason*, in addition to Brunner's own *Dogmatics*, a far more compressed work than Barth's, in only three moderately-sized volumes. In addition there are many shorter works, including *Our Faith*, a short study of the creed, and *The Misunderstanding of the Church*, an influential work in which Brunner attacks the institutionalization of what was in his view meant to be a personal community. Most of his distinctive positions are set out in a clear and illuminating way in *Truth as Encounter*, translated from the second (1963) edition of *Wahrheit als Begegnung*, the 1938 edition of which had previously appeared in English under the less exact title of *The Divine-Human Encounter*.

Brunner believes that his own position, summed up in the phrase 'truth as encounter', is a correct understanding of the Christian idea of truth, and that this has been distorted in opposite ways by the two most famous of contemporary theologians, Karl Barth and Rudolf Bultmann. The opposition between them, which has dominated the German theological scene since about 1950, cannot be properly resolved by victory for one side, since the alternative is a false one. Brunner himself understands truth in the biblical sense as a happening, transcending the opposition, fundamental in all merely human thought, of object and subject. From these two poles of thought derive tendencies running through all the history of Christian thought, the objectivist and the subjectivist. Of the two, it is clearly in practice the objectivist that he regards as the more dangerous, since we meet with this in legalism, the great enemy of all Reformation theology. Subjectivism in its roots is even more questionable, however, for it is based in the human drive to autonomy, to false freedom from God, instead of that obedience which is true freedom. Even objectivism arises out of the desire of the guardians of faith to defend it against the false spontaneity of subjectivism. Objectivism has turned faith into doctrine, the personal correspondence of man with the truth that comes to him as an event in God's word into intellectual adherence to credal formulae, and the personal community of those who thus believe into the false institution of the church, with its fixed orders of ministry, semi-magical sacramentalism, and above all its misguided attempt to become a people's church instead of a community consisting of those who confess Christ.

For Brunner, an abyss separates faith, as the personal correspondence of man with the truth of God, which comes to him in history in an encounter, and not in a set of ideas, from the theology and the dogma of the institutionalized church. Nevertheless, Brunner admits that revelation as God's word does make use of objective doctrine. Doctrine stands in an instrumental relation to revelation; as in the sacrament, God's self-revelation is to be found *in, with and under* the doctrine, and in neither case can there be identity between the presence and its vehicle. Faith can and must make use of doctrine, for when God comes to man, he says something to him. Brunner does not want to repeat the mistake he attributed to Schleiermacher, and dissolve the Word into mysticism. But he is always, it seems, more aware of the opposite risk: he thinks objectivism the most fatal and pervasive error in the whole history of Christianity. That is why his criticism of Barth, whom he identifies increasingly with the error of objectivism, is so sharp, sharper even than his criticism of Bultmann, whom he regards as a subjectivist. His own theology can overcome the false antithesis between these two former colleagues in the dialectical theology, to which he himself remains loyal. Whether all this is in fact an adequate account of the thought of either theologian may be doubted, but it tells us where Brunner himself wants to go.

On the question of revelation, Brunner wants to affirm a general revelation to all men, denied by Barth, as the presupposition of the special revelation in Christ, which enters in to deal with the rejection of general revelation. He wishes to hold a Christological view of creation and even reproaches Barth for basing his doctrine of creation on an exposition of Genesis instead of directly on Christology, but he nevertheless retains the Lutheran doctrine of the orders of creation as the foundation of thinking about society and social justice, instead of following Barth along the Christological path in a doctrine of the Lordship of Christ. It is consistent with this that his actual political stance is well to the right of Barth's, and that he reproaches him for not being sufficiently anti-communist.

Connected with the doctrine of the orders of creation is Brunner's idea of a Christian philosophy, founded on the famous 'principle of closeness of relationship'. Brunner wishes to assert that intellectual work will and must be affected by the Christian revelation to the extent that its subject-matter is related to the theme of revelation itself. Thus, no one has been able to show that there is any foundation for a Christian mathematics, whereas theology must be entirely Christian, without making use of any sources outside revelation. Christian philosophy will show how this relationship operates in various fields of thought. He sees theologians like Tillich and the Niebuhrs, whom he much respects, as Christian philosophers rather than theologians in the strict sense, and from him this is by no means a negative judgement, as it would be from Barth.

BARTH'S INFLUENCE

The breach between Barth and Brunner must be regretted, both personally and intellectually. They do indeed have most things that matter in common, and their aims are probably not so far apart as either supposes. Nevertheless, the intellectual achieve-

144

ment of Barth is on a much greater scale, and he must be regarded as the more important thinker of the two. Though Brunner's influence was once considerably wider, as Barth's work has become better known and understood he has gained an influence going right outside Protestantism. Barth has not had much personally to do with the ecumenical movement, though many who have are among those most strongly influenced by him, among them no less an ecumenist than W. A. Visser 't Hooft, the first General Secretary of the World Council of Churches. Barth has not attended many ecumenical conferences (though he did give an important paper at the founding meeting of the World Council of Churches at Amsterdam in 1948), or written many papers for ecumenical discussions. He has preferred to say: Let the church be the church. When it finds itself under the Word in true obedience, it will also find its unity. On the other hand, it could well be claimed that his theology has played a major part in the development of the ecumenical movement through his influence. Very generally, his theology has done more than anyone else's to persuade Protestants to take the church seriously again, as they did not in the ascendancy of liberal theology. Hence the very widespread discussion of the church in recent Protestant theology, though it is in part the fruit of biblical scholarship, has much to do with the impact of Barth's restoration of the link between theology and church. Specifically, I have already mentioned the use made of the Christological analogy in the discussions of the Faith and Order Commission of the World Council of Churches, in the period between the Lund and Montreal World Conferences on Faith and Order (1952–63). The second form of ecumenical influence arising from Barth's theology has been exercised in the new dialogue between Protestants and Catholics, and this requires consideration at slightly greater length.

The most important critical studies of Barth's theology are the work of Roman Catholic writers, and they precede in time the burgeoning literature now coming from Protestant sources. Among these are Hans Urs von Balthasar's study, *Karl Barth. Darstellung und Deutung seiner Theologie* (1951), regrettably still untranslated, so far as I can discover, H. Bouillard's two-volume study in French (1957) and Hans Küng's bold work, *Rechtfertigung, die Lehre Karl Barths und eine katholische Besinnung* (1957, translated as *Justification*, 1963). Why has Barth's theology attracted so much interest from Catholic theologians? These men regard his theology as 'both the strongest development of Protestantism and the closest approximation to Catholicism'. The former element in this description is not difficult to understand, and alone it makes Barth's thought a fitting partner in ecumenical dialogue with Catholicism. The latter element may cause surprise, in view of Barth's rejection of philosophy, which plays such a part in Catholic theology, and his polemic against the analogy of being, and indeed his generally anti-Catholic tone throughout his work. However, there are points to be made which run counter to these natural impressions.

Most important of all, I think, is the way Barth understands theology. Even though not in the same way as his partners in dialogue, he considers it a rational pursuit. Roman Catholic theologians have until very recently used Thomistic philosophy to provide their theology with its rational structure, while Barth tries to draw out the inherent rationality of the Christian revelation, using any philosophical ideas that come in handy. This was once a decisive difference. Today it is less so, since Roman Catholic theologians obviously wish to shake themselves free from the dominance of Thomism. However, even at its deepest, the difference is not so great as that between Barth and theologians who still hold to the nineteenth-century Protestant tradition. If Barth is sometimes charged with Catholicizing tendencies by theologians of this kind, it is because he wishes to present Christian doctrine rationally and propositionally. Secondly, his respect for rational thought in theology leads Barth to take very seriously the contribution to theology of the church fathers and the ecumenical councils of the early church, in which the doctrines of the Trinity and the incarnation were worked out. Barth's use of the work of the Council of Chalcedon is one of the factors contributing to the marked rise in respect for that Council to be seen in Protestant theology over the past period. So a common acceptance of the fathers unites Barth with Catholic theologians over against the biblicists who condemn them for 'Hellenizing' the

Gospel. Thirdly, Barth's own use of analogy is attractive to Catholic theologians, in spite of his probable misunderstanding of the use made of it in Catholic thought. He seems lately to have given way somewhat on this point.

From the ecumenical point of view, though perhaps not from a strictly theological one, the most remarkable of these studies has been the book of the young Tübingen theologian Hans Küng. His book on Barth's doctrine of justification made his name, and since then his lesser works have been in constant demand by a public deeply interested in the theological renewal of the Roman Catholic church. Since the doctrine of justification was more or less the principal point of difference at the Reformation, any breakthrough here could be of immense importance. Küng proposes the startling thesis that Barth's doctrine of justification and that of the Catholic Church are substantially identical, once the differences in terminology have been overcome. He considers that Catholics were not contending that justification is not a free gift of God, as Protestants believe, but simply that it cannot be separated from sanctification, and he finds this fully accepted and expressed in Barth's doctrine. He is able to print as preface to his book a friendly letter from Barth, testifying that he has correctly understood his teaching. Catholic reviewers too have generally accorded the book a favourable reception. If Küng's thesis can stand up to criticism over a sufficient period of time, he will have shown that the principal issue on which the Reformation was fought out has now been overcome, as least as far as those Protestants who share Barth's outlook are concerned. This does not of course mean that all problems dividing the two traditions have in principle been solved, or that no new sources of division have arisen since the Reformation period. But it would mean that all other differences could be discussed in a climate of much greater mutual understanding, and therefore the ecumenical consequences of the validation of Küng's proposals could be incalculable.

There is reason to believe that in the astonishingly changed ecumenical climate since the Second Vatican Council, the Catholic dialogue with Barth will gather further momentum. Catholic theologians are engaged in re-thinking every doctrine along more biblical lines. As they do so, they are bound to ask the sort of questions Barth has tried to answer, and since his answers are already more acceptable to them than those of other Protestant theologians, it is not improbable that Barth will shortly become a major influence upon many younger Catholic theologians. It is doubtful though if he will long enjoy a monopoly of such influence, for signs of Catholic response to Bultmann and Bonhoeffer can also be seen. What is possible is that in the next period Barth will enjoy more influence among Catholics than among Protestants. The latter have already, especially in Germany, begun to turn away from him, perhaps only temporarily, and just as his work is becoming more widely known in the English-speaking world, new developments are taking place, stemming from the work of younger men, notably that of Dietrich Bonhoeffer. The rising theological generation in Protestantism will have learned a lot from Barth, but it is likely that they will not, at least in Protestantism, follow him very closely.

READING BARTH

How can the lay reader come to terms with so formidable a theological edifice? My first suggestion would be that the attempt should on no account be shirked. Anyone, theologian or non-theologian, who is interested in the themes of theology must know something of Barth's work, and there is no substitute (certainly not in the present chapter) for reading him, at such length as one's time and resources permit. It is not necessary, however, whatever Barth may say to his own critics, to spend the whole of one's leisure time for several years in reading the *Church Dogmatics* right through, unless one wants to become an authority on his theology. I do not wish to suggest that this would not be a thoroughly rewarding enterprise, but I suppose that few will undertake it. He has expressed his major positions in shorter form, and some of these lesser works can be attempted first, to see if one has the taste for profounder encounter through at least some portions of the *Church Dogmatics*. The best introduction to his work is now the lectures which were his academic swansong, published as *Evangelical Theology: An Introduction* (1963), now available in soft as well as hard covers. The most widely read of his works is doubtless the series of lectures on the Apostles' Creed given at Bonn shortly after the war, and published as *Dogmatics in Outline*. I would also recommend a collection of his shorter writings on politics and theology, entitled *Against the Stream* (1954). The next step is perhaps to dip into the *Church Dogmatics* by way of Helmut Gollwitzer's excellent anthology, *Karl Barth's Church Dogmatics, Selections* (1961). This will suggest passages for further reading from the big work itself. I have already suggested that the chapter on the perfections of God in II/1 is of classical significance in modern theological thinking. Many will find the ethical passages in III of absorbing interest. The discussion of religion in I/2 is basic to the contemporary theological debate about religion and secularity. Those who come to be more at home in Barth's work will want to read the great study of reconciliation in IV. Here we find set out more fully than anywhere else what Barth himself has testified is the key to his whole thought, the theme he learned from the Blumhardts, Jesus is Victor.

Three

Bultmann's
Existentialist
Theology

Rudolf Bultmann's contribution to systematic theology is an indirect one, for he is a New Testament scholar, not a theologian in the narrower sense. The study of the New Testament is always relevant, however, to systematic theology, since the theologian has the aim of stating the meaning for today of the biblical message. Bultmann also conceives this as part of his task as an interpreter of the New Testament. Any new view of the New Testament is likely to have far-reaching consequences for systematic theology. We have already noted that the application of historical method to the New Testament documents in the nineteenth century produced a new view of Jesus, which was quickly incorporated into systematic theology. Twentieth-century views of Jesus and of the New Testament church have likewise found their way into theology. One way of describing the whole movement of thought with which this book is primarily concerned is to call it 'biblical theology'. I do not believe that the term is a useful one, since it begs too many questions, but it implies at least that many contemporary theologians have found biblical language useful and meaningful in their own work. Precisely this use of biblical language is challenged by Bultmann, so that his ideas come right into the centre of the theologian's problems. Bultmann believes that many or most of the biblical terms are not usable as they stand: in his opinion they require interpretation, and only if interpreted can they speak to us in their original power. He calls this process of interpretation hermeneutic, and his principal hermeneutic method, demythologizing (*Entmythologisierung*), somewhat misleadingly, since the point of his programme is not, as the term suggests, to get rid of mythology, but to interpret it to the man of today.

If we turn from the reading of Karl Barth's *Church Dogmatics* to one of Bultmann's essays, such as the original article on 'New Testament and Mythology',[1] which sparked off the demythologizing controversy, or to his lectures, *Jesus Christ and Mythology*,[2] we find ourselves immediately in a very different kind of world. As we read Bultmann's sharp, lucid, barely qualified argument, contrasting the picture of the world which modern science and our technological way of life have given us with the picture familiar to the men of the ancient world, in which the message of the New Testament was first expressed, we recognize that we are again in the presence of the nineteenth-century quest for a modern understanding of the Gospel. Barth had been so profoundly aware of the losses which had come about through the nineteenth-century quest for modernity that it is easy to miss the signs that he himself had not renounced the quest. Certainly it is not in the foreground of Barth's treatment of the issues of contemporary theology. In Bultmann's writings the quest for a modern understanding of the message of the New Testament is so much in the foreground that it is almost equally easy to miss the signs that he shares Barth's overriding concern for the substance of the Gospel. Many of Bultmann's critics have hastily concluded that he wishes to set the clock back, and return to the type of theology practised in the nineteenth century, which Barth calls 'Egyptian bondage' to philosophy.

Bultmann is, in short, a highly controversial thinker. In fact, since about 1950 his thought has taken the place of Barth's at the centre of theological debate, not only, though principally, in Germany, but also in America. His thought has given rise to a considerable body of critical and interpretative literature, and it is clear that every theologian must make his mind up on the issues Bultmann has raised. These look relatively simple, especially when expressed with the lucidity Bultmann commands, but raise questions in several related spheres, philosophical, historical and theological.

Among the questions Bultmann forces on the theologian's attention is that of the order in which these questions must be

1. Translated in *Kerygma and Myth* I, ed. Hans Werner Bartsch, transl. R. H. Fuller, S.P.C.K., 1953, 1964.
2. S.C.M. Press, 1960.

dealt with. I take it to be the force of Bultmann's own argument that the historical questions of identifying and describing the cultural background of the ideas of the New Testament, and the related philosophical or hermeneutic question of what those ideas meant then and mean now, must take methodological precedence over the theological task of finding a statement of the Gospel for today. Yet even this impression of Bultmann's very careful method needs to be qualified by the statement that Bultmann himself has always present to his mind a theological criterion, by which even his historical work must be judged, namely, that the Gospel itself is not a product of human culture, but comes to man from the beyond; it is a message and communication of divine grace. His critics, however, often seem to proceed upon the assumption that a very considerable range of theological decisions can be taken before the historical and philosophical questions need be broached, and hence that the answers to them will have largely been determined in the forum of theology. A further difference between them is that Bultmann is extremely interested in questions of scientific method, both in the study of the New Testament and in theology, whereas most of his critics are primarily interested in theological content.

Interest in scientific method, as well as in contemporary meaning, was characteristic of the liberal theologians, whereas Barth and his followers thought that questions of content should take priority over questions of method. This order of priority reflects their fundamental wish to affirm the priority of the object of faith over the act of faith, as well as their confidence that the hermeneutic problem was either non-existent or easily soluble. Although Bultmann was once closely associated with Barth and his friends, and on many key issues still takes just the same view as he did during the period of their association, Barth cannot help seeing in Bultmann a reversion to liberal theology, a contemporary descendant of Schleiermacher. Though Barth has studied Bultmann's theology with his usual thoroughness, he entitles his pamphlet on Bultmann 'An attempt to understand him'.[3] Evidently Bultmann does not consider that the attempt was successful, though he has received attacks upon himself

3. Translation in *Kerygma and Myth* II, S.P.C.K., 1961.

with dignity, and has not replied in kind. Within Bultmann's own Lutheran Church, some of the critics have gone even further. They have accused Bultmann of abridging the Gospel so drastically that he stands outside the Christian community. In answer to these conservative churchmen, who have regained in post-war Germany much of the influence and credit they lost in the thirties, Bultmann's supporters have been forced to insist that the demythologizing controversy is a controversy within the church, about how the Gospel is to be presented, not one between the upholders of the Gospel and its detractors.

Bultmann's own writings are mostly easy to read. Those addressed to a wider audience than his fellow-theologians, such as *Jesus Christ and Mythology*, appear to defy further simplification. One has the impression of being able to agree or disagree without further discussion. If this impression is correct, it is hard to understand why there should be such a literature of interpretation surrounding Bultmann's contentions. Evidently there are issues of great complexity and importance concealed beneath Bultmann's clarity of speech. I cannot therefore follow the otherwise tempting course of directing the reader straight to Bultmann's works, after furnishing him with a minimum of background. Some further attempt must be made at guiding the reader into a fuller understanding of Bultmann's views, though I still believe that he is usually not only easier to read but clearer than his own interpreters. I do not expect what is said here to prove an exception to this generalization.

Bultmann's concern with theological method originates with his work on the New Testament. Though this work as such falls outside the scope of the present volume,[4] something must be said about the issues with which it deals, before we can understand the relevance of what he has to say to the task of the systematic theologian.

4. These matters are dealt with at length in Volume 3 of the present series.

BACKGROUND AND CAREER

Born in 1884, of parents coming from clerical families on both sides – his father was a Lutheran parish minister – Bultmann like Barth was introduced to theological discussion in the home. This early awakened interest was fostered by his work at school. His university studies began at Tübingen, and he went on to Berlin and then to Marburg, which he came to regard as his academic home. Among the teachers whose courses he attended were Harnack, the church historian, the biblical scholars Gunkel, Jülicher and Weiss, and the systematic theologian Wilhelm Herrmann, whose influence on Barth we have already noted. It was Johannes Weiss who encouraged Bultmann in the direction of an academic career. Bultmann's interests have always been wider than theology. He had considerable learning in the field of classics, and while a student went to lectures in philosophy as well as theology.

He qualified as a lecturer at the University of Marburg, and taught there as an instructor until 1916, when he went to Breslau as an Assistant Professor. While at Breslau he wrote his first important book, *The History of the Synoptic Tradition*. This book, published in 1921, was one of three works to appear almost simultaneously which founded a new method and school of New Testament criticism, known as form criticism, which remains controversial, but cannot be ignored by any scholar in the field. It was in 1921 also that he returned to Marburg as full Professor, after an enjoyable year at Giessen. He remained at Marburg until his retirement from active teaching, though not from theological work, in 1951.

Like Barth, Bultmann was trained by teachers of the liberal tradition, and began under their influence, holding views like theirs. His thought has never undergone the striking changes which Barth experienced in his own breach with liberalism; the only really important development in his thought occurred when he came under the influence of Barth himself and of his friend Gogarten in the early twenties. By this time Bultmann was already an established scholar, with a major work to his credit which is still being read. His own criticism of liberal scholarship had matured. It was a criticism from within, doing full justice to the scientific aims of liberal scholarship, but attempting to deal with questions it had not solved. Bultmann's work on the historical criticism of the New Testament can be clearly understood if it is regarded as an attempt, made in common with other scholars in the field, to answer the questions put to New Testament scholars by systematic theologians like Herrmann and Kähler.

The dialectical theology, in the hands of Barth and Gogarten, served to confirm and clarify opinions Bultmann had already reached on his own account, and the existentialist, dialectical idiom he learned then has continued to characterize his thought. Where Barth turned away from existentialism to a new kind of positive theology, Bultmann has incorporated existentialism into his theological method in a very careful and systematic way. Thus the other important influence upon him, the philosophical thought of his Marburg colleague Martin Heidegger, came to reinforce an existing existentialist approach, already reflected in his writings of the period before Heidegger began to influence him. His refusal to follow the later Heidegger into ontology and the philosophy of language, as some of his own pupils are doing, may suggest that he used Heidegger for the clarification of ideas already present to his mind. He deals with him independently as an equal, not as one who is primarily under his philosophical influence.

Thus Bultmann's development was a relatively smooth one. He grew away from liberalism more than he rebelled against it. This is doubtless why he still remains in sympathetic contact with its scholarly aims, and is no stranger even to its theological ones. However, the conclusions he reached about liberalism in the twenties, with the aid of Barth and Gogarten, evidently remain decisive. As he says in his 'Autobiographical Reflections'[5]:

It seemed to me that in this new theological movement, as distinguished from the 'liberal' theology out of which I had come, it was rightly recognized that the Christian faith is not a phenomenon of the history of religion, that it does not rest upon a 'religious *a priori*'

5. In *The Theology of Rudolf Bultmann*, ed. Charles W. Kegley, S.C.M. Press, 1966, p. xxiv.

(Troeltsch), and that therefore theology does not have to look upon the Christian faith as a phenomenon of religious or cultural history. It seemed to me that, distinguished from such a view, the new theology correctly saw that the Christian faith is the answer to the Word of the transcendent God which encounters man, and that theology has to deal with this Word and the man who has been encountered by it. This judgement, however, never led me to a simple condemnation of 'liberal' theology; on the contrary, I have endeavoured throughout my entire work to carry further the tradition of historical-critical research as it was practised in the 'liberal' theology and to make our recent theological knowledge the more fruitful as a result.

And speaking of his relations with Karl Barth, which later became difficult, he adds: 'I remain grateful to him, however, for the decisive things I have learned from him. I do not believe that the final clarification of our relationship . . . has as yet been reached.'[6] The matters on which he and Barth disagree can only be understood, so far as Bultmann is concerned, in the light of this firm affirmation of agreement with the basic aims of Barth's theological revolution. The question must be about the extent to which Bultmann succeeds in his aim, and we can now characterize this as the attempt to carry on the enterprise of historical-critical scholarship in the light of the neo-orthodox understanding of the relation of Christianity to culture. If we keep this basic aim in mind, we shall find it easier to understand why Bultmann takes the line he does in the interpretation of the New Testament.

Bultmann also shared with Barth an early recognition of the spiritual dangers of the Nazi regime. He took his share in the theological resistance of the Confessing Church to the German Christians, though his part was not such a prominent one as Barth's, partly because, as he says of himself, 'I have never directly and actively participated in political affairs.'[7] Among the measures passed by the notorious 'Brown Synod' of the German Church in 1933 was an 'Aryan Law', laying down that persons of non-Aryan descent could not be ministers, while ministers who married non-Aryans were to be deposed. The Marburg theological faculty, of which Bultmann was a member at the time, was asked to comment on this law from a theological point

6. ibid. 7. ibid., p. xxii.

of view; they answered that it was 'incompatible with the nature of the Church as determined solely by the authority of Holy Scripture and the Gospel'. Bultmann was also one of twenty-one professors of New Testament who issued a manifesto saying that according to the New Testament, Jewish and Gentile Christians were equally fitted for office in the church. He also criticized Nazism explicitly in his writings of the period.[8] He was a member of the Confessing Church from its foundation in 1934, though he tells us that along with his friend von Soden he struggled against fundamentalist tendencies in the group, especially in the forties and after the war.

We must now return to the development of his early thought from its liberal origins, and trace the influence upon it of his response to the criticism of the historical-critical research into the Gospels coming from the systematic theologians, his encounter with Barth and the dialectical theology, and the contribution of Heidegger's philosophy to the further clarification of his theological method. We shall then be in a position to study his proposals in greater detail, and to see what their total effect is. We have noted in the first chapter that the systematic theologians were ahead of the biblical scholars such as Schweitzer in drawing attention to the acute theological problems involved in the quest of the historical Jesus. Schweitzer, who is often given the credit for revealing the contradictions and subjectivity inherent in the liberal quest, criticized existing scholarship in the light of his own preoccupation with eschatology, in which he hoped to find the key that would unlock the understanding of the whole New Testament, and above all of the career of Jesus. Bultmann himself characterizes Schweitzer's emphasis on eschatology as extreme, and considers that it is by no means the only clue we need, even to the interpretation of the message of Jesus.

Herrmann and Kähler however offered a theological criticism of liberal research into the life of Jesus, bearing upon the question

8. cf. Ian Henderson, *Rudolf Bultmann*, Makers of Contemporary Theology, London, Carey Kingsgate Press, 1965, p. 3. See also 'The Task of Theology in the Present Situation' (May 1933) in *Shorter Writings of Rudolf Bultmann: Existence and Faith*, ed. Schubert M. Ogden, Collins, Fontana Library, 1964.

157

*pil. of Scrip &
do gi*

of the nature of the sources we have for his life, and what use can properly be made of them. Schweitzer's proposals have been taken up in detail by his fellow scholars in the field, and no one now supposes he can ignore eschatology and understand the New Testament, though few follow Schweitzer in even the majority of his interpretations of the Gospel data. In the terms of Schweitzer's famous alternative, consistent scepticism or consistent eschatology, the influence of the systematic theologians certainly tends towards the former. If their view of the sources is correct, we cannot hope to reconstruct a neutral biography of Jesus offering a factual account of his life, which can be presented to readers so that they can make their own minds up. The New Testament literature was written from faith to faith. From start to finish it has no other aim than to serve the church's proclamation of the exalted Christ. Here is a new alternative: sharing the apostolic faith, or entering into complete historical scepticism. Nor is this necessarily an alternative. A person can believe the church's proclamation, while professing himself unable as a historian to reconstruct a biography of Jesus.

The systematic theologians had shown that faith cannot depend upon historical research. They had also shown that the New Testament sources cannot be detached from the faith in which they were written. The evangelist is primarily concerned, when he writes his Gospel, with testimony to the present Lord of the church. True, he wishes to show that the exalted Christ is also Jesus of Nazareth, who taught in Galilee and Jerusalem and was executed by the authorities. But since the evangelist is primarily interested in the present, though he writes about the past, it will never (according to the form critics) be possible to disentangle from his witness the data needed to make a plausible reconstruction of the life of Jesus of Nazareth as a historical figure. Kähler contended that even if such a Jesus were to be constructed, he would not be the real Christ. 'The real Christ is the Christ who is preached,' said Kähler.[9]

If Herrmann and Kähler were right, the faith of the contemporary Christian could not be founded upon the historical Jesus. It

9. *The So-called Historical Jesus and the Historic Biblical Christ*, Philadelphia, Fortress Press, 1964, p. 66.

must be directed, like that of all Christians in the past, to the Christ proclaimed by the church. His faith need not wait upon the findings of the professors, who were in danger of becoming a new kind of legal authority. But what of theology, whether one means by that systematic theology or New Testament scholarship? Both systematic theology and critical scholarship would be involved in new decisions if they accepted the views now being put forward about the New Testament. Systematic theology would have to begin with the preaching of the apostolic or even the contemporary church, instead of from the objectively established figure of Jesus, and from his original message, undistorted by the concerns of the church. Where the influence of Kähler and Herrmann has been strong, contemporary theology has been *kerygmatic*, i.e. based upon the *kerygma*, the New Testament proclamation. Thus the contribution of the New Testament scholar to systematic theology has been widely understood as the clarification of the meaning and background of the primitive kerygma, not as rendering the theologian independent of the history of the church. What Bultmann and others learned from their teachers at this point was soon to be strongly reinforced by the influence of the dialectical theology, with its unprecedented stress on the Word of revelation. Bultmann remained faithful to this early lesson. In his mature theology, he continues to locate revelation exclusively in the preaching of the church, and to distinguish sharply between the revelation given in the preached Word and believed for no external reasons at all, and scientific scholarship, the inquiry into what may be known by academic methods of Jesus and the early church.

THE THEOLOGICAL SIGNIFICANCE OF SCIENTIFIC SCHOLARSHIP

But what *may* be known, if the sceptical contentions of the theologians are justified by the nature of the data? It might seem that there was no further place for the work of the historical-critical student of the Gospels, since the hope that motivated his work had come to nothing. We could never now obtain a detached view of Jesus as a figure in the history of his time. Then only faith itself could assure the believer that he was in touch with historical reality, and not with the delusions of a sect of religious fanatics. That faith could not be independently confirmed by the historian. The believer's contemporary experience of the forgiveness of sins through Christ would play the decisive part in leading him to accept whatever else he found said about Christ in the documents on which the preaching of forgiveness was itself based. If the historian tried to operate in abstraction from his own Christian faith, he would have to be content with few and meagre assertions about the historical Jesus. Yet some could certainly be made, and they might be sufficient for faith. One could be sure *that* he was. *What* he was one must learn from the church.

Nevertheless, if that were all that could be said, historical scholarship was virtually at a dead end in the New Testament field.[10] The important advance, made almost simultaneously by Bultmann and several other colleagues in the field in the second decade of the twentieth century, lay in seeing a range of fruitful consequences for scholarship following upon acceptance of the new view of the nature of the sources. It followed from the new view that the *Sitz im Leben* (literally, setting in life) of the source material for the life of Jesus was the early church, not the period of Jesus' lifetime to which it explicitly refers. It was good evidence for the concerns and needs of the daily life of the church of the middle and end of the first century. Only indirectly could it be evidence for the life of Jesus, for the material that had been transmitted to the Gospel writers through the oral tradition had been chosen and shaped by the needs of church life, not those of the impartial historian.

It was now clear that the Gospels had to be read in quite a new way. Their view of Jesus was not that of contemporaries observing his ministry, but of worshippers of him as the exalted Lord, ruling the church through the Spirit. The stories of his earthly life were not told to give information about the past, but to influence the present. They were a medium of his rule in the

10. For a fuller treatment of the technical aspects of form criticism, see Vol. 3 of this series. It is dealt with also here because an understanding of it is essential to grasping Bultmann's theological contentions.

church here and now. In the Spirit, they gave guidance to the community in arranging its affairs, while it waited for his rule over the world to become manifest at his return. The early church did not look forward to any lengthy future, and it had little interest in the past. It looked to the present, and to the signs of the End within the present. Its Jesus likewise was a present Lord, who used the stories about his past as an instrument of his rule over his community in the here and now. To understand them properly, and to learn from them what can be learned, we must study the stories from this point of view. Instead of being led astray by their appearance of recording the ministry and death of Jesus as mere history, we must try to guess in what circumstances each particular story would have been told in the life of the church, for these circumstances would have determined both the story's initial preservation from among the vast amount of information about Jesus originally circulating (cf. John xxi, 25), and also the shape it had now assumed.

Only when the stories had been subjected to this kind of analysis would it be possible to determine, though for the most part very tentatively, what the story might have been like before the needs of the church shaped it. In such an inquiry, many stories would have to be set down to the needs of the church pure and simple. If they had a historical core, it would be impossible now to recover it. In other cases, it might be possible to discern that the influence of the church's life upon the story had been less, and to infer something like the original form of the story from its present one.

Bultmann and his colleagues were accordingly able to see more significance for their inquiry than had formerly been customary in the stage during which the tradition about Jesus had been transmitted orally. Their predecessors were exclusively interested in literary sources. They had of course been aware that there had been a period of oral tradition, before the first literary sources were composed. But they could only regard that period negatively, as the gap separating the sources from the events they recorded. The gap represented in their eyes a period of decay, as it were, in the intense spiritual activity which gave rise to the Christian religion. The longer the gap, the less reliable the source. Thus the only significant question about the gap was its length. How far had the decay proceeded, before the church committed its memories to writing and so fixed them? The older liberal scholars had thus missed the significance for critical inquiry of the period of oral tradition, and had developed no tools for investigating it. Now that Bultmann and his colleagues could see the oral tradition as dynamic, they were able to devise the necessary tools.

Form criticism (*Formgeschichte*, literally form history, the history of forms) takes its name from a method of analysing the history of the oral tradition underlying the written Gospels by means of a study of the forms of the stories. Their content is provisionally set aside, and their forms compared, both with one another and those of oral tradition outside the New Testament. By a comparative analysis of oral tradition in the Gospels and in contemporary Jewish and Hellenistic settings, the form critics were able to arrive at a comprehensive classification of the types of tradition, into which any particular unit could be fitted. They found that oral tradition breaks down the information it wishes to pass on into short stories, which are independent of each other. Each concentrates upon a single point of importance; in the case of the tradition about Jesus this might be a parable, an ethical pronouncement made by him, or a healing miracle. The units of tradition underlying the Gospels are reflected in the short paragraphs, or *pericopae*, into which the Gospels naturally fall. Now, as we have them in the Gospels, these originally independent units of tradition have been connected up into a continuous story, although, as the older critics had already noted, the links by which this is done are often exceedingly tenuous. Only in the passion story do we find an intrinsic connexion between many successive paragraphs, building up a consecutive story of any length. (Kähler had already remarked that a Gospel is a passion narrative with an introduction.) The older critics had usually taken the links between the units of tradition more or less at their face-value, and on the basis of those provided in the oldest Gospel, that of Mark, had constructed an outline of the events of the life of Jesus, leading up to his death. Serious doubts had lately been thrown on the reliability of the Marcan outline by the researches of W. Wrede and J. Wellhausen,[11] and scholars were beginning to suspect that a chronological outline of Jesus' ministry could not be derived from the Gospels.

Bultmann and his colleagues, particularly K. L. Schmidt, now took the simple but radical step of separating the individual stories from the outline, like unstringing a necklace: the stories were the beads, the outline the string. They attributed the stories to the oral tradition, and the connecting outline to the evangelist himself. The separation was very easy to make, which confirmed the appropriateness of making it. It was only necessary to remove short phrases (often as simple as 'immediately', 'the next day' and the like) linking each story to its immediate predecessor. Then each paragraph could be regarded as the record of an independent unit of tradition, whose point lay solely in its content, and not in its place in the outline. Deprived of the semblance of chronological sequence which the evangelist had furnished, the stories demanded some other arrangement than the chronological. The simplest available was a classification according to type, and this form criticism could now provide.

Comparison with other oral traditions soon showed that stories of a particular type tended to assume a common form. It likewise showed what sort of development might be expected to occur over a period of time. In the first place, the story would tend increasingly to conform to the form normally assumed by its type. The more atypical it was, other things being equal, the less influenced it would have been by the dynamics of tradition. In general, stories tend to grow in the telling, not necessarily in the sense that the incident is heightened (sometimes the opposite seems to be the case) but that imagination supplies detail wanting in the original version. The better these dynamic and creative forces were understood, the more chance the investigator would have of assessing the degree of their influence. Sometimes he must conclude that the forces at work had effectively obscured the origin of the story. At other times he could believe himself closer to the earliest form of a tradition.

The period of oral tradition could be described as dynamic

11. Bultmann, 'The New Approach to the Synoptic Problem', in *Existence and Faith*, ed. Schubert M. Ogden, Collins, 1964.

and creative in another sense also. This was a period of Spirit-inspired prophets, of whom the author of the Apocalypse in the New Testament is the best known to us. Their oracles, announcing the will of the exalted Lord in relation to circumstances confronting the leaders of the church, might easily after a period of oral transmission be set back to the time of Jesus' earthly ministry. Or the evangelist, receiving such an oracle from tradition with no indication that that was what it was, might give it a place in his outline, furnishing it with the necessary links to connect it with the narrative as a whole. Thus the creation of new stories about Jesus could take place without the slightest dishonesty on the part of the church, and from any other point of view than the historian's, they could be regarded as saying something true about Jesus. Nevertheless, these facts made the critical endeavour to discern the original *Sitz im Leben* of a story all the more necessary, if its historical value was to be correctly recognized. To discover an immediate setting for a story in the life of the church did not mean that in its original form it did not go back to the ministry of Jesus, nor did its attribution to a prophet necessarily mean that it did not represent what Jesus would have said confronted with the same circumstances. But such considerations imposed on the form critic a degree of scientific caution in anything he affirmed that the source critic had not seemed to need.

Form criticism came as a shock to a public brought up on the liberal lives of Jesus. It seemed altogether destructive and sceptical in its effect. The tradition about Jesus had been so filtered, it now appeared, through the life of the primitive church that we can affirm nothing with confidence about him beyond the bare facts of his existence. He might have been quite other than the person depicted in the preaching of the church. Both liberals and conservatives were worried by form criticism, and it is plain that its impact has not yet been fully absorbed, even by theologians. Liberals feared that they could now never get back behind the dogmas of the church to an independent view of Jesus, upon which a rational contemporary faith could be founded. Conservatives feared that Christianity might be losing a historical basis which was necessary to its continued existence.

So form criticism remains controversial, and with it the persons of its originators, including Bultmann. Bultmann is popularly associated with extreme scepticism about the historical Jesus, with a view that asserts that what little we can know of him is at variance with any picture needed by anything like a traditional Christian faith.

In fact, Bultmann's scepticism is by no means as great as is often represented. His own views are to be found in his *Theology of the New Testament*, which opens with the famous and provocative statement: 'The message of Jesus is a presupposition for the theology of the New Testament rather than a part of that theology itself,' but not only there. They are also to be found in his earlier book, *Jesus and the Word*, and in such an essay as his *Jesus and Paul*,[12] in which the continuity between Jesus and historic Christianity is cogently argued for on purely historical grounds. Apparently destructive statements, such as the one just quoted, become intelligible in the light of his wish to deal genuinely scientifically with the sources, at a level of critical sophistication out of reach of an earlier generation of critics. On the other hand, it must be remembered at all times, when assessing Bultmann's total view of the New Testament, that he believes revelation to be an event which occurs exclusively here and now, in the preaching of the church, an event in which God asks the questions of man, and man can only respond to the message in faith or reject it in unbelief. Thus all theology, including that of the New Testament, starts from proclamation, from the kerygma.

Form criticism had among other effects a tendency to focus greater attention on the theology of the early church. The older critics had originally recognized that Paul and John were theologians, but had tended to believe that theological considerations had played little conscious part in writings like the synoptic gospels, though some were ready to declare that even these had been written under the influence of Pauline thought. It was now realized that the material of the New Testament is theological from start to finish; in particular, the period of the

12. *Existence and Faith*, ed. Schubert M. Ogden, Collins, 1964, pp. 217–39.

oral tradition had also been the all-important creative period in Christian theology, when the foundations had been laid that were to determine its whole historical future. According to Bultmann, it was the primitive community, on both Jewish and Gentile soil, that took the decisive steps in the church's understanding of Jesus, and of itself as a community, and of its sacramental rites, before even Paul arrived on the scene.

Bultmann's own pupils, and others who had learned from him, later began to inquire into the theological tendencies of the evangelists themselves, and see in their arrangement of the tradition they had received a precise theological intention, where the earlier form critics had often seemed to regard them as mere compilers. So the new developments tended to bring theological analysis closer to the centre of the scholarly picture than when source criticism had been dominant, and it is not therefore surprising that Bultmann's own most important work in the New Testament field should be his two-volume *Theology of the New Testament*,[13] a work agreed by even his critics to be a most distinguished scholarly achievement.

THE INFLUENCE OF THE DIALECTICAL THEOLOGY

We are now coming closer to the themes with which Bultmann's distinctive contribution to theology is associated. Bultmann had learned from the history-of-religions school of criticism which flourished during his own earlier years not to deal with religious ideas and institutions in isolation from their cultural environment. Thus the question arose of the origin of the theological ideas which the New Testament and its written and oral sources had used to express the Christian experience of salvation through Jesus. Some of these were clearly Jewish. When Jesus was characterized as the Christ, or the Messiah, the Son of God and the Son of Man, these titles, whether or not Jesus had used them of himself, and Bultmann believes that he did not, must be interpreted in the light of Jewish eschatological thinking. Others however came from Gentile sources, and were first incorporated into the thought of the church when the Gentile mission had

13. S.C.M. Press, 1952 and 1955; 1965.

brought numbers of educated people into the community from the Hellenistic environment. When Jesus is thought of as the pre-existent redeemer, the man from heaven, or as the Lord, who reigns over earthly and heavenly powers, we are encountering ideas that originated in the Hellenistic world, and must be interpreted in the light of that background, as we know it from its literature. Similarly, the understanding of the sacraments which developed in Gentile Christianity owed much to the formal similarity which the early Christians, like modern Catholic scholars, recognized between their own baptism and eucharist, and the rites of the mystery religions. Paul, as a cultured Hellenistic Jew, was in touch with all these influences, and knew how to use them in the service of the Gospel.

When we have learned to identify the sources of the major theological ideas of the early church in relation to their cultural background, the question arises, what is distinctive about early Christianity? If the message of Jesus is not itself part of New Testament theology, but only its presupposition, and if all the principal ideas of that theology can be traced to either Jewish or Hellenistic sources, or to a mixture of both, does not Christianity turn out to have been simply an amalgam of contemporary ideas, created by the emotional needs of a community with Jewish roots, but becoming increasingly unpopular with the Jewish community, and with membership now largely Gentile? Was Christianity the creation of the cultural melting-point of the first century?

Bultmann's scientific honesty and methodological scrupulousness had led him to the point where these became pressing questions, but he had a theological answer to give which rested upon the insight he had learned from the dialectical theology of Barth and Gogarten. We remember what he later said about the lesson he had learned from them:

It seemed to me that in this new movement, as distinguished from the 'liberal' theology out of which I had come, it was rightly recognized that the Christian faith is not a phenomenon of the history of religions, that it does not rest upon a religious *a priori* (Troeltsch), and that therefore theology does not have to look upon Christian faith as a phenomenon of religious or cultural history. It seemed to me that, distinguished from such a view, the new theology correctly saw that the Christian faith is the answer to the transcendent Word of God which encounters man, and that theology has to deal with this Word and with the man who has been encountered by it.

If these strictly theological convictions were correct, they could also be connected with what he had learned from the later liberal systematic theologians. Christ is met with in preaching. Thus the preaching of the church is not a phenomenon of cultural history, but the Word of the transcendent God. It cannot be accounted for by analysis of the cultural background of early Christianity, nor is it disposed of by tracing every theological idea back to its source in such a background. On the other hand, it also follows that the theological expression of the message can never be regarded as absolute. Theology is relative, both to the message itself and to the cultural environment in which the message is expressed at a particular time. It is therefore appropriate to ask whether a past expression of the message is the best one for today, or whether the form of the message found in the New Testament itself does not demand interpretation, if it is to convey today what it conveyed to its first hearers. Bultmann wishes to avoid the identification of the message with its expression, precisely because he regards it as the Word of the transcendent God. If the Word cannot be distinguished from theology, then Christianity must be relegated to the history of religions. But it was just this that he had learned from the dialectical theology not to do.

So from the twenties on we find Bultmann discussing the mythological nature of the ideas in which the New Testament theologically expresses the Christian message. We also find him interpreting this mythology, as we should expect from a dialectical theologian, in an existentialist way, in order to discover its contemporary meaning. The term 'demythologizing' itself appears to have been first used in the thirties, and does not become a feature of Bultmann's own writings until the famous 1941 essay, 'New Testament and Mythology'. But if the term is not present, the idea is. From the twenties on, Bultmann states that the New Testament expresses the Christian message in a mythological form, and uses existentialist thought to clarify the meaning of the mythology both for its original users and for man today.

Schubert M. Ogden, one of the best-informed and most perceptive of Bultmann's interpreters, believes that his consistent theological intention, from the twenties onwards, is best summed up in words of Karl Barth from the preface of the second edition of the *Epistle to the Romans*, already quoted in part:

> If I have a 'system', it consists in the fact that I keep in mind as persistently as possible what Kierkegaard called 'the infinite qualitative distinction' between time and eternity in both its negative and positive meaning. 'God is in heaven and you are on earth.' The relation of *this* God to *this* man, the relation of *this* man to *this* God, is for me at once the theme of the Bible and the very essence of philosophy. The philosophers speak of this crisis of human knowing as the primal source, while the Bible sees at this parting of the ways Jesus Christ.

Ogden believes that the key to Bultmann's theology from this time on is to be found in the negative and positive implications of the 'infinite qualitative distinction' between time and eternity. 'Indeed,' he says, 'we must lay it down as a rule that *one ought never to suppose he has correctly understood anything that Bultmann says, as regards either the method or the content of his theology, until he is able to see it as permitted or required by this basic dialectic.*'[14]

Negatively, we have already seen in connexion with Barth, the dialectic affirms the transcendence of God over all religion and philosophy, so that human language is incapable of containing true positive propositions about God. The Word of God is therefore not to be identified with the statements of Christian theology. Positively, the dialectic affirms that the world and human life within it contain analogies, which may be used indirectly to express the relationship between God and man. Barth used many, such as the wholly other, the vertical from above, the mathematical point, and so on. The object of all these is to express the one-way relationship between God and

14. Ogden's introduction to *Existence and Faith*, Collins, 1964, p. 15. Italics his.

man, in which God the primal source knows man, and by letting man know that he is known, in revelation, permits man to acknowledge this divine knowledge in an act of obedient self-commitment. Bultmann came to prefer an analogy drawn from the relation of man to the world, as clarified by existential analysis.

THE INFLUENCE OF HEIDEGGER

At this point in the development of his thought, the philosophy of his Marburg colleague Martin Heidegger helped Bultmann to give much more systematic expression to the existential dialectic than Barth chose to employ. In any case, Barth quickly became dissatisfied with the whole existentialist approach to theology, and with the aid of Anselm moved into a positive theology, in which theological propositions correspond to divine rationality, and so are in a proper sense true. Bultmann remained a dialectical theologian, but used Heidegger to give a precision to his thought that was out of the reach of those of his colleagues who remained eclectic in their existentialism. It was dialectical theology, not Heidegger, that introduced Bultmann to existentialism, but Heidegger permitted him to develop an existing existentialist outlook very much further.

In order to follow Bultmann's thought as he moved to this further stage, it is not strictly necessary to master the details of Heidegger's own complex and often obscure analysis of the being of man. Bultmann takes what he needs from Heidegger, and what he does take can for the most part be expressed without calling on the whole range of technical terms and neologisms Heidegger himself employs; the key ideas are not very difficult to grasp.

Why does Bultmann turn to the philosophy of Heidegger for help in clarifying the problems of theology? He did not, as we have noted, encounter the themes of existentialist thought for the first time in Heidegger. Like the other dialectical theologians, he had already encountered them in Kierkegaard and, under his influence, seen them in the New Testament itself. He already understood faith as grounded in the paradox of the eternal coming to be in time, a paradox which is an offence to the reason, and can only be believed in 'by virtue of the absurd',[15] and not understood. Thus, truth for the existentialist theologian does not reside in the objective propositions of theology, but in the reality which only faith attains, in an act of inwardness, or passionate subjectivity. He had also learned from Kierkegaard that specific sense of *existence*, which refers to life lived in such passionate subjectivity, and not merely passed through. These and many other aspects of existentialist thought were already part of Bultmann's interpretation of the New Testament before he met Heidegger.

In 1927, however, his Marburg colleague Martin Heidegger brought out the first volume of his major work, *Sein und Zeit* (translated as *Being and Time*)[16]; the promised second and third volumes have not yet appeared, though some of their contents have come to light in other ways. As an interpreter of the New Testament, Bultmann read his philosophical colleague's work, and tried to see what it might have to say to him. In Heidegger's account of man he found unmistakable echoes of a view of man with which he was already familiar in the New Testament, though it was expressed in a very different terminology, and its foundations were not religious but secular and even atheist. In Heidegger's philosophy man's existence is described as 'fallenness', 'being-for-death'. The ground of his being is thus said to be anxiety. Man is pre-eminently a *historical* being, who achieves authentic existence only in the courageous resolve to accept his situation in the world and his coming death, and so is freed for life in the world with others. What then is the relationship of this philosophical analysis of man to the thought of the New Testament?

Bultmann came to the conclusion that the difference between what the New Testament says about man and his existence, and what the philosopher says about the same themes, is much the same as the difference between concrete and abstract. The

15. For Kierkegaard's notion of the 'absurd', see *Fear and Trembling*, tr. Walter Lowrie, Doubleday Anchor Books, 1955, pp. 57 ff. etc., and the fuller discussion in the *Concluding Unscientific Postscript*.

16. Tr. by John Macquarrie and E. Robinson, S.C.M. Press, 1963.

philosopher deals with the structures of man's being as such; he finds that it is characteristic of man to exist through concrete choice in time, because he is a historical being. But this abstract analysis, though it show the necessity of choice, does not confront the reader with any particular concrete choice. It assures him that, because he is a man, he cannot choose but choose. It tells him of the conditions of an authentic choice. It explores the kinds of possibility open to man as an existing being, but it does not say if any of these possibilities are realized. In all those respects in which philosophy is necessarily abstract, the New Testament is concrete. It speaks of a particular choice, and of the existence of the man who has made it. Its theme is the realization of authentic existence by a decision for the grace of God in Jesus Christ. It thus points to the Christian proclamation, which concretely addresses actual men, offering them the opportunity to decide and to realize their authentic existence.

In so far as theology offers a conceptual analysis of the event of revelation and faith, it must use humanly intelligible language to do so. For this purpose, Bultmann regards existential analysis as peculiarly suitable, because it gives the best account available of man as a historical being who exists by decision, and so is capable of being addressed by and responding to a gospel. Bultmann chooses existentialism not for apologetic reasons, because the modern unbeliever is more likely to understand the Gospel if it is expressed in existentialist terms, but for theological ones, because the meaning of the Gospel is in fact clarified when it is expressed in this language. The advantages which existential analysis has to offer theology have little to do with the question of whether existentialism is popular today, or corresponds with a certain contemporary sensibility. Perhaps it does, but existentialism is not the easiest of philosophies to communicate to the lay mind, and Heidegger is not overwhelmingly popular among his fellow philosophers. Bultmann has little concern with the questions that would interest the apologist of the cruder sort. The advantages and disadvantages of existentialism as an apologetic probably more or less balance out. They are not the point for Bultmann. It is not for such adventitious reasons, but because of what Heidegger can teach us about man, through his difficult terminology, that Bultmann is interested in his philosophy.

The common ground between Bultmann's existentialist theology and Heidegger's existentialist philosophy is a view of man. Bultmann thinks that theology can be conceptually clarified only if it is expressed in terms of man and his existence. On the other hand, it will be possible to express theology in this way only if man is in fact such that he can be addressed and called to a decision for authentic existence. Hence a philosophy that analyses man in terms of possible ways of being human is peculiarly suited to the exposition of the Christian faith, even though it knows nothing of that particular address to man that comes to him by the Gospel, nor of that particular decision which is Christian faith. By the use of existentialist analysis, faith and its opposite can be exhibited as genuine possibilities for man. If the meaning of the Gospel is actually clarified when it is analysed in the language of existentialism, the suitability of this philosophy in the exposition of theology will have been confirmed. If, for example, it can make sense of the obscure and often mythological talk to be found in the New Testament writers, it will have vindicated itself. Hence Bultmann's *Theology of the New Testament* could be regarded as a large-scale verification of his method as applied to the relevant material.

We are now in a position to sum up the relationship of existentialist philosophy to New Testament theology, as Bultmann understands it. We have spoken of philosophy as abstract and the New Testament as concrete. We can now use the terminology of existentialism itself to make the distinction more precise. Philosophy is existentialist (*existential* in German): it analyses man in existentialist terms. Theology takes over these terms for the analysis of a particular address and a particular choice and decision, open to man within the terms of the existentialist analysis. But when it speaks directly of this concrete choice, it serves the proclamation of the Gospel, and this is a direct call to those particular hearers, whose personal existence is involved in what they hear and in the choice they are invited to make. What happens then is not existentialist but existential (*existentiell* in German). Bultmann insists on the importance of

173

this distinction between *existential* and *existentiell*. The Gospel itself is always *existentiell*, but when we analyse the way it works, and what it implies about the nature of man, we shall use existentialist terminology in our analysis, and thus speak *existential*, not existentially but in the manner of existentialism.

Does the use of existentialism as a means of systematically clarifying the meaning of the Gospel also predetermine the content of theology? Barth, in particular, fears that it must, for he believes that any theology that has struck up an alliance with a philosophical system as close as the one Bultmann has entered into runs the risk that the theology will only be able to say what will go into that particular philosophy. The Gospel in his view always transcends human intellectual schemes, and can only be adequately expressed in its own distinctive language. Barth has no objection to the eclectic use of philosophy, where the Gospel remains in control, and makes use of whatever philosophical ideas come in useful, but uses different ones at different points. It is system he objects to. We shall see reason to think that Bultmann does run into difficulties as a result of his choice of existentialism, which he could avoid by being eclectic, but we must first hear his reply.

A principal function of philosophy in Bultmann's own thought is to furnish a preliminary understanding of the subject-matter of theological discourse. If someone were to speak to me about a subject of whose very existence, let alone the issues arising within it, I was ignorant, I should fail to understand, even if the speaker addressed me in familiar words. A man of the first century would have great difficulty in entering into a discussion about the merits of TV programmes. While he might have some conception of the issues, arising from his knowledge of drama or history, the technical aspects of TV criticism, arising from the use of the medium, would be lost on him. Man today frequently feels in this position when he hears religious talk. But if it can be shown to him that every human being is faced with the question of his own existence, and how this can be realized authentically in the choices that must willy-nilly be made, he can understand a Gospel which calls him to a particular sort of choice, and offers authenticity of existence through that choice.

Now when he hears the Gospel he knows that the problem it answers is his: the preacher is not talking about men of some distant culture, he is talking about him. Bultmann thinks that without some such *pre-understanding*, as he calls it in a technical term, the Gospel would be absolutely unintelligible. The role of Heidegger's thought is to clarify in a systematic way, appropriate to the precise discourse of theology, the pre-understanding of the Gospel latent in me because I am a human being.

Since Heidegger's thought is phenomenological,[17] it bears upon human experience, and does not make judgements about reality, as science does. If it purported to be science or metaphysics Barth's judgement would be decisive. In fact, Heidegger's philosophy is analytical. It does not add to our stock of information about reality, nor does it build a system. It attempts to describe man as phenomenon, and its analysis refers to the existence of man *as we experience it*. It speaks of man therefore not as a nature, but in terms of possible ways of being. If life in Christian faith can be described in terms of Heidegger's analysis of man's possibilities, Christianity can be set forth in a clear and contemporary way.

In this analysis of man, Heidegger wants to stress the uniqueness of *human being*. The being of man is unique not merely because this is the place at which we experience being from within (this will become important in Heidegger's later thought about being). It is unique because man has a different kind of being from what is not man. Heidegger employs special terms to distinguish these different ways of being. He refers to man himself as *Dasein* (literally, being there), which is a fairly colourless word for existence in ordinary German, but Heidegger gives it force by his usage. The proper mode of being of a man is *Existenz* (existing). Man's being is historical. It evades the kind of knowledge we have of things, which can be objective or scientific. Of course man can also be the object of scientific knowledge, but not in his specific capacity as human being, or existence. This specific form of human being, or existence, is revealed by phenomenological analysis, and verified by reference to the experience analysed, which is shared by others.

17. See note to page 92 above.

Heidegger has various terms to describe the being of what is not man, or things. These too are described by him phenomenologically; that is, they are described from the point of view of human experience of them, not scientifically. Thus existentialist categories are devised to speak of their relation to man. A principal category applicable to the being of things is *Vorhandenheit*, roughly, being around, being on hand. This very neutral term stands in sharp contrast to words like *Existenz* and *Dasein*. Heidegger has to introduce new meanings for technical terms like these, and does so by a combination of attention to etymology and root meaning, and careful and striking usage. *Existenz* in its Latin origins is connected with standing out (*ex, sistere*); to exist is to stand out from the world. *Dasein* means to be there, and so carries connotations of presence. Hence the contrast of *Existenz*, which belongs to *Dasein*, and *Vorhandenheit*, which belongs to things, is a contrast between being present and standing out from the world, on the one hand, and merely occurring on the other, in the way that dead things do.

He calls man's being historical. Man exists in time as well as space. He has a past, which can affect his present in various ways, and a future, though this future must one day end in his death. He can remember his past and look forward to his future. The most important fact about man's existence is that it leads to death. It is poised over non-existence, and hence to grasp fully the nature of human existence is necessarily to experience anxiety, to be aware of the threat of non-being, of not existing. In all these ways the being of man differs from the being of the things that make up the world. Though he lives in the world, and this too must be numbered among the characteristic marks of his existence, he is not part of the world of things. He transcends the world, through his existence in time, and also because of the relation he has to himself. Unlike things, which are only objects, man is related to himself. He can be both subject and object to himself, and therefore he transcends in his relationship to himself the subject-object relationship found in his relationship with the world of things. Since he knows himself both as subject, the experiencer, and as object, the one experienced, he can himself be neither of these. But this transcending of the subject-object relationship is not itself given in experience, or it could not properly be called transcendental. It is revealed by phenomenological analysis.

Man's relationship to himself can have various forms. These are the various possibilities that are open to man, because he is *Dasein* and not a thing. Heidegger does not attribute to man a given nature, but thinks of him as constituted by the possibilities open to him. He can choose between these possibilities, and must do so, but only between these. He cannot choose to be a thing, though he can and does choose to treat himself like one. But this is to exist inauthentically, not in accordance with the human way of being. In his relationship to himself, man understands himself. But he can understand himself in various ways, and such a 'self-understanding' (a favourite word of Bultmann's) is actualized in the choice of one of the possibilities open to him.

Man also exists as an individual, not as a member of a group that can be objectively classified. Each individual exists by actualizing through choice and decision some of the possibilities that are open to man, and described by Heidegger's analysis. Philosophy cannot describe the act of choice of an individual, but it can describe man as a being who as such acts and chooses, and it can chart the choices at his disposal. It is part of Bultmann's understanding of the relationship of philosophy to theology that theology can describe phenomenologically the choice of faith and the existence of the man who has made it. Theology from this point of view is the phenomenology of the life of faith.

If he is to use Heidegger's analysis of man, Bultmann must show that faith is among the specifically human possibilities open to man. He cannot do this concretely and remain within the scope of philosophy. Philosophy knows nothing of God or Christ or the Kerygma. But it does know of authentic and inauthentic possibilities, or ways of existing, and it can describe them. To exist authentically, then, is to exist properly as a man. It is to take the inevitability of one's own death upon oneself in an act of courageous resolve, and hence to give one's life a direction. It is to accept the hand one has been dealt – only there is no dealer in Heidegger's philosophy – and play it out. It is to start from where one has been thrown into life. *Thrownness*

(*Geworfenheit*) is an inescapable, if absurd, characteristic of man's way of being. He is like a die that has been cast – by nobody. He arrives in life by no choice of his own, and finds himself moving towards death with every minute that passes. But if he is to exist authentically he must accept this absurdity and live from it.

To live towards one's own death with acceptance is to be free, for it liberates one from seeking false security in what the world has to offer. Nothing that it can offer is in fact secure, since death stands over all. The man who lives towards death is detached, and so free, able to live with others without frantically exploiting them for his own ends. Inauthentic existence also means to live as if one had security in the things of this world, the objects with which one is surrounded. It is to treat oneself as an object among these other objects, to forget that one is a man, not a thing. To exist inauthentically is to be fallen. The shiver of anxiety, which reminds one of death, and exposes the falseness of the security one has built up in the world by inauthentic existence, is a call to leave fallenness and exist authentically.

No reader of the New Testament can encounter Heidegger's themes without a sense of familiarity, in spite of the strangeness of much of the terminology, and the atheistic and despairing tone. In the vivid and concrete language of the parables, Jesus also warned man not to find security in this world, to build up treasure on earth by collecting its things around one. He too warns of death, which will strip man of this false security, and reduce it to nothingness. He calls for detachment from the world, and the seeking of a higher righteousness. Paul echoes the same message, when he says in a passage to which Bultmann attaches the highest importance:

> From now on, let those who have wives live as though they had none, and those who mourn as though they were not mourning, and those who rejoice as though they were not rejoicing, and those who buy as though they had no goods, and those who deal with the world as though they had no dealings with it. For the form of this world is passing away. (1 Cor. vii, 29–31.)

For Bultmann, this Pauline 'as though not' ($\dot{\omega}\varsigma \mu\dot{\eta}$) is the essence of the life of faith, and likewise the concrete actualization of what Heidegger describes under the name of authentic existence.

Bultmann believes, then, that Heidegger's analysis of the possibility called authentic existence provides an abstract description of something that is concrete and actual in the life of faith, and only there. Jesus Christ is the one who makes authentic, properly human, existence an actuality for man. Authentic existence is possible because he is a man, and so the secular philosopher, even if he is an atheist, can describe the life of faith abstractly in a phenomenological analysis of man's possibilities. Philosophy however does not know of the actualizing of this possibility, which happens only through Jesus Christ. It happens, moreover, for Bultmann, only through the kerygma, which announces Jesus Christ to man, in such a way as to invite and empower man to take the decision which will render his existence authentic. Through the forgiveness of sins, the Christian proclamation sets man free from his past, inauthentic seeking of security in the world through reliance on things. His own being has become alienated through this search for security: he has come to understand himself also as an object among objects, and his neighbour as another such object. For Bultmann as a theologian authentic existence, freed by the forgiveness of sins, is ordered not so much to death as to the neighbour. The new life is a life of love. It does also look forward to death, but in hope not despair. The man of faith faces death freely in the forgiveness of sins, rather than being free because he faces death.

We can now see in what sense it is proper to talk of the Gospel in existentialist terms, and to construct an existentialist theology. The Gospel itself is not an existentialist philosophy. But it speaks to man *existentiell*, in such a way as to involve his existence. When this fact is clarified, it will be natural to do so *existential*, using the existentialist terms that bring out the nature of the Gospel as an existential claim and promise. An objectivist terminology, such as traditional theology uses, would be less fitted to bring out the character of the Gospel as an address to man. Such a way of speaking objectively can be assented to with the understanding alone, without any need to commit one's existence. 'The demons also believe, and shudder,' says the Epistle of James, referring to such an objectivized belief. Or with Melanchthon, Bultmann can say, 'To know Christ is to know his benefits, not to look into his natures.' In the opinion of Bultmann, a theology which is faithful to the New Testament will have the character of existential address. It will be the servant of the proclamation; what is not useful in this service must be eliminated. Thus, an interpretation of New Testament Christology which analyses Christ's metaphysical status will have failed as an interpretation of the New Testament's true theme. An interpretation which discloses Christ as the giver of authentic existence to men will have succeeded, however many of the traditional questions of theology it leaves unanswered. Hence theology is always about man and his existence, and any truly theological statement, whatever its original form, can be translated into a statement about man and his existence, and only then will have assumed its clearest and strongest form.

DEMYTHOLOGIZING

We now have the background necessary to understand Bultmann's famous project of demythologizing, and also why he thought it necessary. Demythologizing is the interpretation of statements that in their original form appear to be objective statements about the world, and thus without significance for theology, so as to bring out their latent reference to man's existence. The trouble with the mythological element in the New Testament is not so much that it conflicts with the outlook of modern man (though it does, and we shall see in due course in what way this is also a drawback), but that it represents existential truths objectively. In this form they can be evaded, because the issue then becomes the doubtful one of their objective truth, or conformity to our own outlook on the world. Demythologizing therefore does not mean throwing the mythological statements out, but bringing them to life, in both their original and their contemporary meaning.

Bultmann agrees with those scholars, particularly of the history-of-religions school, who think that the New Testament expresses the Gospel very largely in mythological terms, borrowed from both Jewish and Hellenistic sources. The New Testament wished to speak of transcendent realities, the relation of God to man, and the offer of authentic existence to fallen man. But the vocabulary at its disposal was not one that we should today consider appropriate for speaking about matters of that kind. Nor did it aim to use the precise vocabulary of philosophy. It therefore spoke in mythological terms, that is, it

used imagery to express the other world in terms of this world and the divine in terms of human life, the other side in terms of this side. For instance, divine transcendence is explained as spatial distance. It is a mode of expression which makes it easy to understand the cultus as an action in which material means are used to convey immaterial power.[18]

Bultmann takes this particular definition of myth from the history-of-religions school, and he is well aware that it does not cover most modern uses of the term, in which myth, as he says in the same place, is almost equivalent to ideology. In fact, Bultmann declines to be interested in refining the sense of the word myth, and it would appear that his programme of demythologizing would hold good for him, whatever sense of myth were to be agreed on.

The reason appears to be that however we understand myth, it will still involve objectifying a message that is really an address to man in his existence. Bultmann believes that all such objectification distorts the Gospel for its present-day hearers. So long as the New Testament is interpreted in a way that retains objectified statements, its message will fail to reach the modern reader. He will get bogged down in the question of whether he can or ought to believe the statements with which he is confronted, and the understanding of existence which the mythology was intended by its original users to convey will never come to his attention, in such a way that he can make a decision for or against it.

At the time that the New Testament was written, mythology

18. 'New Testament and Mythology', in *Kerygma and Myth* I, ed. Bartsch, S.P.C.K., 1964, p. 10 n.

was apparently able to communicate an existential message. Evidently however even then its success was not total, for we find the New Testament writers themselves engage in demythologizing, as the writer of the Fourth Gospel does, when he reinterprets the primitive eschatology in terms of eternal life. Today, the only way to preserve the original intention of the New Testament writers who use mythology is to interpret it in terms of the understanding of existence it was intended to convey. 'The real purpose of myth is not to present an objective picture of the world as it is, but to express man's understanding of himself in the world in which he lives. Myth should be interpreted not cosmologically, but anthropologically, or better still, existentially.'[19] To retain mythology in its literal meaning, as conservative interpreters wish to do, will thus involve equating the Gospel with cosmological assertions which modern man has good reason to think false. Worse, it will involve failure to grasp the positive existential meaning concealed in the myth.

The real purpose of myth is to speak of a transcendent power which controls the world and man, but that purpose is impeded and obscured by the terms in which it is expressed. Hence the importance of the New Testament mythology lies not in its imagery but in the understanding of existence which it enshrines. The real question is whether this understanding of existence is true. Faith claims that it is, and faith ought not to be tied down to the imagery of New Testament mythology.[20]

Why then is there a temptation to interpret myth cosmologically, instead of anthropologically or existentially? Myth actually incorporates a view of the world, a cosmology, current at least on the popular level at the time of the composition of the New Testament. Those who wish to take the Bible more or less literally are thus involved in the defence of this first-century cosmology. But to believe this literally today is impossible without the sacrifice of the intellect, because it would commit us to out-of-date science. The simplest and perhaps the most fundamental case has already come to our notice in connexion with Bultmann's definition of myth. In language many readers will have met with

19. *Kerygma and Myth* I, ed. Bartsch, S.P.C.K., 1964, p. 10.
20. ibid., p. 11.

in *Honest to God*, we can say that the myth speaks of God as if he were 'up there', inhabiting a heaven beyond the sky. The myth presupposes a cosmology, that of the three-decker universe, with heaven above our heads, and hell in the basement below our feet. Hence the incarnation is expressed in the idea that Christ came down from heaven, and the end of his presence in sensible form on earth by the statement, he ascended up into heaven. Now, it is not important whether men in the first century understood statements like that literally, but it is important whether we do so today. To do so today contradicts a cosmology we hold non-mythically, which we have good reason to believe corresponds to reality.

Bultmann gives a number of examples of this difficulty in the first section of his famous essay, 'New Testament and Mythology'. There is the activity of good and evil spirits in the world, centring on heaven and hell respectively. There is miracle, and in general any intervention of the supernatural in the course of human history. There is the idea of an approaching last day, in which history will end, the dead rise, and all be judged. The resurrection of Jesus, and even the doctrine of atonement, in which the guilt of one man is expiated by the death of another who is sinless, present fully comparable difficulties. Bultmann expresses the whole difficulty in vivid sentences: 'It is impossible to use electric light and the wireless, and to avail ourselves of modern medical and surgical discoveries, and at the same time to believe in the New Testament world of spirits and miracles. We may think that we can manage to do it in our own lives, but to expect others to do so is to make the Christian faith unintelligible and unacceptable to the modern world.'

Because in the most famous of his discussions of the problem of myth, Bultmann sets the difficulties created for modern man by a pre-scientific view of the world in the forefront of his discussion, it is easy to suppose that he actually equates myth with a pre-scientific cosmology. In fact, there are really two related problems. The first and more important has already been discussed. Myth expresses an existential meaning in an objective form, and calls for intellectual assent instead of for a decision involving one's life. In the second place, and this is the point now before us, the intellectual assent required is unlikely to be accorded because the myth makes use of the cosmology current in New Testament times, instead of that of today. That cosmology ought to be incredible to modern man. If even intellectual assent is refused for good reasons, the modern listener never gets to the point at which he might grasp the existential meaning of the myth. The original readers of the New Testament, sharing the cosmology in which the myth was expressed, did not have the second problem, and in any case were perhaps better at interpreting mythological language than we are today.

That the problems are distinct can be easily shown if we consider a type of interpretation which brought the cosmology up to date, while retaining the mythological form of expression. Some theologians toy with this kind of method, but Bultmann would question its value. Presumably a myth expressed in contemporary cosmology would be read as science-fiction, and certainly some science-fiction seems to be interested in presenting ideas about man mythologically. Would Christ then appear as one of those rescuing beings from outer space that figure in some types of science-fiction? Would God be seen as influencing human minds by telepathy? The original difficulty Bultmann saw in myth would clearly remain. The transcendent would still have been expressed in terms of spatial distance. No decision seems called for by the science-fiction myth.

All myth suffers from the drawback that it presents the supernatural as on the fringes of nature, among the possible but improbable events that entertain the readers of science-fiction. No myth of this type can convey the nearness of God's presence to man in history, of which the Gospel speaks. The difficulty therefore can be reduced to the conception of the supernatural as an extension of the natural, which even a contemporary myth involves. Bultmann prefers not to talk of the supernatural, which he regards as a mythical notion as such, but of the transcendent, of the divine. When the transcendent impinges on man through the Word, it calls him to authentic existence. His response brings about a transition in man from inauthentic to authentic existence, and the theologian is able to speak indirectly of the transcendent by referring to this transition.

The term demythologizing suggests that something has been removed from the New Testament, and thus raises the suspicion that Bultmann is a reductionist in the liberal sense. Now Bultmann was not the first to spot the presence of mythology in the New Testament. The nineteenth-century writers of lives of Jesus were the first to speak of myth, and their way of dealing with it was to eliminate it. Bultmann considers that by eliminating myth altogether, part of the substance of the Gospel is jettisoned, namely, that essential part of it which refers to the approach of the transcendent to man. Thus he is in basic disagreement with his predecessors, and his programme must not be understood as a revival of the liberal project of modernizing Christianity. He thoroughly agrees with Barth and other neo-orthodox theologians that the Gospel is strange, not just to modern man, but to all men. It is not to be accounted for in cultural terms, for it comes to man from outside all culture. This is just what the myth, properly interpreted, safeguards.

The Gospel contains an offence. As Paul said: 'We preach Christ crucified, a stumbling block to Jews and folly to Gentiles' (1 Cor. i, 23). The stumbling block, or offence, is that man is addressed by the Gospel as one who stands in need of total grace, of a salvation that comes to him from altogether outside his own culture and resources, and that this salvation is linked with the particular historical event of the crucifixion of a man in the first century. By eliminating these features from the Gospel, and translating it into a timeless message whose principal content is ethical, the liberals had made it acceptable to modern man at the cost of what was essential to it. They had removed the Gospel along with the offence.

Has Bultmann also removed the offence of the Gospel, in his wish to make it intelligible to modern man? Are the mythological elements of the Gospel part of the offence of its historicity? Must we not take it as it comes to us, first-century cosmology and all? Now Bultmann does appear to have removed something, with his project of demythologizing. The first-century cosmology has gone, and so therefore has its offence. Along with it have disappeared a range of objective statements bound up with that cosmology, including many that have figured largely in the traditional presentation of Christianity. But Bultmann does not consider he has removed the genuine offence of the Gospel; on the contrary, he has brought it into view for the first time, by removing the false and trivial offence of the out-of-date science. This false offence is an effective deterrent, because while it is maintained modern man cannot get close enough to the Gospel to experience its real offence. Only when the false stumbling block of the mythology has been removed can the truly shattering offence of the Cross emerge into view.

Bultmann is thus no reductionist: he intends to preserve the whole substance of the Gospel. The Gospel only appears to have been reduced by demythologizing, because its presentation has been greatly simplified. On the other hand, since the mythology is no longer intelligible, those who retain it have reduced the communicable efficacy of the Gospel to no small extent, even if theoretically they have reduced nothing of the Gospel itself. The conservative is in this sense as much a reductionist as the liberal. On the other hand, if the mythology can be successfully interpreted, everything that is part of the authentic Gospel will be retained, and only what is superfluous, and actually an obstacle to the Gospel, will have been discarded.

Bultmann's aim in undertaking the programme of demythologizing is thus one with the aim of the dialectical theologians. He wishes to break with the liberal aim of presenting the Gospel within the terms of man's religious culture, and express it as transcendent, as qualitatively distinct from the works of man and anything in the world. The objection to myth can therefore also be expressed in terms of the famous antithesis between a quantitative and a qualitative distinction between time and eternity. Myth suggests that the transcendent is only quantitatively distinct from the world of man. It expresses the divine in terms of what is very remote, but in the last analysis still part of the world. Thus to retain myth uninterpreted would be to fail to make that decisive break with religion that Barth and his friends in the dialectical theology tried to make back in the twenties. Thus, although the demythologizing programme has drawn down upon itself the severe criticism of Barth and his supporters, it is a project that follows directly from aims

that were also Barth's at the time that he and Bultmann were in
closer association.

On the other hand, when this aim is kept steadily in view, it is
possible to wonder if Bultmann has been as successful in his
reinterpretation of myth as in his criticism of it. Bultmann does
wish to speak about the divine, or the transcendent. He continues
to believe, with traditional theology, that God is a transcendent
person, while denying that objective statements can be made
about him. God can only be spoken of from within the encounter
of word and faith, and hence in terms of his effects on man. But
Bultmann also goes on to say of God that he acts. Here he
surely goes beyond what can be expressed in anthropology.
Heidegger's philosophy permits Bultmann to express with
compelling clarity a biblical view of man and of the revolution
in his existence the Gospel brings about for the one who hears it.
But is existentialist analysis equally useful in speaking about
God? Bultmann believes that to speak about God and his
action in the world is not a matter of mythology. Here direct, or
more properly, analogical speech is in order. In this too he is at
one with Barth, at least in principle. In a helpful chapter in
Jesus Christ and Mythology, under the title 'The Meaning of
God as Acting', he explains that the action of God is not to
feed into the continuum of history new and alien events, not
subject to its causality. Events which faith calls acts of God are
ordinary events, capable of explanation by appropriate scientific and historical methods. Faith need not deny the appropriateness of such explanations, but it will add that these events are
for it acts of God.

The archetypal act of God, in the light of which other events
may be judged also to be his acts, will be the kerygma. The core
of Bultmann's theology is the notion of the kerygma, the proclamation of the church, as a human event in which God speaks.
Revelation, as we have seen, is now, not in the past, and it is
absolute. No questions can be asked about the qualification of
preaching to be the Word of God. In the questions it asks
about man's existence, and the answers it gives about possibilities
of authentic existence in Jesus Christ, the word brooks no
argument. It must be accepted or rejected. The kerygma is not

the product of human culture but the Word of the transcendent God, though the theology in which it is spoken is always necessarily the product of human culture.

So far, perhaps, so good, but the difficult problem comes when the theologian wishes to speak about the God who thus speaks and acts. Existential analysis helps him to speak about man, but there is no phenomenology for God, since God is not a phenomenon. If the theologian is to go beyond the phenomenology of faith, regarded as the reflection of God's otherwise unintelligible act, he must turn to analogy. God is then conceived as subject, along with the dialectical theology, and his qualitative transcendence is thought of on the analogy of man's transcendence of the world. God's action is conceived on the analogy of human action. When Bultmann speaks directly of God, as he sometimes does, he remains within the framework of ideas of the dialectical theology, and no longer has available to him a conceptual clarification of theological speech, such as Heidegger provided for him in those parts of his theology which can be expressed anthropologically. Hence there is a certain discontinuity in his thought, which has provided an important topic of debate among those who have learned most from him. Some of his followers are looking for other philosophical resources, that will do for theology what Heidegger's existentialism has done for anthropology. Schubert M. Ogden, for example, finds this in the process-philosophy of Whitehead and Hartshorne.[21] Others, such as Herbert Braun, carry non-objectivity in reference to God to the conceivable limit, so that God is spoken of only as the 'whence' of man's disturbance. Such a totally anthropological approach carries with it silence on the question of God.

CRITICISM AND DEBATE

We have noted that Bultmann's thought has always been controversial, and it remains so today. He has stirred up two kinds of controversy. There is debate, among those who accept his basic contentions, about how his insights should be further developed and clarified. Ogden considers that this could be done

21. *The Reality of God and Other Essays*, S.C.M. Press, 1967.

by giving clearer philosophical grounding to what is to be said about God, and also by moving away from the Christocentrism which unites Bultmann with Barth and his other neo-orthodox friends of the twenties. The two criticisms are related, for Ogden not only wishes to say that authentic existence is possible to those who do not know of Christ, he also wishes to find a basis outside Christ for talk of God. He still believes, however, that for Christians God and authentic existence are known in Christ, and that he is the basis for authentic existence in fact, whether men who have it are aware of him as its source or not.

The Swiss theologian Fritz Buri has criticized Bultmann along somewhat similar lines, though his differences from Bultmann seem to be greater than Ogden's since he has moved into a radical position from a liberal one, without ever having been close to neo-orthodoxy. He thinks Bultmann has adopted too little, not too much, of the liberal programme. In particular, he criticizes the prominence of the kerygma in Bultmann's thought, which he considered incompatible with his analysis of man and his existence. It must be possible for man to attain authentic existence without encountering the kerygma, or we could not use this language to explain the effect of hearing the kerygma. So he considers that the Gospel should not just be demythologized, but *dekerygmatized*. The link between Christ and authentic human existence, through the kerygma, should be cut. Buri is also influenced by process philosophy.[22]

If Bultmann is criticized on one side for being too little of a liberal, he has come under even more criticism from both conservatives and Barthians for being too much of one. Barth regards him as a liberal because he thinks Bultmann continues in an exaggerated form the subjectivity begun in Lutheranism by Melanchthon and given systematic form by Schleiermacher. In starting his theology from an anthropology Bultmann has re-entered the liberal trap, and cannot escape the absorption of theology by culture. We have seen that if this criticism were justified, it would have to be concluded that Bultmann had failed to realize his own clearly-expressed intentions. The con-

22. On process theology, see further, below, pp. 334 f.

servative Lutherans, on the other hand, think he has abandoned the objective facts of salvation-history, notably in his view of the resurrection, discussion of which is outside the scope of the present volume. For this controversy, see the volumes of *Kerygma and Myth*, edited by H. W. Bartsch, and translated by R. H. Fuller.

There is I think a great deal to be said for the view that Bultmann in fact stands near the middle in many of the controversies of present-day theology, and this is evidenced by the fact that some regard him as too liberal, others as not liberal enough. Some think he has said too much about God, others too little. All these criticisms appear to be based in Bultmann's continued loyalty to the essential positions of the dialectical theology of the twenties, and his application of them to new problems. Had he moved with Barth into a more positive and rational theology, he would have silenced the latter's objections while attracting others. Had he in fact remained a liberal, he would have been unable to speak of the transcendence of the Word of God over religious culture, and would have had no basis for his reinterpretation of mythology. The difficulties Barth found in dialectical theology Bultmann, as a New Testament scholar and philosophical theologian, does not deal with. On the other hand, his criticisms of the influence of culture upon theology are more searching, because more concrete, than Barth's own.

A more interesting and fruitful debate, perhaps, is the one going on among those who have remained closer to Bultmann's own positions, about how best to carry out hermeneutics in a systematic way. This inquiry has also been associated with a new approach, also based in Bultmann's own work, to the question of the historical Jesus. At the present time, this post-Bultmannian debate in Germany is one of the most lively centres of theology anywhere. It has also led to a fruitful dialogue between American and German followers of Bultmann. In Great Britain, however, his theology has found less response, except in a very generalized way.

Perhaps the most interesting, though undeveloped, criticism of Bultmann is to be found in the prison letters of Bonhoeffer,

to whom we must now turn. Bonhoeffer suggests that, in his
programme of demythologizing, Bultmann went both too far and
not far enough, and makes his own highly radical suggestion for
a replacement for the programme of demythologizing.

Four

Dietrich Bonhoeffer: Religionless Christianity

Of all the writers discussed in detail in this book, Dietrich Bonhoeffer was perhaps the most radical. With the possible exception of Reinhold Niebuhr in the specialized field of social ethics, he is the one whose ideas have had the greatest echo among people outside the circle of professional theologians. Yet his thought nowhere attains full and systematic formulation. He died at the hands of the S.S. at the age of thirty-nine, leaving behind him finished works he had grown beyond, fragments and drafts of what was to have been his major work, and a number of letters and papers smuggled out of prison, in which he expressed revolutionary theological insights that may yet bear their proper fruit in the work of a new generation of theologians. If Bonhoeffer had lived to bring them to fruit himself, there can be little doubt that he would have been the theologian to dominate the post-war scene, instead of Bultmann and Tillich, whose principal insights had already been reached before the war.

Had he lived, Bonhoeffer would only have been in his sixties today. What he would now be saying can hardly be guessed, in view of the rapidity with which his thought developed in his lifetime. Yet even in unfinished form the seminal thoughts of his last period have proved astonishingly difficult for his contemporaries and juniors to assimilate, let alone push beyond the point at which he left them. They have been analysed and interpreted many times, but they remain unfinished, open, a source of continuing disturbance and liberation. Outside the theological community, they have been received with simple gratitude, for more than any other theologian Bonhoeffer speaks directly to the condition of the layman living in the world.

These judgements apply in particular to Bonhoeffer's last work, which is not a book at all in the ordinary sense, but a collection of letters and papers conveyed from a Gestapo prison by guards charmed and bribed by their unusual prisoner, and assembled together after the war by Eberhard Bethge, the friend to whom the most theologically important of the letters were written. Because of the consuming interest of the *Letters and Papers from Prison*, and to a lesser extent of the earlier book *The Cost of Discipleship* (a commentary on the Sermon on the Mount for which Bonhoeffer was perhaps best known in his own lifetime) practically everything he wrote has been published and translated. There has also grown up around these writings, finished and fragmentary, something of a literature of inter-pretation, and there is certainly more of this to come. Yet the interest of the reader will always return to the books I have mentioned, and everything else will seem important only for the light it can shed on the man who wrote them. It may also be said of Bonhoeffer, as of other martyrs (we shall consider later in what sense Bonhoeffer was a martyr) that his life and death together constitute a theological statement as weighty as what he wrote. Perhaps it is in Bonhoeffer's own action and suffering, therefore, that we shall find the completion that cannot be discovered in his writings. In trying to understand the meaning of what he wanted to say, we must pay particular attention, in that case, to the events of his life and their interaction with the books he wrote.

Because Bonhoeffer's ideas developed rapidly and changed more than once under the impact of meditated experience, those who wish to understand his thought as a whole have a problem of interpretation. Is the Bonhoeffer of the prison letters to be interpreted in the light of the earlier, more carefully written but less original works? If so, he can be set in his place in modern theology, and assigned a position among the neo-orthodox inter-preters of Christianity who were his elders and peers. Or must the disturbing novelties of the last period be taken as they stand, and given a context in contemporary Christian experience, rather than in Bonhoeffer's own past and background, so that they can speak directly to us on their own merits? In that case, a rather different Bonhoeffer will emerge, a radical rather than a neo-orthodox thinker, the forerunner of theologians of the sixties who wish to probe beyond the points reached by the writers here discussed. On the whole, the established theologians have taken the former course, the laity and the younger theologians the latter. For our purposes, something like the latter course is also necessary, since the readers for whom this book is intended will probably not read the early works of Bonhoeffer, except perhaps in the hope of finding there more of the thought they have valued in the later books. They will want to use him as a starting-point for contemporary action and reflection. In that case, it is likely that they will find him the most sympathetic of all the theologians they meet with here.

Unlike Barth, Bultmann and Tillich, who came from clerical homes, in which theology was regularly discussed, Bonhoeffer was the son of a professor of psychiatry, and the cultural atmosphere of his home, which had a deep influence on him, was secular and humanist. His father and brothers were agnostics. Dietrich Bonhoeffer was born in 1906, at the same time as a twin sister; they were the sixth and seventh of the eight Bonhoeffer children. Particularly after the elder Bonhoeffer moved from Breslau, where Dietrich was born, to the chair of psychiatry at the University of Berlin, his home exposed him to the influences of German culture at its richest, in the tradition of nineteenth-century liberal thought. Among their neighbours at Grünewald, the Berlin suburb where the Bonhoeffers lived, were Adolf von Harnack, the church historian, and Hans Delbrück, the secular historian. Ernst Troeltsch, who had moved in 1915 from the chair of systematic theology at Heidelberg to one of philosophy at Berlin, frequently visited the Bonhoeffers. Max and Alfred Weber, the sociologists, used to take part in discussions with Bonhoeffer's father and brothers while he was at school and university, and from listening to these discussions he acquired a considerable knowledge of and interest in sociology. Other subjects that were regularly discussed included the ideas of the youth movement, with its philosophy of life and nature, the philosophy of history, Russian literature, and the ideas of Nietzsche, Soloviev and Berdyaev. Bonhoeffer read the whole of Nietzsche in his youth, and was deeply influenced by his thought.

A highly intelligent boy growing up in that sort of home could hardly fail to be influenced in the direction of academic life, but when the time came to decide what field to enter, Dietrich made a choice that could not have been predicted from his home environment. He decided at the age of sixteen to take courses in Hebrew at school, and to aim at the study of theology. After a year at Tübingen he entered the university of Berlin, when its theological faculty was still enjoying the marvellous flowering that had begun in the years before the war, though the liberal tradition it represented was by now under fire from the new forces of the dialectical theology; Karl Barth was already a professor in Germany. In church history and the history of theology, the Berlin faculty could boast of the great Harnack, of Karl Holl, a leading figure in the revival of Luther studies, and of Lietzmann, the historian of the early church, in biblical studies of Sellin and Deissmann, in systematic theology of Bonhoeffer's own teacher, Reinhold Seeberg. Under the latter's encouragement, Bonhoeffer became a specialist in Hegel and a systematic theologian, and completed his dissertation at the early age of twenty-one.

EARLY WORKS

His degree dissertation dealt with the doctrine of the church, a topic of particular interest to Seeberg, and was published under the title *Sanctorum Communio* (the communion of saints).[1] Like other early works of Bonhoeffer, it is academic in manner, and perhaps lacks the consuming interest for the contemporary reader of the works by which he will be remembered. On the other hand, we cannot pass by these early works without brief notice, for they contain the seeds of many of the most striking of his later ideas and foreshadow developments, not just in his own thought, but in that of others in the same movement of thought, including Barth himself. Surprisingly often, we find Barth taking up and developing, after an interval of several years, an idea that makes its first seminal appearance in Bonhoeffer. The themes of Bonhoeffer's early books remain central to his

1. *Sanctorum Communio*, Collins, 1963 (English translation).

interests, although the way he understands them will undergo rapid development over the period of his short career.

Barth would later describe *Sanctorum Communio* as a 'theological miracle'. The miracle he had in mind was doubtless one of precocity, rather than of absolute achievement. In theology very early achievement is exceedingly rare. Bonhoeffer's actual success in this work is perhaps less impressive than the way in which he is able to raise questions that would later become of first-rate importance in the development of modern theology. In this work of 1927, Bonhoeffer already saw the doctrine of the church as the central issue for a modern theology based on revelation. It would be five years more before Karl Barth would bring out the revised edition of the first volume of his dogmatics under the new title of *Church Dogmatics*, and many more before the doctrine of the church became under the influence of the ecumenical movement the favoured theme of every younger theologian.

The key phrase of *Sanctorum Communio* is *'Christus als Gemeinde existierend'* : Christ existing as community, or church. Bonhoeffer wishes to think of the revelation in Christ as concretely as possible, and so he locates it not in ideas but in the presently existing community of the church. This drive to concreteness marks all Bonhoeffer's work, and is among its most distinctive characteristics. At no time in his career had he any patience with airy generalities, which could not be made concrete in the life of this world.

Starting from the thesis of his teacher Seeberg (itself an adaptation of Hegel's thought) that man is essentially a social being, and that each of his communities is characterized by its own 'objective spirit', Bonhoeffer sets out to exhibit the church as both the community of revelation, known as such only by faith, and as an empirical social community, whose 'objective spirit' is the vehicle of the work of the Holy Spirit. As an empirical community, the church lies within the field of sociology, and so Bonhoeffer tries to show by sociological analysis how the community of faith takes concrete shape in the world. The relationship between its character as the community of faith, and its character as an empirical community in this world, is a dialectical one, only to be resolved beyond the history of this world. The strength of the work lies in its drive to make revelation concrete by locating it in the empirical community of the church, which is theologically known as the body of Christ. His attempt to mediate between the liberalism of his own teachers, and the new theology then being discussed, would have been more convincing had he entered into more serious dialogue with those who had thought most deeply about empirical communities, i.e. with Troeltsch among theologians, and with Marx and Weber among sociologists.

After his degree dissertation, Bonhoeffer's next work would be his qualification thesis for an academic post. This work, also submitted in the university of Berlin, marked a further stage in his breach with the liberal theology in which he had been trained, though he never lost a respect for its achievements, and he remained sensitive to ways in which neo-orthodoxy failed to answer its genuine questions. This second book, published in 1931, continued some of the themes of *Sanctorum Communio*, notably the attempt to provide a church form for the idea of revelation; he wished to unite the notion of revelation as coming to man from outside his culture (the new emphasis of Barth and the dialectical theology) with that of its concrete shape in this world (Bonhoeffer's own personal contribution, derived in part from his Lutheran background and in part from the bent of his own theological mind).

Entitled *Act and Being*,[2] the work confronts various philosophical and theological approaches to the doctrine of revelation, grouped together as 'transcendental philosophy' (the tradition of Kant) and 'ontology' (in current German thought the idealism of Hegel and many of the liberals). Barth was associated at that time with the attack on idealism with the aid of neo-Kantian transcendentalism, and Bonhoeffer now allies himself with this approach to a greater extent than before. Nevertheless, his conclusion is that neither 'act', the category of interpretation favoured by transcendental philosophy, nor 'being', the one favoured by the idealist tradition, is adequate for the theological discussion of the Christian revelation. Bonhoeffer's own thesis is that 'the

2. Dietrich Bonhoeffer, *Act and Being*, Collins, 1962.

idea of revelation must be re-envisaged with the concretion of the idea of the church, i.e. in a sociological category where both kinds of analysis encounter each other and are drawn together in one.'[3]

Some of the themes of the prison letters are already present in germinal form in these early works, though they have not yet been liberated from their academic framework to the life which they there enjoy. At all times Christology was of central importance to Bonhoeffer, and his constant wish was to understand Christ and his revelation as concretely as possible. Christ was no more to be reduced to an idea than he was to be regarded as the creation of man's religiousness. His grace and his command were to be found in this world, and to follow and obey would mean action, setting the Christian apart from those who neither followed nor obeyed Christ. Again, it is interesting to notice that Bonhoeffer began to understand revelation not only as wholly distinct from religion but very concretely as revelation in Christ while Barth was still extracting himself from dialectical transcendentalism. Both men were never without what has been called in the mature work of Barth Christological concentration: Barth had learned too much from his own teacher, Wilhelm Herrmann, for that. But it may fairly be said that Bonhoeffer was a little ahead of Barth in this rigour of concentration, even if he could not yet develop his thought with the systematic power of the older man.

Bonhoeffer's thought about Christ, however, differed from Barth's in ways that are partly to be explained from his Lutheran heritage, where it differed from Barth's Calvinistic background, and partly as personal to Bonhoeffer. There is a technical point of difference between Lutheran and Calvinistic Christology which is perpetuated in the difference of approach to the doctrine of Christ in the thought of the two men. We have already observed the importance to Barth of the Calvinist saying, *finitum non capax infiniti*.[4] This tag has its origin in Christology, where it is met by the Lutheran counterpart, its opposite: *finitum capax infiniti*. Over against the Lutheran belief that God entered fully into Christ at the incarnation, the Calvinist maintained the so-called *extra Calvinisticum*, the doctrine that God also re-

3. ibid., p. 16.   4. Above, p. 94.

mained outside (*extra*) the humanity of Christ, and continued to rule the world from heaven as well as to undergo the humiliation of the earthly life and passion of Jesus.

These differences are connected with the differences in eucharistic doctrine of the two forms of Protestantism, on which they separated at the time of the Reformation. The Reformed teaching on both counts emphasizes the transcendence and sovereignty of God and of the ascended Christ, where the Lutheran lays equal stress on his nearness, reality and what Bonhoeffer calls 'haveability' in the incarnation, the Word and the sacrament. Hence the Lutherans held fast to the doctrine of the real presence of Christ in the sacrament of the altar, taking the word 'is' in 'this is my body' literally, where the Reformed taught a spiritual presence, however much they too insisted on its objectivity. Bonhoeffer like his fellow-Lutherans saw the Gospel as bound up with God's self-commitment and availability to man, of which the real presence of Christ in the sacrament is more than a symbol for them.

Bonhoeffer's Christology follows Lutheran tradition in emphasizing the unlimited 'condescension' of God in Christ, where Barth's follows the Calvinist in emphasizing equally God's freedom, even in the incarnation, symbolized by the denial that humanity can contain the infinite God. Thus Barth's Christology can never have the ultimate concreteness of Bonhoeffer's, though in his mature work he too turns in the same direction.

In his later work, Barth sees the dangers of too philosophical a view of transcendence: even transcendence can become an idol. The first two sentences, at least, of this quotation from *Act and Being* might have been written by Barth – but not perhaps until several years after they were written by Bonhoeffer himself: 'God is not free *of* man but *for* man. Christ is the Word of his freedom. God is *there*, which is to say: not in eternal non-objectivity . . . but "haveable", graspable in his Word within the church.'[5] In 1930, when these words appeared in print, Barth himself was still struggling to free himself from eternal 'non-objectivity' with the aid of Anselm.[6] Characteristically Bonhoeffer reaches an

5. Bonhoeffer, *Act and Being*, Collins, 1962, p. 91.
6. See above, pp. 102 ff.

insight very early, expresses it with almost epigrammatic brevity, and passes on to other questions, where Barth reaches the idea at his own pace, and when he does, develops it systematically and at great length. There also occurs at this early stage of Bonhoeffer's development the idea of Christ as 'the man for others', the key to the mature Christology of Bonhoeffer, and also a phrase to be appropriated by Barth in his later work.

There is doubtless a risk in the Lutheran type of Christology, against which the protest of Reformed thought has force. God's transcendence may be lost, and Jesus the man worshipped instead of God. Worse, the Lutheran risks dragging down the concept of God to what human piety can assimilate. Both at this stage and at the end of his life, Bonhoeffer had his own way of guarding against this danger. He does not take refuge in the thought of metaphysical transcendence, as Barth did, especially in his early neo-Kantian phase. Bonhoeffer has his own idea of transcendence, which becomes extremely important in the prison letters. He sees it as a property of persons. I encounter transcendence in the other, the Thou, in my neighbour. Thus Bonhoeffer made his own use, as did others of his generation, of the personalist philosophy current at the time, and particularly associated with the name of the Jewish philosopher Martin Buber, whose influence on modern theology is so pervasive.[7] Bonhoeffer understands the transcendence of God in Christ as such a personal transcendence, carried to the limit. This is a concept of transcendence associated with nearness, not remoteness.

Also common to Barth and Bonhoeffer and to the other theologians of the dialectical school, to which Bonhoeffer now loosely attached himself, was the rejection of religion as a presupposition for the doctrine of revelation. The Berlin tradition, in the persons of Troeltsch and Seeberg, had had a good deal to say about religion, in the form of what they called 'the religious premise' or the 'religious *a priori*'. Both men wanted to use their analysis of religion as the foundation of the theological edifice. Bonhoeffer was always on the side of Barth in

7. On Buber see R. Gregor Smith, *Martin Buber*, London, Carey Kingsgate Press, 1966.

rejecting this starting-point, in asserting the autonomy of the Word of God from all human culture, and its distinction from human religion in any form. Later, he would take the criticism of religion to a point never reached in Barth's theology, and give it a form with which his own name will always be associated.

At this stage, he wanted to assert that revelation did not need to have a space cleared in advance by religion, a landing-strip, as it were, for the Word of God. The Word of God was more like a bomb, that cleared its own space in the world as it landed. Then the church, to push the image a bit further, was the crater left in the world by the explosion of the Word, a radioactive crater, perhaps, that continued to emit energy long after the original explosion.[8] At any rate, in Bonhoeffer's thought the church takes the place of religion, as he himself would later note was true of Barth.

After going down from the University of Berlin, Bonhoeffer spent two years in Spain as an assistant with the German-speaking congregation of Barcelona, and then a year's leave of absence in the United States, working at Union Theological Seminary, New York. He was not impressed theologically by what he found in the United States, and he made it his duty to acquaint his fellow-students with the new ideas associated with Karl Barth, ignoring for the moment his own criticisms of the latter. He did manage to see a good deal of the country, and to absorb something of the social concern of the American churches. He then returned to Berlin to take up the position of lecturer in theology for which the writing of *Act and Being* had qualified him. In the July before he took up his duties he attended a seminar at Bonn conducted by Karl Barth; though he was already under the influence of Barth's ideas, first-hand contact meant much more to him, and he wrote to a friend that he scarcely regretted anything in his career so far more than not having come to Bonn earlier.

At Berlin, he entered upon an extremely busy life. In addition to lecturing upon various theological topics, he was chaplain to

8. The image is mine, not Bonhoeffer's, though I believe it expresses his meaning. He was of course fortunate enough to live at a time when the image of a radioactive crater could not in any case have occurred to him.

a technical college, gave confirmation classes to young workers in a slum area of Berlin, and acted as secretary to the Youth Commission of the World Alliance for International Friendship through the Churches, and of the Universal Christian Council for Life and Work, two of the early ecumenical organizations that led to the founding after the war of the World Council of Churches. His ecumenical work continued through the thirties, and made him many friends outside Germany. The book of lectures on the early chapters of Genesis, published as *Creation and Fall*,[9] and the lectures on Christology,[10] reconstructed from student notes and published after the war, belong to this period.

THE STRUGGLE FOR THE CHURCH

In 1933, Hitler came to power in Germany. Two days after the Nazis took over, Bonhoeffer gave a radio address attacking the leadership principle, which was interrupted by the authorities before it could be finished. A month later he delivered it again in expanded form as a lecture to students in political science. In April 1933 a 'law for the restitution of the civil service' dismissed Jews from government service, including university chairs. This law applied to two of Bonhoeffer's relations by marriage. In July 1933 church elections were held, rigged by the authorities to ensure the success of the German Christian group, who thus secured a substantial majority in the government of the church, led by the notorious Reichsbischof Müller. In September the National Synod[11] put the Aryan legislation into effect for the church and implemented the leadership principle in the government of the church.

Bonhoeffer took some part in the organization of opposition to these developments, but by the time this work bore fruit in November 1933, in the formation of the Pastors' Emergency League, through which Martin Niemöller came into prominence, Bonhoeffer had left Germany in disgust to work as pastor to two small German congregations in London. There he got to

9. *Creation and Fall*, S.C.M. Press, 1959. 10. *Christology*, Collins, 1966. 11. See above, pp. 111 and 156.

know many of the leaders of English church life, and in particular struck up a friendship with G. K. A. Bell, who as Bishop of Chichester led much of the Anglican participation in the ecumenical movement. From his vantage point in London, Bonhoeffer made it his duty to acquaint the churches outside Germany of the significance of what was going on in the church struggle. In 1934, the synods of Barmen and Dahlem drew up a confession of faith, and set up a provisional government for the church, in opposition to the German Christians who controlled the existing structure. Bonhoeffer represented these 'Confessing Church Brethren-Councils' at the ecumenical meetings he was able to attend. In 1935, however, he returned to Germany, partly under the influence of an urgent summons from Barth. The immediate occasion, however, of his return was a call from the Confessing Church Council of the Prussian Union to lead a small seminary for ordinands at Finkenwalde in Pomerania.

At this time the university theological faculties were largely passive under the impact of the new developments, and the brethren of the Confessing Church did not consider the theological training given there an adequate preparation for service in the pastorate at such a time. As opportunity offered they therefore set up seminaries of an unofficial character to train men after graduation, during the period of their *Vikariat*, or assistantship, prior to ordination to the ministry of the Word and sacraments, or pastorate proper. The seminary at Finkenwalde was one of these.

Bonhoeffer had now an even more radical conception of the needs of the time. During his visit to England he had been impressed with the work of Kelham and Mirfield in the Anglican church, houses where religious orders give theological training to young men who share their monastic life to a certain extent during their training. He tried to adapt what he had seen there to a Lutheran context and to the special needs of the Confessing Church. In connexion with the Seminary at Finkenwalde he founded a loose form of community, the *Bruderhaus*. The men were under no vows, and were free to leave at any time. But they declared their intention to live together in a common life for a reasonably long period, and shared their property, living a common devotional life based on prayer together, biblical meditation and open confession of sins. It was at this time that Eberhard Bethge, the editor of Bonhoeffer's posthumously published works, became associated with him.

The object of the community was to strengthen the pastoral life, especially at a time when it might be difficult for a young man to preach fearlessly without this kind of support, and when the Confessing Church needed men who could be sent anywhere at any time. The community provided a focus of fellowship for former members of the seminary, and conducted retreats for pastors and lay people. Both seminary and community were forcibly dissolved in 1937. Bonhoeffer tried to continue the work clandestinely through a team ministry of the assistants, which he directed from the post of a supply teacher, but during this period he had no real home.

In the period of his life in which he worked with the seminary and community, Bonhoeffer's search for the most concrete grasp of the revelation in Christ took a form that could have been called extreme, had the external circumstances been less difficult. In his final period, he too became critical of his views then. He turned theologically from systematic theology to the direct exegesis of Scripture, and even to this in a devotional rather than a critical form. He had learned to pray the psalms as the religious orders do, interpreted as the prayer of Christ in his church; his theological interpretation of the psalms followed the same principles. Though he continued to maintain the theoretical rights of historical criticism as a preliminary to exegesis, at this stage his concern was the classic one, simply to hear and obey the Word of God found in the Scriptures.

He developed a theory of concreteness in ethics which paralleled the Lutheran view of the relation between Word and sacrament. As the Gospel becomes concrete in the sacrament, the Law becomes concrete in precise commandments referring to a particular situation. Matching this concreteness in his understanding of obedience to Christ was a still more intense concreteness in his understanding of Christ in his church. The church now meant the Confessing Church for him, and he became notorious for his contention that whoever knowingly cuts himself off in Germany from the Confessing Church, cuts himself off from salvation. In this he went much further than the Barthians among the Confessing Churchmen, and lost much good-will among the moderates. Yet what he said followed directly from two positions common to himself and to many of his critics. They were in agreement with the old principle that there is no salvation outside the church, without wishing to interpret this legalistically: Bonhoeffer understood this to be a pointer to the place at which salvation *is* offered, rather than a negative judgement on other communities. They also agreed that for Germany at that time, the Confessing Church was the place, and the only place, in which the faith of Christ was rightly confessed, and hence the only place where the true church could assuredly be found.

The books for which Bonhoeffer was best known in his lifetime belong to this period, *The Cost of Discipleship* (*Nachfolge*, 1937), and *Life Together* (*Gemeinsames Leben*, 1938).[12] The former book, the first of Bonhoeffer's works to be published in English after the war, applied the new concrete exegesis to the Sermon on the Mount, a part of the New Testament which had traditionally been something of a theological embarrassment to the Lutherans. In contrast to liberals, who have found the centre of Christianity in the teaching of the Sermon, Lutherans regard it as part of the Law. Jesus' ethical teaching sets a standard so high that it is impossible to keep it literally; hence it does not bind the Christian, who is justified by faith and is not under the Law. In his new mood, Bonhoeffer was prepared to characterize all this as evasion of God's word and commandment.

In passages reminiscent of Kierkegaard's attack upon the Lutheran state church of his time (Kierkegaard had alleged that Luther would have said the opposite had he lived in the nineteenth century instead of the sixteenth) Bonhoeffer characterized as 'cheap grace' the preaching of justification by faith alone to bourgeois congregations. This was 'the justification of sin without the justification of the sinner'. In place of cheap grace, the meaningless words of justification bringing about no renewal of life, he wanted to put what he called 'costly grace'. By this he

12. *The Cost of Discipleship*, S.C.M.Press, 1948, 1959, 1964; *Life Together*, S.C.M. Press, 1955.

meant the grace preached by Jesus himself, which costs a man all that he has, because it is the pearl of great price. The paradox is sharp: how can it be grace if it is costly; how can it be costly if it is grace? Bonhoeffer did not resolve it intellectually: he pointed to discipleship, the concrete following of Jesus, as the resolution. The only way to receive free grace is to follow Jesus. So justification by faith alone could never be, as it had become in the conventional Lutheran preaching, a presupposition, something taken for granted. Justification must always be an answer to an agonizing question, a solution to the problem of how one could satisfy the infinite demands of divine righteousness. Only so could it be understood as genuine, and therefore costly, grace, and truly laid hold of by a penitent sinner. Justification by faith is possible only for the man who has learned by experience that he cannot be justified by the works of the Law.

Bonhoeffer now called for no preaching of justification without the preaching of the Law, and no communion without confession. In place of the Lutheran order, Only he who believes can obey, he introduced a dialectic: Only he who obeys can believe, only he who believes can obey. This dialectic could be applied in pastoral counselling: those who found they could not obey the commandments were to be told to believe in the Gospel; those who could not believe the Gospel were to obey, at least by turning up in church to hear the preaching. *The Cost of Discipleship* made Bonhoeffer famous, and it is still a book of gripping power, even when read by one who is aware of Bonhoeffer's later development, and of the different view he would eventually take on the problems it confronted. Indeed, he never repudiated the book.

Life Together was written out of the experience of the *Bruderhaus*, after its dissolution. It actually sold more copies in his lifetime than anything else he wrote. It tells of the practices he had learned with the brethren of meditation, of free and open confession, of the trust and fellowship a shared Christian life brings. Much of what is said would be familiar to many Anglican and Catholic Christians, though from their point of view its Lutheran emphasis would be unmistakable. To Lutherans themselves it was all fresh and new, disturbing, but, as the circulation of the book shows, richly suggestive of ways to fill a gap in the presentation of Christianity which traditional Lutheranism had left wide open.

GERMANY OR AMERICA?

Since 1935, Bonhoeffer had been liable to conscription under one of the Nazi laws, and at the same time he was coming under increasing suspicion from the authorities. During the thirties he toyed with absolute pacifism as the Christian answer to war, though an answer most untraditional for Lutherans, for they usually make a sharp separation between church and state at the theological level, while coordinating them politically and ethically. He had even intended to go from London to meet Gandhi in India, to discuss with him both the common life as practised in the latter's ashrams, and the techniques of non-violent resistance. In any case, he did not wish to fight for Hitler.

The probability that he would be subject to conscription into the armed forces increased as his activities were gradually restricted by the authorities. In August 1936 he lost his right to teach as a *Privatdozent*, or lecturer, at the University of Berlin. In 1938, after the disbandment by the Gestapo of the seminary and its attached community, he was forbidden to take part in church activities in Berlin. In the summer of 1940, after his return from a second visit to America, he was forbidden to preach, and ordered to report at regular intervals to the police. In the spring of 1941, his books were proscribed and he was not allowed to write or publish. Thus, over this period of five years, he was gradually separated from his work with the Confessing Church, and from contact with professional colleagues and friends. Before this process became complete, however, two other events happened which were of great significance for the final period of his life.

In view of this danger that he might be called up into the army, some of his friends abroad, with the agreement of the Confessing Church brethren, tried to arrange for him to leave Germany and continue his theological work unhindered. Reinhold Niebuhr and others managed to arrange a visit to America for him, in the summer of 1939, which they hoped would lead to his taking up a permanent post there. This second visit promised to be a fruitful one: Bonhoeffer was now much better able to appreciate the value of work being done by American theologians, and he in his turn was obviously going to make a very favourable impression on them. But he was unhappy in himself. He began to feel uneasiness about his presence in America not long after he had arrived. He did not share the hopes of his American colleagues that he would remain permanently in the United States, and did not like to regard himself as a refugee. He began to think that he was in a false position.

In addition to these doubts about the basis of his presence in America, he soon experienced the pull of his friends and of the work they had been doing together in Germany, and he started to plan his return, perhaps for the autumn, or maybe for early in the New Year. As the international situation deteriorated, his wish to be back in Germany grew even stronger. Finally, at the beginning of July 1939, he wrote to Niebuhr:

I have come to the conclusion that I have made a mistake in coming to America. I must live through this difficult period of our national history with the Christian people of Germany. I will have no right to participate in the reconstruction of Christian life in Germany after the war if I do not share the trials of this time with my people. My brethren in the Confessing Church wanted me to go. They may have been right in urging me to do so; but I was wrong in going. Such a decision each man must make for himself. Christians in Germany will face the terrible alternative of either willing the defeat of their nation in order that the Christian civilization may survive, or willing the victory of their nation and thereby destroying our civilization. I know which of these alternatives I must choose; but I cannot make that choice in security. . . [13]

Bonhoeffer left New York on 7 July; in the event, his visit had lasted less than a month. Once at sea, he found that his inner uncertainty had vanished, and he felt once more at peace with himself. After a visit to England, he was back in Berlin before the end of July. On 24 August Ribbentrop signed the German-Soviet pact, and a week later Hitler invaded Poland. Bonhoeffer

13. Edwin H. Robertson (ed.), *The Way to Freedom*, Collins, 1966, pp. 246.

took up once more his work with the younger clergy of his church. His first circular letter to his brethren after his return meditates upon the task of the preacher in a time of trouble and confusion, and moves to the topic of death, which Bonhoeffer had considered adopting for a lecture series in Edinburgh that he had been invited to give. These lectures would never now be delivered.

FROM CHURCH TO WORLD

The second of the two important events of this period was his recruitment to the German resistance movement by his brother-in-law Hans von Dohnanyi. Dohnanyi was serving as assistant to General Oster of the Intelligence Service. Dohnanyi, Oster and his colleague Admiral Canaris, who was later hanged beside Bonhoeffer at Flossenbürg, were using their position as cover for a movement of resistance against the regime, which culminated in the 20 July 1944 attempt on Hitler's life. Bonhoeffer was taken on as a civilian agent for the *Abwehr* (the counter-intelligence department) to save him from conscription into the Army and to use his knowledge for the benefit of the resistance. Bonhoeffer thus entered an altogether different world of activity and associations. Prohibited by the Gestapo from exercising his office as a pastor, and cut off from his church friends and colleagues, he moved about Germany and even abroad as a courier for the *Abwehr* with a freedom not permitted to respectable citizens.

In addition to journeys from Munich, where he was based (he lived for a time in the Benedictine monastery at Ettal, and was astonished to hear his own works read by the monks at meal-times), to the headquarters of his organization at Berlin, where he was able to visit his family, he was also sent abroad. In 1941 he went to Switzerland: he saw Barth, and delivered messages to Visser 't Hooft, later to be the first General Secretary of the World Council of Churches, and then keeping the threads of the ecumenical movement together in wartime from a Geneva office, while acting as a link in the conspiracy of freedom. The following year, on a journey to Sweden, he was able to meet the Bishop of Chichester in Stockholm, and tell him, for the information of the British Government, about the plans of the resistance for the overthrow of the Nazi government.

On his way back to Munich from Stockholm, he wrote to Bethge from the train:

Again and again I am driven to think about my activities, which are now concerned so much with the secular field. I am surprised that I live and can live without the Bible for days. I would say: it is not obedience but auto-suggestion if I should force myself to the daily meditation. I know, such meditation would be of great help – and indeed it is. But I am afraid that I would in this way falsify a real experience and that at last I would not get the real help. If I open the Bible again after such a period, it is new and rewarding as ever, and I eagerly want to preach once again. I know very well that I must only open my own books in order to hear all that there is to be said against it. I do not want to justify myself, and I observe that I have gone through much richer spiritual periods. But I feel the resistance growing in me against all religiosity (*das Religiöse*), sometimes reaching the level of an instinctive horror – surely, this is not good either. Yet I am not a religious nature (*eine religiöse Natur*) at all. But all the time I am forced to think of God or Christ, of genuineness (*Echtheit*), life, freedom, charity – that matters for me. What causes me uneasiness is just the religious clothing. Do you understand? This is no new concept at all, no new insights, but because I believe an idea will come to burst upon me I let things run and do not offer resistance. In this sense I understand my present activity in the secular sector.[14]

The new idea that did indeed burst upon him did not arrive until this activity had been brought to an end by imprisonment.

Bonhoeffer had for a number of years been an object of suspicion to the Gestapo, and his cover as a civilian agent for the *Abwehr* proved insufficient to allay these suspicions. In the autumn of 1942, one of his Munich superiors was arrested by the Gestapo, and talked. Bonhoeffer knew that imprisonment could not be far away. In April 1943 he was arrested, and held in prison at Tegel, near Berlin. He just had time before his arrest to hide some of his papers, and to give his messages to his family, and

14. Eberhard Bethge, 'The Challenge of Dietrich Bonhoeffer's Life and Theology' in *World Come of Age*, ed. R. Gregor Smith, Collins, 1967, pp. 70 f.

to Eberhard Bethge, who was staying with them at the time. The remainder of his life would be spent in prison, but theologically it was the most fruitful period of all.

There is much evidence to suggest that theology is particularly sensitive to the environment in which it is thought out and written. Most theologians, including those discussed in the present volume, have led a stable life in a university or seminary, and their most important encounters have been with other theologians, through their books or in conference. Those Christians who live in the parish ministry, or as laymen in secular jobs, have contributed less to theology so far than their academic brethren. Undoubtedly the demands of scholarly work are heavy, and normally impose upon the researcher a certain withdrawal from the business of ordinary life. It may be, however, that theologians suffer more from this necessary withdrawal than their colleagues in other disciplines, and that theology would have acquired a richer stock of ideas and concepts had it been written by people living in other circumstances.

More than most theologians, Bonhoeffer experienced changes of environment, but he went on reflecting, meditating and giving theological shape to his thoughts through every change. He began his life in the academic world, and everything at first pointed to a brilliant career for him as a professor. But he interrupted the course of this career, first to go to Spain as a curate and to America, then as chaplain to the German congregations in London. When he returned to Germany, he left the milieu of the university for that of an embattled church, and within the church he withdrew still deeper into concentration upon essentials in the life of the brotherhood he led. After this almost monastic phase, which is reflected in the books of the period, *The Cost of Discipleship* and *Life Together*, he found his connexion with the church, to which he had given himself so completely, gradually being severed by circumstances outside his control, until he found himself living a wholly secular life as a plain-clothes agent.

The letter quoted above reflects the impact upon his monastic spirituality of this experience of the 'secular sector'. In prison, he found the last two phases coming together. On one hand, nothing could be more worldly than his existence as a prisoner, without any of the social structures of the church to help him identify as a religious person. On the other hand, his prison cell could also be in part the monastic cell, and he returned to his devotional practices, or to some of them, with gratitude. The theology of the prison letters reflects the tension between this total worldliness, stripping down to the bare bones of human existence, with only vestigial social roles, let alone ecclesiastical ones, left to him, and the continuing religiousness of his inner life in the cell. It was from this tension in his experience that the discoveries of his last period were to come.

THE PRISON WRITINGS

The works of the last period of his life were the *Ethics* and the *Letters and Papers from Prison*;[15] both of these are posthumous works, compiled and arranged by Bethge. The *Ethics* would have been, Bonhoeffer hoped, his most important work so far, and at one point he wrote that all he now hoped for from life was to be spared long enough to finish it. However, what we have is not a finished work, but a collection of drafts and more or less finished essays on particular topics, woven together into something like a book by its editor. Bethge tells us that the material represents four different stages of Bonhoeffer's thinking. The material ranges from technical discussions of matters traditionally treated in Lutheran ethical writing, and of interest to few but specialists, to vivid meditations on the teaching of Jesus. The book is difficult to read consecutively, but full of insights to reward those who persevere with it. All the same, it can hardly be recommended to a non-theologian who has not already acquired a great interest in Bonhoeffer from his other writings. A reader with such an

15. *Ethics*, tr. by N. H. Smith, S.C.M. Press, 1953; Collins, Fontana Library, 1964: this paperback edition has the material re-arranged to follow the order of the later German editions, and is to be preferred. *Letters and Papers from Prison*, tr. by R. H. Fuller, S.C.M. Press, 1953; Collins, Fontana Library, 1959; references here are to this paperback edition. A superior, revised translation was issued by the S.C.M. Press too late for use in this book. The German is *Widerstand und Ergebung*, Munich, Chr. Kaiser Verlag, 1951.

interest will find that the *Ethics* sheds much light on a number of passages in the prison letters, and helps to fill out their thought. Its composition, however, dates in the main from the somewhat earlier period of his life with the *Abwehr*.

We have already noted that the important new discovery of Bonhoeffer's prison period had to do with the deepening of an already traditional neo-orthodox criticism of religion. The question of religion is broached almost at once in the theological passage of the famous letter of 30 April 1944:

> I am constantly moved by the question what Christianity really is, or who Christ really is, for us today. The time in which everything could be said to men by means of words, whether theological or pious, is over. So too is the time of inwardness or conscience, which means the time of religion in general. We are moving towards a completely religionless time. Men as they are simply cannot be religious any more. ... Our entire 1,900-year-old Christian preaching and theology are based upon the religious *a priori* of men.[16]

The way in which Bonhoeffer raises the questions in this letter should occupy us for a moment before we consider the answers he wishes to give. We can detect in the way things are put in the very first sentence of this quotation the influence upon Bonhoeffer of the two great movements of thought in modern theology, liberalism and neo-orthodoxy. 'What Christianity really is for us today' might be the liberal question, but Bonhoeffer at once sharpens it characteristically, and gives it a neo-orthodox and even personal turn, when he asks the question again, in the form, '*who Christ* really is for us today'. To ask the theological question in a Christological form is characteristic of the school of thought of Barth, to which Bonhoeffer certainly felt himself to belong, though as an independent thinker. But it is also worth noting that to ask *who* (as opposed to *what*) Christ is for us, is characteristic of Bonhoeffer's own way of putting the Christological issue, as shown in his early works.

So the question is, who Christ is for us, but it cannot be answered as it has been answered before, on the basis of a religious

16. As translated by R. Gregor Smith, *World Come of Age*, Collins, 1967, Introduction, p. 14.

a priori. Even now, we have moved beyond the scope of Barth's criticism of religion; for the latter, the criticism of religion is part of his continual struggle with the liberals, but Bonhoeffer now speaks of a 1,900-year-old basis for preaching and theology in the religious *a priori*. It is no longer just liberalism that is under criticism. On the contrary, some of the liberal questions are returning, and in a sharper form than before. Instead, the whole of traditional Christian thought is now seen from a new perspective, created by the arrival of a time unknown to all the theologians of the past, a time of no religion at all. That time has not yet fully come, but it is very near, and Bonhoeffer believes that the theologian must do his work henceforward in the expectation of its coming, and so without reliance upon the religious *a priori*.

Karl Barth's criticism of religion helped him to escape from a liberal way of dealing with the problems of theology, and to recover a sense of intellectual community with the Reformation writers and even with the church fathers. Bonhoeffer's criticism of religion set him apart from all previous theologians, including Barth himself. He now saw their work as conditioned by a premise which had disappeared. It is not the content of traditional theology that he questions: in this respect he does not follow the liberals, but is wholly with Barth, against what he understands of Bultmann. What he feels obliged to call in question is rather the religious expression, or interpretation, of Christianity, as he finds it even in Barth, the famous critic of religion. Accordingly, he must call for the reinterpretation without the aid of the religious premise of the whole of traditional doctrine, including the doctrine of God, which had been left almost untouched even by the demythologizing programme of Bultmann. This criticism, not just of his immediate predecessors, but of the whole past of theology, seems to set Bonhoeffer apart from his older contemporaries, and to place him rather with the so-called radical theologians of today, who owe so much to him, even when they do not follow his thought in detail.

The new idea, therefore, is not just the criticism of religion from the standpoint of Christology and the church, for this would not have been new. It had long been a feature of his own theology, and in any case was shared with Barth and others. What is new is the perception that religion is not a universal human premise, that a theologian can use, with the liberals, or reject, with Barth, in the name of revelation in Christ, but a time-conditioned phenomenon, that happens to have co-existed with Christianity throughout its history, but is now passing away. Barth had defined religion as unbelief, and therefore had regarded it as a permanent companion of faith while history lasts. Hence, in spite of the title (as usually translated) of his section on religion, he could not actually look forward to the *abolition* in any complete sense of religion, but must see it as continuing on, under the justifying grace of God. As Bonhoeffer says in the same letter and in the following one, although Barth was the first to begin the criticism of religion, he ends up with a restoration.

Bonhoeffer's own view of religion is nowhere fully worked out, and as Bethge himself points out,[17] cannot stand on its own feet without the companion ideas of his Christology and that of the coming of age of man, to which we must turn in a moment. It is clear, though, that it differs from Barth's in important ways, characteristic of Bonhoeffer's mind. His view of religion is much more concrete, even sociological, than Barth's. Hence he is less concerned with its sinfulness, as unbelief, than with its historically conditioned character. Had he chosen to concentrate upon the question of unbelief, in the manner of Barth, he could still have argued that while unbelief will certainly accompany faith until it becomes sight, there is no reason for it to take the form of religion in every cultural situation. Today, in fact, unbelief much more characteristically takes the form of godlessness. Here is another difference: Barth in his own writings makes it clear that he does not think there is such a thing as godlessness. Everyone worships something, even if only money or sex. For Bonhoeffer, on the other hand, the godless are not covert idolaters. 'The truth is, we've given up worshipping everything, even idols. In fact, we're absolute nihilists' (27 June 1944). Bonhoeffer does not, I think, anywhere spell the argument out,

---

17. Eberhard Bethge, 'The Challenge of Dietrich Bonhoeffer's Life and Theology' in *World Come of Age*, ed. R. Gregor Smith, Collins, 1967, pp. 78 f.

but he alludes to it in the letter of 18 July 1944, when he says: 'When we speak of God in a non-religious way, we must not gloss over the ungodliness of the world, but expose it in a new light. Now it has come of age, the world is more godless, and perhaps it is for that very reason nearer to God than ever before.' This last suggestion makes sense if we remember that in the Gospels the publicans are represented as nearer to God (because God is nearer to them) than the Pharisees. The religious man is, as Barth had shown, an idolater. The godless man is not: he may not have the self-righteous pretensions of the religious man, which get in the way of grace.

But the unbelief, or idolatry, of religion is not uppermost for Bonhoeffer, as for Barth. What concerns him is the fact that religion has always hitherto provided a terminology and a social and cultural framework, within which the Christian faith had automatically been set. If such a framework, or garment, as he calls it, is no longer available, Christianity will have to be understood in a wholly new way, non-religiously. In the last letters, he is searching for this new understanding. It emerges gradually, partly in discussion with the views of his elders, Barth and Bultmann. In the first reference to his new idea, in the letter of 30 April 1944, he mentions 'inwardness and conscience' as marks of religion; in the same sentence he implies that religion could be fully expressed in words. Religion has to do with the inner life of man and his problems of conscience, whereas contemporary men are concerned with outward action and their relationship with others. They are more concerned with social problems than the matters that cause guilt to individuals, and they ought to be, in the opinion of Bonhoeffer. In various letters he pours scorn on the apologists who search out people's weaknesses and peccadilloes in order to label them as sins and offer the religious remedy they have to sell. In this sense, religion becomes what Bethge calls the 'spiritual chemist's shop', full of remedies for sins.[18]

The same letter adds metaphysics as another mark of religion. At first sight, this seems a little odd, if we remember the liberal use of religion to make up in apologetics for the collapse of

18. art. cit., p. 80.

metaphysics in philosophy. What Bonhoeffer here has in mind as religious appears to be the postulation of another, transcendent world beyond this one, in which God is located, and from which this world is to gain completion. Bonhoeffer here identifies metaphysics as something which even the early Barth employs in his neo-Kantian talk about God as beyond human limits. Bonhoeffer calls in question even the notion of the limit, or boundary, of human existence, at least as a presupposition on which talk about God can be based. Science and technology are always extending these limits, and so reducing the area in which a God thus metaphysically conceived can be located. Such a God is always in fact a mere *deus ex machina*, whom man calls on out of laziness or despair, when his own resources seem to have come to an end. But later on human resources will not be so limited, and then the *deus ex machina* will be no longer needed or invoked.

In the next letter, metaphysics is again mentioned, but now alongside individualism. Religion is the concern for individual salvation. 'Today we are under the impression that there are more important things to bother about.' Shocking as this sounds to the pious, Bonhoeffer believes that it is the outlook of the Bible. The Old Testament knows nothing of the salvation of individual souls, and the New is concerned with the whole world, 'as created and preserved and set subject to laws and atoned for and made new'. Christianity is not a religion of salvation, because it is not concerned with the salvation of individuals as such, nor with a hope for man lying altogether beyond this world.

If God is conceived of as beyond human limits, as outside the sphere of man, then religion becomes a special province of life for relating to what is outside the limits, or a special space in which room is made for God. But this is the wrong way to think of God. 'I should like to speak of God not on the borders of life but at its centre, not in weakness but in strength, not, therefore, in man's suffering and death but in his life and prosperity.' The *reductio ad absurdum* of this view of God is the one reflected in insurance policies, where an 'act of God' is an event which cannot be predicted in the statistics, and so insured against. But even the insurance companies know that this kind of event cannot be explained, but must simply be accepted. Bonhoeffer thinks that men should not use religion at points where human resources give out. Such situations ought to be borne with patience and resignation, without invoking religious explanations. Once religion is thought of as a special province of life for relating to the metaphysical realm, those who are religious come to think of themselves as privileged in relation to other men. To be religious is to have a sort of class privilege, which sets one apart from other men, rather than freeing one for solidarity with others.

Bonhoeffer's Lutheran tradition offers him a theological category into which this new view of religion can be fitted. The Jewish law was likewise a time-conditioned garment for faith, which Christ brought to an end. This was a great issue for Paul, who argues in the Epistle to the Galatians that circumcision cannot be a condition for justification. Both Jewish and Gentile Christians are set free by Christ from the obligation to keep the Jewish law, which circumcision entails. Once he is justified by faith, the Jew need not continue to keep the Jewish law, and the Gentile must not be asked to, nor must he voluntarily submit to doing so, as a condition of participation in the church. Bonhoeffer thinks that religion presents the same issue today.

The religionless man of today must not be asked to become religious first, in order to believe in and follow Christ. Similarly, the man who is an inheritor of the religious culture of Christianity can be set free from it by Christ, and liberated for fuller participation in the world.

I often ask myself why a Christian instinct frequently draws me more to the religionless than to the religious, by which I mean not with any intention of evangelizing them, but rather, I might almost say, in 'brotherhood'. While I often shrink with religious people from speaking of God by name – because that name somehow seems to me here not to ring true, and I strike myself as rather dishonest (it is especially bad when others start talking in religious jargon; then I dry up almost completely, and feel somehow oppressed and ill at ease) – with people who have no religion I am able on occasion to speak of God quite openly and as it were naturally. (30 April 1944.)

It follows that the religious premise is useless as an apologetic except among people whose 'conversion' would perhaps not add anything to the church that it should be glad to have (the 'last survivors of the age of chivalry', as Bonhoeffer ironically calls them). At worst it is ignoble and degrading, 'a snuffing about among people's sins'.

What is the relation of Bonhoeffer's view to those of Barth and Bultmann? We have already considered in part the difference between Bonhoeffer's idea of religion and the one we earlier met with in Barth, but we have not yet specifically heard his own criticism of Barth's view, except as a restoration. Barth is the only theologian to have begun the criticism of religion, but he has not (unlike Bonhoeffer) carried it to its proper conclusion. In consequence, he has arrived at what Bonhoeffer somewhat puzzlingly calls a 'positivism of revelation'. He therefore doesn't think Barth's criticism of religion makes any real difference to the way the Gospel will appear to the religionless working man, or indeed anyone in general. What is this 'positivism of revelation' (*Offenbarungspositivismus*)? When Bonhoeffer refers to it again, in the letter of 5 May 1944, he tells us that it is a doctrine which says in effect, Take it or leave it (*Iss, Vogel, oder stirb*): Virgin Birth, Trinity, or anything else, are all equally significant and necessary parts of the whole, which has to be swallowed as a whole or not at all.

Bonhoeffer's point seems to be that once Barth had abandoned religion as a basis for theology and turned to revelation, while preserving the structure of the old orthodoxy, the content of the Christian faith has become foreign to man. Indeed, Barth insists strenuously that that is exactly what it is. It must be accepted on trust from the church, simply because it is revealed or thought by the church to be bound up with revelation, without interpretation, and without a distinction being made (as the liberals were able to) between what is of first importance and what is secondary, or a consequence of other matters. Likewise, no distinction is made between what can be learned at once, and what will only become intelligible later. In German thought, positivity or positivism refers to a presentation of Christianity as simply given, without a rational explanation being offered. The conservatives called themselves positive theologians because they accepted the deposit of faith as given. Barth does not intend to be a conservative, but Bonhoeffer thinks he has fallen back into this bad sense of positivism, when he moved from the dialectic of his early thought into the 'positive' theology of his maturity (here however 'positive' is the opposite of negative, not the opposite of rational). On the other hand, as his criticism of Bultmann shows, Bonhoeffer does not wish to go along with the liberals in distinguishing between the essence of Christianity and its non-essential aspects. Is he trying to have things both ways?

His own answer to Barth is twofold. On the one hand, a systematic reinterpretation of Christian ideas is necessary. Christianity must be interpreted 'in the manner of the world'. What this means Bonhoeffer does not yet know, though he has some preliminary ideas. But perhaps not everything can be reinterpreted at once. To safeguard the continuing worldly interpretation from becoming mere reductionism (as in the case of liberalism) there must be introduced something analogous to what the ancient church called 'the discipline of the secret' (*disciplina arcani*), 'whereby the mysteries of the Christian faith are preserved from profanation'.

The discipline of secrecy, as we may call it, is the second part of the answer, but it is not easy to imagine exactly what Bonhoeffer had in mind. Certainly there is a reference to the practice of the ancient church, from the third to perhaps the fifth century, of keeping secret both what took place in its central rites of baptism and the eucharist, and the text of its sacred formularies, such as the Lord's prayer and the creed. These were only taught to the candidate for membership of the church just before his initiation. In all probability, the practice was learned from the mystery religions of the Graeco-Roman world, and indicates a feeling on the part of churchmen that Christianity was likewise a mystery, open only to the initiated. The matters protected by the discipline were not to be made public, nor to form part of evangelism or apologetics. How Bonhoeffer thought a revived discipline of secrecy could be useful in the non-religious interpretation of Christianity cannot be fully determined from the two references to the matter in the letters,[19] and interpreters of his thought disagree on what he meant. There is, however, considerable agreement that the point is an important one.[20]

The standard English translation of the *Letters and Papers from Prison* translates the German word *Arkandisziplin*, which Bonhoeffer uses here, as 'secret discipline', and almost all interpreters writing in English have followed this usage. If this translation is correct, the meaning will be that a discipline of prayer and worship is to be kept up secretly, to safeguard non-religious Christianity from too great worldliness and loss of spiritual depth. Though the German word is apparently patient of this translation, and some German writings seem to adopt this type of interpretation, the Latin term that lies behind it is not. *Arkandisziplin* is simply the normal rendering in theological German of the Latin phrase *disciplina arcani*, and is so used by writers on the practice of the ancient church just described.[21] Since Bonhoeffer introduced the term without explanation, it is most probable that he was using it in its normal meaning among theologians, and not in some novel one, as the English-speaking interpretations must presume, following the usual translation. In that case, the 'discipline' can hardly be the individual's practice of prayer and devotion, or even the liturgical worship of the church. The Latin phrase does not refer to a discipline which is to be carried on in secret, but to a discipline which consists in the preservation of secrecy about something else. More loosely, it can be taken to mean a teaching which is kept secret. Thus, the usual interpretation that has Bonhoeffer balance his emphasis on non-religious Christianity with a secret discipline of prayer, though it corresponds to his own practice, misses the point he meant to make. That point was primarily a theological one. He wished to find a non-religious interpretation of Christianity, without falling into the reductionism of liberal theology. He might well have thought the usual interpretations in English

19. 30 April 1944, *Letters and Papers*, p. 92; 5 May 1944, ibid., p. 95.

20. So e.g. Bethge himself, art. cit., p. 82.

21. e.g. F. X. Funk, *Das Alter der Arkandisziplin*, Paderborn, 1907. See also the explanation in Duden's *Lexikon*, *Fremdwörterbuch* volume, s.v. *Arkandisziplin*.

open to the charge of 'inwardness', and thus of relapsing into religiousness.[22]

To judge from the few clues available to us, Bonhoeffer thought the *Arkandisziplin* relevant for meeting major difficulties attending the non-religious, or worldly, interpretation of Christianity, during the period when it must remain only partially achieved. Bonhoeffer, let us repeat, did not call for any reduction in the content of Christianity. But he was unable to see, for the present, how some of the central doctrines and practices, such as prayer and worship, could be interpreted in a worldly manner. How, too, does one speak in a worldly manner of God? These matters must not be abandoned, but protected by the discipline of secrecy until they can be reinterpreted. He also links the discipline with a distinction he had made in his *Ethics*, between the ultimate and the penultimate, where the affirmation of the penultimate, the ordinary life of man, governed by morality and justice rather than justification by grace alone, can safeguard the ultimate itself from cheapening.[23]

As against Barth, therefore, Bonhoeffer invokes the function of the discipline of secrecy in preserving what he calls 'degrees of perception and degrees of significance'. To thrust everything before the world at once and as a whole is to make a law out of faith, instead of a gift, as Christ intended. From another point of view, though Bonhoeffer himself does not mention this, to thrust the whole uninterpreted package before the world, as Barth does, comes close to 'casting pearls before swine'; this uncomfortable text might turn out to be relevant precisely in this context. To refuse to make the distinctions implied in a discipline of secrecy, between what may be said to the world and what can only become intelligible to the initiate, does not help the conversion of the world either. It has the effect of 'leaving the world to itself'. Preaching that does not refer to the life of the world, but to the closed and privileged sphere of religion, which the world regards as either non-existent or trivial, will not draw the

22. For another view, see R. H. Fuller in Martin E. Marty (ed.), *The Place of Bonhoeffer*, S.C.M. Press, 1963; also R. Gregor Smith, in (most recently) *World Come of Age*, Collins, 1967, p. 14.

23. *Ethics*, Fontana edition, pp. 125 ff.

world into the church. If all the church can offer is 'positivism of revelation', or uninterpreted religious doctrine taken as an indissoluble whole, the world will have been offered no alternative to going its own way.

As against the older liberal theology, however, Bonhoeffer is with Barth in insisting that the Gospel itself is not to be reduced to what the world can at present comprehend. Thus, the theologian must not identify the content of the Gospel with what he can at present succeed in interpreting after the manner of the world. What is to be done with the all-important residuum, that the theologian cannot yet reinterpret, or the world, by the same token, yet understand? About this there is to be silence, so far as words are concerned. It seems that Bonhoeffer would have liked a moratorium upon evangelism as it is generally understood, in the sense of trying to explain the innermost mysteries of Christianity by rhetoric, and likewise upon public debate among theologians about such topics as God-talk, or the theology and practice of Christian worship. But within the *arcanum* itself, all these things are to be retained intact, presenting a continual challenge to the theologian's task of interpretation. The *arcanum* is not meant to be a shield, therefore, behind which the Christian can hide a religiousness he is in fact afraid to abandon, though he knows he must speak to a world which has already done so. Rather, he must take the *arcanum* with him into the world, in the form of a reticence of speech and deportment, contrasting sharply with the ready tongue of the evangelist. But there is also the hint, to be developed later, that actions may be a more appropriate form of communication.[24]

The idea of a discipline of secrecy is not without its dangers, whether interpreted theologically, as here, or more pietistically, as in the usual explanation. It is perhaps not surprising that the early church did not long maintain its own version of the discipline. At best, it must seem to be a stopgap, and at worst, a means of maintaining after it has become theologically unjustifiable the separation between the church and the world, in

24. My own interpretation of the *Arkandisziplin* received much help from a discussion I was able to have with Professor Hans W. Frei; however, he should not be blamed for any mistakes I may have made above.

the sense that the church inhabits a mysterious religious sphere, altogether apart from the world. That is just what Bonhoeffer wanted to avoid. Bonhoeffer was in agreement with Bultmann about the urgent necessity of interpretation. He calls for fresh interpretation emphatically in his related criticism of Bultmann, which is perhaps even more important for our understanding of his total project than his criticism of Barth, though it is expressed somewhat inadequately in the letters. A recently published letter shows that Bultmann is also among the sources for the new ideas of Bonhoeffer during his prison period.[25] He welcomed Bultmann's essay on 'New Testament and Mythology', which he and Bethge had read when it was circulated in mimeographed form, if only because it 'let the liberal cat out of the bag'. Unfortunately, as this phrase from the letter now published, and the references in the prison writings, suggest, he also misunderstood Bultmann's intentions, supposing that the latter's project implied the reduction of the Gospel to its essence, after the manner of the liberals. As we have noted above, Bultmann in fact deliberately rejected this project for himself, and, just as Bonhoeffer does, associated himself with Barth's criticism of liberalism, that it sacrificed the substance of the Gospel to apologetics. Both men do consider that neo-orthodoxy had begun to shirk the liberal questions, especially in the second phase of the Confessing Church's career, and to move towards orthodoxy in the older sense, becoming conservative, and anxious to protect the church as an institution.

Bonhoeffer thinks that the usual criticism of Bultmann, on the ground that he went too far in his demythologizing project, is mistaken. He did not go far enough, because he supposed, wrongly, that the mythology could be detached from 'the thing itself', the Gospel. You cannot, in the opinion of Bonhoeffer, separate 'God and miracles, but you do have to be able to interpret and proclaim *both* of them in a non-religious sense'. So Bonhoeffer wishes to say that if mythology is the right category, though he prefers religion, even God cannot be exempt from demythologizing: on the other hand, such matters as miracles,

25. Given in German and in English in John A. Phillips, *The Form of Christ in the World*, Collins, 1967, pp. 249 ff.

especially the resurrection, are inseparable from God, and must be retained and interpreted, not discarded along with the pre-scientific picture of the world. Perhaps one of the greatest losses of the post-war theological scene is the debate we should have had between Bultmann and Bonhoeffer, who could have been in far better communication with Bultmann than Barth.

Bultmann and Bonhoeffer share a concern for interpreting the Gospel in a contemporary manner, but they approach the problem from different points of view. They agree, with one another and with Barth, that the Gospel comes to man from outside his culture, and is therefore not to be understood wholly in its terms, i.e. as religion. They also agree (*pace* both Barth and Bonhoeffer, who think of Bultmann as reductionist) that the whole substance of the Gospel is to be preserved in any such reinterpretation. But Bonhoeffer's programme is both more conservative and more radical than Bultmann's. It is more conservative, in that with Barth he wants to retain the miraculous elements in the Gospel, as bound up with God himself. It is more radical, in that he wishes to jettison not just nineteenth-century religion and first-century mythology, but all religion, and thus to reinterpret even God. He regards Bultmann, like Barth, as still implicitly accepting the religious *a priori*, especially in what he takes from Heidegger.

We have now considered what Bonhoeffer meant by religion, and the difference between his view of it and those of his seniors in the movement of contemporary theology. But we have not yet considered the reasons why he thinks religion is coming to an end. To do this will introduce us to what Bethge thinks is the distinctive idea of the prison letters, that of the world come of age (*mündige Welt*). This idea dates back to the Enlightenment, and Bethge here gives a reference to Kant. Bonhoeffer dates the beginning of the fact to the thirteenth century, without wanting to argue about exact dates:

The movement towards the autonomy of man (under which head I place the discovery of the laws by which the world lives and manages in science, social and political affairs, art, ethics and religion) has in our time reached a certain completion. Man has learned to cope with all questions of importance without recourse to God as a working hypothesis. In questions concerning science, art or even ethics, this has become an understood thing which one scarcely dares to tilt at any more. But for the last hundred years or so it has been increasingly true of religious questions also; it is becoming evident that everything gets along without 'God' and just as well as before. As in the scientific field, so in human affairs generally, what we call 'God' is being more and more edged out of life, losing more and more ground.

Catholic and Protestant historians are agreed that it is in this development that the great defection from God, from Christ, is to be discerned, and the more they bring in and make use of God and Christ in opposition to this trend, the more the trend considers itself to be anti-Christian. The world which has attained to a realization of itself and the laws which govern its existence is so sure of itself that we become frightened. False starts and failures do not make the world deviate from the path and development it is following; they are accepted with fortitude and detachment as part of the bargain, and even an event like the present war is no exception. Christian apologetic has taken the most varying forms of opposition to this self-assurance. Efforts are made to prove to a world *thus come of age* that it cannot live without the tutelage of 'God'. Even though there has been surrender on all secular problems, there still remain the so-called ultimate questions – death, guilt – on which only 'God' can furnish an answer, and which are the reason why God and the church and the pastor are needed. Thus we live, to some extent, on these ultimate questions of humanity. But what if they one day no longer exist as such, if they too can be answered without 'God'? (8 June 1944; italics mine.)[26]

Bonhoeffer has been criticized by Barth among others for taking the world too much at its own valuation in passages such as this. The world has no such maturity as is here spoken of, they contend. So it still needs what the church has to offer. But Bonhoeffer does not suggest that the world has the sort of spiritual maturity a man might receive through faith in Christ. The point is that in its own life it is autonomous. It does not need the tutelage of 'God', and to conceive God in turn as that which the world needs for its completion is to misconceive him religiously. Eventually, even if not now, it will become fully apparent that the world does not need such a God, and then where will the apologetic be? Moreover, Bonhoeffer sees the

26. *Letters and Papers from Prison*, pp. 106 f.

movement towards autonomy, towards dispensing with God, as in line with the movement of the incarnation itself.

The important letter of 16 July 1944 adds to the notion of the world come of age, and relates it to the contrast between the religious idea of 'God as a working hypothesis' and 'the God of the Bible', who is made known in the weakness of Christ. The phrase, 'God as a working hypothesis', is a reference to Laplace's famous reply to Napoleon, when the latter asked him what place God had in his new cosmology: 'We have no need of this hypothesis.' Bonhoeffer points out that in every field the same development is to be seen; man grasps intellectually the autonomy of the world, and dispenses with God as a working hypothesis. When he does so, he rapidly comes to understand very much better the laws under which the world in fact operates, and finds that dispensing with God as a hypothesis is justified intellectually by its results.

Men dispensed with God not just in science but in the study of society, in ethics, philosophy and religion. Grotius, the jurist, thought of international law as a law of nature that would still be valid *etsi deus non daretur*, literally, even though God were not given, i.e. if God did not exist. The phrase evidently struck Bonhoeffer, and he repeats it in several contexts. He points out that the idea of an infinite universe has the same effect: though it logically does not rule out the existence of God, it is 'self-subsisting, *etsi deus non daretur*'. So God is totally unnecessary as a working hypothesis in any field at all. Here is the point where the religious become nervous. But the answer is not to take the bolt-hole back to the security of the Middle Ages, before man began to be autonomous.

The only way is that of Matthew xviii, 3, i.e. through repentance, through *ultimate* honesty. And the only way to be honest is to recognize that we have to live in the world *etsi deus non daretur*. And this is what we do see – before God! So our coming of age forces us to a true recognition of our situation vis-à-vis God. God is teaching us that we must live as men who can get along very well without him. The God who is with us is the God who forsakes us (Mark xv, 34). The God who makes us live in this world without using him as a working hypothesis is the God before whom we are ever standing. Before God and with him we live without God. God allows himself to be edged out of the world and on to the cross. God is weak and powerless in the world, and that is exactly the way, the only way, in which he can be with us and help us. Matthew viii, 17 makes it crystal clear that it is not by his omnipotence that Christ helps us, but by his weakness and suffering. (16 July 1944)[27]

This is one of the crucial passages for the understanding of Bonhoeffer's thought in his prison period. Here we find a dialectic between the absence and the presence of God. The God who is absent, who cannot be used as a working hypothesis, is not (as the unwary might suppose) the false God, the God of religion. He is the true God, whom Bonhoeffer elsewhere calls the God of the Bible. The false God of religion, the *deus ex machina*, is present when men want him: he comes when he is called. The true God does not: he is the one who did not come to Christ in Gethsemane and on the cross, to get him out of his difficulties. On the other hand, the false God is an illusion of religion, and therefore not really present. As an idol, he has no effective existence. The true God is present through the cross; by his suffering and powerlessness in the world he is able to give genuine help.

Here Bonhoeffer touches on what seems to be his final distinction between the false God of religion and the true God. It is the difference between weakness and power. Men want an omnipotent God, but they want his omnipotence for the purpose of supplementing their own resources when they run out. God in Christ is weak, not powerful. From the religious point of view, he fails to deliver. But that is the only way, according to Bonhoeffer, in which he really helps.

It is quite clear that the criticism of religion cannot stop short of the criticism of God; indeed, this is precisely what it entails. The most remarkable of religion's creations is its God, and if Christianity has indeed been conceived religiously for 1,900 years, its view of God will have been conditioned by religious expectations. Nowhere is it so important to remove religion from Christianity as in its doctrine of God. Bonhoeffer has clearly now moved beyond the mere observation that because religion is as a matter of fact passing away, Christianity will in future be

27. *Letters and Papers*, pp. 121 f.

interpreted non-religiously. He finds the non-religious interpretation demanded by the New Testament itself. The New
Testament conceives God through Christ, not as the metaphysical
God 'out there', ruling the world from on high. Bonhoeffer
seems to go further than any other modern theologian in refusing
to conceive God outside Christ. Above we have considered how
his Lutheran tradition made such concreteness possible.

To conceive God exclusively in Christ raises problems of all
kinds, with which Bonhoeffer does not deal. But it has two
important consequences with which he does deal. It involves a
non-metaphysical notion of transcendence, and it involves thinking of God in terms of weakness and humiliation, instead of
power and glory. It involves what Lutherans called a theology of
the cross. Bonhoeffer conceives transcendence non-metaphysically
in two ways. First, he calls on his early idea of transcendence as
a property of persons. Transcendence is in 'the nearest at hand',
not in what is infinite and remote. (Bethge translates, in a gloss
that doubtless correctly represents the meaning, the nearest *Thou*
at hand.)[28] Second, transcendence is conceived ethically. It is to
be found in Christ's being for others. As the man for others, who
has no concern for himself, he transcends existence as we know
it. So transcendence is the presence of a person who is for others.
This has nothing to do with the metaphysical notion of the
'beyond', though Bonhoeffer can also refer to transcendence as
'the Beyond in our midst'.

In such passages we already find the beginning of the interpretation of God and of Christ, 'in a worldly manner'. It begins
to be possible to answer the question asked in the 30 April letter,
'How can Christ become the Lord even of those of no religion?'
In the same letter, he already implies that if as Christians we
abandon our notion that we belong to a privileged group, and
consider that we belong wholly to the world, then 'Christ is no
longer the object of religion, but something quite different, indeed
and in truth the Lord of the world'. If we retire into religion,
Christ is also limited by our withdrawal. Only if we think of

28. More literally, 'the presently given, attainable neighbour is the transcendent'. Cf. *Letters and Papers*, p. 165. German in *Widerstand und
Ergebung*, p. 260.

ourselves in complete solidarity with the world, and abandon religious ways of thinking of Christ and of God, can Christ be today what the New Testament claims that he is. He is Lord of the world when worldly men, without ceasing to be worldly, acknowledge his Lordship, from within the world.

In the very first phrases in which the new thoughts are expressed, in the 30 April letter, Bonhoeffer remarks that the time is past when everything can be told in words. It is therefore not surprising to find that his non-religious interpretation of God and Christ is not simply a matter of words. Reinterpretation is also a matter of participation, or what in a former phase he would have called discipleship. On the one hand, Christ is the centre of life, and not a stop-gap. 'He must be found . . . in life and not only in death; in health and vigour, and not only in suffering; in activity, and not only in sin' (25 May). We must rejoice with those who rejoice, as well as weeping with those who mourn. On the other hand, more pessimistically (or realistically) Bonhoeffer refers to the image of Gethsemane, which appears to be the centre of his deepest thought about the new interpretation.

As Jesus asked in Gethsemane, Could ye not watch with me one hour? That is the exact opposite of what the religious man expects of God. *Man is challenged to participate in the sufferings of God at the hands of a godless world.* He must therefore plunge himself into the life of a godless world, without attempting to gloss over its ungodliness with a veneer of religion, or trying to transfigure it. He must live a 'worldly' life and so participate in the sufferings of God. . . . It is not some religious act that makes a Christian what he is, but participation in the sufferings of God in the life of the world. (18 July 1944.)

And more generally: 'Faith is participation in this being of Jesus (incarnation, cross and resurrection). Our relationship to God is not a religious relationship to a supreme being, absolute in power and goodness, which is a spurious conception of transcendence, but a new life for others, through participation in the being of Jesus.' (From 'Outline for a Book'.)[29]

These last passages interpret and are interpreted by Bonhoeffer's own life in the war years, leading to his death. Bonhoeffer

29. *Letters and Papers*, p. 165.

has been called a martyr, and with justification. It is important, though, to remember that he was also a martyr 'after the manner of the world'. Conservative churchmen in Germany after the war refused to honour his memory in church because he did not die for the cause of the churches, but for the political cause of resistance to Hitler. He did not give his life for religion, or even for the God of religion. He died, alongside humanists and secularists, who had been his fellow-conspirators, in the common human cause. This was how he saw participation in the sufferings of God at the hands of a godless world.

After the failure of the conspiracy in which he had been involved, his death became inevitable. When the 20 July 1944 attempt on Hitler's life led to failure and to the discovery of the resistance, the conspirators who were still at large were arrested, and Bonhoeffer's connexion with the plot became known for the first time. He was placed in close confinement in the prison on Prinz Albrecht Strasse. The following February he was removed, first to the concentration camp at Buchenwald, and later to Schönberg. For a while it seemed as if like others he might be taken south to security in the Alps, but he had been placed on the list of those who in no circumstances should be allowed to survive the war. In the first days of April, as the American forces drew nearer, the S.S. took matters into their own hands, and held summary courts-martial, without authorization from higher authority, condemning the most important of the conspirators to death. Bonhoeffer was hanged at Flossenbürg on the morning of 9 April 1945, along with Canaris, Oster and others. The same day his brother-in-law Dohnanyi was executed at Sachsenhausen.[30]

As well as letters and papers, Bonhoeffer wrote poems in prison, and some of them, notably *Christen und Heiden*, the one which begins in translation, 'Men go to God when they are sore bestead',[31] express his theological thoughts as clearly as the letters, and more succinctly. Perhaps the best summary of the meaning of his life and thought as a whole is to be found in the poem called *Stations on the Way to Freedom*:

30. Bethge, 'The Last Days', in *Letters and Papers*, pp. 176 ff.
31. op. cit., p. 174.

Dietrich Bonhoeffer – Religionless Christianity

Discipline:
If you set out to seek freedom, you must learn before all things
Mastery over sense and soul, lest your wayward desirings,
Lest your undisciplined members, lead you now this way, now that way.
Chaste be your mind and your body, and subject to you and obedient,
Serving solely to seek their appointed goal and objective.
None learns the secret of freedom save only by way of control.

Action:
Do and dare what is right, not swayed by the whim of the moment,
Bravely take hold of the real, not dallying now with what might be.
Not in the light of ideas but only in action is freedom.
Make up your mind and come out into the tempest of living.
God's command is enough, and your faith in him to sustain you.
Then at last freedom will welcome your spirit amid great rejoicing.

Suffering:
See what a transformation! These hands so active and powerful
Now are tied, and alone and fainting, you see where your work ends.
Yet you are confident still, and gladly commit what is rightful
Into a stronger hand, and say that you are contented.
You were free for a moment of bliss, then you yielded your freedom
Into the hand of God, that he might perfect it in glory.

Death:
Come now, highest of feasts on the way to freedom eternal,
Death, strike off the fetters, break down the walls that oppress us,
Our bedazzled soul and our ephemeral body,
That we may see at last the sight which here was not vouchsafed us.
Freedom we sought you long in discipline, action, suffering.
Now as we die we see you and know you at last, face to face.[32]

32. Given in verse form in *Ethics*, Fontana edition, p. 15.

Five

Paul Tillich:
Theology on
the Boundary

Tillich's work has sometimes been used to complete Bonhoeffer's unfinished thoughts from his prison period. Readers of *Honest to God* will remember the way in which the ideas of Bonhoeffer, Bultmann and Tillich are there used to supplement one another in building up a total picture of the need for a fresh understanding of God. In view of the considerable diversity of outlook among these three, the critic is at first inclined to demur at such a procedure. Yet if one considers their basic aims, and the diagnosis they offer of the contemporary intellectual and spiritual situation, it is hard not to agree with Bishop Robinson that their work points in a generally similar direction. Moreover we have recognized that Bonhoeffer's own disagreement with Bultmann is based in part upon a misunderstanding of what the older man was trying to do, and the same is, I think, true of his incidental reference to Tillich. How far is it true, as Bonhoeffer suggests, that it was the aim of Tillich to 'interpret the evolution of the world – against its will – in a religious sense, to give it its whole shape through religion?'[1] The context shows that Bonhoeffer is thinking of the early Tillich, during the period when he could be simply identified with the religious socialists. Of Tillich's work as a whole, it might be as true to say that he interprets Christianity 'in the manner of the world', as Bonhoeffer thought was necessary. Undoubtedly he and Bonhoeffer would have differed about what the manner of the world was, and certainly Tillich uses the idea of religion quite differently from Bonhoeffer. Nevertheless, no writer among the group here principally considered goes as far as Tillich in trying to give the Christian faith an expression which will render it intelligible to men of the world, while preserving its unique substance.

1. *Letters and Papers*, pp. 108 f.

Tillich goes so far in expressing Christianity in language drawn from the common intellectual tradition of the West that, even more than Bultmann, he has been taken by the supporters of Barth for a liberal. Many of the best-known books on Tillich are written to prove this thesis. If everyone who is not a strict follower of Barth is a liberal, the criticism is well-founded. Certainly Tillich does not agree with Barth on a number of the most fundamental issues, and in any case he would reject the antithesis between the aims of liberalism and the proper task of theology today, as set up by Barth. Nevertheless, it is hard to ignore the community of intention between Tillich and all the other writers here discussed on a number of crucial points at which they differ from their liberal predecessors, though this is doubtless in part a matter of the interpretation of Tillich. Tillich is as clear as Barth that the substance of the Gospel cannot be deduced from a philosophical doctrine of man. Likewise, Christology is central in Tillich's thought, though the Christology he uses is very different from Barth's. His view of the historical Jesus, though worked out in his own way, is closely related to Barth's, through a common ancestry in the last of the liberal systematic theologians.

Nevertheless, though we may think some Barthian criticisms of Tillich beside the point, it is not easy to remain faithful to Tillich's own interpretation of his work and still place him in the same general tradition as Barth. If on one side he has strong links with the theological concerns of Barth and men who stand close to him, on the other he has connexions with liberal and with Catholic thought, as well as with the philosophers, scientists, psychotherapists and artists. In fact, no sooner has a critic found a way of characterizing Tillich, than he ought, in order to be faithful to the material, to go on to say the direct opposite. This renders his thought peculiarly elusive, and interpreters, not surprisingly, differ considerably on the question of what the key to it is. Tillich's thought is perhaps best characterized therefore in his own words as theology 'on the boundary'. Tillich wishes to mediate between false antitheses, and to offer reconciliation between them.

In magnitude and intellectual calibre, the work of Tillich is comparable only to Barth's among contemporary theologians. In expression, however, it is altogether more concentrated. Into the three volumes of his *Systematic Theology* Tillich probably crams as many ideas as Barth deals with in twelve larger ones. The difference is not due only to greater compression. Tillich does not make use of the lengthy exegetical discussions and reviews of the work of other theologians, past and present, that occupy the fine print in Barth's volumes. He is content to isolate ideas and issues in their sharpest form, and to work with these rather than with the raw material from which they have been drawn. Tillich's work contains few and short footnotes. Though it is as a rule elegantly and clearly expressed, its difficulty lies usually in its abstractness rather than in the quantity of material it is necessary for the reader to understand. To summarize Tillich is even harder than to summarize Barth, for if anything is left out the argument usually suffers. Not many readers will have an equal appreciation of both men, and yet they complement one another. If we turn to Barth for the strongest expression of what the Christian faith is, in roughly its traditional form, we must turn to Tillich for the relationship of that faith to modern man's intellectual life and creative work.

TILLICH'S PRESENTATION OF THE GOSPEL

Tillich believed that men found a different aspect of the Gospel relevant to their condition in each age. The early church was preoccupied with the question of death, and expressed the Gospel primarily as the gift of immortality, through participation in the resurrection of Christ, and union with God, or deification. The Middle Ages, and even more the period of the Reformation, were preoccupied with guilt, and hence the dynamic of the Reformers' understanding of the Gospel lay in its message about the grace of God, overcoming man's separation from God through guilt, and expressed in the doctrine of justification by grace through faith. Today, however, this doctrine is barely intelligible without special training, and the question it answers is no longer central to human existence. Our question today, Tillich thought, comes from our experience of the contradictions

235

and estrangement inherent in man's life as a finite being under the conditions of 'existence'. The Christian message for today is that of the New Being in Jesus the Christ, as our ultimate concern. The New Being in Jesus the Christ is the theological centre of Tillich's thought, and it is this that he believes the church should now proclaim to the world, and of which he himself speaks in the remarkable sermons, collected together in the three volumes, *The Shaking of the Foundations*, *The New Being* and *The Eternal Now*.

The idea of the New Being is intimately connected with Tillich's way of speaking about God, as being-itself, or the power of being, or the ground of our being. Being is that which resists non-being, or nothingness: the power of being, or the ground of being, is what enables the particular beings (of which being-itself is not one) to resist collapse into nothingness. Thus the Gospel for Tillich is concerned with what a well-known existential psychiatrist has called 'ontological security'.[2] Man's being stands under the threat of non-being, but the Gospel assures him that the New Being has appeared under the conditions of finite existence in Jesus, and so his own existence is ever buoyed up by the infinite power of being-itself, or God.

The contemporary question about existence, to which Tillich's theology presents the answer drawn from the Gospel, does not wholly replace or rule out older questions and answers, for each of the questions that has led to the development of a distinctive approach to the Gospel in the time that it was being asked arises from some permanent aspect of finite existence. Yet in different situations in history, different aspects of existence force themselves on man's experience, and in Tillich's opinion, the evidence of writers, artists and philosophers, who see most deeply into the situation at any given time, points to the conclusion that today the question is of being, man's being as poised over the abyss of non-being, and constantly threatened by the destructive power of non-being.

The formulation of the existential question for today includes the questions that were most vivid to the men of the past. That

2. See R. D. Laing, *The Divided Self*, Penguin Books, 1965.

this is so may be concluded from one of the most popular of Tillich's works, *The Courage to Be*, which is closely related to the more esoteric themes of the *Systematic Theology*. In this book, Tillich contrasts the anxiety described by existentialists with that courage with which he identifies the standpoint of faith. The anxiety he has in mind is not the relatively superficial neurotic anxiety which can sometimes be removed by psychotherapy, but rather the anxiety, felt most deeply by the healthiest and most sensitive of people, which arises from the very conditions of human being, poised as it is over non-being. This anxiety takes a three-fold form: there is the anxiety of fate and death, the anxiety of guilt, and the anxiety of meaninglessness. Tillich sees clearly how religion can intensify these anxieties by giving them radical expression. Under their weight and darkness, God himself may disappear from view. Tillich tries to show how the courage to be arises from the very depths to which such anxiety pushes men, when in ultimate concern their questioning goes beyond even the God of religion, to what he calls the God beyond God. The courage to be reflects the consequent realization that God, as being-itself, is at the depth of all finite being, including one's own.

This is a highly distinctive presentation of the Gospel. Its fuller implications will become apparent to us as we examine different aspects of Tillich's thought. Whether it is genuinely contemporary depends upon the reliability of Tillich's intuitions about our existence today, supported by the artists and existentialist philosophers whom he regards as its spokesmen. Clearly, it cannot be separated from a certain way of thinking about human life, which we find in its most distinctive expression in a number of existentialist philosophers and theologians, including Tillich himself. Tillich does not lay the emphasis where Protestant theologians traditionally have, on the question of sin and the forgiveness of sins, yet he does not ignore this question either. As we shall see, he is firmly in the Protestant tradition, but he is also aware of the difficulty of bringing home to the man of today the meaning of the traditional Protestant language. Perhaps Tillich's emphasis upon the New Being, as overcoming estrangement, can be related to Barth's wish to show how God's Yes prevails over every No, and Bultmann's wish to show that the Gospel delivers man from the false security of the world of things, setting him free to live in critical detachment, and openness to the future. All these men proclaim an ultimate and unshakeable security, available to those who can part with self-conferred and illusory security.

Tillich speaks of this Gospel in all his writings. But he does not speak of it in the same way in every group of them. In the *Systematic Theology* he speaks esoterically, to those within the circle of the theologically and philosophically sophisticated, who can interpret the religious symbols and refer them to their ultimate source, beyond the contradictions of essence and existence, and perhaps beyond even such symbols as the personal God of the Bible. To this group belong also a number of his other more academic and philosophical writings. A second group is concerned with the problems of man in his community life and culture, including the interpretation of history. Here the primary theme is religious socialism as the hope for society, in which the estrangements of men from one another and of all human life from God are partially overcome in a society positively related to God, but free of theocratic or class dominance. This group of writings belongs for the most part to his early and middle periods, and is brought to an end by the disillusionment arising from the events of the second world war, and the post-war period. Hope for a society positively related to God has come to seem very remote, and the task is not now to announce that the historic moment of its realization is near at hand, but to wait for it, with no immediate hope for its appearance. The sermons constitute the third group, with *The Courage to Be* as a bridge to the first, and this is the most accessible of the three groups. If the *Systematic Theology* is the esoteric side of Tillich, this is the exoteric. Here the symbols are used almost as they stand, yet the interpretation is always present for the benefit of the initiated reader, and the person who is inclined to take the religious symbols literally is led a little way along the path to a deeper understanding. Most readers would be best advised to begin their study of Tillich with this third group of writings, and even those who find that they cannot come to terms with the esoteric Tillich will discover much to win their gratitude in these beautiful and moving utterances.

In calling the Tillich of the *Systematic Theology* esoteric I have been paradoxical, for Tillich's systematic theology is intended to be apologetic as well as kerygmatic, to explain the meaning of the Gospel in intelligible contemporary terms, as well as to proclaim it as irreducible revelation. Tillich would not want to think of his readers as initiates, but as those who wish to look beyond the intellectual difficulties created by taking religious symbols as they stand, in order that what they symbolize may be better communicated to them. The reader will not be placed in the position of being able simply to decode the symbol, as a result of Tillich's clarifications. If that were possible, it would only prove that the symbol was no longer alive. But he would be able to understand the symbol as a symbol, and perhaps to be grasped by the power of what is present in the symbol. Whether this process is effective will clearly depend in part on one's view of Tillich's philosophy of religion, including his doctrine of the way religious symbols function.

Tillich's influence reached its zenith in the last years of his life. He continued working long past his formal retirement from teaching, and was still active in his eightieth year. His earlier work largely consists of essays and articles on particular topics, and his readers were not presented with his total scheme of thought, on which these earlier contributions had been based, until the last years, when he produced in three volumes the *Systematic Theology* on which he had been at work since 1925. Even in the case of this work, the first volume preceded the others by more than a decade, and it is not surprising that most current interpretations of Tillich find the key to his thought in ideas contained in the first volume of the *Systematic Theology*. A more recent study, taking fuller account of the second and third volumes, suggests however that the real key may be found in the material of the third volume, which deals with the questions raised by life in its actuality, and the Christian answer to these questions in the doctrine of God the Spirit.[3]

3. David H. Kelsey, *The Fabric of Paul Tillich's Theology*, New Haven and London, Yale University Press, 1967.

Support is lent to this view by the formal consideration that the material of the *Systematic Theology* is arranged more or less in a dialectical triad, though there are actually five, not three sub-divisions. The first portion of the work deals with the problems raised by the analysis of essence, the second with those of existence, and the third with those of life, in which essence and existence are mingled – not united, for life is not the synthesis of essence and existence, but the actuality from which these opposites are drawn by an act of abstraction. Likewise it becomes clear in the later portions of the system that Tillich thinks of God more typically as Spirit than in any other way; it is crucial to his view of God that God transcends essence and existence in such a way as to participate in both. Here perhaps the language of dialectic, with its talk of the synthesis uniting the thesis and its antithesis, and of the negation of the negation, may be genuinely appropriate. The living God as Spirit is perhaps the ultimate synthesis to which the dialectic of being and existence points.

However, it will doubtless take as long to digest the significance of the material of the third volume for the interpretation of Tillich's thought as it has for interpreters to come to terms with the earlier portions of the work. It is probably still too early for definitive judgements on the structure of his thought as a whole. It is tempting to suggest, however, that in Tillich's system is to be found just such a theology of the Holy Spirit as the later Barth thought a legitimate and conceivable alternative to his own approach, when he looked back in mellower mood to his controversies with his nineteenth-century predecessors. He was even prepared to suggest that this could have been the true aim of Schleiermacher.[4] In view of the close relationship between Christ and the Spirit, such an interpretation of Tillich would be compatible with the earlier suggestion that Christology is the centre of Tillich's thought.

TILLICH AS A PHILOSOPHICAL THEOLOGIAN

In a more complete sense than anyone else discussed in this book, Tillich is a philosophical theologian, though he does not

4. cf. *The Humanity of God*, pp. 24 f.

call his major work 'philosophical' but 'systematic theology'. In the most thoroughgoing way, he sets out to express Christianity in philosophical terms, and to offer a philosophical analysis of the functioning of what remains irreducibly theological. He analyses the Christian proclamation rather than proclaiming it. His system makes few truth-claims, but often commends attitudes, and offers much analysis. In short, he tells us what the Christian faith means rather than what it is. Of course the two tasks are inseparable, but the distinction shows us where he differs from Barth. The latter's dedicated concern to state what the Christian faith is renders him vulnerable to Bonhoeffer's criticism that his thought is a 'positivism of revelation'. Barth's readers must take Christian doctrine as a whole, uninterpreted, and without gradations of meaning or significance. There is no positivism, in this or just about any other sense, in Tillich's thought. Everything that can be explained, is; nothing is flung at the reader in a take-it-or-leave-it way. Nevertheless, Tillich's theology comes to rest in ultimate mystery, no less than Barth's. The mystery is one that philosophy can only point to, and theology speak of only through its own proper symbols: the mystery of God. This mystery is above reason, though 'ecstatic reason' is grasped by the divine mystery in the moment of faith. Tillich is therefore a theologian first and a philosopher second, and all his great philosophical interest and ability is mobilized to a theological task. It is doubtless for this reason that his philosophy, like that of many of the greatest theologians of the past, is a somewhat eclectic one. The unity of his thought does not lie in the philosophy he uses, as some Barthian interpreters have contended, but in the theology he uses it to clarify. The attempt to find the key to Tillich's thought in any one of his philosophical ideas will almost certainly fail, as the diversity of existing interpretations in any case suggests.

Tillich's undoubted intention is to clarify the Christian faith systematically by philosophical analysis. The greatest difficulty that his thought presents for many readers is that for them the theology is more transparent than the philosophy which is supposed to clarify it. In other words, they find they need greater effort to come to terms with his philosophy than with the theology it expresses. To the (very real) extent that Tillich's thought is apologetic in intention, this is a serious drawback, and for such readers his work must be judged not to have succeeded. Others, doubtless, will find the exact contrary, and will judge him the only intelligible writer among the theologians of the day.

Why is this? Today there is no common philosophy, or philosophical climate, uniting everyone who is interested in philosophical questions. In English-speaking philosophy, the dominant tradition is now empiricist, going back to Locke and Hume, and issuing, through the work of Russell and Wittgenstein, in the contemporary concern for logic and language. Tillich has no sympathy with this tradition, and shows scant appreciation of its aims. He hardly troubles to defend himself against criticisms which could be made of his thought on the basis of thinking of this type. On the other hand, his own indebtedness is to classical philosophy, from Parmenides to Hegel, mediated through the existentialist tradition of Germany. He wants to deal with the classical problems of metaphysics, often characterized as non-sense and pseudo-problems by the exponents of the empiricist tradition in its present form. As one who stands broadly within the existentialist tradition, Tillich also rejects the claims of metaphysics to give information about reality, but he does not for that reason reject its language and the problems it attacked. Worse still, from the empiricist point of view, Tillich's sympathies, where they are not wholly with the existentialists, are with the idealists. It is not accidental that his earliest work dealt with the philosophy of Schelling, for in Schelling existentialism begins to bud off from the idealist stem.[5]

I have already remarked that Tillich's philosophical thought is somewhat eclectic – perhaps it would be better to say original – and what has just been said may begin to substantiate this

5. Schelling (1775–1854), a friend of the young Hegel, after a period of eclipse by the latter, developed a version of idealism in opposition to his, in which essence was replaced by existence, and the negative by the positive, and in which revelation became a central idea. Kierkegaard and Marx were among those who heard his Berlin lectures. Most of Schelling's works have not been translated.

description. One might venture to suggest that if any general characterization of his philosophical position is possible, it could be called a ruptured idealism. On his own testimony, the point of departure for his philosophical thinking is the subject–object relationship, as analysed by Kant in a way that proved to be the historical basis of German idealism. The subject does not simply know the object as it is, but contributes to the act of knowledge from the material of his own subjectivity. Knowledge is therefore not of things-in-themselves, but of empirical objects, or phenomena, through the categories furnished by the knowing mind.

This relationship provides for Tillich the clue to the understanding of being. The clue to being lies for him as for the idealists on both sides of the subject–object relationship, and not just on the object side, as for realists. In relation to the history of Christian thought, this places Tillich with the Franciscan and Augustinian thinkers of the Middle Ages, and in relation to antiquity, with Parmenides and Plato rather than with Aristotle or the Stoics. So he has links with a tradition running from Parmenides to Hegel, and thence to Schelling, the critic of Hegel, and to Kierkegaard, Marx and Heidegger. This is a complex filiation, and it relates him to a family of thinkers who are at present apt to be dismissed out of hand by one very influential school of philosophers, especially in Britain and to some extent also in America. Moreover, it is this latter school whose representatives have the best claim to be the spokesmen of science on the territory of philosophy, so that Tillich's appeal is not likely to be so great for scientists as for readers on the arts side.

Tillich's philosophical thought begins in idealism, and he conceives being in the last resort in the manner of an idealist. But his thought does not remain on the idealistic plane. He agrees with the criticisms of Hegel offered in various but related ways by Schelling, Kierkegaard, Marx and Nietzsche. Hegel thought he could offer an ultimate conceptual synthesis of reality, through the reconciliation of all contradictions and negations in the Absolute Spirit, with which man's subjective spirit is ultimately one. His critics attacked from their various standpoints his claim to express the reconciliation of all contradictions in a concept. Kierkegaard saw reconciliation as above reason, to be grasped only by faith, in an act of supreme subjectivity; for the reason, it can only be absurd. The union of God and man was not an eternal truth of reason, but actual in the historic incarnation and cross of Christ, to be believed in in spite of its scandal to the reason. Like Kierkegaard, Marx believed that history as we know it does not contain reconciliation. He differed from Kierkegaard in locating the cause of estrangement or alienation not in unbelief but in private property under the conditions of class struggle. He considered that in his dialectical materialism he had turned the dialectical idealism of Hegel the right way up, so that it stood for the first time with its feet on the ground. Nietzsche seems to have seen reconciliation if anywhere in the ecstatic acceptance of Eternal Recurrence, when a man is strong enough to will not only the present moment, but its infinite repetition. Nietzsche's atheist mysticism has perhaps in the end more in common with its theistic counterpart that he so passionately rejected than at first appears.

The existentialist tradition stemming from Schelling and Kierkegaard could not accept idealism as it stood, even while it used the language of idealism to refute it. Existentialism sees the idealist reconciliation as ruptured in man's historical existence by the chasm of estrangement. Tillich shares this view. It seems to me that when he thinks of God he thinks like an idealist, but when he thinks of man he thinks like an existentialist or even at times like a Marxist. The critics of Hegel supply the categories in which he thinks of man and history. This does not mean that he identifies God with essence and man with existence, but he discovers in his ontological analysis a contradiction between essence and existence, which only the New Being, or God as being-itself, can reconcile. Ontology cannot speak directly of God, still less establish his existence, but it can show that finite existence, in spite of or because of its contradictions, points to the ground of its own being. Revelation is the answer to the question set for reason by the contradictions of finite being. What is revealed however, the power of being-itself, is conceived with the aid of idealist thought. God is not a being, and therefore does not exist, as particular beings do. As being-itself, he transcends essence and existence and also the subject–object scheme, but he does so in part by being on both sides. He is not static essence, but living Spirit.

BACKGROUND AND CAREER

Paul Tillich was born in August 1886, in the province of Brandenburg, Germany, the son of a Lutheran minister. His childhood was spent in the small cities of the province, which to a great extent still preserved their medieval character. He tells us that his childhood experience of these cities laid the foundations of a romantic feeling for history, as later experiences of the countryside and seashore did for his feeling for nature. His almost mystical feeling for nature sets him apart from other contemporary theologians, who generally set man and his history in opposition to nature. From the worshipping life of the church his father served he drew a sense of the holy, later to be clarified in his thought by Rudolf Otto's famous phenomenology of the holy.[6] In 1900 the family moved to Berlin, and Tillich was equally impressed with the dynamic character of city life.

Tillich's relationships with his parents, like almost everyone else's, were of great importance for the subsequent development of his personality and thought, though in view of his later interest in depth-psychology, perhaps he has greater awareness of these influences than most people acquire. His home was a rigid one, both doctrinally and morally. 'Every attempt to break through was prevented by the unavoidable guilt consciousness produced by the identification of the parental with the divine authority. There was only one point at which resistance was possible; namely, by using the very principles established by my father's authoritarian system against this system itself.' (This passage is significant in the light of some ideas of the adult theologian.) The element from his father's system of thought that he chose as his weapon to attack the system as a whole was philosophy, for which his father had great respect, and in which

6. *The Idea of the Holy*, Oxford University Press, 1923, 1950; 1958.

he was well-trained. In discussing philosophy with his father, Tillich broke through into independence, and finally extended this independence over the whole area of life. 'It is this difficult and painful breakthrough to autonomy which has made me immune against any system of thought or life which demands the surrender of autonomy.'[7]

After attending high school in Berlin, Tillich studied theology at Berlin, Tübingen and Halle. He gained the degree of Doctor of Philosophy from Breslau, and of Licentiate in Theology from Halle. In 1912, the year he received his theological degree, he was ordained in the Lutheran church. He began his academic career at the University of Berlin after the war, having served as a chaplain during the war years.

The period following the defeat in the 1914–18 war was one of great disillusionment and bitterness for Germany. For a while, however, it seemed to some to hold out hopes of a successful revolution against much that had been wrong in the old imperial Germany. Tillich allied himself with the social aspects of the revolution of 1918, and soon joined with the religious socialists in supporting the social-democratic party, in spite of its Marxist and atheist outlook. Tillich's sympathy with the left dated back to his childhood, and it was profoundly religious in character, influenced by the words of the prophets against injustice, and of Jesus against the rich. Moreover, though Tillich was never a communist, much less a Stalinist, his attitude to the thought of Marx himself always combined a Yes with the customary No. Even when it was dangerous to say so, in America in the fifties, Tillich could not refrain from giving Marx his due, as the one whose ideas were responsible for the transformation of the social situation in many countries, the raising of the lot of the industrial masses, the application of economic and sociological analysis in a variety of historical and contemporary fields, and even the awakening of a social conscience in the churches. Tillich's interpretation of the religious situation in the 1920s centred on religious socialism, for which he believed the historic moment had arrived.

7. 'Autobiographical Reflections', in Charles W. Kegley and Robert W. Bretall (eds.), *The Theology of Paul Tillich*, New York, Macmillan, 1952, p. 8.

For a variety of reasons the moment did not come. Instead, the Nazis came to power in Germany, and their Christian supporters were able to use much of the theological basis of the ideas of religious socialism to justify their support of the Nazi revolution. Tillich never lost the hope for religious socialism, though in later years the hope was 'mixed with resignation and some bitterness about the division of the world into two all-powerful groups between which the remnants of a democratic and religious socialism are crushed. It was a mistake when the editor of the *Christian Century* gave to my article in the series "How my Mind has Changed in the Last Ten Years" the title "Beyond Religious Socialism". If the prophetic message is true, there is nothing beyond religious socialism.'[8]

Tillich lectured at the University of Berlin from 1919 to 1924, his main interest lying in the development of a theology of culture. In the following year he moved to Marburg as professor of theology, and there began work on the *Systematic Theology*, the first volume of which appeared only in 1951. His stay at Marburg did not last long, though it was important in the development of his thought. He experienced the challenge of neo-orthodoxy through his students, who were by this time radically influenced by the new ideas, and inclined to dismiss with contempt everything that did not fit in with them. This experience, though depressing at first, encouraged him to come to terms with the new ideas more than he had so far done. During the brief period he was at Marburg he was also a colleague of Heidegger. The impact of existentialism on his own philosophical thinking, for which his studies of Schelling had prepared him, took a long time to absorb, but in due course he accepted existentialism as a way of thinking, though he did not accept its answers.

After one year he went to Dresden and then to Leipzig. Then in 1929 he accepted the post of Professor of Philosophy at Frankfurt, the most modern and liberal university in Germany. His early work had qualified him at least as much in philosophy as in theology; at Frankfurt, which had no theological faculty, he lectured on topics on the frontier between philosophy and theology, as indeed he always had. His lectures and addresses

8. ibid.

brought him into conflict with the Nazis, and when Hitler came to power in 1933 he was immediately dismissed. Reinhold Niebuhr happened to be in Germany that summer, and, as he was later to do in the case of Bonhoeffer, offered Tillich a chance to move to the United States. In 1933, at the age of forty-seven, Tillich emigrated to the United States, and became first visiting, then associate and finally full Professor at Union Theological Seminary, New York. He began a new career, in a new language and in a new country. Yet it was only in the setting of the United States that he attained his full powers, and achieved the reputation and intellectual influence they deserved.

Tillich remained at Union as Professor of Philosophical Theology until 1955. He was also a member of the faculty of philosophy at Union's neighbour, Columbia University, and participated fully in the life of that distinguished university also. From 1955 to 1962 he was at Harvard, holding one of its rare university professorships. Then he moved to the Divinity School of the University of Chicago. He died in 1966.

TILLICH AND MODERN THEOLOGY

During his student days at Halle Tillich had been profoundly influenced by Martin Kähler, whose importance as one of the forerunners of contemporary theology we have more than once noted. In his autobiographical work *On the Boundary*[9] Tillich has this to say of Kähler:

Kähler was a man whose intellectual ability and moral and religious power were overwhelming. As a teacher and writer he was difficult to understand. In many respects he was the most profound and most modern representative of the nineteenth-century theology of mediation. He was an opponent of Albrecht Ritschl, a proponent of the theological doctrine of justification, and a critic of the idealism and humanism from which he was himself intellectually descended. I am indebted to him primarily for the insight he gave me into the all-embracing character of the Pauline-Lutheran idea of justification.

In a foreword he contributed to the translation of Kähler's

9. New York, Harper & Row, 1966, pp. 47 f.

The So-called Historical Jesus and the Historic Biblical Christ,
Tillich expresses indebtedness to his ideas about the problem of
the historical Jesus in the light of scholarly research into the
sources, but adds:

There was another element in this thought which was even more
important for several of my friends and myself, namely, his application
of the principle of the Reformation to the situation of the modern man
between faith and doubt. He taught us that he who doubts any statement of the Bible and the creed can nevertheless be accepted by God
and can combine the certainty of acceptance with the actuality of even
radical doubt. This idea made it possible for many of us to become or
remain Christian theologians.

Both Kähler's views on the historical Jesus and the historic
Christ, and his idea, later to be developed by Tillich himself with
great eloquence and power, of justification by doubt, derive from
his perception of the central importance and universal application
of the idea of justification by faith. Tillich accepted from Kähler
this generalization of Reformation doctrine, and it pervades his
own theology. In speaking of the influence Kähler had on him,
Tillich has more to say about the idea of justification by doubt
than about his views on Christology. Tillich was a philosophical
theologian, not a New Testament scholar. However, when Tillich
later came to develop his own Christology, the theme of Kähler
was unmistakably present in it. Whether the debt was direct or
not, Kähler's contention that faith cannot depend upon historical
research into the life of Jesus is taken as basic by Tillich, and this
too sets him alongside men like Barth and Bultmann, instead of
with the liberals, where many of his critics wish to place him.

Kähler does not account for all Tillich's ideas on Christology
in relation to history. He tells us that his understanding of
modern critical work on the New Testament was mediated
through Schweitzer and through Bultmann's *History of the
Synoptic Tradition*. In the foreword I have just quoted, he
remarks that Kähler's answer is insufficient today, in view of the
problem of demythologization. When we consider Tillich's
Christology, we shall see that he has built a distinctive personal
view on foundations that he shares with the majority of neo-
orthodox theologians. As early as 1911, Tillich had raised the

question of the possible consequences for Christian faith if the non-existence of the historical Jesus were to become probable on critical grounds. In his own words, 'the foundation of Christian belief is the biblical picture of Christ, not the historical Jesus.'[10] In essentials, this is pure Kähler, but Tillich later greatly develops the idea of the biblical *picture* of Christ.[11]

This position on the relation of revelation to historical studies brought Tillich close to Barth in certain important respects, and in liberal circles he has sometimes been taken for a Barthian, as he is commonly taken for a liberal in Barthian ones. He actually found himself closest to Barth in the early nineteen-twenties. In an article written in 1922, he expresses agreement with Barth and Gogarten in a rejection of the attempt of idealism to bring God and man under a common intellectual understanding. On the contrary, as Tillich thought then and continued to think, there is no way from self to God, either by natural theology or by any other way in which God and man are set alongside one another. As Tillich contended, merely to set God above man is still to coordinate them in a common system. Revelation comes from God to man, and theology can express it only by way of systematic paradox.

Tillich has not departed from these basic positions of the dialectical theology, but his alliance with Barth, if it could be called that, was short-lived. Barth was troubled by Tillich's insistence on autonomy, which Barth described as his unnecessary fight against the Grand Inquisitor in Protestant theology, and he thought Tillich's fear of heteronomy exaggerated. On the other hand Tillich himself increasingly saw in what he called Barthian supranaturalism just such a tendency to heteronomy. He accused the dialectical theologians of not being truly dialectical, in their refusal to engage in dialogue with the cultural situation of the day: 'The message must be thrown at those in the situation – thrown like a stone' (cf. Bonhoeffer's rather similar criticism of Barth).[12] The dialectical theologians have plenty of

10. *On the Boundary*, p. 50.

11. Cf. M. Kähler, *The So-called Historical Jesus and the Historic Biblical Christ*, Chapter 2, esp. p. 77, and see pp. 253–4 and 266–7 below.

12. *Systematic Theology*, I, p. 7.

No, but no Yes. So Tillich came to believe that only his type of method could be called dialectical, and in spite of his great respect for Barth, moved far from him.

Nevertheless, in a number of important respects Tillich's theology shares characteristic positions of neo-orthodoxy. We shall see in a moment that Tillich wishes to balance these positions with others more characteristic of a liberal or a Catholic approach to theology, but the neo-orthodox elements are there. Indeed they occupy a crucial position in his thought as a whole, as such positions must if they are present at all. In addition to his view that faith has its foundation in the biblical picture of Jesus as the Christ, instead of in the Jesus of History, there is the centrality of Christology as a whole in his scheme. Granted that it is an original one, and much further from the dogmatic formulations of tradition than those of the other writers so far dealt with, Tillich's Christology occupies the same position in his total scheme as the Christologies of the neo-orthodox theologians do in theirs. For Tillich too, Christ is the place of a revelation of God unique in fullness and finality, reaching men as the result of a divine initiative which man does not deserve and cannot bring about, but can only accept with gratitude. The New Being has appeared in Jesus as the Christ, to save man from the contradictions and estrangement of his existence. The revelation in Christ is the criterion by which all other revelation is to be understood and judged. It follows that Tillich's theology, philosophical as it is in expression, is theology, not philosophy of religion. It serves a Christian message that, because it comes from divine revelation, can only be proclaimed, never argued for or deduced from some general philosophical analysis. We shall shortly see what Tillich means by his claim that his theology is apologetic as well as being in this neo-orthodox sense kerygmatic.

Another characteristic mark of neo-orthodoxy is its criticism of religion in the light of revelation, and the consequent distinction it makes between faith and religion. Tillich also makes this criticism and distinction, though, like Barth, he does not wish to carry the criticism of religion so far that he is unable to use religion as a category of interpretation. Tillich describes Christianity as religion that denies religion. Tillich is able to put things in this way because he means by religion something different from what Barth means. We have seen above that Barth understands religion as man's attempt (always unbelieving and idolatrous) to do for himself what only God can do for him. Through religion man forms an image of the God he will worship, and tries to establish his own righteousness in relation to this God. When Barth afterwards restores religion in the form of Christianity under grace, it seems that he thinks of it more empirically, as such things as worship and ethical activity. Bonhoeffer views religion in a complex way, owing something to Barth, something to his own teachers, and something to his knowledge of sociology and intellectual and social history. His idea of religion cannot therefore be reduced to a single key notion, unless it is the completion of man by some kind of *deus ex machina*, a God who will act as man's decision-maker and problem-solver.

Tillich regards religion as 'a state of being grasped by an ultimate concern, a concern which qualifies all other concerns as preliminary, and which itself contains the answer to the problem of the meaning of our life. Therefore this concern is unconditionally serious and shows a willingness to sacrifice any finite concern which is in conflict with it.'[13] But this ultimate concern is not only present in religion; it may be found throughout man's cultural life. From this broader point of view, religion is 'the depth of culture'. A religion embodies in a historical institution a particular understanding of the way in which this ultimate concern has been answered. Christianity, however, constantly criticizes its own historical embodiment as a particular religion, in the light of the New Being that has appeared in Jesus the Christ. Thus Christianity sharpens its perception of what is ultimate in ultimate concern, and denies itself as a religion, because in the light of its knowledge of the New Being it understands how all religion including its own can become falsely absolutized.

Tillich's interest in and emphasis upon history also sets him

13. *Christianity and the Encounter of the World Religions*, New York, Columbia University Press, 1963, p. 4. Similar statements are to be found in almost all Tillich's books.

with the neo-orthodox group of theologians. History is the key to the understanding of man, and the place of God's self-communication and address to man. Under God, it moves towards a goal, the Kingdom of God, though since Christ this goal is also present in history as its depth. So history has a direction, its movement towards the Kingdom of God, and a centre, Christ, in whose light the direction can be known. Man's freedom in history is taken up in the providence of God and woven into the meaning and destiny which God confers on history.

All these neo-orthodox elements in Tillich's thought are balanced, however, by others which seem to be their contraries. But the balance is not, I think, a static one. The neo-orthodox elements are decisive: the way Tillich relates the two sets of elements, neo-orthodox and liberal/Catholic, identifies him as a contemporary theologian, and not a continuing exponent of the essential positions of the nineteenth century. Rather than thinking of Tillich as a liberal, it might actually be less misleading to think of him as a radical. His combination of nineteenth-century questions with twentieth-century theological answers actually points beyond, not behind, the positions of neo-orthodoxy, as does Bonhoeffer's late theology, to a new kind of theology endeavouring to synthesize the strongest elements in the nine-teenth- and twentieth-century traditions. In the last years of his life Tillich asked his younger followers to remember that 'the real Tillich is the radical Tillich'.

If Christology is in the neo-orthodox manner central to Tillich's thought, his is nevertheless a Christology which sets out to solve quite different problems from the traditional ones. In regard to the relation of Christology to history, Tillich means what he says when he states that the foundation of faith is the biblical *picture* of Christ. He is less interested in preaching as a starting-point than either Kähler or indeed any of the men so far discussed. For him the biblical picture functions as a religious symbol – not, of course, a *mere* symbol, for all symbols that are alive participate in what they symbolize, and thus convey its power as well as suggesting its meaning. The picture of Jesus as the Christ is itself revelation, independently of its relationship to the historical Jesus. The picture is built up out of various forms of biblical testimony to Christ, but the governing ideas are those of his cross and resurrection. Christ is the final revelation because he sacrifices himself as Jesus to his mission as the Christ. So his personal identity and concerns become transparent to what he reveals. This revelation is unique in that the symbol denies itself completely for the sake of what is symbolized. It thus completely fulfils what is partially effective wherever there is revelation. In the cross Jesus sacrifices himself, in the resurrection this sacrifice is fulfilled in the power of the New Being, appearing when human resources come to an end. This biblical picture becomes the symbol which is the foundation and centre of distinctively Christian faith and theology. Tillich believes that there was an appropriate history giving rise to this symbol, but the symbol, not the history, is the foundation of faith.

Tillich's Christology then is not concerned with the traditional problems of how God could become man without impairing the fullness of Godhead or manhood, or splitting the individuality of the incarnate Lord. In Jesus as the Christ, the paradox to be explained by Christology is the union of essential and existential humanity, not the union of God and man. Like the idealists of the Hegelian school, Tillich believes that essential humanity is already united with God: it is Godmanhood. Jesus the Christ is essential humanity, the New Being, appearing under the conditions of existence (and therefore undergoing crucifixion). But because he is the New Being, he overcomes the power of estrangement and death, in the resurrection, and opens up participation in the New Being to man. Man's participation in it is real but partial; though the New Being grasps man, evoking faith, we constantly allow ourselves to slip away into estrangement once more. But the appearance of the New Being is final, and it does not desert us.

The New Being in Jesus the Christ is not only final reconciliation, but final revelation too. The revelation in Christ is not the only revelation there is: wherever there is religion, there is revelation. Ultimate concern is grasped by revelation of that which concerns us ultimately, i.e. that in which our being or non-being is involved, and this is God, however the one who has

254

the concern may express it. All the religions are the result of a revelation, in which the object of ultimate concern has manifested itself in a sign-event, or miracle, or in a holy object, grasping man's reason in an act of response and commitment.

In such a miracle, or holy object, the power of being is manifested, drawing reason beyond its customary limits, set by the polarities of finite being, into what Tillich calls ecstatic reason. He contrasts ecstatic reason with the technical reason we use for solving problems, and the ontological reason we use in metaphysical analysis. In ecstasy, reason is grasped by what is beyond reason, and therefore cannot be manifested to it directly in a concept, but only through such a symbol or holy object. The symbol is either an event in history (miracle) or an object confronting us in the world (holy object), which has been caught up into the communication between God and man which is revelation.

That is why it is never a mere symbol, unless it has ceased to be involved in revelation; it contains the power of that which it symbolizes. On the other hand, the object or event does not become supernaturalized; it remains worldly and historical, and Tillich does not mean a miracle in the sense of an event interrupting a sequence of natural causes. The object or event in which the power of being manifests itself is effective for the purposes of revelation to the extent that it does not obscure that which is symbolized, by becoming important in itself. If it does, it loses the power to mediate the ultimate, and becomes simply an idol. This principle, which can be understood from a phenomenological study of the revelations in all religions, shows us also that Jesus Christ is the final revelation, for he alone by sacrificing himself entirely to his mission, according to the biblical picture, is completely transparent to the New Being.

The core of Tillich's disagreement with the dialectical theologians is to be found in his own dialectic, between the 'kerygmatic' and the 'apologetic' element in his theology. At the same time, the 'correlation' he makes between them is one in which the balance falls decisively towards that which can only be proclaimed. The apologetic element in Tillich's theology derives from his analysis of what he calls the 'situation'. This is not a simple empirical reading of what life is like at a given epoch, in particular our own. It is an analysis in depth, derived from the artists, writers and philosophers, more than from popular culture. Such an analysis furnishes an existential question, which can be addressed to revelation. The question cannot determine the answer: in this Tillich firmly agrees with other contemporary theologians. But the question does determine how the answer will be formulated and understood: in this Tillich disagrees with Barth and his friends, and comes closer to liberal thought. The two elements, the existential question, and the answer of revelation, are systematically 'correlated' in Tillich's theology, and this is what gives it its characteristic shape. He calls it a 'theology of correlation', and his method is one which yields existential questions from an analysis of the situation, leading through the hearing of the proclamation to a particular kind of understanding considered by Tillich to be the one which is most relevant and 'existential' today.

In the formulation of the questions, and in the understanding of the answers which they find in the revelation of Jesus as the Christ, Tillich makes abundant use of the philosophy of religion, including ontological analysis and aesthetics. So pervasive is his use of ontology that some of his interpreters think it is determinative for his whole thought. Both Barthian and Catholic critics of Tillich have thought of him as shaping his whole understanding of theology in the light of a preconceived ontology.

Against this interpretation stand a number of features in his thought that range him rather with Barth himself. First, Tillich's philosophy, like that of the classical theologians of the early church and Barth's own, is an eclectic one, though it leans in a particular direction. He takes elements from the whole history of western philosophy, and it is not possible to call him a consistent realist, idealist or existentialist. Unity is given to his thought, therefore, not by his philosophy but by his understanding of the object of Christian faith. Second, this philosophy appears to be analytical, and to make no claims to add to our information about reality. Tillich's ontology is not therefore a natural theology. On the other hand, he does not relate God and man together in a common intellectual scheme in which the possibility of revelation could be grounded in advance. Anthropology is only one starting-point, not *the* starting-point of his thought. In fact, the questions of the old natural theology are taken up into the system and integrated with the exposition of the revelation. The analysis of man discloses the need for revelation, if there is to be reconciliation of the contradictions of finite being under the conditions of existence, and may even point inconclusively to the presence of being-itself within finite existence as its depth. Actual revelation alone makes concrete discussion of it possible. Third, there is the statement of the second volume of the *Systematic Theology* that the only non-symbolic statement theology can make about God is that all statements about him are symbolic. This must be taken to modify a statement in the first volume, that the only non-symbolic statement theology can make about God is that he is being-itself.[14]

The significance of this change of position for the interpretation of Tillich's thought has not yet been fully discussed, still less agreed on, but it must be considerable. If the statement of Volume I stood uncorrected, it would be possible to say that Tillich's theology informs us that God is to be identified with something known to us by philosophical analysis, namely, being-itself. In that case, Tillich would have told us what the name of God refers to, and would incidentally have translated the traditional term God by the new philosophical term, being-itself, in such a way as to make the old symbolic term superfluous in a modern presentation of Christianity. He would have offered the reader both connotation and denotation for the name of God. He would have told us its sense as well as its reference.

The interpretations of Tillich which take Volume I of the *Systematic Theology* as normative must make this assumption. If they are right, Tillich must finally be judged to be a philosopher, who translates all his theological statements into clear philosophical terms. If the newer statement is taken as correcting the older, as it would be reasonable to suppose it does, different conclusions will follow. The first statement is a statement about God: all the symbols can be cashed (or at least known to be symbolic) if we say that God is being-itself. The second state-

14. *Systematic Theology*, II, p. 4; I, p. 239.

ment, on the other hand, tells us nothing new about God. It tells us something about statements about God, namely that they are all symbolic. Now in Tillich's thought, the elucidation of the functioning of symbols is a theological task. If all statements about God are symbolic, they are theological statements. It would appear to follow that even the statement that God is being-itself will have to be taken symbolically, and therefore theologically. It will have to be given the same sort of interpretation as similar statements in classical theology, i.e. taken as a predicate of a subject who remains mysterious, and whose meaning is not exhausted by this predicate, or even by all such predicates together. If the two statements are taken together, it must be concluded that the statement, 'God is being-itself', cannot be converted into the statement, 'being-itself is God', without error, as could presumably have been supposed before the second and corrective statement appeared.[15]

Although the kerygmatic or proclamatory element in Tillich's theology is decisive over the apologetic, or existentialist element, with which it is systematically correlated, no contemporary theologian, not even Bultmann, makes so much use of philosophy as Tillich does. It is certainly his conviction that theology has everything to gain from the clarification philosophy can offer it, and at no point should it be content simply to repeat biblical language without philosophical clarification. The language of Canaan, as Barth calls it (the technical vocabulary of the Christian church), is never for Tillich the language most adequate to theology. The apologetic element in his theology is not a search for the justification of Christianity on the assumptions of the world; it is an attempt to speak clearly and relevantly to the theologian's own time, by answering, from the treasury of Christian faith, the questions old and new which are put to it, and it answers them in the language in which the questions are formulated.

Tillich also shares with many contemporary theologians an intense interest in history, as the arena of man's life, and of

15. In the same way, the Thomistic statement that God is *ipsum esse subsistens*, or *actus purus*, does not explain away the biblical attributes of God.

God's shaping of his destiny and freedom. Again, however, we find Tillich balancing this interest by one in nature, stemming from romantic elements in his thought, and setting him quite apart from his leading contemporaries. Tillich thus thinks of Christianity more sacramentally than do his peers, and he expects to find the holy manifested in nature as well as in historical revelation. Such ideas link him with Catholic thought, and differentiate him from even older Lutherans. It would appear both from his theological writings and from what he has told us in autobiographical passages that a certain nature-mysticism is one of the most important sources of his thought. This sacramental way of thinking is actually characterized by Tillich as primitive, and he admits that it stands in considerable need of correction by other elements. The most important of these is the 'Protestant principle' itself, which denies ultimacy to any concrete manifestation of the Holy, except the final revelation. None the less, the sacramental, or Catholic, element in Christianity supplies its substance, whereas the Protestant principle, which denies ultimacy to it, is a formal principle, not a substantial one. Catholicism needs Protestant correction, but the substance must be there before there is any point in correcting it.

Tillich's religious socialism also sets him apart from other neo-orthodox theologians. Barth was also a social-democrat in politics, and did much with his doctrine of the Lordship of Christ to overcome traditional Lutheran conservatism among his colleagues in the Confessing Church, and analogously among Christians elsewhere. But he was far from giving socialism, or any other political programme, a religious connotation, as Tillich did. To be a socialist could not be related directly to his theology; it was a concrete choice for which his theology freed him, made on pastoral grounds and in the light of a human reading of the political circumstances. Other circumstances might lead to a different political commitment. Hence perhaps his refusal to be anti-communist in the same way that he had been anti-Nazi. For Tillich, on the other hand, socialism is the hope for a society truly free and positively related to God, a hope for whose realization within history the opportunity had seemed to him to have come. That it did not arrive in the inter-war period, when he and his friends believed it had, is not in his opinion a criticism of religious socialism, but of his own political judgement.

TILLICH'S DOCTRINE OF GOD

So far, we have looked briefly at the general character of Tillich's presentation of Christianity, and have considered how his theology is related to his personal history, and to the influences he underwent from circumstances and from the theologians under whose guidance he was trained, and we then turned to consider some of the formal and structural elements in his thought as a means of relating him to the other theologians discussed in this book. In doing so we have touched upon a number of his leading ideas. In the space that remains we must concentrate on a few of the most important of these, and look at them in greater detail. We begin by gathering up what has been said about his doctrine of God, and relating it to current discussion.

In his view of God, most of the leading themes of Tillich's theology meet, and what is most puzzling and most illuminating about him are united. One would be tempted to call Tillich's view of God a mystical one, especially in view of the writers he uses as sources, were it not for the fact that he emphatically repudiates such a view as leading to polytheism. Clearly, he intends his own view of God to be more concrete than the one he attributes to mystics. At the same time, he acknowledges his own debt to mystical writers such as Nicholas of Cusa and Jacob Boehme. It is in keeping with the paradoxical and dialectical character of Tillich's thought that there should be difficulty in deciding whether he believes in a personal God or not. Certainly he does not believe God to be *a* person, if only because he does not think he is *a* being. He chooses to speak first of God as being-itself, since something must be, before anything else can be said about it. But he wants to say also that God is personal, even if not a person; his approach to man is not less than personal but more, and so justifies the symbols of loving fatherhood.

As we have seen, being-itself is not one of the beings. It is beyond the polarity of essence and existence, though it participates in both poles, as in the poles of infinity and finitude. To attempt to prove the existence of being-itself, as if it were a particular existent, is to justify the protest of atheists. God is not a separate person, a being beyond and additional to (and therefore really alongside of) all the beings that make up the world. Being-itself is at the depth of being, giving to all concrete being its power to resist non-being. To discuss the existence of God is therefore absurd. Being-itself does not *exist*, for it is beyond the realm of existence, as it is of essence. That being is, is perhaps an unnecessary tautology. In any case, the protest of atheism against the assertion of God as a separate person additional to the totality of particular beings is justified and must be taken seriously by theology.

Critics of the point of view Tillich holds have said that to define God into existence in this way is illicit. By identifying God with ultimate reality Tillich makes it impossible to deny his existence, though he has begun by tactically conceding the atheist's arguments. This objection rests upon a complex misunderstanding of Tillich's argument. Tillich is not attempting to define God into *existence*, since he does not assert existence of him, but a mode of being for which our ordinary vocabulary has no words. Nor is he attempting to *define* God into existence. His analysis does lead him to talk about being as well as particular beings, but this is an implication of something that will generally be conceded to be true about the beings, except by those who reject such language out of hand, that they are both vulnerable to, and also partially resist, non-being. Tillich's analysis yields the idea of being-itself by pointing to characteristics of existent beings as known by common sense. Finally, as we have seen, to speak of being-itself as actual is to go beyond philosophical analysis and depend upon revelation.

God is for Tillich our ultimate concern. This term has caused much confusion, since it is the same as the one Tillich uses for our subjective concern, which is religion. But he does not mean to equate God and religion. Religion is a state of being ultimately concerned. God is what ultimately concerns us, that which remains when all finite concerns have been negated. Ultimate concern is the depth of finite concern, and what concerns us ultimately is the depth of all that concerns us conditionally. Especially in his earlier writings, Tillich can speak of God as the unconditioned, and the term is to be interpreted in the present context. He does not think of God simply as the Absolute, a term he rejects, but as that for which our concern cannot be conditioned. The fact that we find ourselves ultimately concerned does not entail, as Tillich sometimes seems to suppose, that our concern has an object. But by showing that no finite or conditioned object can concern us ultimately, he has raised a question which revelation can answer in the proclamation of the New Being, as that which does concern us ultimately. In such ultimate concern, our own being and non-being is involved. Being-itself enables us to resist the threat of non-being.

I have suggested that Tillich's final concept of God is idealistic. I do not mean that he confuses God and man pantheistically, as has been suggested, or that like Hegel he simply believes Christ to be the historical source of the eternal idea of Godmanhood. I mean that he finds God on both sides of the polarities of finite being, and in particular on both sides of the subject–object relationship. Unlike the oriental mystic, Tillich does not identify God with the 'I' as opposed to the world. Nor does he, in the manner of personalist philosophers such as Buber, who have been so influential in modern theology, identify God with the 'Thou' who ultimately confronts us through our relationship with finite 'Thous'. He finds God in both the I and the Thou, and also in nature, as the holy ground of its being. To understand God in this way makes it impossible to conceive of him anthropomorphically, or indeed in any way in which he is regarded as a particular object whose existence could be denied or proved. It also makes him the ground of personality, though not a particular person. As Tillich points out, his way of conceiving God has significance for prayer and meditation. It prevents one making the ultimately disappointing mistake of thinking of God as a higher person who is present to one in devotional practices, as an object of consciousness. Rather, he is at the depth of one's own being, as at the depth of all being. He can never become an object to the mind, except symbolically.

It may now be possible to understand Tillich's well-known

polemic against what he calls supranaturalism, later echoed for English readers in *Honest to God.* Tillich criticizes Barth and all traditionally-minded theologians for the error of supranaturalism. What does he mean? The *supra*natural is evidently not identical with the *super*natural. The denial of the supernatural presumably entails the assertion of naturalism, and this Tillich clearly rejects. He objects to thinking of God alongside man, as if he belonged to the same order of being, and, as we have seen, he considers that to assert that God belongs to a higher order than man is to fall by implication into this mistake. 'Above' is in a sense also 'alongside'. Just as God is not a separate being alongside all the beings, so there is no special realm of existence for God along-side that in which everything else exists. What Tillich wishes to assert over against supranaturalism is 'self-transcending' or 'ecstatic' naturalism. Ecstatic or self-transcending reason can be grasped by and acknowledge being-itself. But reason cannot and should not affirm the supranatural. If theology does so, it is holding on to its traditional assertions in a positivist way, without coming to grips with the question of what they really mean.

Now, it is important to realize that Tillich's doctrine of God is trinitarian. Moreover, like the system itself, the doctrine of God is conceived dialectically. When we say that God is being-itself, we have only spoken of him as the revealed answer to the questions that arise out of finitude. True, the question of being has particular importance because it is always the first question. But it is not the only theologically important one. We have not yet considered the answers of revelation to the questions arising out of man's estrangement, nor those arising out of the ambi-guities of life. These will also call forth in appropriate parts of the system affirmations about God to be set beside what has been said about being-itself. God is not only creator, or being-itself, he is also Christ, and Spirit. The trinitarian elements in Tillich's doctrine of God do not seem to be primarily the products of ontological analysis. They come from revelation. Indeed, we might not be mistaken if we supposed that the very arrangement of the ontological analysis in a three-fold shape is determined by the fact that questions of man's finitude and estrangement and of the ambiguities of his life have been answered through revelation in a disclosure of God as Creator, Reconciler and Spirit. We have to remember that in Tillich's theology the question does not determine the answer any more than the answer determines the question, but the two are correlated, so that the question determines the form and not the substance of the answer. Perhaps the substance of the answer can affect the form of the question.

When Tillich concentrates on his ontological analysis, he is inclined to think of God primarily as being-itself, and to stress this way of thinking of him over the more obviously theological symbols he employs elsewhere. When this way of thinking is uppermost, Tillich is inclined to regard other ways of thinking as symbolic in relation to this one. Where the analysis of revelation is uppermost, he thinks of God trinitarianly, or in the way that turns out to be his favourite, as the Spiritual Presence. When this way of thinking is uppermost, he says that all ways of thinking about God are symbolic. God reveals himself as the Spiritual Presence; as such he is ultimate mystery, and everything whatsoever that is said of him is symbolic in relation to the revealed actuality of this mystery. In the later volumes of the system, Tillich's attention turns away from the thought of God called forth by the analysis of finitude, and moves to the actuality of God's presence to man's life.

If we follow up the insight that Tillich thinks dialectically about God, as well as about the questions the situation sets to the Christian kerygma, we shall perhaps conclude that for him the term Spirit is not just the name for one of the persons of the Trinity, just as being-itself is not merely a name for the creator, but for God. God is Spirit, or Spiritual Presence. As life brings together the aspects of finitude and estrangement in man's being, the actuality of God's presence in his self-disclosure unites being-itself with the power of reconciliation. God as being, and God as reconciler, may be regarded as a dialectical pair whose root is in the doctrine of God as Spirit. Tillich's doctrine of God is evidently not trinitarian in the traditional sense. What he says about God is always said about the Godhead itself, not about persons in God. It follows from his Christology that there is no need to think of the Son as a special person, since Christ is not

God made man, but essential humanity manifested under the conditions of existence. So the three aspects of the doctrine of God do not correspond to three persons of a traditional Trinity. They are dialectically related manifestations of one dynamic, living Godhead, who is best thought of under the symbol of Spirit, or better, Spiritual Presence. God revealed is God present.

REVELATION

Tillich's doctrine of revelation is clearly all-important for the understanding of his thought as a whole. In his systematic correlation of the Christian kerygma, as the answer, with the questions arising from the existential situation of man in the present, revelation is also correlated with reason, but not in the traditional way. Traditionally, revelation and reason complemented each other. Reason told one of the existence of God, while revelation furnished the predicates by which we can know of his character and relation to man. In Tillich's thought, this scheme is characterized as supranaturalist. It sets God and the world alongside one another, even while it affirms that God's sphere is higher than the world's. It thus renders God incredible. The earlier Barthian solution, of simply suppressing the role of reason in the knowledge of God, while leaving the scheme otherwise undisturbed, strikes Tillich as no less supranaturalist. (Perhaps he never came to terms with the mature Barth's Anselmian answer, which is much closer to his own.) For Tillich, revelation and reason must be neither coordinated, nor the one subordinated to the other, whether in the manner of neo-orthodoxy or of naturalism. They must be correlated. Like religious experience, reason becomes a receptive organ for revelation.

To do this, Tillich makes a distinction between technical reason, ontological reason and ecstatic reason. Technical reason is occupied with solving problems. It has created the modern world through its use in science and technology. Tillich has no quarrel at all with science. But he wishes to avoid theological disputation with it, of a kind that would place theology in a supranaturalistic relation to science. The propositions of theology can never come into conflict with those of science. Theology, like ontological reason, makes no such fact-claims as science might disprove by its own methods. Indeed, it is not clear that Tillich's theology makes any empirical claims, whether in the realm of history or science. The empiricist philosopher will therefore feel justified in classifying the whole of his thought as analytic or even empty. Whether Tillich would object to the former classification (obviously he must resist the suggestion that his statements are empty) is not altogether clear. In the page or two he devotes to the question of verification, in the form that interests the empiricist philosopher, he suggests that the propositions he is interested in cannot be verified by any ordinary appeal to fact, or sense experience. They receive what he calls 'verification in life'. What exactly this is, and how it differs from the kind of verification assertions have, when they propose anything that can significantly be disagreed with, does not become clear. By the same token, when Tillich makes statements on the ground of ontological reason, it is not clear whether he thinks they are such that disagreement with them would be significant, or whether he is offering an analysis of the meaning and structure of reality compatible with all contemporary pictures of how things are in the world.

In any case, ecstatic reason is not concerned with this kind of verification. It is reason operating beyond the limits of its normal functioning, precisely at the point where normal functioning has come to an end in irreconcilable contradictions. Ecstatic reason comes into play when miracle occurs. The miracle is not an interruption of the normal course of nature, for Tillich does not believe that there are such interruptions. It is the coincidence of a sign event, involving a holy object, with ecstatic reason, in which meaning and power are disclosed through the object, which participates in the power of being. The holy object *par excellence*, and the revelation basic to the Christian religion, is Christ. Christ is the originating revelation, but there are also dependent revelations, to which the original revelation gives rise. In these, the biblical picture of Christ, created in the minds of those who experienced the original revelation through ecstatic reason, itself functions as a holy object for new believers. When this happens, the original power and meaning of the New Being, first disclosed historically in Jesus the Christ, are now disclosed in the *picture* of Jesus as the Christ. Ecstatic reason receives this picture. So reason is grasped by the power of the New Being, and finds healing through it. Ecstatic reason is in effect Tillich's name for faith, and it is a clear one.

The holy object, as Tillich calls it here, can also be called a symbol. Strictly speaking, the holy object appears in the structure of miracle, the symbol in that of religious understanding, but the two function so similarly that we are justified in relating them closely to each other. If Jesus the Christ is the most important holy object in Christianity, the biblical picture of him provides its most important symbol. As we have seen, the biblical picture gives rise to other symbols also, including those we apply to God, such as creator and spirit.

The biblical picture of Christ, the primary source of those symbols theology analyses and relates to one another, stands on its own merits as a medium of revelation. It does not need the external validation of historical investigation. Just as for Bultmann revelation occurs now in the proclamation of the church, not in the historical reconstruction of Jesus by the critic, so for Tillich the biblical picture furnishes revelation, and the reconstruction of the scholar is of scientific not of theological interest. There is however, in his view, an analogy (*analogia imaginis*) between the picture and the historical person who evoked it. If we could have a photograph of the historical Jesus, the image we have in the Bible would correspond to it analogically. Jesus was in fact such that he could be called the Christ, even if there is nothing of interest to religion in reconstructing from the Gospels any fresh historical picture of him.

THE PROTESTANT PRINCIPLE

Tillich's theology is not only a theology of the Christian revelation, but a theology of culture and history. This aspect of his thought comes from his understanding of what he calls 'the Protestant principle'. In spite of the many points at which he enters sympathetically into contact with Catholic thought, Tillich is emphatically a Protestant, and a Lutheran, not a Calvinist. He tells us that one boundary he never moved on was that between the Lutheran and the Reformed traditions. His Protestantism centres on what he learned from Kähler about the pervasive significance in Christian thought of the doctrine of justification by faith. Though he regards the terminology of the doctrine as unintelligible to modern man without theological training, he does not for that reason regard the idea as unimportant, or incapable of relevant restatement. On the contrary, in one form or another, it is a basic category of his own theology.

The Protestant principle is based on the negative and positive implications of justification by faith. Negatively, it forbids the identification of the ultimate with anything whatsoever that participates in it in this world. Nothing that is not divine may be given divine value, so that it becomes an idol. Thus, Protestantism will be critical of the sacred sphere, even while affirming its existence and value. Neither the church, nor any of its functions such as preaching and the sacraments, are to be confused with what they mediate. In a recent formulation of the Protestant principle, Tillich shows how the negative side implies the positive: 'The Protestant principle [is] that the sacred sphere is not nearer to the ultimate than the secular sphere; both are infinitely distant from and infinitely near to the Divine.'[16] Thus the secular sphere, the sphere of culture, can be given equal value with the sacred, the sphere of religion. 'As religion is the substance of culture, so culture is the form of religion.'[17] Religion and culture therefore belong together, and theology is concerned with both. Both are under grace, and in both the Ultimate may be manifested. Both also stand in need of grace.

The Protestant principle stands within Christianity as a permanent and always relevant warning against the tendency of religion to idolatry. Accordingly, its function in Tillich's thought is somewhat similar to that of the criticism of religion in Barth's; but it includes a positive aspect, not present in Barth's polemic against religion, and stemming from Tillich's Lutheranism.

16. *Christianity and the Encounter of the World Religions*, p. 47.
17. *On the Boundary*, pp. 69 f.

Tillich extends the principle, *finitum capax infiniti*, from its original setting in Christology to cover the whole world. But Lutherans are traditionally more open than Calvinists to the positive theological significance of culture, including philosophical thought. Tillich's Lutheranism helps him to see the positive implications of his Protestant principle for literature and art as well as philosophy, and to relate all of these to the Ultimate, which is originally manifested in the preaching and sacraments of the church. Further, he conceives of religion as having substance and continuity in history. So long as the Protestant principle is at work to ward off idolatry, the substance of religious culture can be affirmed as confidently as by any Catholic.

Tillich therefore understands grace not simply as the vertical descent of the divine favour upon sinful man, but as taking shape in history through structures. The divine judgement over everything finite does not reduce human creativity to meaninglessness. What he calls a structure of grace is not identical with anything finite, but it is the breaking of the unconditional into the conditional, to be perceived by faith in nature and history, in social life and of course in the church. We might say that a structure of grace is not a further element within the totality of finite being, but a binding together by grace of particular elements within finite being to serve its own purposes. Grace itself maintains the protest, which must always be inherent in grace while it is grace, against confusion between finite and infinite, which always turns the finite into an idol. The concept of a structure of grace is admittedly an obscure one, but it is useful to Tillich in making the positive affirmations which follow from his understanding of the Protestant principle, while making them follow genuinely from this principle, and not simply from liberal humanism. He thus avoids the negative judgements on culture of the early Barth, while joining with him in his protest in the name of divine judgement upon the absolutizing of anything within this world.

When anything finite, no matter how good in itself, becomes absolutized, it becomes in Tillich's language *demonic*. Tillich has no doctrine of the devil, as a quasi-positive ground of evil. Non-being has for him an evil connotation, as it has for much Christian tradition. Conversely, evil is destructive, and tends to pull down being into non-being. Estranged existence is self-destructive. The demonic, like grace, is structural: it appears in human culture and institutions, as well as in individuals. Like the structures of grace, demonic structures are not things along-side other things, but unite existing elements into a formal pattern, or *Gestalt*, to use the German term, which now has some currency in English. The demonic structure appears in the first instance, therefore, not as directly destructive, but as the tendency to absolutize the finite. Thus 'the demonic is a power in personal and social life that is creative and destructive at the same time.'[18] The eventual goal of the demonic is to set up the finite in place of the infinite, as an object of ultimate concern, which it cannot be. Hence the demonic can be used to explain symbols like Lucifer or the Antichrist, giving them a concrete and identifiable meaning for human history and institutional life.

THE INTERPRETATION OF HISTORY

Structures of grace and demonic structures appear within history, and participate in its drama. For Tillich, history has a meaning and direction, given it by its centre, Christ. Its destiny is the Kingdom of God, the presence of the Spirit within historical life. 'The meaning of history is the process whereby the divine, through the instrument of human freedom, overcomes estrange-ment through love.'[19] The dialectic of history is given by the interaction of the divine purpose, or destiny, with human freedom, in which a positive tendency is imparted to the latter by the appearance of reconciliation within history at its centre in Christ. History is the theatre of a drama in which man in his freedom encounters the divine and the demonic, and has the opportunity for significant decision. Men who accept the limitations inherent in finitude can participate through grace in the positive movement of the divine within history.

18. *On the Boundary*, p. 79.
19. James Luther Adams, 'Tillich's Interpretation of History', in Kegley and Bretall (eds.), *The Theology of Paul Tillich*, p. 300.

Not every moment of history is equally significant. There are moments laden with opportunity, where decision is above all called for and potentially fruitful. Such a moment Tillich calls a *Kairos*, borrowing a term from biblical Greek. *Kairos* is not mere time, but significant time, right time, opportune time, fulfilled time. History throws up such *kairoi* in the interaction of divine purpose and human freedom. The appearance in history of Jesus as the Christ was the central and normative *kairos*. Though the dialectic of history will only be completed beyond history, in the fulfilment in the Kingdom of God, the New Being in Christ has invaded history, overcoming estrangement and re-uniting human beings and human life to the divine ground. In a *kairos*, the on-going dialectic is heightened and speeded up, so that society has the opportunity to become significantly less estranged.

Along with thought and culture generally, society can exist in one of three relationships to the divine ground: heteronomy, autonomy and theonomy. Theonomy is the root or ground from which the other two have split off, or perhaps their dialectical synthesis. Hence the others are not really true alternatives, though autonomy is to be preferred to heteronomy. Heteronomy is authoritarian. In its literal meaning, it sets the law of being in *another*. Kant in the sphere of ethics set up a contrast between heteronomy and autonomy. As against heteronomy, autonomy stands for the power of man to discover the universal law of being in *himself*, without dependence on external authority. So autonomy means literally finding the law in *oneself*. This does not mean that the law one finds is self-made or subjective. It is the true and universal law, as Kant was concerned to affirm. Only by discovering it in oneself and freely obeying it can one act ethically. Autonomy is also manifested in all free thought and institutions, just as heteronomy is in all dogmatic and authoritarian thought and institutions.

Kant did not speak of theonomy. The synthesis of heteronomy and its negation, autonomy, in theonomy was the discovery of nineteenth-century Hegelians, and was taken over by Tillich, both as the synthesis of principles he finds inadequate in isolation, and in his later thinking as the true root from which the opposed pair have broken off. If we follow the dialectical order, autonomy protests freedom as against authority, but contains contradictions in itself which lead to estrangement. If society revolts against ecclesiastical domination, it may become secular and religiously impoverished. The denial of the sacramental leads to the profane, even to nihilism.

Tillich does not agree with a number of more recent theologians who have celebrated secularity and the profane world whole-heartedly. He looks beyond autonomy to the recovery of values inherent in heteronomy. Heteronomy stood for the presence and power of the divine ground, though it tended to absolutize the mediation of that ground, thus provoking the protest of autonomy. But by its protest autonomy cuts itself off from the presence of the divine. Theonomy, the negation of the negation, reaffirms the presence in man of the divine, but no longer in the authoritarian form which absolutizes the means. Theonomy relates man and society to the divine through freedom, not authority, a freedom in which man discovers that the divine is not alien to him, but coincides with what is most truly his own life. In reconciliation from estrangement, man is united once more to the divine ground, without threat to his freedom.

If a Calvinist had been able to conceive of the notion of theonomy, which is hardly possible, he would have located it strictly in the Christian life, and probably as a hope not actually realized in history. Tillich sees theonomy as historical possibility for man in society. He believes it is realized religiously in worship, where the authority of the divine comes to man not in binding doctrinal statements, but in a set of symbols equally accessible to the primitive and to the sophisticated mind, preserving for the latter his intellectual freedom.

He also considers theonomy a possibility for whole societies. He thinks it was in fact realized in the Middle Ages in Europe. The present hope for a theonomous society lies in religious socialism, though there are remnants of theonomy in all democratic societies. It is worth noting how precisely the theonomous society is intended to meet the original Marxist criticism of bourgeois-capitalist society as producing estrangement. For

Tillich, the estrangement is a fact, but it is to be overcome not by the dialectic of the class struggle, but by that of grace, in which the New Being, as reconciliation over estrangement, unites men to the divine and to one another in a free association, which he calls socialism. 'Religious socialism,' he wrote in the thirties, 'is more than a new economic system. It is a comprehensive understanding of existence, the form of the theonomy demanded and expected by our present *Kairos*.'[20]

THE LATENT AND THE MANIFEST CHURCH

Because the New Being is present in history as a whole, not merely in a delimited sacred sphere, Tillich can speak of its social form as anticipated in other groups than the church. This anticipation is the 'latent church', as he calls it, in contrast to the 'manifest church', in which the New Being is explicitly and consciously received. Because the institutional church is not the only social embodiment of the New Being, it can be criticized by the latent church, for the latter sometimes embodies the New Being more completely and effectively than the church itself, which can at any time become demonic.

Through the idea of the latent church Tillich is able to explain the common experience that other groups than the church often appear to express human community more adequately than the church itself, especially when the latter becomes 'demonized' by giving itself absolute value and defending its institutional interests as if they were identical with the cause of God. If the church is not the only manifestation of reconciliation in social form, it is not surprising if sometimes it is not the best available. Likewise, if other groups do at times manifest human community more successfully than the church, this is also to be attributed to the power of the New Being, overcoming the estrangement of men from the divine ground of their being, and so from each other. Nevertheless, the distinction between the latent church and the manifest church is to be maintained. The latter is the society where the New Being is recognized in its final appearance

20. *On the Boundary*, p. 81.

as Jesus the Christ, and because of this the renewing power of reconciliation is uniquely present there.

DIALOGUE OF RELIGIONS

Tillich's analysis of religion through the Protestant principle also permits a dialogue of religions, in place of the imperialistic relation of Christianity to other religions that goes with heteronomous thinking, and the indifference to them which might go with autonomy. Tillich assumes that all religions are based on revelation, and that the power of being-itself is therefore manifest in each of them to some degree. Their differences are not of the order which must preclude dialogue and demand a struggle for the conversion of the other. The dialogue must deal with polarities in religion, as the reception of the divine by man. In the light of such a dialogue, Christianity, as the religion which is already most self-critical of its character as a particular religion, can increasingly learn to free itself from the limitations of its own particularity. Today the dialogue of the religions will not be so much about their differences with one another, as about the problems each encounters in its relationship to the contemporary challenge of the quasi-religions, as Tillich calls them. The most important of these today are nationalism, sometimes radicalized into fascism, and communism.

Secularism embodies the autonomous protest against religion inherent in Christianity itself, but it is liable to become demonized as a secularist ideology. There can be a secular myth and a secular cult, and against these Christianity must protest, even while it accepts and turns against itself the secular protest against heteronomous religion. 'Religion cannot come to an end, and a particular religion will be lasting to the degree in which it negates itself as a religion. Thus Christianity will be a bearer of the religious answer so long as it breaks through its own particularity. The way to achieve this is not to relinquish one's own religious tradition for the sake of a universal concept which would be nothing but a concept. The way is to penetrate into the depth of one's own religion, in devotion, thought and action. In the depth of every living religion there is a point at which religion itself loses its importance, and that to which it points breaks through its particularity, elevating it to spiritual freedom, and with it to a vision of the spiritual presence in other expressions of the ultimate meaning of man's existence.'[21]

We have tried to understand Tillich's thought as existing, in his own words, 'on the boundary'. We have looked at a number of such boundaries, that between neo-orthodoxy and liberalism, between theology and philosophy, between religion and culture, between Lutheranism and Marxism, between Christianity and other religions. Each of them is important to Tillich, and can be understood as creative, because of the more important, indeed fundamental, boundary situation each points to, 'a boundary for human activity which is no longer a boundary between two possibilities, but rather a limit set on everything finite by that which transcends all human possibilities, the Eternal. In its presence, even the very centre of our being is only a boundary and our highest level of accomplishment is fragmentary.'[22]

READING TILLICH

Most readers will find it best to begin their study of Tillich by reading the three volumes of sermons. If they then wish to go further, they could next read *The Courage to Be* and *The Dynamics of Faith*. Some readers will want to go from there to his works on culture and society, such as *The Protestant Era* and *The Theology of Culture*. I have several times quoted from the valuable autobiography, *On the Boundary*, revised from the earlier chapters of *The Interpretation of History*, and issued in the year of Tillich's death. Another late work, his Bampton lectures at Columbia University, *Christianity and the Encounter of the World Religions*, forms a valuable introduction to his ideas on religion and revelation, as well as to the subject-matter indicated in its title. Finally, the more adventurous, or philosophically educated, could attempt the summits in the three volumes of the *Systematic Theology*. As I have implied, this work is not for everybody. For those who can cope with it, it

21. *Christianity and the Encounter of the World Religions*, pp. 96 f.
22. *On the Boundary*, p. 98.

offers intellectual pleasures not exceeded in modern theology, and clearly no one can be said to understand Tillich who has not come to terms with it. It contains far more than it has been possible to mention here, and is written with lucidity and elegance, given the highly technical nature of the subject-matter.

Six

**Theologians
of Scandinavia
and America**

The writers we have considered so far are the ones who have
exerted the greatest influence on contemporary theology, and it
is no accident that they are all German in background and
training (though Barth and Brunner are Swiss, and Tillich did
his most important work after he went to the United States).
Before turning to consider, in a final chapter, how younger men
have responded to their influence, we must look more briefly at
the work of several men outside Germany, though still largely
heirs of the German tradition, who have made contributions
only slightly less important than those of the men so far discussed.
Among these the most significant thinker is Reinhold Niebuhr,
whose contribution in the specialized field of social ethics and
the doctrines immediately related to it has been no less influential
than those of the men considered already.

Scandinavian theology can be considered almost as part of the
German tradition. The closeness of the Scandinavian languages
to German makes it easy for their theologians to read German
books quickly, and men from Scandinavia have frequently gone
to German universities to study. On the other hand, the church
situation in Scandinavia is a unique one, with Lutheran state
churches embracing, nominally at least, a high percentage of the
population. These churches, like the Church of England, remain
in close historical continuity with their pre-Reformation past,
partly because the Reformation in Scandinavia was exceptionally
gentle. Unlike the Church of England, however, the Scandinavian
churches acquired a confessional tradition from the influence of
Lutheran theologians on their early history as separate bodies,
and the interaction of this with their sense of the Catholic past
produces interesting results.

It may be more surprising to find American theologians

regarded as heirs of the German tradition. The difference of language, and the physical distance between America and Germany, might have been expected to preclude any great cultural influence coming from Germany. The explanation lies in a variety of factors. The British visitor to North America will constantly be struck by the extent to which cultural influence from his own country has been Scottish rather than English, and this is particularly true in theology. Scottish theology differs from English, as a result of its links with the Continent through its Calvinist tradition, in being much more aware of German work, and responding to it much more quickly. Most of the foremost interpreters of Barth and Bultmann writing in Britain are Scots. Beyond this, the American educational system has more in common with the German than the English, and this also facilitates the exchange of ideas. Perhaps most important of all, a high proportion of the American churches owes its origin to immigration from the Continent of Europe, and the membership of these churches still retains a high proportion of recent immigrants, who keep in close touch with their original language and culture, though they become Americans and take on the characteristics of American culture too. For these and other reasons, American theologians are usually better-informed than their English counterparts about German theology, and more strongly influenced by it. There has always been a time-lag between the creation of a new theological position in Germany, and the appearance of its counterpart in America, but the interval has usually been shorter than in Britain, and it is shortening rapidly at the present time, owing to the general speed-up in communications. By the same token, it is only lately that we are seeing the emergence of distinctively American types of theology, which we shall look at, along with other developments, in the final chapter.

THE 'LUNDENSIAN' THEOLOGY

So far as Scandinavia is concerned, we shall make no attempt to offer a general survey of the interesting things going on there, but concentrate upon a single group of men, who have been widely associated with the movement of revolution against liberalism described in connexion with Barth and his friends, and who have exerted a world-wide influence. Because of their association with the University of Lund, in south Sweden, they have become known as exponents of a 'Lundensian' theology. The men who made this kind of theology famous are Anders Nygren and Gustaf Aulén. The current representative of Lundensian thought, Gustaf Wingren, is so much its critic that it is probably better not to regard him as its follower.

Lundensian theology arose at about the same time as German neo-orthodoxy, and has commonly been regarded as a parallel movement of thought. This is a correct judgement to the extent that these men also opposed liberalism in the content of their theology, and restored orthodox ideas, especially of grace, to centrality. But the Lundensians were far from being neo-orthodox in method. Here their aims were in direct continuity with those of their liberal predecessors. Their goal was to render systematic theology scientific, as the liberals had done for historical criticism. The application of scientific method to systematic theology disclosed Christianity objectively as very different from the picture of it drawn by liberal thought. In the result, we find in Lundensian theology a remarkable combination of liberal method with neo-orthodox content, which rendered its work accessible to many who saw the defects of the older liberalism, but were not prepared to go all the way with Barth in his revolution.

Many of the characteristic marks of neo-orthodoxy are missing in Lundensian theology, such as the sharp distinction between Christianity and religion, the emphasis on revelation in Christ to the exclusion of general revelation in history and culture, and the related distinction between the Jesus of history and the Christ of faith. On the other hand, we find near-equivalents of these ideas, stemming from the famous (and no less sharp) distinction made by Anders Nygren between *agape* and *eros*, two kinds of love, the first distinctive of Christianity, the other of Hellenistic mysticism, which Nygren discovered in various combinations in historical Christianity. Nygren understood *agape* as the love which flows down from God to undeserving man, and so from man to his neighbour; *eros* on the contrary meant the hunger for God characteristic of mysticism, neo-Platonic and Christian. Once this distinction is made systematically, *eros* becomes a category under which much that Barth and others call religion can be conveniently subsumed. Any movement of the spirit from man to God can be called *eros*, so that the term becomes a catch-all, closely resembling natural theology in the early thought of Barth. Thus the differences between the two schools of thought become less important in their total impact, than if one concentrates upon the methodological differences. In their later work, Barth and Nygren both moved away from the polemical positions with which they are commonly associated. Nygren's later work is strongly biblical in tone, and very close to the thought of large numbers of men within the general movement of 'biblical theology'.

Anders Nygren was an approximate contemporary of the older men so far discussed. He began to publish his major works at the beginning of the nineteen-twenties. His most important and best-known work is his two-volume treatise, *Agape and Eros*, though his commentary on the Epistle to the Romans has been widely read in English translation. In 1948 Nygren became bishop of Lund in the Church of Sweden, having been Professor of Systematic Theology and Ethics at the University of Lund since 1924. He took a leading part in the ecumenical movement since the Lausanne Faith and Order Conference of 1927. From 1952 to 1963 he chaired the Faith and Order Theological Commission on Christ and the Church, and produced a book of that name to help its deliberations.

Nygren's basic aim was to render theology a scientific discipline. Clearly one does not mean by this that he sought to approximate it to the natural sciences, which would hardly be possible, but he did wish to give it the objective and disciplined character of a science. If theology is to be a discipline in this sense, it must meet the criteria applied in other fields: it must have a distinctive object, a specialized interest in that object not shared by other disciplines, and a distinctive method. Barth also regards theology as a science, and his own thought endeavours to meet similar criteria: the object of theology is the Word of God, God revealing himself in Christ; theology's interest in this subject arises from the need to criticize the church's proclamation in relation to its governing norm; the method is determined by the nature and structure of the object. At the outset Nygren takes a different view from Barth, which unites him instead with the nineteenth-century thinkers, from Schleiermacher on, whom Barth so strongly criticizes. Nygren accepts Kant's Copernican revolution in philosophy, which entails that there can be no science of God, since man has no rational knowledge of metaphysical realities.

The object of theology as a science cannot therefore be God as such, even in his revelation, but must be the phenomenon of the Christian faith. For Nygren, as for Barth, theology is a critical science, but what it inquires into is not the relation between proclamation and revelation, but the experience expressed in the Christian faith. The aim of systematic theology will be to discover what distinguishes Christianity as a religion from other religions, to expose Christianity in its distinctiveness, rather than to discuss it in its totality, which includes much that is in fact not distinctive. There is an implication here which is perhaps less strictly scientific: what is distinctive in Christianity is implicitly taken as normative, what is less distinctive is regarded as unimportant or even illicit.

Nygren's approach resembles Schleiermacher's in beginning with a philosophy of religion, in which the validity of religious experience is first defended, and then what is distinctive about Christian experience sought for and expounded. His theology must deal, as Schleiermacher's did, with the content of the faith of Christians, not with the object of faith, which cannot be directly known by the reason at all. The neo-Kantian aspects of this philosophy of religion, rather than what it owed to Schleiermacher, were probably the reason why its readers saw in Nygren an ally of the early Barth in restoring the transcendental mystery of Christian thought in a time when it had been humanized by liberals. Both affirm the transcendence of God over the powers of the human reason, and lay a classical, or neo-Reformation, stress upon sin and grace. But whereas the early Barth tried to escape from Schleiermacher by setting up his diastasis between revelation and culture, and the later Barth escapes altogether, with the aid of Anselm, into dogmatics properly so-called, Nygren continues to discuss the distinctiveness of the Christian experience of faith, with the aid of the contrast between *agape* and *eros*.

Nygren regards religious experience as the communion of man with the eternal (within the philosophy of religion he prefers this term to God, since its implications are wider than theism). This communion is realized within religion, which is a specialized area of human life, distinct from science and morality, and of no concern to the scientist or moral philosopher as such, though he may also in another capacity be a religious man. Man's communion with the eternal is incapable of empirical verification, and in this it resembles the experience of ethical obligation. Its enjoyment depends on personal decision and commitment, as does ethical experience, though religious experience is distinct from ethical experience. Accordingly, religious experience cannot validly be criticized in the light of norms drawn from outside its own universe of discourse. Similarly, each particular religion has its own form of communion with the eternal, and the decision to regard one of these as right and the others as wrong can only be made by an act of choice, in which one is preferred to the others. Hence, a statement which is 'true' within the universe of discourse of one religion may well be 'false' from the point of view of another. No theoretical reason can be given for the choice of a religion.

The task of systematic theology will be neither to speak positively and rationally about the object of Christian faith, in the manner of later Barth, nor to offer an apologetic for Christianity as the best or highest religion, in the manner of much liberal theology, but to describe the Christian form of communion with God in such a way as to bring out what is central and distinctive in it, and to show how everything else is related to this centre. Though Nygren is a Lutheran, and strongly influenced by Luther in his conception of what is in fact authentically Christian, his intention is not to produce a Lutheran systematics. He wishes to give a scientific account of Christianity itself, not just of the Lutheran form of it, or of the thought of Luther. These narrower tasks are easier to perform, since one's interpretation can here be checked against the writings of the men under consideration.[1]

To analyse Christianity as a whole Nygren developed a new technique which he called 'motif-research'. He attempts to discover the distinctive motif of Christianity in its communion with the eternal and finds this in *agape*. Motif is a word not much used in English, but common in other European languages. We are most familiar with it in music, as for example in connexion with Wagner's *Leitmotive*. In German *Motiv* can also be used for the subject-matter of a photograph. The aim of motif-research is to discover the identifying theme of Christianity. Where this is present, we shall know that Christianity is present too, and where it is absent, we may assume that we have left the Christian universe of discourse. If the right motif has been identified, we shall be able to see how the subordinate themes can be systematically organized by relating them to this. The motif is not just an element in the thought of a particular writer, but runs through the history of a religion. The material studied by motif research is thus very broad, including the Scriptures, the work of theologians past and present, and the life of the church. In spite of its complexity, it is an objective, scientific study, verifiable against the material, and systematic in its organization of the results.

Nygren finds the distinctive motif of the Christian communion with God in the idea of the love of God as *agape*. Other religions also speak of the love of God, but they mean something different. In particular, Nygren finds a sharp contrast between the idea of love in Hellenistic religion and that in the New Testament and Luther. The difference is summed up in the distinctive terminology employed to express the two contrasting motifs, though Nygren realizes that the difference of meaning is more fundamental than the difference of language, and would exist even if the same words were employed by both. This can happen to Christianity in languages with a less rich vocabulary for love than Greek.

1. Nygren's writings on the philosophy of religion have not been translated into English. For a clear account, to which I am indebted, see Philip S. Watson, 'The Scientific Theology of Anders Nygren', in *Theologians of Our Time*, ed. A. W. and E. Hastings, Edinburgh, T. & T. Clark, 1966.

Modern theologians have frequently held that the first translators of the Bible into Greek deliberately chose the comparatively obscure and colourless word '*agape*' to render the Hebrew word for love. The more common words available to them, *eros*, love, and *philia*, affection or friendship, would not do, it is contended, to convey the highly distinctive idea they had in mind. (However, Hebrew cannot render these distinctions, and it is at least possible that the translators were influenced by the fact that the word *agape* resembles in sound the Hebrew word it is used to translate.) At any rate, the New Testament writers follow the practice of the Greek Old Testament, and use the word *agape* when they want to say that God is love, or its verbal cognate when they speak of the command to love the neighbour.

Nygren understands *agape* as love motivated by grace, not need. According to the Christian conception of the communion between God and man, God does not need man, and does not love him because of his intrinsic worth, which he has lost by sin, even if it had ever been great enough to merit the love of one so infinitely removed in value from man as God. God loves because he is love; his love overflows to unworthy objects, bringing men into responsive communion with himself. Thus the Christian conception of love is bound up with the character of Christianity as a Gospel, with its message that God has come to save lost man. Everything in Christianity can be understood in the light of this motif.

In contrast, Hellenistic religion works with the motif of love as *eros*. *Eros* is the love of God for himself, and the love of man for God, while *agape* is the love of God for man and the love of man for his neighbour. *Eros* is based on delight and need. Its classical expression is found in Plato's *Symposium*, where love is depicted as poor and needy, as ugly and lacking in all those ideal qualities it seeks in the beloved, for its own completion. *Agape* comes not from want and need, but from overwhelming fullness. Both *agape* and *eros* are contrasted by Nygren with *nomos*, or law, as the motif of Judaism. Now all three motifs appear in historical Christianity, in various combinations as well as separately. Augustine's concept of *caritas* or charity, which has profoundly influenced all subsequent thought in Christianity on the subject, was in Nygren's view a fusion of *agape* and *eros*, with *eros* playing the determinative part. Luther's thought restored the centrality of *agape*, placing *nomos* and *eros* on a secondary and provisional level.

Nygren's view has had decisive importance for contemporary theological discussion of love, and at present it is equal in influence to Augustine's own account of the matter. This is a remarkable achievement, whatever criticisms can be made of his view. Such criticisms cannot relevantly be dogmatic ones, on the ground that love ought not to mean *agape* as defined by Nygren. His contentions are scientific: he holds that this is what love does mean in Christianity, when the relevant data are considered. Thus his contentions can be falsified only by reference to the evidence of the data. Here the issue must be whether *agape* as he defines it is indeed distinctive and determinative in the Christian idea of love, and whether, granted this, it is the one central motif in Christianity.

Nygren did not carry through the Lundensian method to a complete systematic account of the Christian faith. In his early years he concentrated on laying the philosophical foundations of a scientific method for theology, and after the completion in the thirties of *Agape and Eros* he turned to biblical theology. His colleague at Lund, Gustaf Aulén, later bishop of Strängnäs, made use of the method over the whole of systematic theology. He is best known in the English-speaking world for two books, *Christus Victor*, a historical study of the doctrine of the atonement, making use of Nygren's method to elicit the motif defined in the title of the book, and his systematic volume, *The Faith of the Christian Church*.

Christus Victor appeared in Swedish in 1930, and rapidly gained a considerable influence. Aulén finds three principal motifs in Christian thought about the atonement. He contrasts the favoured motif, in which Christ's work is understood symbolically as the divine victory over the powers of evil, with the Latin or objective view, associated with the thought of Anselm's *Cur Deus Homo*, and Aquinas' later treatment of the theme, in which God is reconciled to man by the satisfaction of Christ's sacrifice, and also with the subjective view, associated with

Abelard and modern liberal theology, in which man is reconciled to God by the influence of God's forgiving love. The idea
Aulén prefers is found notably in Irenaeus and Luther, though in
one form or another it is very common in the early fathers. He
calls it, on this account, the 'classic view', and believes it to be
primary in the New Testament, while admitting that other views
are also present. He perhaps does insufficient justice to the
presence of the other two motifs in Luther himself. According
to the classic view, Christ brought about the redemption of man
by a victory over the powers of evil, consummated in his death
on the cross, and vindicated in the resurrection. This essential
motif can be distinguished from the garb in which it is also
found, where Christ's death is understood mythologically as a
ransom paid to the devil which he had not the right to retain.
The classic view combines the advantages, and escapes the
disadvantages, of each of the other views: It is objective in that
the atonement is the work of Christ, not just a change in the
heart of man, but God's *agape* remains the constant source of
the work of atonement and God throughout does not change his
attitude to man. God is the author of the whole movement of
atonement, so that man is reconciled to God, as in the
subjective view, but by a work of God in Christ, as in the
objective view. Hence this view is best able to do justice to a
text like Paul's, 'God was in Christ reconciling the world
to himself'.

Aulén's systematic theology combines the descriptive method
of Lundensian theology with the use of the motif of *agape* as the
organizing feature of the system. Translated as *The Faith of The
Christian Church*,[2] Aulén's book has not had the influence of
his *Christus Victor*, but has been found very useful for teaching
purposes, where a good one-volume systematic theology is
needed. In Aulén's view, systematic theology is a science, whose
object is defined in the title of his book. It describes the faith of
the Christian church systematically by organizing it around its
central motif. As we have seen, this is *agape* for the Lundensians,
and in the intellectual realm the equivalent of *agape* is revelation,

2. G. Aulén, *Faith of the Christian Church*, Philadelphia, Fortress Press,
rev. edn, 1961.

God's free self-disclosure to man, who cannot attain him by the upward movement of his spirit in reason, history or culture. Systematic theology cannot prove that revelation is true, but it can show that revelation is central in the faith of the Christian church. Only a fully Christ-centred theology can do justice to this motif, and all merely confessional theologies fail.[3]

REINHOLD NIEBUHR

In America, the term neo-orthodoxy is perhaps most commonly associated with the thought of Reinhold Niebuhr. Since the thirties, he has dominated the American scene as the most prominent native-born theologian, though he disclaims for himself the title of theologian, and regards himself as a teacher of Christian social ethics. Certainly he has not found it necessary to work out his total understanding of Christianity in a systematic way, and his main contribution to theology proper lies in his doctrine of man. His work cannot therefore be strictly compared with that of men like Barth and Tillich. If we are to follow the fashion and apply the term 'neo-orthodox' to Niebuhr, we can do so if we recognize that it can only apply loosely, and that he himself is far from sure that he welcomes it. What joins him to most of the other men described in this book is his criticism of liberalism, though not so much in the field of systematic theology as in the special areas of man and society. Certainly there is little if anything in his thought to justify any of the connotations of 'orthodoxy' as authoritarian or rigidly dogmatic. On his own confession, he stands closest to Brunner of the men so far discussed.

Of German descent, Reinhold Niebuhr was born in 1892 in Wright City, Missouri, a state with a considerable proportion of German immigrants in its population. His father was a minister in a small Lutheran denomination which in 1934 merged with a Calvinist group in the same area to form the Evangelical and Reformed Church; this in turn joined in 1956 with the Congre-

3. For a fuller account of Aulén's thought, see Nels F. S. Ferré, 'The Theology of Gustaf Aulén', in *Theologians of our Time*, ed. A. W. and E. Hastings, Edinburgh, T. & T. Clark, 1966.

gationalists to form the United Church of Christ. After studying at Elmhurst College, Illinois, and at Eden Theological Seminary, Niebuhr went to Yale Divinity School, graduating in 1915. He was ordained to the pastorate of Bethel Evangelical Church, Detroit, and spent thirteen years in its ministry, before going to Union Theological Seminary, New York, as Professor of Christian Ethics; he remained there until his retirement in 1960.

His father was not himself a liberal, but he introduced him to the work of Harnack. Niebuhr learned in his parental home to combine a strong faith and piety with intellectual freedom. He failed, however, to become interested in the questions, largely epistemological, which at the time occupied his teachers at Yale, and chose not to go on to a doctoral degree. Indeed, his academic interests seem to have been first aroused by his experience of the life of the church and society, and he remarks that it was a hazardous choice when Union called him to its chair of Christian ethics in 1928, and that for a number of years he felt like a fraud standing up before a class that attributed to him far more knowledge than he in fact possessed.[4]

However, he gradually became exceptionally well-read in his chosen field, and his intellectual influence extended far outside the theological circles of his professional colleagues. He is widely regarded as one of the foremost of American political philosophers. Beyond this, he is a political thinker and strategist with a real engagement in politics, operating on the Left Wing of the American Democratic Party, and there associated with many of America's leading politicians and political theorists. In addition to the body of his theological writings, he is the author of a great number of articles in monthly and quarterly journals of opinion, and for many years edited the fortnightly *Christianity and Crisis*, which acquired under his leadership considerable influence in intellectual life and politics, even outside nominally Christian circles.

His autobiographical writings, such as *Leaves from the Note-*

4. 'Intellectual Autobiography of Reinhold Niebuhr', in *Reinhold Niebuhr, His Religious, Social and Political Thought*, ed. Charles W. Kegley and Robert W. Bretall, New York, Macmillan, 1956, 1961, pp. 8 f.

book of a Tamed Cynic[5] and the chapter from Kegley and Bretall's symposium, already referred to, show clearly the great importance in his theological development of the Detroit pastorate. 'During my pastorate of thirteen years in the city,' he wrote in the chapter referred to, 'Detroit was to expand from a half to a million and a half population. The resulting facts determined my development more than any books which I may have read.' His own congregation increased in size many times, and came to contain men and women from the most varied circumstances, from workers in the automobile industry, to two millionaires. More importantly still,

the social realities of a rapidly expanding industrial community, before the time of the organization of the workers, and under the leadership of a group of resourceful engineers who understood little about human relations, forced me to reconsider the liberal and highly moralistic creed which I had accepted as tantamount to the Christian faith. . . . My first interest . . . was to 'debunk' the moral pretensions of Henry Ford, whose five-dollar-a-day wage gave him a worldwide reputation for generosity. I happened to know that some of his workers had an inadequate annual wage, whatever the pretensions of the daily wage may have been. Many of them lost their homes in the enforced vacations, which became longer and longer until the popular demand for the old Model T suddenly subsided, and forced a layoff of almost a year for 'retooling'.

He also experienced the ruthless use of power by industry to fend off the organization of the workers into trade unions. 'In my parish duties I found that the simple idealism into which the classical faith had evaporated was as irrelevant to the crises of personal life as it was to the complex social issues of an industrial city.'[6]

When he began to write, his publications were therefore full of criticism of the liberal view of the world, whether expressed in secular or Christian terms. At the same time, his thought then contained many remnants of the culture he sought to criticize. He became prominent in a well-known pacifist organization, the

5. Chicago, Willett, Clark & Colby, 1929.
6. 'Intellectual Autobiography', in Kegley and Bretall, *Reinhold Niebuhr*, N.Y., Macmillan, 1961, pp. 5 f.

Fellowship of Reconciliation, which he ultimately headed. Later, his criticism of pacifism would bring out some of the essential aspects of his mature doctrine of man. He also fell into a somewhat naïve acceptance, as he later felt, of Marxism as a weapon against liberal moralism applied to society. His first major work, *Moral Man and Immoral Society*,[7] made considerable though not uncritical use of Marxist ideas, along with some (well-criticized) pacifist ones. He afterwards considered that it revealed 'a failure to recognize the ultimate similarities, despite immediate differences, between liberal and Marxist utopianism'.[8]

Moral Man and Immoral Society was the first systematic fruit of Niebuhr's involvement in political and social life, as reflected upon from his new academic environment. He was in no way less active than before in all political matters: apart from his involvement in organized pacificism, he founded the Fellowship of Socialist Christians, and ran for Congress as the candidate of the Socialist Party in the New York constituency in which he resides. The book itself is a classic of modern theology. It has been said that 'its explosive effect in American theological circles is perhaps unequalled by the impact of any other single book of the last half-century'.[9] Like the early work of Barth, the book struck the prevailing liberal establishment as wholly destructive. As against the secular liberalism typified by the philosopher John Dewey, Niebuhr contended that education and scientific intelligence could not of themselves bring about a better society. The egoism not just of individuals but of collectives was such that a decent balance in society could not be attained without giving each group enough power to defend itself against exploitation by other groups. Politics and power relations will always be necessary in the most enlightened society.

His critique of Christian liberalism was even more devastating. He simply denied, on the ground of his understanding of human nature, the applicability, taken for granted by liberals, of the

7. New York, Charles Scribner's Sons, 1932.
8. 'Intellectual Autobiography', p. 8.
9. Nathan A. Scott, Jr, *Reinhold Niebuhr*, University of Minnesota Pamphlets on American Writers, Minneapolis, University of Minnesota Press, 1963, p. 15.

ethic of the Sermon on the Mount to a political programme. The ethic of *agape* does not suggest one political programme rather than others: it is equally distant from all, for all must involve power and coercion. Not love but justice is the ethical norm for society. Justice is concerned with the distribution of power, and so the major theme the book had to attack was the problem of power and its use. In these terms he discusses (very topically) the techniques of non-violent resistance then being devised and used by Gandhi. 'Though it may be possible . . . to establish just relations between individuals . . . purely by moral and rational suasion and accommodation', in 'inter-group relation this is practically an impossibility. The relations between groups must therefore always be predominantly political rather than ethical, that is, they will be determined by the proportion of power which each group possesses at least as much as by any rational and moral appraisal of the comparative needs and claims of each group.'[10] Thus a responsible Christian social ethics must be concerned with the right use of force to secure a just distribution of power within a community.

To the liberalism of the time, perfectionist and pacifist to the point of sentimentality, such ideas seemed remote from any possible application of the Gospel to society, though some of Niebuhr's ideas had come from Rauschenbusch and other theologians of the Social Gospel in America, who had sharpened their liberalism with a certain infusion of Marxism. To liberals as a whole, reversion from love to power as a norm meant to go back on the Gospel. Was Niebuhr indeed, as they supposed, a pessimist about man and the power of Christianity to transform him? The thesis of *Moral Man and Immoral Society*, he wrote recently, was 'the obvious one, that the collective self-regard of class, race and nation is more stubborn and persistent than the egoism of individuals. This point seemed important, since secular and religious idealists hoped to change the social situation by beguiling the egoism of individuals, either by adequate education or pious benevolence.'[11] To admit the obvious, and to adjust

10. *Moral Man and Immoral Society*, New York, Charles Scribner's Sons, 1960, pp. xxii f.
11. *Man's Nature and his Communities*, Bles, 1966, pp. 14 f.

one's doctrine of man and one's ethics to fit it, was Niebuhr's aim. His thought was not so much pessimistic and cynical, as realistic, and because it was realistic it increasingly won the respect of those actually engaged in political life.

Meanwhile the events of the thirties were rapidly sweeping away the liberal utopianism that Niebuhr attacked in his writings, and it seemed important to think out a doctrine of man that would do justice to the permanent aspects of his life and behaviour, and neither be simply optimistic, with the secular and Christian liberals, nor simply pessimistic, in reaction. During this period his study of the revelant classical texts of Christian theology proceeded hand in hand with his political involvement, while his view of man deepened, especially under the influence of Augustine, whose thought answered many of his unanswered questions, and emancipated him from both liberal and Marxist views of human nature. On the eve of the war he was invited to give the Gifford Lectures at Edinburgh, and chose as his theme *The Nature and Destiny of Man,*[12] under which title the lectures appeared in two volumes. They are his most substantial contribution to theology, and the work by which he will be remembered, though he has tried to correct the views he expressed in the Gifford Lectures as a result of the criticism they received when they came under world-wide notice.

In this major work Niebuhr tried to give theological expression to the political and social realism he had long embraced, which was now coming to be widely shared under the impact of events. His aim was to describe the human situation, making use of the biblical imagery, and to show that this mythical and dramatic presentation of the condition of man as a self in history was more adequate to experienced reality than its philosophic rivals. Theologically speaking, his Gifford Lectures contain his doctrine of man and his eschatology, but they contain much else besides. Of the rich material Niebuhr wove together into the texture of these lectures, the topics most closely related to his stated theme itself were Christology and the interpretation of history. Though Niebuhr never attempted, or felt the need to attempt, a systematic

12. Vol. I, New York, Charles Scribner's Sons, 1941; Vol. II, 1943; one-volume edition, 1949. English edition, Nisbet & Co. Ltd, 1943.

theology, *The Nature and Destiny of Man* actually deals with several of the key problems of modern theology, though always with the doctrine of man in view.

Niebuhr's thought is profoundly dialectical. If ordinary dialectic is two-sided, Niebuhr's is often many-sided. Even when he is thinking dialectically in the ordinary sense, he often splits the two sides of the dialectic into polarities, and cross-relates them to their partners on the other side of the dialectic. The strength of his thought lies in part in his ability to keep many relevant aspects of a complex issue in mind and under control, avoiding the distortions that come either when one of these gets out of hand, or several are crassly synthesized. Not only does he constantly see theological and philosophical issues in this way, but he sees them as dialectical wholes in dialectical relation to the complexities of historical life. It is his constant criticism of ways of thinking he finds inadequate that they smooth out this harsh and complex dialectic of reality into something that can easily be grasped by the mind, but is inapplicable to human life and history.

His first dialectic in relation to man is that of nature and spirit. Niebuhr gives fresh life to the insight that man exists on the borderline of the natural and spiritual worlds. Man's nature is essentially ambiguous. As a creature of nature, he is subject to the laws and limitations of the natural world, 'unable to choose anything beyond the bounds set by the creation in which he stands'. Like all other natural beings, he needs time and space, warmth and nourishment. At best his life is short, above all in contrast to the immensity of the time and space of the universe. Unlike other natural creatures, however, he can transcend all this through his consciousness. As spirit, he can know and order in his mind the structures of the universe that physically dwarf him, and can use them as instruments of his own creativity. He can think himself, and the self which thinks itself, and so on, into an infinite regress of self-transcendence. Thus man is both 'free and bound, both limited and limitless'. He is both conditioned as nature by the natural laws that govern his existence, and free as spirit to transcend them. In biblical terms, man is a creature, but a creature in the image of God.

The ambiguity of man's existence as nature and spirit is the source of his moral dilemmas. Man lives in *possibility* (readers of Kierkegaard will remember what the latter did with possibility in *The Concept of Dread*), and so in anxiety. If he were but a child of nature, he could not know possibility, for he would simply actualize the laws governing his existence. If he were simply a spirit, he could actualize his possibilities in freedom. In his ambiguous situation as a man, he has possibilities which are none the less limited, but part of the possibility which surrounds him is that he does not know at what point he will or will not encounter limitation. 'Man is anxious not only because his life is limited and dependent, and yet not so limited that he does not know of his limitations. He is also anxious because he does not know the limits of his possibilities. He can do nothing and regard it perfectly done, because higher possibilities are revealed in each achievement. All human actions stand under seemingly limitless possibilities. There are, of course, limits, but it is difficult to gauge them from any immediate perspective. There is therefore no limit of achievement in any sphere of activity in which human history can rest with equanimity.'[13]

Like Kierkegaard, Niebuhr sees man suspended vertiginously between finitude and freedom, both of which he must accept if he is to live in spiritual health. The vertigo expresses itself as anxiety, and anxiety is the condition from which all sin arises. Man is constantly tempted to escape the discomfort of this anxiety by abolishing (though he cannot in fact do so) one or other of the aspects of his dual nature, which gives rise to his anxiety. He will either be a god or a beast: either he will make himself the basis of his own security, or he will try to renounce freedom by plunging into his natural condition. In so far as he yields to the temptation to renounce his proper manhood in its painful ambiguity, he falls into sin: if he tries to evade nature and finitude, he falls into pride; if he tries to renounce freedom, he falls into sensuality. In general, Niebuhr is more concerned with pride than with sensuality, since this is the form of sin which is principally at work in the social relations he studies.

13. *The Nature and Destiny of Man*, Vol. I, London, Nisbet & Co. Ltd, 1941, pp. 195 f.

However, we must not suppose that like some theologians of the past he identifies sin with pride, still less with inherited sensuality. Sin for him is the evasion of the human condition.

In this connexion Niebuhr has recently confessed to a pedagogical mistake.[14] Supposing, not unreasonably, the truth of the observation formulated some years ago by a writer in the *Times Literary Supplement*, 'the doctrine of original sin is the only empirically verifiable doctrine of the Christian faith', he tried to express for a wider audience the inevitability, though not the ontological fatedness, of sin so conceived, by making use of the biblical image of original sin. He tried to demythologize the old myth and to exhibit the resulting perspective on man as the truest realism. The upshot was that the remaining liberal optimists thought him a religious authoritarian, while the social realists who agreed with the political philosophy of the lectures felt obliged to say that they could not agree with his theological presuppositions. Yet what he meant to say, and did say, should have commanded their agreement at this point too, and doubtless would have done, if he had not made the 'mistake' of using the biblical term. He wanted to speak of sin as utterly pervasive in every moment of human existence, yet as always entered into in freedom. Original sin 'can therefore not be attributed to a defect in (man's) essence. It can only be understood as a self-contradiction, made possible by the fact of his freedom, but not following necessarily from it.'[15]

Original sin was widely taken to be *all* Niebuhr wanted to say about man, and once again he was hailed, like so many of his theological contemporaries in those days, as a prophet of gloom, cynicism and depression about the human race. But he had also much to say about grace, as operative here and now within human history, though it has not yet achieved its final destiny, so that human life is a real drama, and no theologian's melodrama. He sees even the tragedy of man as grounded in that which gives him his greatest dignity, his radical freedom. Niebuhr works the myth of original sin along with the most concrete reflection upon experience. It is no theological abstrac-

14. *Man's Nature and his Communities*, Bles, 1966, pp. 15 f.
15. *Nature and Destiny of Man*, Vol. I, p. 18.

tion for him, but precisely a poetic myth, which refers to the life we actually live, and can be verified in our experience of our condition. The superiority of the Christian view of man, as sinner through his radical freedom, lies in its capacity to preserve the agonizing ambiguity of human nature, without resolving it, and so becoming unfaithful to the experienced tension of being human. It will stress to the exclusion of its opposite neither man's dignity nor his wretchedness, neither his freedom nor its limitation.

Niebuhr once said that his theology is nothing more than the analysis of the truth about *Christus pro nobis* (Christ for us) and *Christus in nobis* (Christ in us). If this is so, Christology must be the key to Niebuhr's thought too, as it is to that of so many of his contemporaries.[16] Since he is not a systematic theologian, he does not offer a systematic presentation of his Christology, nor relate what he does say explicitly on the topic to a fully worked-out Christology. Nevertheless, when his Christological thought is all assembled, as by Lehmann in the article referred to, it appears as a whole which is both original and highly relevant to the themes of man and society with which Niebuhr has constantly been occupied.

Christ is the final revelation, and therefore the key to the understanding of man, both in relation to God and in relation to his neighbour in personal and social life. In the biblical imagery, Jesus is both Son of God and Second Adam. As Son of God, he embodies God's sacrificial *agape* in history. This is the way Niebuhr understands what has traditionally been called his divinity. As Second Adam, he shows us what man really is. The Second Adam presupposes the first – mythically, man under the conditions of sin. Thus Jesus connects man's original and ultimate perfection, showing us that he is made for love.

As Niebuhr explores the applications of Christology to his theme, he is led to further dialectics. The dialectic of Christ for us and Christ in us has already been mentioned. Lehmann shows how Niebuhr's thought moves backwards and forwards between

16. For an interesting attempt to see Niebuhr's whole thought from this angle, see Paul Lehmann, 'The Christology of Reinhold Niebuhr', in Kegley and Bretall, *Reinhold Niebuhr*, New York, Macmillan, 1961.

these poles, starting from human historical experience and so interpreting Christ's significance for us in terms of his grace within human life, then moving to the other pole to show that this grace is intelligible only because Christ carries out his atonement on man's behalf, before its fruits can enter human life as grace. On the other hand, if he starts by expounding the work of Christ for man, he must move at once to show how this is operative within man. Similarly, he is concerned to show the relationship of Christ not only to the self, in the salvation of the individual but (and surely this is much more difficult to do) to the world and its redemption. Christology must be related to history, and it is here that he finds it necessary, as we shall see, to revive the symbol of the second coming of Christ, almost totally discarded by liberal thought.

Both *pro nobis* and *in nobis*, Christ embodies the grace of God. Niebuhr likes to talk of grace dialectically in terms of power: grace is the power of God *over* man and the power of God *in* man. So it is both the forgiveness that overcomes man's estrangement from God through his sin, and also the enabling power that lets him overcome his actual sins. Similarly, he wants to show how sacrificial love, or *agape*, the love that does not count consequences or reckon on being returned, is necessary to the creation of mutual love, both in the love of Christ and the love of man for man. Love which reckons only with mutuality cannot elicit mutuality.

Man's nature is related to his destiny. He lives in history, which extends the ambiguity of his existence into the time dimension. The true meaning of history has been disclosed in the cross of Christ. The sacrificial love of the cross is the final norm of human life, whatever Niebuhr may also want to say about proximate norms, in his treatment of social and political issues. We see the character of history as interim precisely in the inapplicability of the final norm to proximate social situations. History stands between the first coming of Christ, in which its meaning is disclosed, and his second coming, in which it is fulfilled. *Agape* does not rule here and now. 'Sin is overcome in principle but not in fact.' Here is a statement which has drawn down more criticism on Niebuhr from his fellow-theologians than any other, yet it is easy to see what he meant, though there may be better ways of saying it. Of course, Niebuhr means to say that sin is also overcome in fact, in the lives of individuals at least, but his realism forbids him to exaggerate the extent to which this has happened, even in the saintliest of men, and *a fortiori* in their institutions, including the church. In history love cannot simply triumph, as the liberals thought. It 'has to live in history as suffering love, because the power of sin' makes triumph impossible.

The interpretation of history and of man's social life in history requires a realistic assessment of the persistence of original sin in spite of redemption. Imperfection will dog every human effort, and the holiest of men and groups will be betrayed by their egoism into sin. This egoism will express itself in the rejection of finiteness, in the sin of pride and idolatry of self. Here is the theological root of Niebuhr's constant polemic against utopianism, Christian, secular or Marxist. Increasingly he has come to see in such utopianism greater depths of evil; more recently he has been led to the judgement, unusual in a contemporary theologian, that communism is more evil than Nazism, precisely on the ground of its aggravated utopianism, and the acts into which such utopianism betrays its political exponents. In his later years, Niebuhr has moved a long way from the semi-Marxism, and even to some extent from the socialism, of his earlier period. On the other hand, he has had increasingly to struggle against the conservative implications of the doctrine of original sin, which have so strongly marked the political attitudes of traditional Christianity. In later life, he moved close to the conservatism of the British Conservative Party, though never to that of the American Right, which he regarded as a profoundly decayed liberalism.

His justification of democracy is based on his dialectical view of man. In a famous sentence, he said: 'Man's capacity for justice makes democracy possible, but man's inclination to injustice makes democracy necessary.'[17] Political philosophers who underestimate man's capacity for justice think he should be protected from himself by some form of authoritarian government. But the conventional liberal democrat grounds his faith

17. *The Children of Light and the Children of Darkness*, p. xiii.

in democracy on faith in human nature, totally underestimating the possibilities of chaos, always latent in society, and the need for structures of law and for sanctions to keep them at bay, precisely for the sake of democracy. When the sentimental liberal is exposed to the shock of reality, and sees what man is really capable of, he panics, and falls into a pessimism as great, and as ill-founded, as his former optimism. Hence he can be as dangerous as the professed authoritarian.

The dialectical view of man also leads to the conclusion that history contains neither its own fulfilment nor its own meaning. This meaning has been disclosed in Christ, but history as we know it awaits its fulfilment. 'Symbolically this is expressed in the New Testament in the hope that the suffering Messiah will "come again" with "power and great glory."'[18] The hope of the second coming of Christ is certainly a symbol, not a literal truth. But if, as a symbol, it cannot be taken literally, neither can it be dismissed as unimportant. Either error tends to obscure the biblical dialectic of time and eternity, either reducing the ultimate vindication of God over history to a point in history, or presupposing an eternity which annuls rather than fulfils the historical process.[19]

The resurrection is a symbol that discloses related truths about man and history. 'The hope of the resurrection embodies the very genius of the Christian idea of the historical. On the one hand, it implies that eternity will fulfil and not annul the richness and variety which the temporal process has elaborated. On the other it implies that the condition of finiteness and freedom, which lies at the basis of historical existence, is a problem for which there is no solution by any human power.'[20] Man's final fulfilment cannot be imagined as annihilating the duality that constitutes his nature. It must include nature as well as spirit, body as well as soul. Even in history, the power of the resurrection is seen in the rebirth of man. Faced with the sacrificial love of God, man's prideful self undergoes a shattering dissolution. From this death man can be reborn in the power of grace to be

18. *The Nature and Destiny of Man*, Vol. II, London, Nisbet & Co., Ltd, 1943, p. 298.
19. ibid., p. 299.   20. ibid., p. 305.

a real self, living in and for others and in relation to God. In fact, justification by faith occupies so important a place in Niebuhr's thinking that some have regarded it as an adequate single principle of interpretation. In its negative and positive implications, it does sum up what Niebuhr wishes to say about the nature and destiny of man. He is a sinner under grace, who remains sinner even while the power of grace is at work in him, and sins most when he denies his own sinfulness.

We have several times referred to Niebuhr's use of myth. Myth belongs to the essence of his theological method, and brings him into superficial disagreement with Bultmann, who means by myth something very different. What Niebuhr himself means is something much closer to what Tillich calls 'symbol', a term which Niebuhr also uses when he is thinking primarily of myth in its verbal expression. 'This is perhaps the most essential genius of myth, that it points to the timeless in time, to the ideal in the actual, but it does not lift the temporal to the category of the eternal (as pantheism does), nor deny the significant glimpses of the eternal in the temporal (as dualism does). When the mythical method is applied to the description of human character, its paradoxes disclose precisely the same relationships in human personality which myth reveals, and more consistent philosophies obscure, in the nature of the universe.'[21]

Niebuhr uses myth as a primary theological category. Myth must be 'taken seriously but not literally'. By his use of myth, the theologian is enabled to speak, poetically and dramatically, as he could not if he tried to express himself philosophically, of the presence of the transcendent within human life. A philosophical expression of the myth would necessarily have to translate the transcendent into terms of immanence, whereas the myth can suggest what cannot be said literally. So myth relates the category of the *pro nobis*, the transcendent initiative of God's grace, to the *in nobis*, the human and historical experience of grace. Without seeking to give impossible precision to its description of the realities with which theology is concerned, myth relates them to historical experience in such a way that it is not meaningless to talk about verification, at least where the doctrine

21. *Interpretation of Christian Ethics*, S.C.M. Press, 1937, pp. 82 f.

of man is concerned. Perhaps in Niebuhr's handling of theological ideas through the medium of myth we find one of his most original contributions to the contemporary discussion of theological method.

RICHARD NIEBUHR

Reinhold Niebuhr's brother, H. Richard Niebuhr, did not achieve the world-wide fame of the older man. Born two years after Reinhold, he moved sooner into the academic world, to which he was more naturally suited, becoming a professor at Eden Theological Seminary, where both men had been trained, before he went on to Yale to do his B.D. and PH.D. After a period as President of Elmhurst, the small college in which both Richard and his brother did their undergraduate work, he returned to Eden, and eventually, in 1937, became a member of the faculty at Yale Divinity School. From 1953 he directed Graduate Studies in Religion at Yale University, and continued on the faculty of the Divinity School and University until his death in 1962. Reinhold Niebuhr wrote of him: 'He was always a few paces ahead of me in theological development; and all my life I have profited greatly from his clearer formulation of views I came to hold in common with him.'[22] It cannot therefore be concluded that the achievement of the elder brother is by any ultimate standard superior to that of the younger, though the latter's reception has been much quieter. To the professional theologian, at least, Richard Niebuhr's solutions of the problems of modern theology are always of absorbing interest, and they bear upon a wide range of questions on many of which Reinhold had little or nothing to say.

His best-known works reflect many interests held in common with his brother, as well as making his own distinctive contribution to the understanding of the topics with which they deal. *The Social Sources of Denominationalism* (1929) was the pioneer study of the influence upon Christian disunity of sociological forces, sometimes called the 'non-theological factors in dis-

22. 'Intellectual Autobiography of Reinhold Niebuhr', Kegley and Butall, *Reinhold Niebuhr*, New York, Macmillan, 1961, p. 4.

unity'. In 1932 he issued his translation of Tillich's *The Religious Situation*, in which Tillich's thought on history and politics was first introduced to American readers. *The Kingdom of God in America* (1937) continued his studies in church history using sociological tools. The book brings out a distinctive strain in American Christianity, a theological 'myth' that has inspired and directed a great deal of social action over the centuries of American history. *The Meaning of Revelation* (1941) is his subtle and many-sided contribution to the discussion of the topic which is perhaps of greatest interest to contemporary theologians. *Christ and Culture* (1951) takes up his interest in the social teaching of the churches, dating from his doctoral work on Troeltsch, and offers a revision and refinement of Troeltsch's categories in his own famous work. In the 1950s he turned to the question of the ministry of the church and theological education, and joined with colleagues in editing a succession of books on the history and purpose of the ministry, and the relevant ways of training men for it today. His last works, *Radical Monotheism and Western Culture* (1960) and *The Responsible Self* (published posthumously), returned to constant themes of his thought. He was active on the theological side of the ecumenical movement, but became critical in his last years of its then prevailing Christocentrism, which he believed threatened the Trinitarian and therefore the monotheistic character of its theology.

As will already be apparent, one of the distinctive features of Richard Niebuhr's thought is the way in which he works theological and sociological analysis together in a unity. He addresses himself to churchmen who want to think out their faith in the modern world, offering them the instruments for doing so scientifically, but without concern for apologetics. He thinks critically rather than defensively. In addressing the Christian, Niebuhr is constantly aware not only that he is a member of the church, but that he is also a member of many other communities. By taking these communities into account, his theology deals with culture as well as with the Gospel itself. In taking account theologically of the culture in which Christians live, the theologian is enabled to address others with whom they share membership of these various communities. But Niebuhr has no intention of speaking to them from neutral ground. His standpoint is the church and its faith, and from there he describes the Christian faith and its relevance to culture as it appears to him, without attempting to prove or justify it.

In all these connexions, Niebuhr wishes to speak as a 'radical monotheist'. Because he attaches such importance to his monotheism, he can and must regard all that is not God as relative. He is freed by his radical faith for the most sensitive awareness of all the relativities of time, place and cultural belonging which influence the social life of man and his thought. He is thus able, since he does not absolutize his own position, to enter into dialogue with other members of the communities in which he participates. Increasingly his own relativism finds expression in an existentialist outlook, which he uses to understand appropriately the interaction of selves in community, and of man with God, the person who confronts him finally.

Niebuhr wrote in the preface to *The Meaning of Revelation*: 'Students of theology will recognize that Ernst Troeltsch and Karl Barth ... have been my teachers. ... These two leaders in twentieth-century religious thought are frequently set in diametrical opposition to each other; I have tried to combine their main interests, for it appears to me that the critical work of the former and the constructive work of the latter belong together.'[23] As Hans W. Frei wrote in his masterly study of the background of Richard Niebuhr's theology: 'The result of Niebuhr's encounter with these two thinkers has been that one of his major tasks is to unite a doctrine of radical monotheism and Christocentric revelation with an understanding of our life as responsible persons in an endlessly varied cultural history.'[24] It may be that Niebuhr does not altogether succeed in bringing his response to these two very different men into a unity, as it would have been immensely fruitful to do. The influence of Barth is more apparent when he thinks about revelation and confessional theology in general, that of Troeltsch in his social thought, including the fact

23. *The Meaning of Revelation*, New York, Macmillan, p. x.
24. 'Niebuhr's Theological Background', in *Faith and Ethics*, ed. Paul Ramsey, New York, Harper, 1957, 1965, p. 64.

of its pervasiveness in his theology. Had he succeeded in relating the critical work of Troeltsch more effectively to the basic issues of theology (and this is the point at which Troeltsch's own thought broke down) while perhaps integrating more fully the constructive work of Barth into his study of communities (for here he seems to owe more to Kierkegaard) his achievement might have been even greater. Indeed, he might then have been the key figure in contemporary theology. As it is, these problems remain unsolved in the form that Niebuhr might have been uniquely fitted to solve them, though he raises them more suggestively than thinkers with more integrated and systematic theologies are able to.

Niebuhr's radical monotheism arises from his conviction that the fundamental question for theology is God. Neither man himself, nor history, nor sin raise the problem of God: God himself does, for man finds him intervening in his natural religiousness to confront him, first as his enemy and then as the bestower of grace. Theology must therefore reckon with the existence of natural religion but never speak from the ground of natural religion. If there is natural religion, there is no natural theology for the Christian. The Christian must see natural religion only through faith in Jesus Christ. God is the enemy of what we naturally want and value. Only in Jesus Christ can we be related to this enemy-God in faith. In Christ the goodness and grace of God has been revealed for Christians, and this alone gives them the ground for speaking of him. 'Christian theology today must begin with revelation, because it knows that men cannot think about God save as historical, communal beings and as believers. It must ask what revelation means for Christians rather than what it ought to mean for all men, everywhere and at all times. And it can pursue its inquiry only by recalling the story of Christian life and by analyzing what Christians see from their limited point of view in history and faith.'[25] In this passage we can see the connexion between Christocentric revelation and relativism. The confessional standpoint of the Christian is represented (perhaps a little ironically) as relativistic.

The third strand in Niebuhr's thought, his existentialism, also

25. op. cit., p. 42.

appears when he thinks of God. For him there can be no question, as in Tillich, of regarding God as transcending the subject–object distinction, so that he is no longer thought of as *a* person, or *a* being. 'We must think and speak in terms of persons.' God confronts us in 'irreducible selfhood' as a person. Though God is always subject, he is fully objective to us. As subject, he is the centre of his own free and purposive activity, and he initiates and acts, never becoming passive to the actions of others. In relation to us he is a genuine other. If he transcends in any sense the self-other relationship, it is not by entering both sides of that relationship as a participant, but by confronting us in an original self-other relationship in which all other such relationships are grounded. Niebuhr thinks of our knowledge of God realistically and non-metaphysically. For him, God is still a transcendent person, who is other than us and to us, as in traditional theology. However, since the divine person is unique, our relationship to him is unique. In this unique relationship, and there alone, we have knowledge of God.

Radical monotheism arises from man's perception of God's confrontation of his natural religion, which is always polytheistic, as its enemy. Looked at from this point of view, God is always power, hostile power, defeating everything outside himself. Such an emphasis on the power of God, going back to the traditional self-abasement of the Calvinist before the glory and majesty of God, divides Niebuhr from liberal theologians who can conceive God only in terms of love. Power and love must meet in the divine unity. Only in faith can we see them to be one, when God reveals himself in Christ as the Father of the Son, and our Father. Paradoxically, radical monotheism must be trinitarian. Niebuhr believed that less radical monotheisms prevail in modern theology, in the form of (covert or open) unitarianism of the Son or of the Father. But these raise acutely the question either of God's power or of his goodness, according to whether one starts from the Son or the Father. The God of nature seems not to be good: the God of the cross seems to lack power. Together in the Trinity they are almighty goodness and holiness. The doctrine of the Trinity is a reformulation in the light of revelation of our natural conception of unity. God reveals himself, then, as a single person who is altogether powerful in his goodness, and good in his power.

'Just as faith knows no absolute standpoint it can therefore accept the relativity of the believer's situation and knowledge. . . . To deal as we must with the relative values of persons, things and movements does not involve us in relativism, when we remember that all of these realities which have a relation to each other also have a relation to God that must never be lost to view.'[26] Relativism is here thought of as total relativism, which Niebuhr disclaims. Even his relativism is relative to his radical monotheism. Relativism for the Christian is both grounded and overcome in the relation of all relatives to the absolute God. Radical monotheism renders all other distinctions relative by distinguishing God ultimately from everything else.

On the other hand, in the relation of things and persons in the world, who are all relative to God, relativism means limitation. There is no absolute standpoint, except God's, and other persons can only think from their own time, place and situation. To consent to this relativity makes possible fruitful social and historical thinking. No one can think as a historian or student of social organizations who thinks in absolute terms, for he cannot understand the past as different from the present, or another society as operating according to different norms from those of his own. Such relativism makes possible the distance in the observer, which allows him to see what is different from himself as different. Having once learned to do this he can see how other beings and societies differ not only from himself but from one another.

Existentialism provides a way of understanding the interaction of relative selves and societies, without absolutizing any. Niebuhr gains his existentialist insights from Kierkegaard, rather than from the latter's twentieth-century successors who have used existentialism to construct a phenomenology and even an ontology. Niebuhr learns from Kierkegaard to think of the responsible self, and of the acts and decisions on which his thought must follow. The self exists in moral relation to other selves: it is always together with others, but always other than

26. *Christ and Culture*, New York, Harper Torchbooks, 1956, pp. 239 f.

they. This given relationship of persons is the foundation of knowledge and thought, and leads to the understanding of our confrontation by God as person and as other. It follows that truth, above all theological truth, can never be detached from moral act and responsibility: it is never merely intellectual or theoretical. Theological truth, then, is relational.

Unlike some existentialists, Niebuhr finds that insights of this kind cut him off from neither history (in the sense of the past) nor reason. The self is to be understood as not just in the present, but existing in time. The past endures in the present, and in part makes it what it is. Hence Niebuhr's view of revelation does not oblige him to break the relationship between the historical and the historic in Christ in the same sharp way that many neo-orthodox writers do, especially those who are existentialists in the manner of Bultmann. For Niebuhr, revelation lies not just in the 'now' of preaching, but in the historical existence of Jesus Christ, and its enduring effect. Because his existentialism permits the thought of other selves not just as subjects but as objects too, it allows him to regard God objectively, as one who can be thought about, though only within the relationship of faith. On the other hand, the same existentialism forbids him to take Barth's way into ontology. He would doubtless echo the criticisms of Brunner and Bonhoeffer against Barth's positivism of revelation. Nor does Niebuhr work out any doctrine of analogy that would permit him to lay out a rational statement of what we can know about God. In this respect, at least, he remains at one with the thought of the nineteenth century.

Seven

Language
and God

Modern theology has been dominated by men whose work is now finished. Either old age or death has brought their creative powers to an end. Fortunately, we may still hope to read a little more of the work of some of the greatest of them, but even from these no fresh ideas can reasonably be expected. But the stature of these men is so great that no younger writer can yet be discerned who appears to belong to their company and to debate with them on equal terms. On the whole the theology being produced today moves within the set of problems defined by these men and their own nineteenth-century predecessors. Those writing today see the problems in the same way as their elders, though they try to improve on or refine their answers. For a further generation of creative theologians to appear, equal in originality and power to those discussed above, it would be necessary to escape from the problems dominating the neo-orthodox generation, and define fresh ones. Such developments usually arise from cultural changes to which writers respond with fresh questions and solutions. My own guess would be that the next important movement in theology is more likely to come from America than Germany, for that is where the culture is changing fastest. Hence it may be significant that the most radical theology being written today comes from young American writers.

The writers now in their prime are mostly pupils of or strongly influenced by the group of men considered in the central portion of this volume. The easiest way to understand their thought is to relate them to their predecessors, and to notice how they modify the questions or the answers they have inherited. When we turn to younger men, whose thought is not yet fully developed, but

308

who are the ones most likely to lead theology in new directions, we can still trace the influence of the great men of the neo-orthodox generation, but it has now become more confused. Influences criss-cross or are combined in unexpected ways. There is a widespread tendency to view the nineteenth century with renewed respect, and to assert that its questions have remained unanswered during the period of neo-orthodox ascendancy. A search is to be discerned for a theology that will continue the nineteenth-century quest for intelligibility and modernity, while taking into account the criticisms of twentieth-century writers of the solutions offered in the previous century. New ways of thinking are being tried out in several quarters, but there is still little sign of anything so radically new that it would be possible to speak of a third phase of modern theology. Even the most original work appearing at present seems capable of being set in the context of questions we have already examined in the work of previous writers. Those who are most inclined to describe their own work as radical probably differ from their elders most in taking with much greater seriousness the unanswered questions of the nineteenth century. The thought of that century seems to be assuming greater importance, after its criticism by neo-orthodoxy has been absorbed.

It is not surprising if neo-orthodoxy failed to dispose conclusively of the theology of the nineteenth century. The origins of the twentieth-century world lie in the nineteenth. Most of the philosophical implications of the culture of today were already apparent to nineteenth-century thinkers. While our culture remains based on industry, technology and science, these problems will remain paramount for theology. Only a philosophical revolution, reflecting a new perception of man's relationship to the world, and therefore perhaps a new stage in the development of science, is likely to render the problems of the nineteenth century wholly obsolete. As a matter of fact, it is possible that such a revolution is on the way. In the last few years there has been converging interest, from a number of angles, upon the question of communication, and hence a sharpened interest in how the human mind itself works. The vitality of the pop culture in Britain and the West Coast of

North America, fascinated with extending the bounds of experience, the work of the communications experts like Marshall McLuhan on media, as extensions of the nervous system of man, and the rapid rise of interest in oriental religion and its techniques of meditation, may be straws in a wind blowing in the same direction. But these influences are strongest in people under thirty, and very few theologians have anything distinctive to say until they reach their forties at least.

It may be a while, therefore, before we read any theological work expressing this altered outlook. For the present, we may expect theologians to continue to confront the problems raised by science, and by its empirical method. The revolution in culture generated by the systematic application of scientific method to every possible area of life is still accelerating. Its benefits can hardly be contested. However, the empirical approach to reality raises acute problems when applied to man. It turns him into an object, a thing. We know that we are not simply objects, since we experience ourselves also as subjects. It is useful to regard man as an object for certain purposes, but if we refuse to take into account the immediate knowledge of ourselves that consciousness affords, we become less than human. As the empirical method is currently understood in the natural sciences, only objective facts count as evidence. Thus an empirical psychology will discount the evidence of introspection, and deny the relevance of consciousness to the scientific study of man. Radically empiricist man is behaviourist (and atheist). He sees himself as a part of the natural world that lies open to his dominance. Like the world, he must first be understood as a mechanism (in this case a biological one) and then made to function better through the mastery given by scientific understanding. But thus to objectify man is also to rob him of what is distinctive in his humanity, and to impoverish his personal life.

Hence there is widespread discontent with the way of life brought about by the scientific revolution, in spite of its benefits. People have a hunger that science does not appease. No previous culture has consumed art on such a scale as our own. We look to painting, music and literature to provide us with a way into a world whose doors science has almost closed to us. The currently renewed interest in the practices of both eastern and western religions indicates a feeling that consciousness and personal life were perhaps better understood in the period in which these religions took shape. Yet the way of introspection, and the study of consciousness (even 'cosmic consciousness') does not seem to lead to intellectual conclusions about the nature of reality. Science remains the way we know about how things are. By contrast, every other route to understanding appears subjective, telling us about the way we feel, and adding nothing to our stock of reliable information, about the world, man or God.

There is nothing here for the theologian to make apologetic capital from; he is caught in the same dilemmas himself. As the problems just discussed present themselves to the theologian, they raise for him the question of language. In the tradition which has so far led modern theological writing, it has been common ground that God speaks to man in his Word. The questions that arise from this starting-point have already been noted. What is meant by the Word of God? How is this word related to the Word made flesh, to the written word in Scripture, and to the word of proclamation? And how are these in turn related to the language of theology? Against the background of the dominant empiricism, theology is forced to re-examine its language. Must the theologian throw in his lot with the scientist, and speak only of publicly ascertainable facts? If so, theology is likely to become confined to historical investigation and to analysis of religious literature. It will no longer be able to speak directly about human life, still less about a God who created and redeemed it. The alternative seems to be to open itself to the realm of the imagination, restoring a mythical dimension to religious thought, at the expense of being classed with poetry and fiction, instead of with those disciplines that can find out what we do not already know about reality.

One possible way of overcoming these dilemmas has recently been gaining ground among writers engaged both in theological work and in the study of religion and religions. This way, no less empiricist in its aims than scientific thinking, endeavours to make available for rigorous study a wider range of experience than the 'facts' to which science must be confined. It stems from the phenomenology of Husserl, Scheler and Heidegger in Germany, and of Sartre and Merleau-Ponty in France. Phenomenological analysis begins by provisionally renouncing concern with reality and truth, attending without prejudice to whatever appears in consciousness. Thus, the objects of the religious consciousness can be studied with great exactness, since the perceptions of the investigator are not blurred by premature concern with explanation. This method is particularly useful in studying religious literature, especially that coming from the past or from another culture than our own, since it can free us from the assumption that we already know what is or is not real. But the method is by definition confined to the analysis and description of phenomena as they appear to consciousness, and if the ultimate aim is scientific, must be supplemented with the attempt to explain what has been described.

Among contemporary theologians, Bultmann and Tillich in particular have made abundant use of phenomenological method, especially in the form of the 'existential analysis' associated with Heidegger.[1] The influence of Heidegger, including the later Heidegger passed over by Bultmann, is even stronger in more recent writers. Their interest is focused on the relation between consciousness and language. The problem of interpretation, or hermeneutics, raised for modern theology in classical form by Bultmann and his associates, centres on the attempt to reconstruct the contents of a writer's religious consciousness as it was before its conceptualization in language. The ultimate point of reference is no longer language itself, but the experience of the self in relation to the world. Language is not that experience, but its expression, whether adequate or otherwise. So, if the original experience of a religious writer of the past can be reached, behind his own language, it can be re-expressed in our own, and thus 'interpreted', or even 'understood'.

Theologians of another sort have remained close to scientific ways of thinking. They have tried to explore the significance for theology of the philosophy, especially influential in Britain and

1. See above, p. 170.

America, that is concerned with language from another point of view than that of hermeneutics. European phenomenological and existentialist philosophy is interested in language as expressing man's self-understanding and his experience of his world as it appears to him; English-speaking linguistic analysis is interested in language from the point of view of its logic. It classifies language into types of utterance, examining the criteria by which they can be identified, and the logic appropriate to each. Its hope is to clear away many of the old puzzles of philosophy, which (it holds) result from what Wittgenstein called 'bewitchment' by language. This method of working has attracted a large group of men of outstanding ability, though perhaps Russell and Wittgenstein, among an older generation, remain the most influential writers. The thought of the group is now quite complex, and suffers (particularly in theological writers) from over-simplification by those who wish to debate its positions from the outside. In particular, it is a mistake to identify a whole philosophical tendency with the logical positivism of the inter-war period. The latter in effect asserted that thinking is scientific thinking, alleging that all (genuine) assertions are verifiable in sense experience; utterances lacking such (actual or possible) verification were held to be either tautologies, like the propositions of mathematics and logic, or emotional noises. Theological statements were placed in the latter class.

Some of the most interesting work now being done in English-speaking theology endeavours to confront the issues raised by the philosophical analysis of language from the point of view of its logic. If linguistic analysis can clarify (and hence in some cases sweep away altogether) longstanding problems in philosophy, perhaps it can do the same for theology. Analysis of the meaning and logic of theological utterances could lead both to clearer statement and to fresh insight about what should be said. As the philosophers who practise linguistic analysis have themselves moved from the crudities of logical positivism into a more sophisticated grasp of the subtleties of language, they have become open to dialogue with theologians once more, and challenged theologians to respond by using these methods to explain what they are doing. As we compare the European and the English-speaking types of theological concern with philosophy, we cannot fail to be struck by the fact that each is concerned with language, though so far in a very different way. Across the gulf which has so far separated the two philosophical tendencies, occasional signals pass which indicate dawning realization that the problems are ultimately held in common. Theologians likewise, though strongly differentiated in the same way, are becoming aware that both approaches may be useful to them, and are perhaps not mutually exclusive.

THE INFLUENCE OF THE NEO-ORTHODOX GENERATION

To isolate, as I have, the problem of language as the most important now facing theologians is not to underrate the importance of what is being done by those who continue to occupy themselves with more traditional problems. Enough has been left over for their successors by the men discussed above for their influence to remain paramount. Among the theologians of the last generation, the most influential seem to have been Barth, Bultmann and Bonhoeffer. The influence of Tillich and the Niebuhrs is present, especially in American theology, but in subtler ways. In particular, there is widespread recognition that Tillich is the father of 'radical theology', even if it adopts no position associated with Tillich himself. The influence of the Niebuhrs is to be traced more in the continuing interest of American theologians in ethical questions than any particular positions they have taken up. In tracing the influence of the theologians of the last generation upon the younger men, it may be useful to ask, firstly, which of them a writer is most indebted to, and then whether he belongs on the left wing or the right wing of those influenced by him. The left wing takes a writer's methodology as normative, and uses it to generate new positions often quite different from his own, as the left wing of the young Hegelians did in the nineteenth century. The right wing takes the substance of his thought as normative, and either refines his own positions in detail, or pushes on to questions he had no time or inclination to deal with. This way of classifying younger theologians is naturally very schematic, and is only meant to serve the purposes of preliminary study. Moreover, the division between the left and the right wing sometimes tells us more than identification of a principal influence does. All radicals, and all conservatives, seem to have a great deal in common with their fellows, whatever specific influences they have undergone.

Barth's influence is perhaps too massive for any highly creative writer to submit to it; accordingly, those who remain close to him are seldom radicals. As we noted in the chapter on Barth, the most important area of his influence seems to be ecumenical theology. Though ecumenical questions have ceased to be of major interest for most Protestant theologians, they have suddenly become so for Catholics. We may expect the influence of Barth to be most strongly felt where Catholic and Protestant theologians are in dialogue on the central issues raised by the confrontation of their traditional theologies.

Is there a left wing among those influenced by Barth? If there is, I think it can be identified among those who have learned from him that theology is a 'science', whose assertions refer to a given object, but who now wish to relate this conception of theology to the discussion among philosophers about the criteria for assertions, or (in the terminology of Wittgenstein) to identify theology's 'language-game'. If that is so, we may regard Paul M. van Buren, who was actually a pupil of Barth himself, as a very left-wing Barthian. His book, *The Secular Meaning of the Gospel* (S.C.M. Press, 1963), which has attracted a great deal of attention, will be discussed below in a fuller treatment of the contemporary interest in the logical analysis of theological language. While this interest is shared by theologians of diverse background, the thought of Barth is one part of that background.

Among those influenced by Bultmann we must class some of the most important theologians now writing. In the chapter on Bultmann we observed that since 1950 theological debate in Germany has centred round the questions raised by him; even the debate between Barth and Bultmann is about Bultmann's questions, not Barth's. The discussion on hermeneutics is carried on principally among those in debt to him. Influences from

Barth and Bonhoeffer have also, however, been introduced into that discussion. In general we may regard as right-wing Bultmannians those who hold to the neo-orthodox features of Bultmann's own thought, concentrating upon hermeneutic problems. The left wing both in Europe and America has called in question matters taken for granted by Bultmann himself, such as the Christocentrism of his view of revelation, and the rather traditional view of God as a transcendent person which seems to underly his discussion of the action of God in the world. Noting that Bultmann's doctrine of God does not fit easily into a perspective governed as his in other respects is by an existentialist anthropology, a group of younger writers sharing the hermeneutic concern has tried to work out a doctrine of God less dependent upon a Christological revelation in history. Thus the neo-orthodox contrast between man as historical being, and nature as the somewhat alien background to history, is now called in question. Among these writers the doctrine of God is given conceptual form by means of a philosophy of process, grounded in an analysis of nature as well as of history. This tendency, to be considered at greater length in its appropriate place below, is certainly a strong growing-point at the present time. Though the adherents of process-theology are not all left-wing Bultmannians, it is especially prominent among them.

The influence of Bonhoeffer is perhaps more diffuse, or rather pervasive; like that of Tillich and the Niebuhrs, it leads to interest in certain questions, more than to close community in answers. In this case the questions are those raised in the prison letters. I think it is now becoming evident that the influence of Bonhoeffer, like that of Barth, is too captivating for an original writer to submit to without creative paralysis; it is noteworthy that among the younger men the influence of Bonhoeffer is widely acknowledged, but his exact positions seldom retained. Among older men there is a right wing, which has done a great deal to interpret the seminal thought of Bonhoeffer to a wider audience. First among them should be placed Ronald Gregor Smith, who has done more than anyone else, both as publisher and as writer, to make Bonhoeffer's thoughts widely known to an English-reading public.[2] In this group, too, we may perhaps place two writers not usually regarded as right-wing in any sense, J. A. T. Robinson and the young American writer Harvey Cox. These are probably the most influential theologians now writing in English. My excuse for placing these men among the right wing of those influenced by Bonhoeffer is that each has given vivid and penetrating expression to ideas first conceived by him, as well as by others of the neo-orthodox group, notably Bultmann and Tillich, and successfully demonstrated their relevance to large numbers of non-theological readers.

Though neither Robinson nor Cox has put forward a position of real originality in the books with which their names are at present most associated, the former in *Honest to God* (primarily for British readers) and the latter in *The Secular City* (primarily for North American readers) have together brought about nothing less than a theological revolution at the level of the 'common reader'. By emphasizing the radical implications of the thought of a group of neo-orthodox writers of the last generation, they have created a climate in which the need for fresh answers is widely recognized. Thus the historical importance of these two best-sellers may prove greater than the originality of their proposals. They may turn out to be the last influential works of the school of thought to which this book has been chiefly devoted, and to have brought its dominance to an end. The way is thus open for these men or others to open up theological perspectives invisible from neo-orthodox ground.

Thus, while we have certainly not heard the last of either Robinson or Cox, we can without injustice regard their work so far as trail-blazing for a more radical group of left-wing followers of Bonhoeffer (and to some extent, as I have already suggested, of Tillich), who have taken up Bonhoeffer's criticism of the traditional doctrine of God, and pushed it to limits he does not appear to have considered, making their own Nietzsche's phrase, God is dead. The importance of this group, in my judgement, lies at present less in the proposals they have put forward, which

2. See his *The New Man*, S.C.M. Press, 1956, and *Secular Christianity*, Collins, 1966. Gregor Smith was Editor of the S.C.M. Press during the period that it published translations of Bonhoeffer's most important works.

must certainly receive considerable refinement and elaboration in the next few years, as in their attempt, not so far very successful, to escape from the set of questions and answers that have characterized the leading theologians of our time, and to write a new sort of theology for the last third of the twentieth century.

We thus find a convergence among contemporary writers, various as are the influences they have received from the immediate past, upon two major problems, neither of which is new, for both have been inherited from both nineteenth- and twentieth-century theologians. However, in the past decade the cultural changes that have been going on since the beginning of the nineteenth century have been accelerating, and have rendered these inherited problems ever more urgent. In this sense it may be said that the issues we defined at the end of Chapter One have narrowed down and become simplified. What must be the language of theology in our time, and how can the theologian speak of God in the language he chooses to employ? To each of these questions we must now turn in greater detail. Clearly they are inter-related.

THE NEW HERMENEUTIC

We begin with the discussion of language in relation to hermeneutics which has dominated German theology in the last decade and a half, occupying the attention of almost all the leading men. The main focus of the discussion has been the journal, *Zeitschrift für Theologie und Kirche,* under the editorship of the systematic theologian Gerhard Ebeling, of Zürich and Tübingen. Ebeling was at first a church historian, and in turning to systematic theology has given it a novel meaning, in which the hermeneutic problem is central. Essentially he sees systematic theology as the study of the principles to be used in translating and explaining ancient texts, and in particular the Bible, for the comprehension of modern readers. The task *par excellence* of the systematic theologian is the interpretation of the New Testament. Thus in spite of a highly professional knowledge of the theology of the past and present, Ebeling seems to have little interest in system-building in the traditional manner, and his work has mainly taken the form of essays on particular topics.

In his editorship of the *Zeitschrift für Theologie und Kirche*, Ebeling has provided a forum for the discussion of all the topics arising in the post-Bultmannian debate. Many of the articles that originally appeared in the *Zeitschrift* are now being reproduced in English in the related American annual, *Journal for Theology and Church* (New York, Harper and Row, 1965–). The hope of the American group of writers which has joined with Ebeling and his German collaborators in this new venture is that the issues of the German discussion will become better known through the journal in the English-speaking world, and that theologians from there may become able in due course to make significant original contributions to the debate.

A number of Ebeling's own works has been translated into English. The most important of these are *Word and Faith* (S.C.M. Press, 1963), *The Nature of Faith* (Collins, Fontana Library, 1966), *Theology and Proclamation* (S.C.M. Press, 1966), and *The Problem of Historicity* (Philadelphia, Fortress Press, 1967). The titles of these books clearly show how Ebeling has started from the set of problems raised by Bultmann. In attacking them he employs a wider range of ideas than those specially associated with Bultmann himself, pulling into the debate some ideas of Barth and Bonhoeffer, as well as those of the so-called 'New Hermeneutic', of which he is himself the principal exponent, along with his close associate Ernst Fuchs of Marburg. Less closely allied than Ebeling and Fuchs, but belonging to the same general tendency, are Heinrich Ott, Barth's young successor at Basel, and a number of others, including Americans like James M. Robinson, John A. Cobb and Robert W. Funk. The American series *New Frontiers in Theology* (New York, Harper and Row, 1964–), has made a number of important articles available in English, along with fresh contributions by American writers.

We may fairly take the questions raised by the New Hermeneutic as typical of the most interesting work being done in Germany today. The hermeneutic issue is certainly not new in itself. Apart from the attention focused on it by the work of Bultmann, it goes back to Schleiermacher, and was further developed in the nineteenth century by Dilthey. The contemporary discussion on hermeneutics largely stems from the article on the problem by Bultmann in the *Zeitschrift für Theologie und Kirche*, later reproduced in translation in his *Essays Theological and Philosophical* (S.C.M. Press, 1956). It is not difficult to agree with these men that hermeneutics or the problem of interpretation is of fundamental importance for theological thinking, without necessarily conceding that it is *the* problem, or that it must be solved by means of an existential ontology. Interpretation is necessarily involved in the study of any document, particularly an ancient one, if it comes to us from another culture. Interpretation is more than just translation. Within a common culture, translation is a relatively simple problem. It can be assumed that to each word in a given language there corresponds a word or phrase in a language into which it is to be translated. There will be minor differences of outlook and vocabulary, but equivalents will exist. American and Soviet scientists can communicate by translation machine. Where there is a cultural gap (as between American and Soviet politicians) matters are not so simple. The writer of the document to be interpreted experiences himself in relation to the world differently from his new readers; even words that appear to be equivalents belong in a different context. If the original contentions of the writer are to be understood today, they must be reinterpreted, so that the writer will say what he would have wished to say in our own culture and time.

Every reader of the New Testament engages in interpretation, but many do so unconsciously. The naïve reader may fail to realize what must be involved if his interpretation is to succeed. He must decide first of all what the words meant for the first-century men who wrote and first read them. Only when he has thus discovered, so far as is possible, the original meaning of the text can he go on to the second part of the task, and attempt to render the same meaning in contemporary terms. Without the resources of scholarship, it is unlikely that either task can be satisfactorily discharged. The first depends on a knowledge of the literature, social customs and philosophical outlook of the ancient world, which together provide the context for the thought of the New Testament writers. The second depends on a correct analysis of contemporary culture and *Existenz*, in which personal judgement must necessarily be involved. The common reader usually concentrates, whether he is aware of it or not, on the second task. He makes the biblical writers mean what he thinks it would be appropriate for them to say today, without controlling this by proper exegesis of what they did in fact say to the men of their own time. He fails to grasp the first-century meaning of the text; if in addition he is a conservative, and wishes to reject a twentieth-century one, he is most likely to end with one appropriate to the eighteenth century.

To ignore the problem of communication between cultures is therefore not to escape it but to become its victim. If we assign to the New Testament a meaning it did not have for its first readers, and can have for only a minority of present-day ones, we have failed to bring its message to the life which the believer claims it possesses for all men in every culture. The group of theologians principally associated with the hermeneutic task considers it the duty of the theologian to work in the service of the proclamation of the Gospel to twentieth-century man by performing this double act of translation, or exegesis and commentary, and by making it as truthful as possible. It can only be this if it is as faithful as present-day resources allow both to the original meaning of the text and to the meanings which are possible without our present culture.

What distinguishes these men from other theologians, for all theologians, like all readers of the Bible, are engaged in some form of interpretation, is first, that they conceive of the theological task as such as one of hermeneutics rather than system-building or philosophical analysis, and second, that they employ for this purpose a broadly existentialist philosophy of language, which in the case of some of them, notably Ott, owes an explicit debt to the later Heidegger, whose work Bultmann, as we have noted, did not find so useful. In his later writings Heidegger conceives the philosophical task as the study of being. By this he means, if we have correctly understood him, neither the transcendent being formerly ascribed to God (this he thinks has collapsed) nor the individual beings which can be known empirically, but that which *enables them to be*, in the sense of resisting non-being. What Heidegger wishes to understand under the term being appears to be closely connected with what Tillich called the depth of being, or the ground of being, of being-itself. Heidegger, unlike Tillich, explicitly refrains from calling being God.

On the other hand, if Heidegger does not call being God, he does ascribe to being the quasi-divine capacity to disclose itself in an event, which is manifested in a development of language. Hence a revelation can be called, as by these theologians, a word-event, or a language-event. In a new constellation of language, being discloses itself afresh. If revelation is a language-event, the aim of the interpreter is to mobilize contemporary language in the service of the Word, so that the original word-event of the primitive kerygma becomes word-event again in our language, for us and for our contemporaries. For Heidegger, poetry becomes exceedingly important philosophically. The kind of thinking which leads to poetic composition is that which renders a man open to the disclosure of being and to the event in which that disclosure takes on expression in fresh language. Authentic preaching, and indeed theology, ought to have something of this poetic quality, in which language is new minted under the pressure of the Word.

In his later thought, Heidegger remains an existentialist, but his existentialism is now largely focused in language. As John Macquarrie puts it: 'As time has gone on, language has become in Heidegger's philosophy the existential phenomenon *par excellence* and the very key to Being.'[3] Thus, a follower of Heidegger can speak of the language-character of reality, or 'the linguisticality of existence'. Communication becomes, as in some very recent developments in scientific thought, the basic category for the understanding of the world. If this is so, the theologian will be entitled to consider his own work of very special relevance, but he may be inclined to stress its distinctive, even professional aspects more rigorously than before. He will see himself, as have most Protestant theologians, including those here described, as the servant of the Word. He need no longer concern himself with

3. *Principles of Christian Theology*, New York, Charles Scribner's Sons, 1966, p. 113.

giving a metaphysical clarification to the Word in terms of substance, or any such understanding of being. Just by concentrating on the study of language, for which his training has pre-eminently equipped him, the theologian will fulfil the interpretative task, while at the same time satisfying the requirements of the philosopher. Hence the Word and its answer in faith becomes everything in this theology, and systematic theology becomes a dimension of biblical exegesis and historical study, rather than a theological discipline in its own right.

The exponents of the 'New Hermeneutic' go beyond Bultmann in two ways. They resist his tendency to separate language and reality in his demythologizing programme. Reality in their opinion does not exist for man except in its expression in language. Hence demythologizing, though admittedly necessary, is not so simple a matter for them as for Bultmann. It involves a new language-event, or perhaps better, the repetition of the original event in new language. The nature of language itself must provide the principles of interpretation. Secondly, they consider that Bultmann's notion of what is involved in the preliminary understanding of the subject-matter of the Gospel, which permits the hearer to know what is being talked about, and to ask a question which the Gospel answers, is too explicit; they think it implies that the necessary pre-understanding for the New Testament is faith itself. In their opinion, all that is needed for the understanding of the New Testament message is the perception that the self is a problem to itself. The problem of understanding the self, to which the understanding of human existence given in the New Testament is the answer, is thus a universally human one. This idea is one that goes back to Wilhelm Herrmann, the teacher of Bultmann in systematic theology.

The way these men conceive the problem of self-understanding and self-communication goes back through Dilthey and Schleiermacher to German idealism. They are preoccupied with the problem of objectivization. The self objectified in language is for them distorted, and hence any interpretation must somehow go back behind the language to the original act of the self reflecting upon itself. On the other hand, language is the way in which such a self-understanding finds expression, even for the self that understands itself. It is not altogether clear, therefore, whether the hermeneutic problem, thus understood, can even in principle be soluble.[4] These writers hope to solve it existentially, by understanding the Gospel as a communication of a new self-understanding through language from subject to subject. But the language is misunderstood if it is thought to confer an objective understanding of either subject, God or man. A major preoccupation of this group therefore is the overcoming of the subject–object scheme in proclamation and its reception by faith. This is understood to be achieved if God as subject addresses man as subject through the proclamation in such a way as to evoke faith as a total response of the self to the Word. Faith as gift then becomes as much God's act as man's, and the preaching ceases to be objectified doctrine and becomes a medium of inter-subjective communication. It must be acknowledged that some readers will continue to find this idea somewhat obscure.

THEOLOGY AND LINGUISTIC ANALYSIS

The problem of language also arises for those who approach theology through an encounter with empiricist philosophy in its contemporary form. Perhaps the best way to understand the problems that arise in this context is to look at the contentions of a particular book, Paul van Buren's *The Secular Meaning of the Gospel*, which has been widely read and discussed in both America and Britain since its publication in 1963. When language is approached from the angle of finding out what is and can be said in it, that is, through an analysis of its logic, we at once find that the problem of language raises the problem of God. The two problems we have isolated as most important in contemporary discussion turn out to be connected. It will be impossible to avoid anticipating, in a discussion of language, questions that arise when theologians deal directly with the topic of God. But there will be no harm in this, since the connexions are manifold.

4. Cf. Hans W. Frei, 'Theological Reflections on the Gospel Accounts', in *The Christian Scholar*, xlix/4, 1966, pp. 303 ff.

When van Buren returned to America after completing his doctoral dissertation with Barth at Basel, it seemed for a time as if he might develop into a right-wing Barthian, but his thought rapidly became more radical. If we start from the assumption of Barthian influence, his book will appear as an attempt to understand what has been believed with the aid of techniques of philosophical analysis drawn from the (largely British) logical empiricist tradition. In Barthian and Anselmic terms, his programme seems to be one of seeking understanding. But it is stipulated that faith is to be understood in strictly secular terms, since in the author's opinion these are the only terms in which we can understand it at all. Here the themes (though not the specific positions) of Bonhoeffer are also invoked. For van Buren, secular interpretation involves some philosophical commitments, which he makes clear at the outset. These include rejection of all forms of idealism, and a consistently empirical approach to the understanding of reality. In consequence, what began apparently as a fresh analysis of the meaning of Christian faith rapidly turns into fresh proposals for its content.

These are so radical as to involve dispensing with a doctrine of God. *The Secular Meaning of the Gospel* sets forth a systematic Christology in which those elements formerly ascribed to God are reinterpreted as expressions of the universal significance the Christian sees in the life and death of Christ. It is impossible to speak about God, for language about God cannot be assigned a clear meaning, when thus analysed. Or rather, it can be assigned a clear meaning, once it is recognized that this language is not cognitive, that sentences about God cannot be taken as making assertions about how things are. God-talk can be given a meaning, so long as we refer it not to the object, 'out there' in reality, but to the subject and to his response to the reality he experiences in Christ. Talk about God refers to particular experiences which are felt to have universal significance. It is the way in which the speaker qualifies his commitment to certain disclosures of meaning as absolute. Thus although there is now nothing left of the traditional assertive meaning of propositions about God, they are by no means simply discarded. In their new meaning they play a role in van Buren's systematic Christology formally similar to, though of course substantially different from, the one they used to play in traditional theology.

Van Buren seems to have moved a long way from his starting-point in a very short time, and it is worth while asking how he got there. Once he has taken the decision to be strictly empirical, he is really committed to his atheist conclusions. God is by general agreement not a verifiable phenomenon in man's world, who can be the subject of a hypothesis analogous to those produced by scientists in their work of understanding and controlling the world. Both on theological and philosophical grounds, an analysis of theological statements as hypotheses for the understanding of the world will be rejected. If all that can be said about reality must be said in a scientific manner, in statements that can be checked rigorously against how things are in the world, it would appear that nothing can be said about God. If God is not part of the world, statements about him can neither be verified nor falsified by reference to the world. In that case, it is contended that nothing at all can be said of him.

Van Buren does not commit himself to statements in the radical idiom like 'God is dead', nor to those of the simple atheist such as, 'There is no God', or 'God does not exist'. Nevertheless, it seems inevitable to group him with the radicals, in spite of the distance he has maintained from them and their work. His book is most compellingly interpreted as that of a Barthian who has freshly discovered that the God who is only spoken of in positivistic statements drawn from revelation cannot be spoken of at all when a secular positivism is substituted for the 'positivism of revelation', as Bonhoeffer called it. But van Buren does not follow Bonhoeffer in retaining God as an object of faith and worship behind the screen of the discipline of secrecy, while seeking for a worldly interpretation. Rather, the worldly interpretation demolishes the old doctrine. God is reinterpreted without remainder. God becomes simply a symbol for the absoluteness of the Christian's commitment to a new perspective on the world, drawn from his vision of Christ.

About Christ van Buren, like other radicals, speaks clearly and movingly. He sees freedom as his most salient characteristic: Jesus was a free man moving among the bound. After his death, he became able to convey this freedom to his original disciples, and to fresh ones. Thus the event of Christ's freedom becoming contagious, as it was not before his death, corresponds in van Buren's theology to the resurrection in the traditional scheme. Indeed, the whole book is shaped around a systematic though highly reinterpreted Christology, in which all traditional doctrines reappear, but in novel guise. Like Barth's, van Buren's theology is systematically Christocentric. It may be objected to his project, like that of the other radicals, that without God there is no reason for the central place assigned to Christ. Van Buren might reply that no reason can ever adequately account for faith. The radicals have, like millions before them, taken the decision to be Christians, and this is the way that they as twentieth-century men have understood that decision.

Is van Buren, as all Barthians would unhesitatingly say, yet another theologian who has reverted to the nineteenth century and taken the high road from anthropology to the atheism of Feuerbach? Perhaps, but certainly not in his own understanding of what he has done. He does not adopt the atheist position any more than the theist. He simply interprets traditional doctrines in the only way possible today, a secular one. If it is contended that this interpretation 'reduces' what is interpreted, so that it means less than before, he will ask what the missing 'more' could be. If he has said all that can be said today in secular terms, he cannot say 'more'. To purport to say more by uttering apparently cognitive statements about God would be to say less, for such statements are false if they are scientific hypotheses, verified by how things are in the world, and empty if they have no such reference, and are thus compatible with all possible conditions of how things are in the world. At least everything van Buren says has a clear meaning.

What is not so clear is whether the use of the sort of philosophy van Buren favours necessarily leads to dispensing with talk about God, at least in its traditional acceptance. The philosophy in question is not such a simple or homogeneous one as might appear from van Buren's use of it. One indication of this is the variety of names by which it is known, such as linguistic analysis, logical analysis or logical empiricism. We have so far used them somewhat indiscriminately, and the time has come to be more precise. If a theologian wishes to use the work done by these philosophers for his own purposes, he must decide which aspects of it are most significant for him. Van Buren, searching for a secular way of understanding the Gospel, seized on logical empiricism, as reflecting the science-oriented way in which secular thought views language and reality. Hence his interpretation of the Gospel is more than an analysis of the way its language functions. As we have noted, he accepts norms to which its language must conform if it is to be judged secular. But theology could also choose to analyse the way in which its language has traditionally functioned, and let the issue of secularity fall where it may. One of the most useful pieces of work for a theologian today, in preparation for any fresh advance in understanding, might be to look at the writings of some traditional and modern theologians from this more strictly analytic point of view. John Macquarrie has now made a beginning with Athanasius in his *God-talk*.[5]

However, a more strictly analytical approach to the nature of theological language would probably raise the question of the meaning of talk about God almost as quickly and acutely as van Buren did. Even if we have no norms to which we insist language must conform, our analysis will aim at clarification of what is obscure. One form of clarification is to sort propositions out into categories. We ask about any proposition purporting to say something whose truth or falsity can be discussed how it may be known to be true. Some statements are true in virtue of the meaning of their terms. To deny them is simply to utter a contradiction. But such statements are not generally thought to add to our stock of information about reality. Statements which do this are usually thought to be verified by looking at the state of things in reality to which they refer, in order to see if the statement conforms to it. The old logical positivists thought that an assertion, as this kind of statement is usually called, is verified by reference to sense experience. Further discussion showed the inadequacy of this criterion, even to the statements

5. J. Macquarrie, *God-talk: An Examination of the Language and Logic of Theology*, S.C.M., Press, 1967.

logical positivists wanted to make. But I do not know that it has shaken the fundamental principle that a statement, to qualify as an assertion, must be such that things would be different if it were true from how they would be if it were false. A statement compatible with all possible states of things in reality does not assert anything. Hence an assertion may also be recognized by the fact that it can significantly be denied. Assertions, and those statements which are true in virtue of the meaning of their terms, do not exhaust the possible categories of language by any means, and under the influence of Wittgenstein philosophers have sought to distinguish the subtle varieties of tasks language performs, and to identify the many 'language-games', as he called them.

Now all this has a great deal to do with the question of God. There can be no doubt that past theologians have supposed that statements they made about God were neither empty nor lacking in significance. They intended to say something true, and it mattered a great deal to them that they should not say something false. Were they 'bewitched' by language, leading them to think that they were saying something, when by the nature of language they could not be? This is more or less van Buren's contention, and certainly many philosophers who have examined theological language along the lines just described have concluded that it is impossible to construe talk about God as cognitive, or as making assertions. Why is this? There are, I think, two principal reasons for theological language running into difficulties of this sort, one traditional and one modern. The traditional source of difficulty lies in the kind of things theologians have wanted to say about God. They have wanted to say that he is the creator of the world as a whole, not just of particular things within it. Thus, if what is said about God were not true, there would be no world at all, and no theologians or philosophers to discuss the matter. But this criterion of falsification is a very difficult one to deal with. The possibility suggested as capable of falsifying talk about God is practically speaking an impossibility, and is intended to be taken as such. The theologians do not consider it possible that there should be no God. From another point of view, they have wanted to say that nothing that could ever happen would (or ought to) shake their faith in God. Hence no particular event in the world, no matter how evil, could count against God. Or if it could *count* against him, it could never be decisive: it could never amount to a falsification. It thus appears that the traditional doctrine of God takes the form of statements that are compatible with all possible states of affairs in reality, and thus do not assert anything of significance. Neither their assertion nor their denial postulates any other state of affairs than that which everyone agrees is the case. Hence, whatever the meaning of the traditional statements, it cannot, apparently, be assertive. Nothing factual is being alleged.

The modern source of difficulty is related to the traditional one, but arises from the wish of the contemporary theologian to avoid getting into unnecessary conflicts with science. Many traditional theologians, and some conservative ones today, have so constructed their doctrine of God that it could apparently be verified or falsified by reference to miraculous events. If the miracle happened, the existence of God is confirmed: if not, it is rendered less probable. A vivid example of this kind of logic is to be found in the story of Elijah's contest with the prophets of Baal in 1 Kings xviii, 19–40. Here the reality of the living God of Israel over against the gods of the Canaanites is confirmed by a miraculous answer to prayer. Few contemporary theologians would be willing to risk a similar experiment. Indeed, they would deny that the reality of God can or ought to ever be tested by deliberate experiments on man's part. No miracle could in itself confirm God, no failure to produce miracles on demand could falsify faith. In short, faith is fidelity even in circumstances where *everything* seems to count against it. Hence theologians are, especially today, not at liberty to use the usual criteria to establish the cognitive character of what they want to say about God. Talk about God is 'logically odd'. It purports to be assertive, but does not submit to the usual criteria for assertions.

The phrase 'logical oddity' occurs frequently in the works of I. T. Ramsey, a British philosopher of religion (now Bishop of Durham) who has in a series of books contributed much to the discussion we have begun to look at.[6] Ramsey is concerned to analyse in contemporary, that is, broadly empirical, terms a much more traditional position than that of van Buren. He is not, I think, concerned to innovate theologically, but to explain what is going on when theologians think and talk on behalf of the Christian community. His influence is widespread, and he is one of the sources van Buren uses for his notion of 'a disclosure' on which the Christian bases his perspective on the world. Such *disclosures* are for Ramsey the source from which talk of God comes. A disclosure occurs, usually after sustained but for the time being fruitless efforts at apprehension, when a set of existing features of the world, or of events, suddenly assumes a new meaning for the seeker. No fresh information is conveyed in a disclosure, but the existing information is now perceived in a pattern formerly not perceived, one possessing power and significance, so that it imposes itself as the *right* pattern. Such disclosures have the force of – precisely – revelation. Disclosures occur in many contexts, from scientific research through literary criticism and creative work to philosophical speculation and religious experience.

What is disclosed in a disclosure? So far we have implied that only pattern, or form, is disclosed, but this must include meaning. If I see a large sign in a foreign city, where I know a very little of the language, but am not at present at all familiar with it, I may stare at the letters uncomprehendingly, until they assume a pattern which is significant and even in a sense familiar – perhaps HOMMES. The letters have not been added to, nor has a translation flashed on below them, but there has been a disclosure of meaning which in an appropriate context may be of importance, even urgency. (The example is my own, not Ramsey's. It may also serve to illustrate Bultmann's point about the necessity of preliminary understanding. I must have personal experience of the context in which this word becomes significant, and as a male human being I possess this.) Similarly, I may wrestle with a problem in my own work, until suddenly I have 'the answer'. But having the answer may not involve knowing anything I did

6. See his *Religious Language* (1957), *Religion and Science: Conflict and Synthesis* (1964), *Models and Mystery* (1964) and *Christian Discourse* (1965).

not know already. It is the significant arrangement of what I know that I have to see in the disclosure of the answer. Ramsey himself several times makes use of a famous example from the Old Testament, where Nathan says to David: 'Thou art the man.'

In this conversation David suddenly obtained new insight into himself and his moral situation. Thus the words of Nathan were a disclosure for David, bringing to light both objective features of reality – the moral obligation David stands under – and also aspects of himself and his conduct he had previously been ignorant of. These aspects of reality had been present all along, and even in a sense known to David, though he ignored them, but it required a disclosure to bring them to full perception. However, the most important kind of disclosure is what Ramsey calls a 'cosmic disclosure'. In this case the elements that re-arrange themselves into a pattern in the disclosure are those of the universe. Here too, no new information is given, but Ramsey regards a cosmic disclosure as a self-disclosure of God through the universe. He sums up his position succinctly in a passage from a recent journal article: 'God is other than the Universe (let alone the world) as he who discloses himself in and through it, something like, though not exactly like, the way we disclose ourselves through our bodily behaviour. Self-disclosures are matches, subject-wise, for that which cosmic disclosure discloses, object-wise' (*Theoria to Theory* I, p. 268, 1967).

Ramsey makes use of the scientific term 'model' for the constellation of language that arises from a disclosure. In a limited disclosure, the feature of the existing pattern of objects or events highlighted as significant in the moment of disclosure is likely to be taken as the key term in the language of the model. In the case of cosmic disclosures, no single term is adequate. Hence Ramsey regards theological language as 'multi-model discourse', each model modifying the others. The result will be a 'logically-odd' type of language, whose oddness, exhibited in constant qualification, will suggest that it points, not just to objective features of reality, but to a disclosure, past or future.

Evidently Ramsey intends to speak of God as other than the Universe, and as a transcendent person, though he does not particularly favour such language. But the disclosure situation which gives rise to theistic language (Ramsey is not here analysing specifically Christian disclosures) is one which adds no new information, as is also the case with the other disclosures he has analysed. Our existing knowledge of reality, gained outside the disclosure situation, provides the empirical grounding for whatever statements may be made as a result of the disclosure. Ramsey says such statements are tested by what he calls 'empirical fit'. This does not mean that they can be tested, like scientific statements, by verification or falsification of predictions derived from them. His testing will be much more like testing historical statements to see if they fit all the evidence at our disposal. This is, to be sure, an empirical operation, but it is not in the narrow sense a scientific one. The evidence against which theistic language must be tested must ultimately be the sum of human experience. If theistic language does not make sense out of all this experience, it will presumably be dropped.

It emerges from Ramsey's discussion, as from van Buren's, and from those of a number of philosophers of religion who have written on these questions, that the oddity of the concept of God makes it extremely difficult to analyse by means of criteria designed for other purposes. God is obviously not a fact, in the sense in which facts are dealt with by science, nor is it at all clear that he is within our experience, especially today. Some have therefore advocated silence about God. But the theologians principally discussed in earlier chapters would find this unacceptable, since they base their talk of God on his *Word*. The prevalence of writing which calls in question the traditional way of talking about God suggests that the neo-orthodox doctrine of God's self-revelation in his Word is breaking down. It can no longer be taken for granted that God speaks in the Word of proclamation, and since the neo-orthodox theologians appear to have effectually barred any other road to the knowledge of God, there is an impasse. Barth's doctrine, the purest form of neo-orthodoxy, is found to be bound up with the assumptions of religion, or to be 'positivism of revelation'. Those who follow Bultmann are much stricter than he in speaking of God only through anthropology, as the reflection in man of a divine act that cannot be spoken of directly. So there is a search going on in various directions for a new way.

PROCESS THEOLOGY

One approach, as we have noted already, is to break with the Christocentrism of the neo-orthodox doctrine of revelation, which Barth, Bultmann and others inherited from the last great liberals such as Herrmann. If revelation is no longer tied to the preaching of Christ by the church, it can be related to a new kind of natural theology. This is the way taken by the various exponents of process theology, many of whom have been under Bultmannian influence. To make use of process theology is to break in more than one way with the traditions of neo-orthodoxy. Apart from going back on its Christocentrism to reinstate metaphysics in a contemporary form, it abandons the strong preference for history over nature as a category of philosophical interpretation. On the other hand, it could be said that process philosophy, or theology, is an application of historical thinking to the understanding of nature.

Whitehead, the founder of process philosophy, made a breach with classical metaphysics analogous to that which Newton made with medieval and ancient science when he conceived of motion instead of rest as the fundamental state of matter. For Newton, a body will continue to move indefinitely in a straight line unless acted on by some force. The metaphysics of the ancient world, on which the classical philosophy of Christianity was founded, assumed that rest was more fundamental than motion, and that motion could only be explained by an unmoved mover. For post-Newtonian physics, motion requires no explanation; rest does. At the very primitive level of thinking from which abstract philosophies arise, there is a fundamental change here which must affect any post-Newtonian metaphysics. Whitehead makes this change when he takes process instead of substance as the way he conceives the fundamental metaphysical reality. For Whitehead, becoming includes being, instead of the other way round. Thus the time dimension is incorporated into the concept of being for the first time, and metaphysics becomes a history of nature.

The American process theologians rely on the 'di-polar theism' constructed by the philosopher Hartshorne on the basis of Whitehead's metaphysics. This theism incorporates into God the pole of being formerly contrasted with him. Not just becoming but finitude and temporality are attributed to God, in addition to being, infinity and eternity. In Hartshorne's thought this has the further consequence that language about God is predicated in its ordinary meaning, and there is no need for a doctrine of analogy. God is then regarded as process-itself, in an analogous way to that in which Tillich regards him as being-itself. Process has now replaced being as the ultimate category. Hence the theistic philosopher thinks that he is justified in applying to God the new ultimate category, as his predecessors did the old one. However, not every past philosophical theologian has identified God with being, and there is in fact an important tradition, represented by Platonists, and strong in the Greek fathers and the Eastern church, which refuses to do so, claiming that God is beyond even being. The risk in identifying God with being, is that being may turn out to be a feature of the world, and to identify God with part of the world would be idolatry. If this risk exists with a philosophy of being, in spite of all the careful qualifications which have been built into it in many centuries of discussion, it is even more plainly present in a philosophy of process, which avowedly starts by analysing features of the world known by scientific method. Thus the process theologians are regarded by some as semantic atheists, who simply deify a feature of the natural world. They would not of course agree with such a criticism, but would take process philosophy as simply providing a conceptuality in which the God of Christian faith can be understood in a contemporary way.

RADICAL THEOLOGY

There is even, it seems, an affinity between process theology and the other way out of the breakdown of the neo-orthodox doctrine of revelation, the radical theology of the death of God.

335

Its most systematic exponent, Thomas J. J. Altizer, who calls himself a Christian atheist, is quoted in an interview as identifying himself with 'dynamic process pantheism'. Altizer is far less explicit in his identification with process philosophy than the post-Bultmannian theologians referred to above, but the fact that he can understand his own thought in this way suggests that process philosophy is susceptible of an atheist as well as a theist interpretation. Altizer makes no reference to process theology in his books, of which only the most recent, *The Gospel of Christian Atheism*, has been published in Great Britain. Whether Altizer's description of himself as an atheist is entirely correct is also a matter which can be debated, if the evidence of his books and articles is to be taken as decisive. What he denies is not necessarily any view of God, but the traditional view of Christian theism, that God is a transcendent person. It is not clear in what sense he can describe himself both as a pantheist and as an atheist; of the two descriptions the former seems borne out by his writings, though they celebrate atheism. Atheism is of course a relative term, and it must not be forgotten that the early Christians were called atheists, because they refused to worship the gods that other people worshipped.

What Altizer and his colleague in the radical movement, William Hamilton, really stand for is a theology of the death of God. To call this atheism would be too simple, though in the relative sense that they consider the God of Christianity to be dead, the term applies. The most puzzling feature of their thought is the assertion that God was once alive and is now dead. Clearly these statements can hardly be taken to refer to the being of God as traditionally understood. They refer in the first place to a change in the character of authentic human experience. The radicals believe that there was a time when it was authentic to believe in, worship and trust in God, but that this time has passed. The death of God is a historical event. In the words of Altizer: 'God has died in *our* time, in *our* history, in *our* existence.' The death of God is therefore a recent event, belonging to the nineteenth and even to the twentieth centuries. Nietzsche's phrase, which they have taken over for Christian and theological purposes, is a poetic way of summing up the whole process of cultural transformation which we have been considering all along as the background to modern theology. The fact that it cannot be taken literally does not mean that it lacks force, including intellectual force. The radicals have put the problems of Christian theology in the modern world in the simplest possible way: how are we to be Christians when God is dead?

Their theology therefore starts from two ideas, which cut through much of the debate among contemporary theologians, and reduce the issues facing theology today to their ultimate simplicity. The first idea is that Christianity is alive in the modern world. The radicals are Christians, and they assume that they belong to a Christian community, though they do not identify this with the institutional church. There is never a time in which it is impossible to be a Christian. Altizer, in particular, will have nothing to do with the idea of a post-Christian era, which is popular among some contemporary writers, including many Christians. In this and all possible cultures, Christian faith continues. The second idea seems clean contrary to the first, but it has the same kind of radical realism. This is the idea that God is dead. The ultimate honesty that Bonhoeffer called for discloses that God is really and truly not given any more. Our experience is atheist. But since this is the experience of Christians, who belong to a community which has known and worshipped God, it is not identical with the experience of the secular atheist. Hamilton expresses the difference, in one of his articles, by saying that it is not 'the absence of the experience of God, but the experience of the absence of God'.[7] The first position may lead to secular atheism, but the second leads to Christian atheism. The Christian atheist experiences a sense of loss, though he does not repine, or try to live in a world which has passed. Nor does he rule out the possibility of the recovery of a sense of the presence of God, but he is sure that it will not be in any form recognizably in continuity with the Christian past. In relation to the God of traditional Christianity, the radicals are atheists. But they are not rationalists, and they are open to the possibility of a fresh manifestation of the divine in an unfamiliar form. Mean-

7. See 'The Death of God Theologies', in Altizer and Hamilton, *Radical Theology and the Death of God*, Penguin Books, 1968.

while the first idea, that they are unconditionally Christians, keeps them loyal to Christ, and they still find in him the centre of their faith. Here they remain closer to the neo-orthodox group than do the process theologians.

Clearly van Buren, for all his disavowal of Nietzsche's language, on the ground that it is as meaningless as its contrary, belongs with this group at least as much as with the left-wing Barthians. He shares with them the confidence that, however radically we interpret the implications for theology of the cultural transformation of the modern world, it is still possible to be a Christian. He shares too their strong Christocentric piety, for I do not know what else to call it. But his philosophical background is different from Altizer's. It is one in which neither theism nor the death of God can be expressed, and it would be equally impossible for him to expect a new manifestation of the divine. Altizer on the other hand draws his philosophical inspiration from the nineteenth century. Hegel and Nietzsche provide him with the dialectical idiom that pervades his thought, and in his most recent books this is filled out and made more concrete with the aid of William Blake's poetic mythology. Underlying Altizer's highly complex thought is his project of finding a contemporary form of eschatological faith. He wants the contemporary Christian to learn once more to negate this present world, in the hope of an imminent future in which God will be all in all.

HISTORY AND HOPE

Altizer's interest in eschatology links him with another young radical of a very different stamp, Jürgen Moltmann of Bonn, and to some extent with a group of German writers in various theological fields, whose names are often linked with Moltmann's outside Germany, though their differences with him are considerable. This is the group around Wolfhart Pannenberg, of the University of Mainz. Altizer, Moltmann and the Pannenberg circle also have in common the wish to break the dominance of Kantian thought in modern theology, and to return to the subtle dialectic of Hegel.

Perhaps the most interesting feature of the work of these

young writers, from our present point of view, is their attempt to isolate assumptions common to the prevalent German neo-orthodoxy, in spite of the differences between its leaders, which have assumed such prominence in recent German debate. Thus, most of the features which we have singled out as characteristic of neo-orthodoxy in Germany are now coming under criticism from these younger writers, and they are trying out various alternatives. In Pannenberg we even seem to find Protestantism itself being called in question, though it is not yet clear how far Pannenberg realizes that he is doing this. Moltmann, on the other hand, remains closer to Barth, especially the very latest Barth of the fourth volume of the *Church Dogmatics*, where he is most strongly influenced by the Blumhardts, the pietist theologians of Württemberg. Nevertheless, it is difficult to escape the impression that at present Moltmann is the more radical thinker of the two, even if his thought presents fewer points of divergence from his immediate predecessors. His work is at present attracting a great deal of attention in the United States, both from relatively conservative thinkers, and from radicals like Harvey Cox.

Both Pannenberg and Moltmann wish to escape from the view of history which has dominated neo-orthodoxy. This view was inherited by men like Barth and Bultmann from the dogmatic theologians of the Ritschlian school from whom they received their own training. Both Barth and Bultmann, it will be rembered, studied at Marburg under Wilhelm Herrmann, and it is becoming increasingly clear that any advance beyond the dialectical theologians will have to begin by noting what they took from Herrmann and the Ritschlians, and asking whether these features of their thought are still acceptable. The Ritschlian view of history, largely taken over by Barth and Bultmann, in their different ways, depends upon a Kantian analysis of the relation of mind to reality, a relationship which leads and has led to a separation between the two which Moltmann calls, following the title of a book by another scholar, *subjectivity* and *objectification*. According to this view, in its strictest form, history is intrinsically without meaning. Meaning resides only in the subjectivity of the human mind. The professional, or 'positivist', historian can only tell us what happened, and if he assigns a cause to what happened, it will only be further happenings of the same kind, occurring a little earlier. Ritschl, it will be remembered, made a sharp distinction, still familiar to scholars, between judgements of fact and judgements of value. The historian makes judgements of fact, the believer adds to these his judgement of value. In the same way, for the existentialist who follows Kierkegaard, objective reality is absurd and meaningless, mere 'facticity'. It is the 'leap of faith' which arrives at truth, in the form of subjectivity. There is, it seems, no intrinsic truth for either. From this Kantian way of looking at reality springs also the famous distinction between *Historie* and *Geschichte*, though it was not a Ritschlian but the 'mediating theologian', Martin Kähler, who made it famous. Existential history, or *Geschichte*, is made by human subjectivity, working on the otherwise objectified *Historie*. As Moltmann (quoting Hegel) says, for this view the forest becomes firewood, and sacred history a tale of events. How can the firewood again become a forest? Not, according to these writers, in any of the ways attempted by their immediate predecessors, but through a different view of reality, in which the opposition between subjectivity and objectification is overcome and transcended.

Such a project at once puts those who entertain it upon Hegelian ground. While none of the men I have mentioned is a thoroughgoing Hegelian, like some of the nineteenth-century theologians, and each is also very seriously preoccupied with the contemporary statement of the New Testament message, Pannenberg and his friends, and Moltmann wish to follow Hegel, not Kant, in a view of history as a process having inherent meaning and direction, perceived, not inserted, by the human mind, in this case the mind of believers. They wish to follow Hegel in seeing dialectical process not only in thought but also in history. Thus their view of revelation cannot be the same as that of Barth or Bultmann.

From this point on I must distinguish between the two men. Pannenberg has for the present at least diverged further from his predecessors than Moltmann. He calls in question not merely the famous distinction between *Historie* and *Geschichte* but even the priority, in a Christian view of revelation, of the Word and hearing over other possible models of reception of divine communication, such as those associated with sight. To the extent that he does this he diverges from the whole Protestant tradition, and enters territory traditionally colonized by Catholics. It is thus not surprising that his view of history has been compared to that of Augustine, rather than to the thought of the Reformers. Moltmann on the other hand remains a theologian of the Word.

Pannenberg tells us that his willingness to consider other models of communication as having equal value with that of hearing a Word stems from the very same reasoning that has led others to insist upon it. When you see, you can choose what you will look at. When you hear, you can only hear what has been said. Thus, the listener is in a greater state of dependence upon what he is told than the looker who can range over whatever is within his field of vision. The looker is more free than the listener. The neo-orthodox theologians, in insisting, as both Barth and Bultmann do, on man's helplessness and inability to question the proclaimed Word, are thus speaking in an authoritarian way inappropriate to modern man, who has been through the Enlightenment rejection of all authority based on status alone. In the German tradition this authoritarian character in religion is known as positivity, or positivism. It will be remembered that Bonhoeffer charged Barth with having a revelation-positivism. Pannenberg wishes to overcome this positivism. Indeed, he suggests a programme of 'de-positivization' of Christianity, which he suspects may render Bultmann's programme of demythologization unnecessary, because his own project will turn out to be the more radical of the two. If Pannenberg is able to carry out this programme effectively, he will efface a certain impression of conservatism which at present undeniably clings to his work, and is responsible for his popularity with conservative theologians in the United States.

Pannenberg seems, rightly or wrongly, to be a conservative because of the kind of commitment to history he wishes to have. His view of the resurrection of Jesus brings this commitment into sharp focus. The neo-orthodox theologians were agreed that the resurrection is an event not susceptible of verification by the methods of the historian. Hence it must be located, if indeed it is to be retained as a crucial element of Christian faith and thought, somewhere else than in ordinary history. Barth locates it in primal history, more real than the ordinary history accessible to the historian, but accessible only to the believer. Bultmann locates it, if he has been correctly understood, in the subjectivity of the believer, and protests against the objectification inherent in the conservative insistence on the empty tomb. Thus for Bultmann the resurrection is reduced, for theology if not for faith, to the Easter faith of the believers, in which the cross is for the first time understood as victory, not defeat. To attempt to verify this insight of faith by proofs from visions, let alone the empty tomb, is to turn faith into a work, and to prove idolatrously what can only be received in unquestioning faith, as proclaimed Word. Pannenberg, in contrast to both, considers the resurrection to be a historical fact. Clearly he can only say this if his view of history is different from theirs.

For Pannenberg the resurrection is the centre of a panorama of universal history, in which God vindicates his own truth and reality, indirectly, inasmuch as he never appears upon the stage of history, but still objectively. When this history is rightly seen, it contains its own meaning. The believer, who sees universal history as a progressive revelation of God, is not inserting into it what is not there. He is seeing it as it really is. Thus, true historiography, or historical method, must be capable of picking up the inherent meaning of history. At first sight, especially to a critic brought up on Barth and Bultmann, this looks like a move to render faith unnecessary, and to hand over Christian belief once more to the professors. The work of historical insight is apparently slated to replace true faith in God's unsupported Word. This is not Pannenberg's intention, but he does mean to understand faith differently from his critics. Faith has confidence in God himself on the basis of his self-revelation in factual history.

How can the resurrection be regarded as a historical fact, in any ordinary sense of the word fact? Pannenberg attacks the assumption common to nineteenth-century historians and those who follow them today, that we can decide whether reported events are facts by analogy with other known facts. Since the resurrection lacks analogies, except in legend, it is usually dismissed as, if not impossible under some immutable laws of nature, so improbable as to be incapable of verification by the historian. Now Pannenberg does not wish to follow the conservatives and Barth, by saying that the resurrection is a miracle, which none the less actually happened. He says it is not a miracle, but a unique historical event. As such, it cannot be dismissed, if the evidence is good enough, merely because of an absence of analogical events; if it is unique, it will not have analogies. But Pannenberg admits that if there were sufficiently strong negative analogies, i.e. analogies to reported events which turned out on investigation not to be what they purported to be, the resurrection could be falsified. In his later work he makes things somewhat easier for himself by admitting that the New Testament evidence centres on the resurrection appearances, not on the empty tomb, and that these are best interpreted, on the basis of the documents themselves, as visions.

We have called Pannenberg's view of historical revelation a progressive one. Strictly speaking, he does not consider history as the revelation of God in the sense that many modern theologians do when they have in mind the history of Israel culminating in the event of the coming of Christ. This 'history of salvation' view Pannenberg rejects. For him, God reveals himself, indirectly as we have noted, not through a special, quasi-miraculous salvation-history, but through universal history. However, this revelation is not complete, and therefore not recognizable as the revelation of *God*, until the process of history is complete. Only at the end of history does it appear that God is God, and the Lord of all the history that has happened. In that case, it might seem that we cannot believe in God on the basis of revelation in history. Here we must return to Pannenberg's analysis of the resurrection. He reminds us, following the British philosopher R. G. Collingwood, that there can be no presuppositionless history. Every achievement of historical meaning is the result of asking a specific question, based on a previously held assumption about reality. The presupposition for the resurrection of Christ was the hope (called 'apocalyptic' by the New Testament scholars) which first-century Jews of the Pharisaic school held of a future general resurrection. The end of history will be the general resurrection, and this will be the final revelation. The resurrection of Jesus assumes meaning and intelligibility against the background of this expectation of the general resurrection. Jesus' resurrection was not understood as an isolated miracle, but as the proleptic beginning of the general resurrection. In this sense, God is thought to have vindicated Jesus' apocalyptic hope of the nearness of the resurrection of all mankind in the Messianic age. The end of history, though future for mankind as a whole, is thus present in the archetypal case of Jesus. But for this reason those who know of the resurrection of Jesus can believe in God, since in Jesus his self-revelation is complete.

In his later work Pannenberg makes a further attempt, and in the judgement of many critics a fruitful one, to close the gap between event and meaning by understanding history as *Traditionsgeschichte*, or *Überlieferungsgeschichte*, terms which his American translators render by 'the history of the transmission of traditions'. The events of history are not bare events, but include the tradition in which they are interpreted. The course of history is likewise characterized by the changes and transformations that traditions undergo. But this course is continuous, and links the believer today with the original events and traditions in which God revealed himself through the resurrection of Jesus.

Pannenberg's thought can be most effectively studied so far in the volume, *Theology as History*, in the American series 'New Frontiers in Theology' edited by Robinson and Cobb (New York, Harper and Row, 1967). Like other volumes in the series, this centres on a major article by the theologian under discussion, introduced by the editors with a systematic review of the German literature, and followed both by a number of critical articles and a reply by the author. A translation is expected both of the symposium by the Pannenberg school, *Revelation as History*, and of his *Foundations of Christology*.[8] Much more will undoubtedly be heard of Pannenberg and his colleagues.

The differences between Pannenberg and Moltmann have not been fully clarified so far, and Pannenberg's replies show that he

8. Now available as *Jesus-God and Man*, tr. Lewis L. Wilkins and Duane A. Priebe, Philadelphia, Westminster Press, 1968.

is sensitive to the considerations on which Moltmann's criticism of his position is based, and that he does not consider himself vulnerable to it. Moltmann wishes to understand eschatology, like Schweitzer, as bearing upon the future, and he refuses to follow the writers of the last generation in reducing it to the impingement of an eternal now upon the historical present. He considers Pannenberg leaves no room for this future history of Jesus in the world, when he understands the resurrection as the proleptic appearance of the end of history within historical time. Moltmann's project in his *Theologie der Hoffnung* (1964, 1965) now translated as *The Theology of Hope* (S.C.M. Press, 1967), is to rethink the whole of Christian theology in eschatological terms. This had never been done before, even by Schweitzer, who called for consistent eschatology, and the writers of the last generation, in Moltmann's view, were incapable of moving radically away from the Greek view of time and eternity into the Hebraic view of history as moving towards a goal that is future, and therefore the object of hope.

For Moltmann, God is likewise the God of the future. He reveals himself, not in history, as for Pannenberg, nor in the proclamation of a past event, but in the Word of promise. God is the one who promises to do things in history. Faith is thus propelled forward towards the future, and characteristically takes the form of hope for the fulfilment of the promises. Theology becomes hope seeking understanding, *spes quaerens intellectum*, and the goal is a *docta spes*. If this is so, Christianity can never settle down in any present, as if it were a time of fulfilment, but however many of God's promises are kept, it must ever be drawn forward to the final fulfilment. More than any theologian before him, Moltmann orients faith towards the future, including the historical future. Accordingly, the resurrection is as central for Moltmann as for Pannenberg, but in a somewhat different way.

The resurrection is both the ground of hope and a new promise that Jesus as the exalted Lord has a further history to fulfil in the world. History is at present continuing to move towards the final triumph of Jesus, through the world mission of the church in which his Lordship is proclaimed and his triumph, along with the final redemption of believers, promised. Is Moltmann likewise vulnerable to the charge of revelation-positivism, introducing at the heart of his interpretation of Christianity a sheer miracle which can only be believed on authority, though the authority is discredited for modern man? Here we approach one of the most interesting features of Moltmann's thought, though I am not sure that it provides an adequate answer to the question just posed. Moltmann introduces into his treatment of the resurrection a searching discussion of the hall-mark of the modern sensibility, the experience of the death of God. But where the radical theologians in America understand the death of God through Nietzsche, Moltmann goes back behind Nietzsche to the young Hegel, and thus is able to understand the death of God dialectically as a moment within a historical process. He considers that the romantic discussion of the death of God, culminating in Nietzsche and his modern followers, abstracted a phase from a continuing process, and that we must say with Hegel that the concept of God can and must rise again from the 'speculative Good Friday', the godforsakenness of all being. Moltmann wants to understand the resurrection of Jesus in this way. Jesus is to be announced to modern man as risen again even from the death of God. Hence, again following Hegel's dialectical thought, Moltmann understands the death as still contained in, and not simply abolished by, the resurrection. The God of the resurrection is therefore an 'atheistic' God. He is the one Bonhoeffer speaks of as the true God, before whom we stand *etsi deus non daretur*.

Both Moltmann's dialectical atheism and his insistence on historical hope bring him to a point from which dialogue with Marxism is possible. The most important contention of the Marxist in the contemporary world is that there is genuine hope for man, that historical action is not meaningless and barren, but can and will lead to a more truly human condition of society. Without such a hope, and the conditions of our time render it peculiarly difficult to entertain one, there is no incentive to political action. Among young people, many choose the subjectivity that Moltmann wishes to overcome, and 'drop out' into a mystical pursuit of individual enlightenment, or of love between persons in a small community. Only the Marxists, and the near-Marxist 'New Left', seem able to maintain faith in political action in a situation where the democratic process seems no longer to provide expression for any will to radical change. There is thus a high probability that the next form of popular Christianity will be subjective and mystical, largely or altogether lacking the dimension of social ethics. Moltmann would regard this as a disaster, and thus attaches great importance to his dialogue with the Marxist philosopher Ernst Bloch. The latter, in his esoteric revision of current Marxism, himself moves close to Christian thought in his discussion of the future. The final section of Moltmann's book, unfortunately not translated, moves into discussion with Bloch on the basis of the latter's *Der Prinzip Hoffnung*, itself urgently awaiting translation. Bloch speaks of the 'thermal current of hope' which links the present to the future. Moltmann evidently wishes to understand the Christian hope in similar terms. It is for him a historical not a transcendental hope, and its guarantee is the promise contained, even for an atheistic world, in the resurrection of Jesus.

Both in America and in Europe, the younger theologians are now offering deep criticism of their elders, and are trying to move beyond their positions through questioning what they took for granted. It would be premature to say whether any of the men I have mentioned, or some others not yet so much in the public eye, will prove capable of renewing systematic theology for a new period, in the way that Barth and his friends did in the twenties. If I were laying bets on younger theologians, however, I would certainly place a considerable proportion of what I had to risk upon the future of Altizer, Pannenberg and Moltmann, though I should perhaps admit that I do not agree with any of them. Perhaps the way forward will lie in calling in question even more of the structure of nineteenth- and twentieth-century German Protestantism than any German has yet done, or even perhaps than the very American Altizer has so far seen the way to do. The urge to innovate is not dead among theologians, and the times seem to call for it as urgently as they did when Barth began to write. If this generation is to produce a Barth, and this is doubtless unlikely, since men of his stature do not occur very often, such a man is not yet in view. However, if our survey of contemporary theology has taught us anything, it is surely that theology does not stop when the culture continues to move, and our own culture is moving very rapidly indeed. New theologians must be expected, perhaps more radical than any that I have described. It cannot even be affirmed that their direction will at all resemble the one we have been examining. The future is wide open, and with it the future of theology.

Further Reading

This short list of books supplements the references given in the text to the work of the writers dealt with, which will normally be found at the first mention of the book in question. These books are suggested for those who want to go a little deeper, both into the period as a whole and the individual writers. (Where two dates of publication are given, the second refers to a paperback edition.)

Works dealing with all or several of the writers mentioned.

[a] Background
The Pelican History of the Church, vols. IV and V.
B. M. G. REARDON, *Religious Thought in the Nineteenth Century*, Cambridge University Press, 1966.
H. R. MACKINTOSH, *Types of Modern Theology*, London, Nisbet, 1937.
JOHN MACQUARRIE, *Twentieth-Century Religious Thought*, S.C.M. Press, 1963. A little about everyone, with the accent on philosophy.
HANS W. FREI, 'Niebuhr's Theological Background' in PAUL RAMSEY (ed.), *Faith and Ethics, The Theology of H. Richard Niebuhr*, New York, Harper & Row, 1957. The best introduction, but not for beginners!

[b] Two collections of essays on individual authors, including some not mentioned here.
A. W. HASTINGS and E. HASTINGS (eds.), *Theologians of our Time*, Edinburgh, T. & T. Clark, 1966.
LEONHARDT REINISCH (ed.), *Theologians of our Time*, Notre Dame, Indiana; University of Notre Dame Press, 1964. The authors of the first of these two collections are mostly of British origin, those of the second German. The latter gives more attention to Catholic theology than the former.

[c] JOHN BOWDEN and JAMES RICHMOND (eds.), *A Reader in Contemporary Theology*, S.C.M. Press, 1967. Short extracts, with even shorter introductions, covering a wide range of thought.

Further Reading

Barth

GEORGE CASALIS, *Portrait of Karl Barth*, Garden City, N.Y., Doubleday Anchor Book, 1963. On the whole, the best book to begin Barth on.

HERBERT HARTWELL, *The Theology of Karl Barth, An Introduction*, Philadelphia, Westminster Press, 1964. Reliable, densely packed, better for students than the general reader.

T. F. TORRANCE, 'Introduction to Karl Barth', *Theology and Church*, S.C.M. Press, 1962;

> *Karl Barth, An Introduction to his Early Theology*, S.C.M. Press 1962. Material for more advanced study, by a committed supporter of Barth.

Bultmann

IAN HENDERSON, *Rudolf Bultmann*, in the series Makers of Contemporary Theology, London, Carey Kingsgate Press, 1965. Short introduction, of about the level of my own chapter, but containing different materials.

SCHUBERT M. OGDEN, Introduction to S. M. OGDEN (ed.), *Existence and Faith, Shorter Writings of Rudolf Bultmann*, Collins, Fontana Library, 1964. Short, clear and reliable.

JOHN MACQUARRIE, *An Existentialist Theology*, S.C.M. Press, 1955; New York, Harper Torchbooks, 1965. Very useful on Heidegger, less so on Bultmann.

CHARLES W. KEGLEY (ed.), *The Theology of Rudolf Bultmann*, New York, Harper & Row, 1966; S.C.M. Press, 1966. Indispensable to the serious student, this volume follows the format of the series Kegley edited with Robert W. Bretall for Macmillan, in which the author joins in a critical symposium on his own work, with eminent contributors.

Bonhoeffer

E. H. ROBERTSON, *Dietrich Bonhoeffer*, in Makers of Contemporary Theology, London, Carey Kingsgate Press, 1966. See note on Henderson's book in the same series.

MARTIN E. MARTY (ed.), *The Place of Bonhoeffer, Problems and Possibilities in his Thought*, New York, Association Press, 1962. Some indispensable articles, e.g. Berger on Bonhoeffer's sociology, but as a whole offers a very conservative interpretation, with the accent on his middle period.

JOHN D. GODSEY, *The Theology of Dietrich Bonhoeffer*, S.C.M. Press, 1960. Pioneering study, based on everything Bonhoeffer wrote, but not very sensitive to the revolutionary aspects of Bonhoeffer.

JOHN A. PHILLIPS, *The Form of Christ in the World, A Study in Bonhoeffer's Christology*, Collins, 1967. Preferable to Godsey, but at times reads like the Ph.D. thesis it originally was.

RONALD GREGOR SMITH (ed.), *World Come of Age, A Symposium on Dietrich Bonhoeffer*, Collins, 1967. Contains a number of well-known and important essays on Bonhoeffer, brought together for the first time. The best book on Bonhoeffer yet, but not for beginners.

Tillich

J. HEYWOOD THOMAS, *Paul Tillich*, Makers of Contemporary Theology, London, Carey Kingsgate Press, 1965. See above.

CHARLES W. KEGLEY and ROBERT W. BRETALL (eds.), *The Theology of Paul Tillich*, The Library of Living Theology, Vol. I, New York, Macmillan, 1952. Indispensable for the student; but only carries the study as far as *Systematic Theology I*.

DAVID H. KELSEY, *The Fabric of Paul Tillich's Theology*, New York and London, Yale University Press, 1967. The most up-to-date study, and the only recent comprehensive one written from a viewpoint sympathetic to Tillich's thought.

ALEXANDER J. MC KELWAY. *The Systematic Theology of Paul Tillich*. New York, Delta Books, 1964. Reliable account, with Barthian evaluations.

The Niebuhrs

NATHAN A. SCOTT, JR, *Reinhold Niebuhr*, University of Minnesota Pamphlets on American Writers, No. 31, Minneapolis, University of Minnesota Press, 1963. An excellent short introduction.

CHARLES W. KEGLEY and ROBERT W. BRETALL (eds.), *Reinhold Niebuhr, His Religious, Social and Political Thought*, The Library of Living Theology II, New York, Macmillan, 1956. See above.

PAUL RAMSEY (ed.), *Faith and Ethics, The Theology of H. Richard Niebuhr*, New York, Harper & Row, 1957.

More recent writers

S. PAUL SCHILLING, *Contemporary Continental Theologians*, S.C.M Press, 1966. For the student.

Further Reading

DAVID JENKINS, *Guide to the Debate about God*, Lutterworth Press, 1966. Affords useful background, drawn from thought of major contemporary theologians, to *Honest to God* discussion.

THOMAS W. OGLETREE, *The 'Death of God' Controversy*, S.C.M. Press, 1966. A reliable guide to the American radicals, but much less exciting to read than the authors discussed.

Philosophical background to contemporary theology

[a] Existentialism, etc.

CARL MICHALSON (ed.), *Christianity and the Existentialists*, Scribner Studies in Contemporary Theology, New York, Charles Scribner's Sons, 1956. Reliable studies by eminent contributors, e.g. H. Richard Niebuhr on Kierkegaard, Erich Dinkler on Heidegger, Tillich on modern art.

DAVID E. ROBERTS, *Existentialism and Religious Belief*, New York, Oxford University Press, 1957.

EMMANUEL MOUNIER, *Existentialist Philosophies*, London, Rockliff, 1948.

R. G. SMITH, *Martin Buber*, Makers of Contemporary Theology, London, Carey Kingsgate Press, 1966.
> Introduction to MARTIN BUBER, *Between Man and Man*, Collins, Fontana Library, 1961.

MAURICE FRIEDMAN, introductory essay in MARTIN BUBER, *The Knowledge of Man*, New York, Harper & Row, 1965.

[b] Linguistic analysis, etc.

A. FLEW and A. C. MACINTYRE (eds.), *New Essays in Philosophical Theology*, S.C.M. Press, 1955. Contains a number of basic essays in the contemporary discussion of language, logic and God.

ANTONY FLEW, *God and Philosophy*, in series 'Philosophy at Work', Hutchinson, 1966. Sharp and comprehensive account of philosophical objections to theism, with attention to contemporary theological writing.

R. W. HEPBURN, *Christianity and Paradox*, London, C. A. Watts, 1958. One of the few non-Christian philosophers who shows a knowledge of major contemporary theologians.

JOHN HICK, *Philosophy of Religion*, Englewood Cliffs, N.J., Prentice-Hall, 1963.

BASIL MITCHELL (ed.), *Faith and Logic*, Allen & Unwin, 1957.

Index of Names

354

Index of Subjects

Index of Subjects

Index of Subjects

Index of Subjects

Some other books published by Penguins
are described on the following pages

The Study of Religions

H. D. Lewis and Robert Lawson Slater

'To maintain that all religions are paths leading to the same goal, as is so frequently done today, is to maintain something that is not true. Not only on the dogmatic, but on the mystical plane, too, there is no agreement.'

These downright words from an expert on oriental religion reflect the modern, realistic approach to the comparative study of religions. The results of western re-appraisal of three great living traditions – Hinduism, Buddhism, and Islam – are outlined in the first part of this Pelican by Professor Slater, who discusses the history, literature, beliefs and practices of these religions and comments on their internal diversity and their attitudes to divinity. In the second part Professor H. D. Lewis relates trends in philosophy to the study of religions, examines the Hindu and Buddhist concepts of God and questions whether such Christians as Paul Tillich have done well, in the high-minded cause of fraternity, to generalize their faith to the point at which it loses its essential Christianity. This book was originally published under the title *World Religions*.

The Pelican Guide to Modern Theology

Volume 2

Historical Theology

J. Daniélou, A. H. Couratin and John Kent

Christianity is not simply enshrined in the Bible; nor is it
merely doctrine, nor merely worship. It has formed and
been formed by history. In this second volume Cardinal
Daniélou provides a modern commentary on patristic
literature (in which can be found the genesis of the classic
dogmas of the Christian Church); Canon Couratin
outlines the development of Church liturgy and the
manner of Christian worship, particularly for baptism
and communion; and, in his discussion of ecclesiastical
history written in the last forty years, John Kent clearly
reveals the modern trends in one aspect of theology. The
whole volume evidences the weight of tradition which
necessarily influences the modern Christian theologian.

Volume 3

Biblical Criticism

Robert Davidson and A. R. C. Leaney

In the third volume two theologians closely survey the
results of modern study of the Old and New Testaments.
They show how the Bible, after more than a century of
critical and historical analysis, still retains a central
literary position within the Christian Church but can no
longer be accorded the inerrant authority of the word of
God. Neither history, linguistics, nor archaeology,
however, have been able to settle every problem, and
this volume introduces the reader to a modern 'Bible
industry' of unprecedented activity.